'A very sensible and fair-minded assessment of a uniquely controversial organization . . . Not only a definitive history of the I.R.A. itself, but also, by a natural extension, a penetrating study of the Irish psychology.'   *The Times*

'As historical reportage it is very good indeed . . . The book strikes many responsive chords and lightens with anecdote the weight of scruple, devotion, killing. If it does no more than dissuade potential martyrs and victims from that rocky, heart-breaking road, then it will have fulfilled a humanitarian purpose of a high order.'

Irish Post, London

'Far, far more than a mere chronology. It paints a vivid picture of a fascinating slice of Irish history, often grim, sometimes gay, enlivened on every page by the personalities of the I.R.A.'

Universe

'Remarkably comprehensive . . . Will provide some badly needed enlightenment and dispose of many hoary myths.'   *Economist*

TIM PAT COOGAN

The I.R.A.

FONTANA / Collins

First published by the Pall Mall Press Ltd, June 1970
First issued in Fontana Books 1971
Second Impression June 1971
Third Impression October 1971

© 1970 by Timothy Patrick Coogan

Printed in Great Britain
Collins Clear-Type Press London and Glasgow

*Dedicated to the memory of my
Aunt Josephine Toal and to the
friendship of John Taylor and
Barbara Mullen*

CONTENTS

ILLUSTRATIONS

PREFACE

Lion-faced old Dan Breen sat up in the bed of his nursing home and took his automatic pistol away from me. It was unloaded but he had become alarmed at the inexpert way I had been waving it about.

' 'Tis easy seen that you've had little experience of guns,' he said.

He was right. I probably had less experience of weapons than any man in Ireland. He probably had more. During the War of Independence the British offered a reward of £10,000 for his capture, dead or alive, after he and his comrades shot down two policemen on the day the first Dail was meeting in 1919 thereby triggering off the military stage of the Anglo-Irish war and helping to bring to the public consciousness for the first time the term I.R.A.

Apart from this episode Breen's symbolic value to a writer on the I.R.A. was the way in which to the public mind he personified the uncompromising dissidence which has always been the heart of the movement—even though for most of his life he renounced force in favour of constitutionalism. After he had replaced his gun in its usual place in a drawer beside his bed we began talking about the Church. He thundered, 'No be God I don't have anything to do with the Church. I've told them I don't want Extreme Unction either. The last time I had a heart attack and they brought me round I asked them what the hell did they save my life for? I'm not afraid to die. There was another patient down the corridor here, always saying his prayers. A real crawthumper. We made a promise that whoever went first would come back and tell the other if he found life on the other side. I'd have had Extreme Unction if he'd kept his bargain but the bastard's gone three months now and he's not shown up since.'

Dan Breen as a symbol was to be greater than I had imagined. A year later Dan made his peace with the Church and a year later still, on December 28, 1969, newspaper headlines revealed that I.R.A. policy had so changed that it was attempting to make peace with political reality and would recognise the parliaments of Dublin, Belfast and London. At the time of writing the I.R.A. has not found its peace, though I hope Dan Breen has.

Before going on with this book, which I hope will explain why I believe Dan Breen's life is symbolically important, I should like to deal with a matter which vitally concerns any reader of any book—the author's point of view. A story told me by the old rebel may help to make this very clear. He said, sensing my lack of enthusiasm for the gun as a political weapon, 'Remember Benedict Arnold, the great traitor? But he was a great patriot too before he went wrong and his home town decided to put up a statue to his hand —*that* had fought for them before the head went wrong!' And he kept repeating, 'Remember Benedict Arnold's hand.'

Well, I remembered the hand all right but my fundamental conviction concerning Irish unity is that it will come about, if it comes, not through force but through agreement, in the manner envisaged by the Irish flag: green for the Catholic South, orange for the Protestant North and white for peace between them.

I think this book will bear out my contention. That was why I wrote it. I haven't attempted to disguise my opinions, but I hold facts to be more important than opinions and I have tried to present these as fairly as possible. I would not willingly write a line which would induce any young man to spend five minutes in the I.R.A. and thus risk his life and liberty or those of someone else, but neither would I willingly detract one iota from the integrity and courage of those who thought otherwise and followed in one of Ireland's oldest traditions, risking health and happiness and even life itself not for themselves but for an ideal.

I would stress here that not everyone I met in the I.R.A. was an idealist. There were some I found who along with the courage of their convictions had acquired the prejudices resulting from being convicted, and who through drink and detention had turned into disquieting characters to be at large with guns. However the vast majority of those I met and disagreed with were decent and surprisingly law-abiding men and women who met me with hospitality and frankness on what was for many of them a very painful topic. I am grateful to them all.

ACKNOWLEDGEMENTS

I am under a heavy debt to a great many people for the assistance I have received in writing this book. Some, because of the nature of the subject matter, must remain anonymous; in the case of others it is inadvisable to be too explicit about who told me what. I shall, therefore, for the most part merely name them, with my sincerest gratitude for their help:

Anthony Heade, Frank Carty, Michael Traynor, Brian O'Neill, Frank Edwards, the late Seamus Byrne, the late Dan Breen, Laurence de Lacy, the late 'Pa' Murray, W. Roe, Pat Clare, Con Lehane, Sean MacBride, the late Mick Fitzpatrick, Seamus G. O'Kelly, Colonel Roger McCorley, Frank Driver, Pearse Kelly, Eoin MacNamee, the late Hugh McAteer, Paddy MacNeela, Tearlach O'Huid, Joseph Deighan, Sean O'Broin, Rory Brugha, General Sean Mac-Eoin, Eamon MacThomas, Joseph Clarke, Charles Murphy, Eamon Boyce, Tom Mitchell, Donal Murphy, Pat O'Reegan, Myles Shevlin, Joseph Christle, Danny Donnelly, Terry O'Toole, Gerry Higganbotham, Lord and Lady Brookeborough, Noel Kavanagh, Harry Short, Stephen Hayes, Harry White, J. P. MacGuinness, Jimmy Steele, Jack Mulvenna, Roddy Connolly, J. F. Reegan, 'Micksey' Conway, Mrs Carmel O'Boyle, Lieutenant General M. J. Costello, General Michael Brennan, Jim Killeen, Jack Brady, Seamus Sorahan, Senator Gerald Boland, the late Peter Kearney, Detective Inspector James Fanning, Francis Stuart, Colonel Dan Bryan, Ambrose Martin, Sean Dowling, Sammy McVicker, William McMullen, Miceal O'hAodh, Charles Gilmore, Anthony Butler, Pat Shanahan. (As Lord and the late Lady Brookeborough are included in this list it is probably superfluous to point out that not all the foregoing are connected with the I.R.A.)

I am particularly indebted to Commandant General Tom Barry for his lengthy, handwritten reminiscence of the Civil War; to An tAthair Columcille for much research on sources and, in particular, for a long dossier on the Civil War in Co. Tipperary; to Eamon Timmoney and Seamus Ramsey for their long assessment of the border campaign; and to the family of Fergal O'Hanlon for letting me examine his diaries. If I did not always quote from the material these (and others mentioned above) supplied me with it was invaluable as background.

For American source material, I am indebted to Joseph McGarrity's daughter, Mrs Elizabeth de Feo of Philadelphia; to Sister Bernard Mary Tarpey, who has written a thesis on McGarrity; and again to Eoin MacNamee and Harry Short. For checking references and carrying out research, I must thank Professor Samuel Fanning and his colleagues at St John's University, New York, Professors Hogan and Griffith. Attorney Charles T. Rice of New York was helpful in checking information. My thanks are also due to Jim Ballance for much research and checking and to Sean Nunan for information on the role of the Clann na Gael in 1919-21. Professor Robert Stewart of the Fletcher School of Diplomacy, Tufts University, Boston, guided my hand through the State Department's volumes on American foreign relations that deal with wartime Ireland. To Dr Alan J. Ward my thanks for giving me his fine paper, 'America and the Irish Problem 1899-1921' (reprinted from *Irish Historical Studies*, March, 1968).

In London I must thank the British Museum for providing photostats of material not available in Dublin and my friend Denis Lynch for being such a diligent and uncomplaining consulter of files and reference works.

In Belfast Jack Mulvenna and Andrew Boyd were unfailingly helpful in providing introductions or looking up information for me. The former editor of the *Belfast Telegraph*, the late Jack Sayers, his librarian Mr Gilbert and Mr Gilbert's successor also deserve my thanks for providing photos and cuttings.

In Dublin I must thank my many journalistic colleagues who covered I.R.A. trials or inquests for giving me their impressions and, for helping me with material and photographs, the staffs of the libraries of the *Irish Press* and the

Irish Times. For providing me with other sources and reference books the staffs of the National Library and, in particular, of Dun Laoghaire Public Library are entitled to my gratitude.

And particular thanks are due to Ciaran Mac An Ali, Matt Russell and Maurice Manning for the time and care they devoted to checking the manuscript and proofs.

The opinions expressed in the book are, of course, entirely my own responsibility.

T. P. C.

1 / THE ORIGINS OF THE I.R.A.

What is Ireland? To many people it is a green and misty isle far out in the western Atlantic. A nation of saints and scholars, of drunkards and blasphemers, of priests and publicans, of piety and machine-minded politicians. A land where Christ and Caesar are hand in glove so that churches are full, and homes empty into the emigrant ships, leaving behind saddened mothers consoling themselves on the diaspora of their vast families with the three great reassurances of a peasant people—mystery, miracle and religious authority.

All of these stereotypes reflect an Ireland that can still be seen behind the façade of Cathleen Ni Houlihan's latest expression—the neon Ireland of office blocks and traffic jams, the fashionable eating places and the tourist trade. You can still find the Ireland of your choice in the pinking masses of cumuli that shift and melt into purples and greys under a blue sky over the Sugar Loaf, in the shy smile of the mantillaed girl who, unhappy in a love affair, joins the thronged congregation in Whitefriars Street Carmelite Church in Dublin to hear the priest read her petition 'that a friendship may be restored', along with other petitions seeking God's mercy on a mother suffering from an incurable illness, His help for a wife who is a dipsomaniac, or a pregnant wife's prayer that her first child be a red-haired boy. All these form a pattern forged many years ago from great issues involving conquest, land, religion and politics.

In the North Christ and Caesar are commonly—though not inevitably—honoured in roars of bigotry and defiance to the rattle of the Lambeg Drum as preachers such as the Rev. Ian Paisley call down contumely on the head of Pope and Papist whom they see as working to overthrow the constitution of Ulster and the Protestant religion, aided by a constantly cited organisation known as the

I.R.A. It is an organisation which more than any other shows us what the real Ireland is like.

Why should God elicit such a different response from a congregation in Whitefriars Street Church in Dublin, the capital of Southern Ireland, and from a congregation in the Rev. Ian Paisley's church on the Ravenhill Road in Belfast, the capital of Northern Ireland?

To understand it is necessary to turn to Irish history and to look particularly at the Irish Home Rule movement, the formation of the Ulster Volunteers and the 1916 Rebellion. As taught in the South, Irish history has tended to portray Irish revolutionary movements as occurring in cycles which always ended in disaster until the triumphant self-immolation of the 1916 leaders, whose sacrifice and courageous example put new heart into the Irish people, and gave rise to an independence movement from which came liberation and prosperity. This over-simplified view is true to a certain extent in so far as liberation goes, but it overlooks the central fact that the 1916 Rebellion by the Irish Volunteers was in fact an armed gesture by a body which came into being only *in reply* to an earlier gesture by the Protestants of Northern Ireland—the formation of the Ulster Volunteer Force to frustrate the British Liberal government's plans to introduce Home Rule to all Ireland. Had the Protestants of the North not acted thus Home Rule would have been passed, and it is difficult to see what force would have existed to stage the 1916 Rebellion. It seems certain however that there would have been no Irish Republican Army; no I.R.A.

The partition issue that helped to keep the I.R.A. alive for fifty years after 1916 dates back to the 'Plantations' begun under James I, in which six Ulster counties in north-eastern Ireland were handed over to 'Undertakers' to be colonised by Protestants, mainly Scots Presbyterians. In other parts of Ireland land was also given over to 'Planters' but in the North tenants as well as landlords were dispossessed and the plantation was therefore most complete.

The ensuing centuries of rebellion and massacre, when Protestant fought Catholic, were as much an effort by the native Catholic landowners to win back their land from the usurping English and Scots as they were religious wars, but they imparted to Irish affairs an all-pervasive tint of religion. The most notable Protestant victory was that of the Battle of the Boyne, July 12, 1690 (July 1 in the Julian calendar of the day), which is commemorated annually and vigorously in Ireland today. 'Good King Billy', William of Orange, routed James of England and enthroned in power in Ireland a Protestant ascendancy. For long this was Anglican in character regarding Presbyterianism with only a little less disfavour than Roman Catholicism.

By the last generation of the eighteenth century a situation similar to that with which we are now familiar in Rhodesia prevailed in Ireland. There was a parliament of planters largely independent of England and equally largely indifferent to the sufferings of the Catholic peasantry whom they ruled and exploited. (This is not to say, however, that had an independent parliament ruled it might have evolved into a more democratic and equitable form of government.) Then in September, 1791 a young Trinity graduate from Kildare named Theobald Wolfe Tone attempted to change the existing situation by issuing a pamphlet, *An Argument on Behalf of the Catholics in Ireland*. Tone was himself a Protestant and the pamphlet met with an immediate success. Within a month of its appearance societies of 'United Irishmen' were formed in Dublin and Belfast.

In 1795 Wolfe Tone and his fellow United Irishmen— Russell, Neilson, Simms and McCracken—stood on Cave Hill overlooking the present Stormont parliament and swore 'never to desist in our efforts until we have subverted the authority of England over our country and asserted our independence'. The United Irishmen hoped to form a 'brotherhood of affection, a communion of rites and union of power among Irishmen of every religious persuasion, and thereby to obtain a complete reform of the legislature founded on principles of political and religious liberty'.

Wolfe Tone was a gay, ardent, outgoing spirit, clear-headed and far-seeing in his political thinking. The failure of his movement was to be a tragedy for Ireland. His effort at revolt in 1798 cost him his life and set in train many consequences which have their effect on Ireland yet. First there was the Act of Union in 1800 whereby Pitt and Castlereagh linked Ireland with England, greatly to Ireland's detriment. Ireland could no longer legislate for herself under the British crown, and the hundred or so members that she sent to Westminster were able to make very little impression on an assembly of 670 when it came to matters affecting Irish interests. Irish trade and industry were discriminated against in favour of British interests throughout the nineteenth century and several evils flowed from this. The Irish system of land tenure resulted in the parcelling out of land into minute, badly worked holdings and to rack-renting by landlords, many of them absentees who did nothing to improve their lands. Then, in the 1840s an ignorant population, grossly inflated beyond what the economy could support by the Catholic birthrate, was struck by famine and a new chapter of horror in Irish history was written.

Between 1841 and 1951 the population fell by two million people; approximately one million died, and another million emigrated. Many of these died on the way to England, Scotland or America, but enough survived to give rise to a tradition of emigration which continues to this day, and created in America the political force of the Irish Americans which subsequently provided much of the impetus and finance for Irish revolutions against England.

The Act of Union was to have three major effects. One was that by its very presence it generated a current in Irish affairs dedicated to the destruction of the act by armed force. It was this current which gave rise to

Robert Emmet's rebellion in 1803, that of the Young Irelanders in 1848, and of the Fenians in 1867 whose lineal descendants, the Irish Republican Brotherhood, blossomed forth again in 1916.

The second great development was the growth of a constitutional movement for the repeal of the Union and for Home Rule. First Daniel O'Connell, then Isaac Butt, and finally Charles Stewart Parnell made repeal of the Union and Home Rule for Ireland their political platform. It was under Parnell that the constitutional and revolutionary movements began to coalesce. In 1879 he launched, through the initiative of John Devoy and Michael Davitt, a new departure whereby the revolutionary and constitutional movements met and mingled with the third force in nationalist Catholic Irish affairs, the Land League. This was begun under the ex-Fenian Michael Davitt at Irishtown, Co. Mayo, on April 20, 1879, and although it immediately fell foul of the Church—its first success was to get a parish priest, Canon Burke, to reduce his rents—the League prospered, and was a principal force in introducing the Land Acts through which by the opening of the twentieth century Irish farmers had won the 'three Fs': Fixity of Tenure, Fair Rents, and the rights of Free Sale.

This largely settled the land issue in Southern Ireland and as there were fewer Protestants than in the North conflict between Catholic and Protestant was also rare. Thus despite the fact that Parnell's fall after the O'Shea divorce scandal left the Home Rule issue in the doldrums, the South became relatively peaceful. The North, however, was less peaceful. O'Connell's Catholic agitation in the South and his conjuring up and utilisation of Catholic power accelerated the drift of Protestant wealth and interest from the South to the North—the third effect of the Act of Union. Industrialists moved North, although land owners retained their holdings in the South. As the industrialists moved North, bringing with them knowledge, drive and initiative, they created jobs in the linen, shipbuilding, and rope-spinning industries which they founded.

Catholics flocked to Belfast in pursuit of these jobs and sectarian feeling was aroused by their arrival.

Beginning principally with the activities of the Rev. Henry Cooke, who died in 1868 and whose statue stands in Belfast today, there arose a line of Protestant clergymen agitators which stretches from Cooke to the Rev. Ian Paisley in a line of unbroken turbulence. From Cooke's day on, one can date no less than seven occasions between 1857 and 1912 when Belfast was the scene of full-scale sectarian rioting resulting in tragedy, loss of innocent lives, evictions, destruction of property and an embittering of relationships between the Catholic and Protestant sects. As Emrys Jones says, in his *Social Geography of Belfast*: 'the support which was given to the extreme anti-Papist attitude of Henry Cooke was probably an expression of Protestant dismay at the great increase in the numbers of the other sect. Tensions certainly rose as their numbers increased.'

These tensions focused upon an Orange Order founded by the Protestant privileged classes 'to maintain the laws and peace of the country and the Protestant constitution' as a reply to Wolfe Tone's United Irishmen.

The Order became such a force in Northern life that at the time of writing its influence in jobs, politics and religion is commonly held to be all-pervasive, and at all times its intent is to divide Catholic from Protestant so that the working classes of either sect will never unite to overthrow the Protestant ascendancy. In times of peace, the Order may only be used to ensure that Catholics do not get houses or to see that the Orange Brethren circulate through the lodges such choice items of anti-Catholic propaganda as the more incautious utterances of some Southern Irish Catholic bishops or cases involving prosecutions for the use of contraceptive methods in the South.

In peacetime one only becomes publicly aware of the Orangemen when they stage their annual picturesque march on July 12, the anniversary of the Battle of the Boyne, to commemorate 'Good King Billy' and Orange triumphs such as the routing of Catholics at the 'Battle of the Diamond' in Co. Armagh in 1795, after which the Orangemen were encouraged to take over Catholic land. But at times of civil disturbance the Order becomes an instrument of savagery, and burnings, lootings and shootings bestrew its unlovely history.

It was to this history and this Order that the English Conservatives under Lord Randolph Churchill turned in 1886 when they seized on the issue of Home Rule for Ireland to smash Gladstone's Liberal government. Lord Randolph summed up the Conservative policy in the historic letter he wrote to his friend James Fitzgibbon: 'I have decided some time ago that if G.O.M. [i.e. Gladstone] went for Home Rule, the Orange card would be the one to play.'

He played it in Belfast, giving to the Orangemen their still emotive slogan: 'Ulster will fight; Ulster will be right.' Gladstone, under pressure from Parnell, took up the issue and foundered under the weight of Tory opportunism and Ulster bigotry in the 1886 elections. The fall of Parnell in 1890 wrecked his Irish Parliamentary Party and years of painstaking reconciliation and manoeuvring lay ahead before the party, under John Redmond, again brought Home Rule to the edge of realisation.

Herbert Asquith, the British Liberal prime minister, became dependent on the Irish Party for support against the Conservatives and attempted to implement his Home Rule pledge with such determination that the House of Lords' veto, an habitual stumbling block for Home Rule proposals emanating from the House of Commons, was removed in 1911. Once again, however, the Orange card was played.

As a result of religio-economic clashes, and the rantings of political priests the average Protestants of Ulster were conditioned to believe that Home Rule was Rome Rule, which would deliver them into the power of the Papacy, the bishops, the priests.* (To further incite these fears

---

* The actual measure of Home Rule to be granted was quite

circa 1910-12 there was a controversy involving the *Ne Temere* decree promulgated in 1908, which declared that marriages between Catholics and Protestants were null and void if the children were not brought up in the Catholic religion.)

George Bernard Shaw correctly summed up the feelings of the Protestant rank and file in Ulster when he wrote:

. . . political opinion in Ulster is not a matter of talk and bluff as it is in England. No English Home Ruler has the faintest intention, in any event, of throwing actual paving stones at any English Unionist . . . the Ulsterman is not like that. He is inured to violence. He has thrown stones and been hit by them. He has battered his political Opponent with fist and stick, and been battered himself in the same manner . . . he has to avenge not only the massacre of St Bartholomew and the wrongs of Maria Monk, but personal insults, injuries and blood lettings of quite recent date and considerable frequency. Consequently, when he sings 'Oh God Our Help in Ages Past', he means business. And there is a strength in his rancour which lifts it above rancour.

Bonar Law, the Conservative leader, was unquestionably largely motivated by political expediency in his espousal of the Unionist cause, but he was also the son of an Ulster Presbyterian clergyman, the Rev. James Law, born in Coleraine in 1822, and he was a frequent visitor to Ulster. He was not altogether indulging in mere rhetoric, when

minute. Ireland was really only to have been granted local government powers under the Crown with severe limitations to her autonomy in the spheres of law, education and finance. The king was still to rule and Westminster to control the British troops who would defend the country in time of war and the Royal Irish Constabulary would police it in time of peace, although after six years this control was to be ceded to Dublin and in peace time the Irish parliament was to make its own laws relating to law and order.

at a Unionist rally at Blenheim Palace in July, 1912 he said 'I can imagine no length of resistance to which Ulster can go in which I would not be prepared to support them, and in which, in my belief, they would not be supported by the overwhelming majority of the British people.' And though the leader of the Unionists may have been a Dublin man, Edward Carson, one of the two members returned to the House of Commons for Trinity College, Dublin, he was also totally convinced that Ireland's future lay in union with England, and he advocated this view with all the forensic skill which had destroyed Oscar Wilde, and remade Archer-Shee.

It was Carson who, in 1912, standing on the steps of Craigavon, read the Ulster Covenant:

Being convinced in our consciences that Home Rule would be disastrous to the material well-being of Ulster as well as the whole of Ireland, subversive of our civil and religious freedom, destructive of our citizenship, and perilous to the unity of the Empire, we, whose names are under written, men of Ulster, loyal subjects of His Gracious Majesty King George V, humbly relying on the God whom our fathers in days of stress and trial confidently trusted, do hereby pledge ourselves in solemn covenant throughout this our time threatened by calamity to stand by one another in defending for ourselves and our children our cherished position of equal citizenship in the United Kingdom, and in using all means which may be found necessary to defeat the present conspiracy to set up a Home Rule Parliament in Ireland. And in the event of such a Parliament being forced upon us we further solemnly and mutually pledge ourselves to refuse to recognise its authority. In sure confidence that God will defend the right we hereto subscribe our names. And further, we individually declare that we have not already signed this Covenant. God Save the King.

This document owed as much to memories of the Reformation and the Scottish Covenanters as it did to any loyalty to the King. Imbued with this spirit during 1912 some 471,414 people are said to have signed this Covenant, some of them with their own blood. This was the origin of the Ulster Volunteer Force.

The Unionist lawyers were not long in discovering that an anomaly in the law allowed two justices of the peace to authorise drilling and other military operations within the area of their jurisdiction, provided that the object was 'to render citizens efficient in military arts for the defence of the United Kingdom Constitution and protecting their rights and liberties under this Constitution'. Ulster justices granted licences so enthusiastically that it was possible for the Unionists to recruit, arm and drill upwards of 100,000 men. Behind them was a network of sympathisers who provided contingency plans, transportation, an army of nurses in case of war, and sufficient manpower to immobilise every bridge, road and canal in the Province. A fund of over one million pounds was set up—Rudyard Kipling sent £30,000 and the Unionists were able to call on powerful support in high places in England also, men such as F. E. Smith, Lord Charles Beresford, Lord Salisbury, James Campbell, Lord Hugh Cecil and Lord Willoughby de Broke.

Moreover the army signified its sympathy with the Ulstermen during the celebrated 'Curragh Mutiny' affair of March, 1914, when a group of cavalry officers stationed at the Curragh, Co. Kildare, the largest British garrison in the south of Ireland, decided they would not engage in hostilities against the Ulster Volunteers. In fact, the Unionists had a staunch if devious champion in the very highest echelons of the army command in Sir Henry Wilson, the Director of Military Operations. Wilson was himself an Ulsterman and an archetype of those many senior British officers who felt that it was shocking to throw the loyalist Ulstermen to the Southern Papist wolves with their history of disrespect for the Crown and perhaps more important to the military mind, disrespect for British uniforms. Wilson openly connived with Bonar

Law and supplied him with military intelligence and guidance.

Behind the Ulster Volunteer Force there was an Ulster provisional government set up by the Ulster Union Council, and this government gained some teeth by the Larne gun-running of April, 1914, in which the Unionist Volunteers landed 35,000 rifles at Larne, Co. Antrim, unloaded them, distributed them and secreted them without the loss of a rifle or a single arrest. The Home Rule movement was visibly grinding to a halt.

Southern Irish historians of the old school, even those who like P. S. O'Hegarty and Frank Gallagher took opposite sides in the Civil War, have since described the Ulster preparations as mere bluff, which a more vigorous line on the part of the Asquith government could easily have suppressed. And they, and a great many like them, always regarded the Ulster problem as one which would be solved not by a softening of Orange sentiment, but by the British getting out of 'occupied Ireland'. There is no doubt that such men were and are sincere in their belief, but equally there is no doubt that they are allowing their passionate wish for a united Ireland, and a Republican one at that, to blind themselves to the realities of the Ulster situation. I trust I have outlined enough of the Orangemen's preparations to explain why. The word 'bluff' is as inappropriate in this context as the words 'right' and 'wrong' are irrelevant.

In so far as the Liberal vacillation was concerned, Asquith was afraid that an attempt to put down the Ulster Volunteers by force might provoke a civil war in England as much as a war between the Crown and its Ulster subjects. Also he doubted, possibly with good reason, whether he had sufficient backing in English public opinion to invoke the Crown against a minority of the King's subjects whose crime was that they wished to remain under the Crown! A poem by Rudyard Kipling in the *Morning Post* articulated the sentiments of those who felt that to drive Ulster out would be wrong:

The blood our fathers spilt
Our love our toils our pains,
Are counted us for guilt,
And only bind our chains.
Before an Empire's eyes,
The traitor claims his price.
What need of further lies?
We are the sacrifice.

We know the war prepared
On every peaceful home,
We know the hells declared
For such as serve not Rome—
The terror, threats, and dread
In market, hearth, and field—
We know, when all is said,
We perish if we yield.

Believe, we dare not boast,
Believe, we do not fear—
We stand to pay the cost
In all that men hold dear.
What answer from the North?
One law, one land, one throne.
If England drive us forth
We shall not fall alone.

However it was not England that drove the Home Rule issue forth, but Germany and the onset of the First World War. John Redmond, leader of the Nationalist Party, agreed to postpone the implementation of the Home Rule Bill until after the war and there the matter rested until 1916. By then a number of things were established concerning the Irish question. One was the form Home Rule was intended to take. Another was the extent of Northern Irish resistance to it, which prior to 1916 had the important effect of raising though not defining the question of partition.

On June 11, 1912 when the Home Rule Bill discussions had reached the committee stage a Liberal M.P., Agar-

Robartes, had moved an amendment to exclude Antrim, Armagh, Down and Londonderry from the Bill because he said he didn't think that 'Orange bitters will mix with Irish whiskey'. The Unionists supported the amendment which was ultimately defeated, but it brought home to the Unionists the fact that effective resistance to Home Rule could only be carried on in certain Ulster counties: in fact in the six ultimately decided on, the four mentioned above, with the addition of Fermanagh and Tyrone although they have large Catholic populations.

Most importantly it also convinced a group of young men in Southern Ireland that if they wanted independence they would be better off fighting for it rather than waiting for the constitutionalists at Westminster to decide how little and how late would be the amount of Home Rule which they could enforce upon the alliance of the Orangemen and Conservatives.

These young men, and one Thomas Clarke who was not so young, were all Fenians or members of the Irish Republican Brotherhood. Padraig Pearse, Sean MacDiarmada, Joseph Plunkett and many others were to give their lives in a tradition of revolutionary activity which had flickered sporadically and unsuccessfully since Wolfe Tone's rebellion in 1798; during Robert Emmet's insurrection of 1803; the Young Irelanders' outbreak of 1848; and the abortive Fenian uprising of 1867. The latter degenerated into a debauch of floggings and firing squads as the British scotched plans for what was intended to be a year of destiny for Ireland with an efficiency made easy by equal parts of Irish bungling and British spies.

The Fenian tradition still persists in Ireland in the form of the I.R.A. and it merits examination. The movement was originally founded in Ireland on St Patrick's Day, 1858, by James Stephens and Thomas Clarke Luby, following the suppression of an earlier revolutionary group, the Phoenix National and Literary Society. The Phoenix Society had been set up by Jeremiah O'Donovan, better known in Irish history as O'Donovan Rossa after his birthplace at Rosscarbery, Co. Cork. Stephens and Luby called their organisation the Irish Republican Brotherhood, or I.R.B. The American wing became known as the Clann na Gael. (In Ireland it was sometimes called 'the Organisation' and sometimes the I.R.B.) Both wings came under the blanket description of 'Fenians' because John O'Mahony, the Clann's principal leader in America, was a man of literary tastes, who saw in the Fianna of Irish legend (who were something of a cross between the knights of the Round Table and Japanese Samurai) an appropriate title for an Irish republican organisation. Stephens saw the Fenians as being part of the same revolutionary movement which had shaken the Continent but in Ireland the Fenians depended for their support on the Catholics. In America and in England, their propagandists and financial supporters were also Catholic emigrants.

The I.R.B.'s organisational plan was as follows. In each parish there was a circle of nine men, one known as the centre or leader. The county centres were elected from the parish centres and the idea was that only the centres knew each other or knew who the members of each circle were—how far in fact this was true could only be judged by having recourse to the files of the British Intelligence Corps of the time! Membership of the I.R.B. was confined to Irishmen who were sworn to accept the organisation's constitution and who were prohibited from joining any other oathbound society without its permission.

The following are key extracts from its constitution:

1. The Supreme Council of the I.R.B. is declared to be the sole Government of the Irish Republic.

2. The President of the I.R.B. shall be in law and in fact the President of the Irish Republic.

3. The Supreme Council being the sole Government of the Irish Republic retains the right to make treaties and declare war, and negotiate terms of peace.

Penalties for breaches of these stipulations were to be 'in accordance with the nature of offence'. These penalties were framed to include death, banishment, or lesser punishments. Sentence of death could only be carried out for treason, and then only with the permission of the Supreme Council. (Treason was defined as being disloyal to the objectives of the I.R.B.—not to the Republic.)

In so far as the social philosophy of the Fenians' founders was concerned, it was arguably international and beyond mere separatism. Writing in his recollections of Fenians and Fenianism John O'Leary, himself a Fenian, said of O'Mahony that he was 'an advanced democrat of socialist opinions'. The *Flag of Ireland*, published in London following the suppression of the Fenians' own organ the *Irish People* in Dublin, 1865, said of the Fenians: 'It took its rise in the Latin quarter of this city when John O'Mahony, Michael Doheny and James Stephens were here in exile after 1848.' (The paper was quoting from a Paris correspondent.)

The ranks of the Catholic laity were keenly defended against Fenian recruitment by the upper echelons of the Irish Church. Some clerics went to extreme lengths in their condemnations. Bishop Moriarty of Kerry said that 'Hell was not hot enough nor Eternity long enough to punish such miscreants'. Others such as the ultra-montane Cardinal Cullen, archbishop of Dublin, saw Fenianism as a kind of Irish manifestation of Mazzini's views and opposed it by more subtle, but no less effective, methods, a pattern which continues to this day. However, in another pattern which also still exists, the Fenians found many supporters among the younger clergy, who returning for their holidays to their home towns from seminaries in which they were acquiring a Jansenistic brand of theology, found that these horned Fenians were, in fact, no more startling personages than their younger brothers, cousins and friends.

The Fenian Brotherhood displayed all the characteristics of Irishmen throughout the ages. The Fenians had colos-

sal energy, daring, flair, suspicion, illogicality, a tendency
to disunity and splits, lack of organisation, courage, naïvety
and sometimes a high degree of shrewd commonsense
coupled with an extraordinary tenacity that did occasionally bring spectacular consequences. Despite the damp
squib at home Fenians were active abroad. The Fenian
invasion of Canada in 1867 was a full-scale affair involving some thousands of men (predictably estimates of their
numbers differ). The sailing ship *Catalpa* was chartered
to sail around the world to western Australia in 1876 to
rescue a group of Fenian prisoners. And it was the Fenians
who commissioned the first American submarine, the
Fenian Ram, designed by John P. Holland and launched
in 1881.

The Fenian movement or off-shoots of it, such as the
'Invincibles', or members of the Clann na Gael, known as
the 'Triangle', were also associated with some darker
activities. To the Invincibles may be ascribed the murder
of T. H. Burke and Lord Frederick Cavendish the newly
appointed chief secretary for Ireland, on May 6, 1882.
It was a terrible deed and a great setback for the Irish
Home Rule movement because of its effect on British
public attitude. In America members of the Triangle were
eventually sentenced for the murder of Dr Henry Cronin,
a fellow-member of Clann na Gael who had been asking
awkward questions about the misappropriation of Clann
funds.

But there were other incidents which served to give both
heroes and a folk memory to the movement, such as the
execution of the 'Manchester Martyrs', Allen Larkin and
O'Brien, hanged in Manchester Jail for the death of a
constable who was accidentally shot as a group of Fenians
attempted to rescue a prisoner from a police van. (It was
their deaths which inspired the ballad 'The Smashing of
The Van', which I first heard sung by Brendan Behan,
who had himself walked in the footsteps of the Fenians.

On the heroic side also the Fenian movement gave
tradition such figures as that of O'Donovan Rossa. Arrested

in 1865 on the suppression of the *Irish People*, of which he was business manager, he was sentenced to life imprisonment on December 13, 1865. He was released on January 5, 1871 after experiences in various British prisons that were authenticated by the Devon Commission. These included having had his hands handcuffed behind his back for thirty-five days in Chatham Jail, and being kept naked day and night on a punishment diet of bread and water, in solitary confinement in a darkened cell, because of his intransigent attitude towards his jailers—an attitude which many Republican prisoners afterwards attempted to emulate.

After his release Rossa went to America and became a prominent member of the Clann na Gael, and one of the prime movers behind the 'dynamite campaign', a series of dynamitings carried out by young Irishmen throughout England for approximately two years beginning in 1903. Like its later offshoot, the I.R.A. bombing campaign in England of 1939, the dynamiting campaign seemed to end with small loss of life, the alienation of English public opinion, and the imprisonment of a number of patriotic young Irishmen, with no other effect than to embitter them and deprive their friends and families of their company and support.

But when an amnesty was granted to the Fenian prisoners in 1898 one such young man emerged from jail determined that this would not be the full story. Following the amnesty Thomas Clarke went to New York, but he returned to Ireland in 1907 because foreseeing a European war he decided that a time was coming when John Mitchel's doctrine 'that Ireland's opportunity would come when England was in difficulty' might have a chance to prove itself.*

* John Mitchel, the leading polemicist of the 1848 militants, had outlined his theory in his paper the *United Irishman*. The idea of striking at England while she was preoccupied with war was used again in 1939 when Sean Russell master-minded the I.R.A.'s bombing campaign against England.

In the colonial Ireland to which Clarke returned opportunities for revolution were few. Free primary school education was widespread throughout the country, County Councils and Urban District Councils were controlled by members elected by the Irish themselves by democratic franchise and generally supported the Irish Party. Tenant farmers were buying back their holdings from the landlords by a system of annuities payable to the British government which had compensated the landlords in the first place. Granted, slum conditions in Dublin were appalling—twenty thousand families were living in one room each according to a survey in 1910, and the infant mortality was 142 per thousand as compared with 103 in London— the bulk of the country was peaceful. Men of Clarke's generation in the I.R.B. did little for the movement beyond talk of the old days which grew more heroic with each telling.

However a group of young men—Denis MacCullagh, P. S. O'Hegarty and Bulmer Hobson—had been active in the north in setting up Dungannon Clubs, called after the town in Co. Tyrone where the Irish Volunteers were founded in 1782. These literary and debating clubs were a cloak for I.R.B. activities which consisted of little more than preaching separatism and republicanism and introducing new recruits to the writing of other authors of either a revolutionary or nationalistic nature—the Republican and separatist Wolfe Tone, John Mitchel, nationalists Charles Kickham, who had edited the Fenian newspaper the *Irish People* and Thomas Davis the leader of the Young Irelanders of the 1840s. The poetry of Ethna Carbery and Alice Milligan and James Fintan Lalor's writings on the land issue all helped towards creating a body of opinion, however small, in favour of staging a rising against the British.

This opinion was shared by very few people outside I.R.B. circles, and though they had a newspaper, *Irish Freedom*, Clarke and the young I.R.B. men cannot have had more than a handful of active members spread throughout the country at the onset of the Ulster crisis. None the less using the Communist tactic of infiltration they had manipulated themselves into positions of influence in a number of what might be termed 'Irish Ireland Societies'—notably the Gaelic League and the Gaelic Athletic Association, both of which had a nation-wide following by 1912. They were non-sectarian (the Gaelic League in fact was founded by a Protestant, Douglas Hyde) and in the period of relative peace and prosperity that followed Parnell's death these associations combined with the influence of the Abbey Theatre and W. B. Yeats to arouse a very definite awareness among young people of a distinctively Irish culture and identity.

The I.R.B. seized its chance to capitalise on this sense of identity when Eoin MacNeill, vice-president of the Gaelic League, wrote an article in the organ of the Gaelic League, *An Cliadheamh Soluis* in October, 1913, proposing that a body of Southern Volunteers be formed on the same line as the Ulster Volunteers. Using the respected name of MacNeill as a front, the I.R.B. organised a meeting to which all parties were invited, at the Rotunda Hall, Dublin, on November 25. At the meeting MacNeill said: '. . . the more genuine and successful the local Volunteer Movement in Ulster becomes, the more completely does it establish the principle that Irishmen have the right to decide and govern their own national affairs. We have nothing to fear from the existing Volunteers in Ulster nor they from us. We gladly acknowledge the evident truth that they have opened the way for a National Volunteer Movement . . .'

It was put to the meeting that the formation of the Southern Volunteers was a reply to the course of action 'deliberately adopted by one of the great English Parties . . . to make a display of military force, and a menace of armed violence the determining factor in the future relations between this country and Great Britain'.

Unlike the Ulster Force which was unified in a single aim under the discipline of regular British army officers the

Volunteers suffered from conflicting motives behind their creation and different views as to who should control them.

MacNeill and the vast bulk of those who joined believed, until the 1916 Rising, that the Volunteers would only be used to fight if by some chance the Conservatives and Orangemen were to use the U.V.F. to attempt to frustrate the introduction of Home Rule. Redmond insisted that the Volunteers should be controlled, at least in part, by himself, not wishing an armed force to spring up in Ireland, and thus jeopardise the prospect of Home Rule. The Volunteers split after he made a recruiting speech in favour of the British army at Woodenbridge in September, 1914, leaving the Republican element in control of approximately 10,000 men against Redmond's estimated 170,000. Next, on the very eve of the 1916 Rising itself there were splits, postponements and the capture of arms being sent from Germany at the instigation of Clann na Gael and Sir Roger Casement, who paid with his life on the scaffold for his enterprise. These setbacks clearly doomed the movement to failure and Eoin MacNeill, learning at the last moment of the I.R.B.'s plans for rebellion, countermanded their orders for a mobilisation of Volunteers on Easter Sunday. Consequently when the Volunteers marched out to challenge the might of the British Empire on Easter Monday, April 24, 1916, under the leadership of Padraig H. Pearse, poet, schoolteacher and principal source of inspiration of Republicans thereafter, the total force comprised roughly 1,200 Volunteers and members of James Connolly's Citizen Army.

This army had been founded by Captain Jack White, a son of White of Ladysmith fame, to defend the workers in the great 1913 lockout in which the strikers were finally defeated, forcing their leader James Larkin to emigrate to America. However, Connolly stayed, having succeeded Larkin as head of the Irish Transport and General Workers Union, and having himself founded in 1896 the Irish Socialist Republican Party. (In 1903, while living in

America he was to become a co-founder of the International Workers League.)

However Connolly himself would never have got much widespread support had the revolution of 1916 been confined to his followers only. In a small-farmer economy, strongly influenced by the Church, the emasculated Labour Party which succeeded him had to expend so much of its time assuring the hierarchy that it wasn't Communist that it never even gave the appearance of being likely to form a government until, after Pope John, its leaders felt it safe to declare that the Labour Party was in favour of socialism and a workers' republic and as a result was beaten badly in the elections of June 1969. Nevertheless by 1916 Connolly's continual incitements to riot and rebellion were such an embarrassment to the I.R.B.'s plans that it co-opted him onto the Supreme Council, and he, with Joseph Plunkett, worked out the plans for the Rising of April 24.

There is no need to go into the oft-told story of the events of that week. The insurgents fought with a typical Irish gallantry, attacked by soldiers using artillery and outnumbering them twenty to one. Cut off from all possible support from the country, or from reinforcement of any kind, they held out for almost a week, during which Dublin was badly damaged and over three thousand people died. The leaders knew their rising was bound to fail, but they were prepared to barter their lives against the possibilities of their various dreams coming true after their deaths.

Some, such as Pearse, Plunkett and MacDiarmada wanted to set up an Ireland that would be 'not merely free but Gaelic as well, not merely Gaelic but free as well'. In so far as his anti-British separatist feelings went Clarke was still the same young man who had gone to jail nearly thirty years earlier. Connolly, a long-time exponent of force, also hoped for the dawning of a socialist republic that would guarantee equality of opportunity to every citizen. Other activists, such as sixteen-year-old Sean

Lemass, a strange mixture of idealist and ruthless political opportunist, who later became a successful Irish prime minister and principal architect of Southern Ireland's industrial drive, merely wanted to carry on the tradition of a rising in every generation, a tradition which had lapsed in their parents' generation because of the Conservative policy of 'killing Home Rule by kindness', a carrot and stick policy of ameliorative and coercive legislation.

All found their aspirations expressed in large measure in the 'Declaration of the Republic' drawn up by Pearse and Connolly and read outside the General Post Office on the morning that the Rising began.

Poblacht na h-Eireann

The Provisional Government
of the
IRISH REPUBLIC

To the people of Ireland

Irishmen and Irishwomen: In the name of God and of the dead generations from which she receives her old tradition of nationhood, Ireland, through us, summons her children to her flag and strikes for her freedom.

Having organised and trained her manhood through her secret revolutionary organisation, the Irish Republican Brotherhood, and through her open military organisations, the Irish Volunteers and the Irish Citizen Army, having patiently perfected her discipline, having resolutely waited for the right moment to reveal itself, she now seizes that moment and, supported by her exiled children in America and by gallant allies in Europe, but relying in the first on her own strength, she strikes in full confidence of victory.

We declare the right of the people of Ireland to the ownership of Ireland and to the unfettered control of Irish destinies, to be sovereign and indefeasible. The long usurpation of that right by a foreign people and government has not extinguished the right, nor can it ever be extinguished except by the destruction of the Irish people. In every generation the Irish people have asserted their right to national freedom and sovereignty: six times during the past three hundred years they have asserted it in arms. Standing on that fundamental right and again asserting it in arms in the face of the world, we hereby proclaim the Irish Republic as a Sovereign Independent State, and we pledge our lives and the lives of our comrades-in-arms to the cause of its freedom, of its welfare and of its exaltation among the nations.

The Irish Republic is entitled to, and hereby claims, the allegiance of every Irishman and Irishwoman. The Republic guarantees religious and civil liberty, equal rights and equal opportunities to all its citizens, and declares its resolve to pursue the happiness and prosperity of the whole nation and of all its parts, cherishing all the children of the nation equally, and oblivious of the differences, carefully fostered by an alien government, which have divided a minority from the majority in the past.

Until our arms have brought the opportune moment for the establishing of a permanent National Government, representative of the whole people of Ireland, and elected by the suffrages of all her men and women, the Provisional Government, hereby constituted, will administer the civil and military affairs of the Republic in trust for the people. We place the cause of the Irish Republic under the protection of the Most High God, Whose blessing we invoke upon our arms, and we pray that no one who serves that cause will dishonour it by cowardice, inhumanity or rapine. In this supreme hour the Irish nation must, by its valour and discipline, and by the readiness of its children to sacrifice themselves for the common good, prove itself worthy of the august destiny to which it is called.

Signed on Behalf of the Provisional Government,

Thomas J. Clarke

Sean MacDiarmada   Thomas MacDonagh
P. H. Pearse   Eamonn Ceannt
James Connolly   Joseph Plunkett

It will be seen that this document, which has subsequently become the Magna Carta of all Irish Republicans, North or South, whether constitutionalists or not, was irreconcilably opposed to the claims of the signatories of the Ulster Covenant. The proclamation of 1916 expressed a distillation of the traditions and hopes of Catholic Ireland, leavened by Connolly's socialism, and asserted independence from England, equality of opportunity, and sovereignty over the whole country. The Ulster Covenant of 1912 spoke for Protestant Ireland, descendants of English and Scottish settlers. Its signatories wished to maintain their link with the Crown with all its consequent liberties and safeguards. To the Northerners 'equality of opportunity' in the Southern document meant putting the Catholics in a position from which they could overthrow Protestant hegemony. And in fact, revolution, time and the Catholic birth rate did do just this. In the North the Protestants circumvented the Catholic birth rate by gerrymandering the electoral system, and a policy of discrimination in employment whereby the Catholic and Protestant ratios remained almost static from the time the northern state was set up in 1920 to the time of writing. To the Northerner the proposed Irish Republic was a cloak for 'Catholic authoritarianism'. To the Catholic 'Protestant liberties' meant Catholic enslavement. It is an interpretation of terminology on which the Irish are still far from agreement.

After the 1916 Rising events took their predictable course. Great roaring fires of patriotism banked up as the British executed the principal leaders of the revolt, imprisoned others, imposed martial law, and hanged Sir Roger Casement in August, long after any danger of another Easter Rising had passed.

British efforts to arrest the development of events were swept aside. An attempt, shortly after the Rising, to forge an agreement between Carson and Redmond on the introduction of Home Rule, with the exclusion of the northern counties until after the war, broke down.

In this new atmosphere public opinion began to focus on the prisoners in English jails. The uncommon-sounding name de Valera, elected leader of the prisoners in Dartmoor, and the last commandant to surrender in Easter Week, became familiar. In Ireland people began to turn their eyes away from Westminster and to examine the doctrines of Sinn Fein, founded in 1905 by Arthur Griffith, who was neither Republican nor a revolutionary. In social and economic matters he was inclined to capitalism, believing in protection and condemning strikes. He was influenced by the writings of Deak, a Hungarian patriot, and saw a link between Hungary and Austria and Ireland and Britain. Griffith proposed that the Irish members withdraw from Westminster, rejecting that parliament's claim to legislate for internal Irish affairs. He advocated a dual monarchy similar to that of Austro-Hungary, in which the British monarch would act as king of Ireland and England, with separate parliaments in both countries—in effect restoring the pre-Act of Union position in Ireland.

In February, 1917 a by-election fell due in Co. Roscommon and Count Plunkett, father of the executed Rising leader Joseph Plunkett, was elected on a platform of non-recognition of the British parliament. Using the banner of a monarchist he inspired the party to press a demand for the implementation of the 1916 declaration of an all-Ireland republic. In May Sinn Fein won another seat when a prisoner in Lewes Jail, Joseph McGuinness, was elected in a campaign during which the Sinn Fein supporters largely based their appeal on 'putting him in to get him out', and overruled the appeals of the Irish Parliamentary Party veteran Joseph Devlin, a Belfast man who could see the difficulties of implementing the Sinn Fein policy and warned the electorate that Sinn Fein stood for 'a hopeless fight for an Irish Republic'. In June and August the two men who were to lead the political struggle on opposite sides of the fence in post-Civil War Ireland, William T. Cosgrave and Eamon de Valera, were elected for Kilkenny and Clare.

Behind the scenes I.R.B. organisers, principally Michael Collins and Thomas Ashe, both of whom had taken part in the 1916 Rising, were directing this activity as they went about the country reorganising the I.R.B. and enlisting more and more young Irishmen in a volunteer army sworn to fight for an Irish republic. Ashe was arrested and died of forcible feeding while on hunger strike. Collins, a guerrilla chieftain of Mao-like stature escaped the net, and day by day the Volunteers grew stronger, drilling more openly and waving tricolours. The clang of prison doors on the ever increasing numbers of young rebels picked up under the Defence of the Realm Act (D.O.R.A.) failed to drown the defiantly swelling chorus of 'Up the Republic'.

A Lloyd George-inspired Irish convention set up to frame proposals for Irish self-government within the British Empire on July 25, 1917, was boycotted by both Sinn Fein and Labour on the grounds that its membership was representative neither of Sinn Fein nor of post-revolutionary Irish sentiment. Sinn Fein held its own convention (known in Irish as an 'Ard-Fheis') at the Mansion House in Dublin on October 25, and de Valera was elected president of Sinn Fein. Then on April 16, 1918, the British delivered the initiative to the Sinn Feiners by passing the Conscription Act. The Irish Party immediately withdrew in protest. The party then joined Sinn Fein and Labour in drawing up a joint anti-conscription pledge which was signed, with a solidarity like that accorded to the Ulster Covenant, at church doors following Sunday Masses. Even the Catholic hierarchy denounced conscription, a major shift in authoritative opinion as prior to the 1916 Rising Cardinal Logue's name had appeared on recruiting posters urging young Southern Irishmen to join the British army. To compound this error of judgement on May 19 the British authorities cooked up 'a German plot' and used it as an excuse to arrest Griffith, de Valera and many other prominent Sinn Fein leaders.

The election of December 14, 1918 completely dis-

credited parliamentarianism on the old British model.
Redmond's party won only six seats, and over a hundred
years of Irish political development disappeared, taking
with it Redmond's health, happiness, and, most unfairly,
his reputation, which deserves to stand high with Irishmen.
The newly elected Sinn Fein deputies held their first Dail
(parliament) on January 21, 1919 in Dublin. This revolutionary parliament was not, of course, recognised by the
British. Thirty-six of its seventy-three members were in
jail, including de Valera, but it appointed delegates to
the peace conference in Versailles and it adopted a 'Democratic Programme' based on the proclamation of Easter
Week, watering down James Connolly's socialistic principles, but retaining the 1916 proclamation's demand for
an all-Ireland republic. (To some members of the I.R.B.
its constitution meant that the Irish republic was in fact
established before 1916 and had existed *de jure* if not
de facto since James Stephens had set up a provisional
government in February, 1867 to take command of the
revolution which failed to take place the following March.)

The I.R.B. had joined Sinn Fein seeing it only as
another nationalist society that might help its aims. But at
the Sinn Fein convention of October, 1917, working
towards an Irish republic within a political party which
advocated setting up a king in Ireland, the I.R.B. agreed
to frame an article in the Sinn Fein convention declaring
the movement's aim to be the securing of international
recognition of Ireland as an independent Irish republic.
The Irish people would then 'by Referendum freely
choose their own form of Government'.

Constitutionally therefore the party kept its options
open on the form of settlement it was prepared to make
with England. In character however it was becoming a
markedly republican organisation. Parallel to the rebirth
of Sinn Fein after 1916 there occurred the reorganisation
of the Volunteers, formed to defend Home Rule but now
directed by I.R.B. men such as Collins and Richard
Mulcahy. By 1918 the August issue of *An tOglach*, the

Volunteer organ, could declare that 'The Irish Volunteers are the Army of the Irish Republic'.

The Volunteers however had their own executive and constitution, and though there was some overlapping of membership between individual volunteers and other national organisations they had a largely autonomous existence from Sinn Fein and the Dail. The first shooting of policemen, for instance, was not sanctioned by the Dail. It took place at Soloheadbeag, Co. Tipperary, on the day the first Dail met. A number of volunteers, led by Sean Treacy and Dan Breen, decided to strike a blow for Ireland and shot two policemen dead in a hold-up for gelignite.

The attitude of many rural volunteers, who subsequently took action like that of Breen and Treacy, was summarised in a remark made to me by one of the most famous guerrilla leaders—Tom Barry—who said of the Volunteers' relationship with headquarters, 'if we pulled off some action that worked they sanctioned it'.

However, this fairly typical reaction of the man in the field to a G.H.Q. anywhere does not minimise the fact that G.H.Q. did co-ordinate policies which emerged from leaders in the field, such as Liam Lynch who advocated the mass destruction of R.I.C. barracks, or Dick McKee who thought up the flying columns, small highly mobile groups of guerrillas, or Collins himself who originated the most effective weapon of all, the destruction of the network of spies which the British used as their eyes and ears in keeping control of the country.

Throughout the course of the Anglo-Irish War the Volunteers and the Sinn Fein party pursued separate though complementary courses of action. Sinn Fein gradually took juridical control of the many county councils, setting up courts and settling land disputes, and the Volunteers sought to achieve military supremacy where they could.

During all this period the question of the Dail's control

of the Volunteers remained one of some doubt and even controversy, partially through the antipathy which some members of the cabinet, notably Cathal Brugha and Austin Stack, felt towards Collins in particular, and the idea of secret societies generally. Brugha had left the I.R.B. after the 1916 Rising, as had the 'Priomh Aire' or First Minister of Dail Eireann, Eamon de Valera, and after his election as minister for defence in the First Dail Brugha sought to bring the Volunteers under Dail control. Collins rejected the idea of trying to run an army under a civilian council. (Michael Collins was president of the I.R.B., the Dail's minister for finance, the Volunteers' director of intelligence and adjutant-general.) The clearest statement of the position, which de Valera felt free to make a few months after the setting up of the Dail, was a statement to the Dail on April 10 that the 'Minister for Defence is of course in close association with the Voluntary military forces which are the foundation of the National Army'—'in close association with' only, not 'in control of'.

Brugha, who disliked and mistrusted Collins, tried again on August 20 when he proposed to the Dail that Volunteers and Dail deputies alike should take an oath 'to support and defend the Irish Republic and the Government of the Irish Republic, which is Dail Eireann against all enemies, foreign and domestic, and I will bear true faith and allegiance to the same'. Arthur Griffith, acting in place of de Valera, who had gone to America on a publicity tour, backed the proposal and the Dail approved the oath. However under pressure of the military situation the Volunteers never made a similar formal acceptance of the oath. The individual commanders were left to discuss it with their troops, most of whom, in the light of their subsequent alignments during the Civil War, seem to have decided in favour of the oath.

The I.R.B. in secret session amended its constitution to delete its claim that the president of the I.R.B. was also president of the Irish Republic, and to recognise that the Dail set up as a result of I.R.B. policy was a 'duly elected public authority competent to declare the will of the Irish people'.

But still the issue of autonomy of the Volunteers persisted. It was not until March, 1921, only a few months before the truce which ended the Anglo-Irish hostilities, that the Dail agreed with de Valera that the Dail should take public responsibility for the Volunteers' military actions, and formally accept the fact that a state of war existed. It was left to him to issue a statement to this effect saying that the Volunteers were 'under the Civil Control of elected representatives, and that their officers held their commissions from these representatives. The Government therefore is responsible for the actions of this army.'

During the course of the war, backed by a sympathetic population, the I.R.A., as the Volunteers became known after the first Dail, carried out a campaign of ambushing, raiding police barracks, and inflicting casualties which were estimated, between the time of the sitting of the first Dail and the truce, at 600 killed, and 1,200 wounded on the British side, and 752 I.R.A. men killed and 866 wounded. In the South these incidents were coupled with midnight police searches, martial law and a fear and tension which were grim enough, but as nothing compared to the situation in the North. There the I.R.A., being fewer in number and relying almost exclusively on Catholics for recruits, was unable to make much progress. The sectarian question continually threw itself across the path of the conflict in the north-east. Derry was the scene of a fierce Protestant onslaught on the Catholic quarter on July 19, 1920 after Carson made a speech at an Orange celebration on the 12th, during which he said, 'I am sick of words without action'. The rioters carried the Union Jack and were not halted by the military over the five-day period during which looting and street fighting went on unabated. When the military did intervene, it was to fire on I.R.A. men who were standing guard on Catholic property.

Other Ulster towns had a similar story. In Belfast, after prominent Unionists had addressed Protestant workers in the Belfast shipyards on July 12, calling for a 'show of revolvers' to drive the 'Fenians' out, an orgy of looting, shooting and petrol bombing broke out. Catholic workers were driven out the shipyards, homes were burned and, again, the military did not offer protection to the beleaguered Catholics. Commenting on these incidents in a report to the *Westminster Gazette* in London on July 24, 1920, a correspondent wrote: 'It is common knowledge in Belfast and had frequently been admitted by individual Unionists, that plans were matured at least two months ago to drive all the Home Rule workers in the shipyards out of their employment.'

The steps towards the truce were initiated in a conciliatory speech which King George V made at the Stormont parliament which he opened on the coming into force of the Government of Ireland Act on May 3, 1920. What this act did in real terms was to recognise that there was in Ireland a large Protestant element in the North who did not want to be governed by the South and, in fact, it effectively partitioned the country from that time on. Under the act, by which Northern Ireland is still governed, the South was to send thirty-three members to Westminster and to have 128 members in a Dublin parliament. The North was to send representatives to Westminster and to have its own parliament. Both Irish parliaments were to have senates. However, the Dail refused to recognise the elections for the Southern senate because the act entitled the Crown to nominate some of the members. It regarded the elections for the lower house as being held for the second Dail, not for the Dublin parliament. In the South, the 124 Sinn Fein candidates were returned unopposed, the only non-nationalist candidates being the four senate members for Trinity who were unopposed. When the Dublin parliament opened, on June 28, only the Trinity representatives and the Crown-nominated senators turned up. This 'parliament' sat for fifteen minutes and was adjourned *sine die*.

This act was both a tragedy and a triumph for the Unionists, a triumph because it prevented them from being placed under any Dublin government in the future, a tragedy because the North, no more than the South, wanted Ireland partitioned. However, partitioned it was and the treaty which the Irish negotiators signed with the British on December 6, 1921 accepted this fact.

How strongly extremist Republican feeling ran against the treaty may be gauged from Brugha's speech against it on the day he left the Dail, never to return:

If instead of being so strong, our last cartridge had been spent and our last man was lying on the ground and his enemies howling round him and their bayonets raised, ready to plunge them into his body, that man should say—true to the traditions handed down—if they said to him: 'Now will you come into the Empire?'—he should say, and he would say: 'No, I will not.' That is the spirit which has lasted all through the centuries and you people in favour of the Treaty know that the British Government and the British Empire will have gone down before that spirit dies out in Ireland.

The treaty set up an Irish Free State, as a self-governing dominion of the British Empire, with the same constitutional status as Canada, Australia, New Zealand and South Africa.

A representative of the Crown was to be appointed in the same way as a dominion governor-general and the members of the Irish parliament were to take an oath of allegiance to the constitution of the Irish Free State which pledged them to 'be faithful to His Majesty King George V, his heirs and successors'. The Free State was to assume responsibility for part of the United Kingdom's public debt, yield certain defence facilities to the British forces and in time of war give whatever assistance might be required by the British.

Furthermore, the treaty granted to Northern Ireland the right to withdraw from the jurisdiction of the Dublin parliament. Of these provisions, the oath, partition and the office of the governor-general were clearly incompatible with the republican aspiration of the nationalist movement and the affection with which Collins regarded it may be seen from his prophetic statement that he was signing his own death warrant. He felt, however, that it was the best 'stepping stone' as he put it, that could be got for the time being towards a full republic.

Moreover while to the public mind the I.R.A. seemed all-powerful the guerrillas were in fact almost at the end of their tether. Losses had been heavy and arms were running dangerously short. Unlike the contemporary Viet Cong who have a friendly landmass at their backs from which arms and medical supplies can readily be secured, the nearest landmass to the Irish was that of their enemy, England, and all military and other supplies had to run the gauntlet of British ships. Once the truce was signed and the I.R.A. lost the momentum and anonymity which had been among its greatest assets in the struggle, any attempt to restart the war would have been disastrous— precisely the consideration which has made Hanoi turn down so many American offers of a cease-fire pending negotiations on the Vietnam war.

The treaty was ratified by the Dail on January 7, 1922, by sixty-four votes to fifty-seven, and an administration was formed three days later led by Arthur Griffith. The constitutional opponents of the treaty, including de Valera, Austin Stack, Cathal Brugha, Robert Barton and Erskine Childers, left the Dail in protest. Outside the Dail the Church, big business, labour and a large proportion of the general public supported the treaty and peace. Opposed to it were the deputies who had left the Dail under de Valera, a high proportion of the I.R.A. and the women's organisation Cumann na mBan, an auxiliary of the I.R.A.

The great polemicist on the Republican side was Erskine Childers, and his influence coupled with that of the women deputies led to those who supported de Valera becoming derisively tagged as 'The Women and Childers Party'. He was not as influential on the Republican side as the pro-treatyites supposed as they winced under his barbs,* but in addition to his polemics they blamed him for using his influence with his cousin Barton who had signed the treaty later to reject it, and for having much to do with influencing de Valera's attitude also. Consequently when he was captured during the Civil War he was executed on a trumped-up charge of being in possession of arms—a revolver given to him by Michael Collins.

But it was not the de Valera faction or the constitutional group which now proceeded to make the running against the treaty. This opposition came mostly from the advocates of physical force—young men who had sworn an oath to an Irish Republic. Their leaders were men such as Liam Lynch (the only member of the Supreme Council of the I.R.B. to vote against the treaty), Tom Barry, Rory O'Connor, Liam Mellows, Sean Deasy, Joseph McKelvey, Earnan O'Malley, Sean Moylan, Sean Dowling, Peadar O'Donnell, George Gilmore, Maurice Twomey, Sean Russell, Sean MacBride and many others.

Though the Irish Civil War like any civil war was a terrible business it was not an unmitigated evil. At first sight it might appear difficult to see how this might be. Reports of deaths and damage so fill the columns of contemporary newspapers that little space remains for other news. The bill in money for the cost of the war was

* Childers' high-pitched polemical style continued to be emulated by Republican controversialists down the years and even today the style of the *United Irishman* is evocative of that employed by Childers in the broadsheets which he turned out against the treaty and its upholders.

probably £20 million, in deaths approximately 700 and in long-term effect the embittering of Southern political life has still not entirely run its course. But at the same time a democratic two-party system did emerge from the Civil War as first the victorious and then the vanquished formed political parties, and above all the Civil War, centring as it did on the refusal of young men who had taken an oath to an Irish Republic to accept anything else, diverted Southern energies from the possibility of a North-South, Orange against Catholic conflict which would have been much greater in scale and horror, and which would also have inevitably brought in the British again on the side of the North. (As matters turned out the Conservative-Unionist section of the British cabinet so disliked the treaty that everyone who signed it was out of office in four years.)

Inevitably, also, given the Northern background, sect-arian strife did break out in places and neither police nor army did very much to help the Catholics. Sir Henry Wilson was so active in his unofficial post as military adviser to the Northern Irish government that Collins had him shot dead in June, 1922, on the steps of his London home by two former British service men named Dunne and Sullivan. This shooting was held by Republicans to be the precipitating factor of the Civil War, but in fact a state of virtual civil war had existed for some time earlier. From February and March of 1922 groups of Republicans, most notably those in the South who gave, nominally at any rate, allegiance to Liam Lynch, and those in Dublin who followed Rory O'Connor, were conducting operations of a para-military nature to obtain funds either to main-tain the troops or the republic—the staffs of the various post offices and banks which involuntarily provided the money were never quite clear which.

Attempts to bring the I.R.A. into line with the Dail failed when the cabinet refused to sanction an army con-vention timed for March 15 lest it lead to the setting up of an army dictatorship. General Mulcahy suggested on

March 20 that a joint council be set up 'to frame definite
proposals for associating the I.R.A. with the government
elected by the Irish people'. The militants' acceptance of
this proposal was conditional on a provision which the
cabinet found totally unacceptable: that recruiting for the
new Irish police force, an unarmed body known as the
Civic Guard, be suspended.

Following this the militants made a clean break with
the cabinet section. And on March 23 a manifesto signed
by leading anti-treaty I.R.A. men appeared in the public
press summoning the convention for March 26 in defiance
of the cabinet's order. At a press conference on March 23,
Rory O'Connor said 'that the Army would not obey
President Griffith' because 'he had violated his oath'.
He said that there was no government in Ireland to which
the army gave allegiance, that the holding of the convention meant that 'we repudiate the Dail' and he announced the setting-up of an executive which would issue
orders to the I.R.A. all over the country. In response to
a question as to whether this betokened a military dictatorship he said, 'You can take it that way if you like.'

The convention was duly held at the Mansion House in
Dublin on March 26. Only anti-treaty men attended, and
the meeting unanimously reaffirmed allegiance to the
republic, and placed its forces under the supreme control
of an executive to be appointed by the convention. It
adjourned when a new constitution was drawn up stipulating that:

The Army shall be known as the Irish Republican Army.
It shall be on a purely volunteer Army basis. It objects
shall be:

1. To safeguard the honour and maintain the independence
of the Irish Republic.

2. To protect the rights and liberties common to the people
of Ireland.

3. To place its services at the disposal of an established
Republican Government which faithfully upholds the above
objects.

A sixteen-man executive was chosen and it was to this body that the anti-treaty Volunteers were to subsequently hold themselves responsible. The executive established an Army Council, composed of Liam Lynch, chief of staff of the Irish Republican Army; Joseph McKelvey, deputy chief of staff; F. O'Donoghue, adjutant general; Earnan O'Malley, director of organisation; Joseph Griffin, director of intelligence; Liam Mellows, quartermaster-general; Rory O'Connor, Seamus O'Donovan and Sean Russell, directors of engineering, chemicals and ammunitions.

On April 13 this council decided to occupy a number of strong points in Dublin, the principal one of which was the Four Courts, the seat of juridical control in Ireland. There ensued a confused dangerous period with barracks being seized around the country, banks being raided, people being shot, and in the South an effort by the Four Courts garrison to countermand the authority of the constitutional authorities. These derived their authority as follows: as required by the treaty the Southern parliament met on January 14, 1922. This parliament was composed of the sixty-four pro-treaty members of the second Dail who were elected in May, 1921, in the elections called for by the Government of Ireland Act. There were also the four representatives of Trinity College. This parliament elected a provisional government for the twenty-six counties and declared itself in favour of the provision in the treaty whereby the provisional government was to evolve into the government of the Irish Free State the year after the signing of the treaty. That much was settled although not of course in the minds of the dissident Republicans. The second Dail never met as the Republican deputies never returned to it, but it was to this 'second Dail' that a number of Republicans subsequently looked for legality—not the meetings which stemmed from the provisional government.

The shades gathered around their aspirations during what was to prove to be all too literally a flaming month of June. Collins had kept in touch with a section of the

dissidents, those led by Liam Lynch who was nominally
the commander-in-chief of all the Republican forces, to
the extent that with Lynch he arranged the planning and
armament for a campaign in the North in support of
the beleaguered Catholics. This was in March. In May he
concluded a pact with de Valera, both sides agreeing to
go into the elections of June 10 under a shared Sinn Fein
banner calling on the electorate to vote only for pro- or
anti-treaty candidates and to forget about such light
considerations as the interests of farmers, labour, Unionists,
etc. The pact also provided for the enactment of a republican constitution after the election, although the day
before the Four Courts was seized Winston Churchill
had declared in the House of Commons that: 'If a
Republic was set up, that is a form of Government in
Ireland which the British Empire in no circumstances
whatever can tolerate or agree to.'

Understandably therefore the pact displeased the British
who exerted pressure to have it abrogated—which Collins
did on the eve of the election, in a speech in which he
urged the electorate to vote for anyone it fancied, thus
ending the prospect of a coalition government about which
his colleagues had been unenthusiastic anyway.

Three days before the elections were held Sir Henry
Wilson was shot and on the same day the Four Courts garrison arranged for the kidnapping of General O'Connell,
the Free State army chief of staff. Either happening would
have provided a catalyst for momentous events. Together
they were irresistible and, on June 28, field pieces borrowed
from the British loomed across the Liffey and blasted
the Four Courts garrison from their fortress. The bombardment brought the issue of the treaty from the debating
table to the sterner tests of ambush, reprisal, military action
and execution.

It was a war of young men. Kevin O'Higgins, the
strong man of the Free state government, said that: 'The
Provisional Government was simply eight young men in
the City Hall standing amidst the ruins of one administra-

tion, with the foundations of another not yet laid and with wild men screaming through the key hole.' The Republican leaders were young men also, in their late teens or early twenties. They hadn't the cohesion and resources of their opponents, nor did they have the backing of a sympathetic population. Houses that were friendly to the I.R.A. during the Anglo-Irish war were closed to them during the war of brothers. The worst of them contributed to the statistics of death and crime of the period and all the best of them had to fight a war were the qualities exhibited in these extracts from his last letter to his mother, written by Liam Mellows:

> Mountjoy Prison, Dublin.
> Dec. 8th 1922.
> 5 a.m.

My dear Mother,

The time is short and much I would like to say must go unsaid but you will understand in such moments heart speaks to heart. At 3.30 a.m. this morning, we (Dick Barrett, Rory O'Connor, Joe McKelvey and I) were informed that we were to be executed as a reprisal. Welcome be the will of God, for Ireland is in His keeping despite foreign monarchs and treaties. Though unworthy of the greatest human honour that can be paid an Irishman or woman, I go to join Tone and Emmet, the Fenians, Tom Clarke, Connolly, Pearse, Kevin Barry and Childers. My last thoughts will be on God, and Ireland and on you.

You must not grieve Mother Darling. Once before you thought you had given me to Ireland. The reality has now come. You will bear this as you have borne all the afflictions the cause of Ireland brought you—nobly and bravely. It is a sore trial for you, but that great courageous soul of yours will rejoice for I die for the truth—life is only for a little while, and we shall be returned hereafter.

Through you I also send another message: it is this, let no thought of reprisal or revenge dominate Republicans because of our deaths. We die for the truth, vindication will come, the mist will be cleared away, and brothers in blood will before long be brothers in arms, against the oppression of our country and imperialist England . . . in this belief I die happy forgiving all, as I hope myself to be forgiven. The path the people of Ireland must tread is straight and hard and true, though narrow; only by following it can they be men. It is a hard road, but it's the road our Saviour followed—the road of Sacrifice. The Republic lives, our deaths make that a certainty.

I have had the Chaplain to see me. It is sad but I cannot agree to accept the Bishops' Pastoral, my conscience is quite clear, Thank God, with the old Gaels. I believe that those who die for Ireland have no need for prayer.

God Bless and Protect you,
Your Loving Son Willie.

Mellows' reference to the bishops' pastoral concerned the issuing by the hierarchy on October 10 of a joint pastoral letter condemning the Republicans' war effort as 'morally only a system of murder and assassination of the National forces'. The bishops wrote of the Republicans' oath that 'No oath can bind any man to carry on a warfare against his own Country in circumstances forbidden by the law of God.' Following the publication of this pastoral many priests began to refuse confession to Republicans who would not repent of their ways. As a result men under sentence of death sometimes could not receive communion and died without the Viaticum, although as in Fenian times there were always some priests who defied the ban and heard Republican confessions.*

* It is still not clear whether or not he did receive the sacraments but a letter to the press in Dublin on April 24, 1968, from Captain Ignatius O'Rourke who was present at the execution, seems to indicate that he may have. According to the letter, a few minutes before Mellows was executed he sent for the prison chaplain, Father McMahon, and O'Rourke describes how, 'A few minutes later' he saw Father McMahon leaving the room 'accompanied by Liam Mellows with his right arm around Liam's shoulders and they walked along together leading the group as we all walked to the sandbags. Liam and Father McMahon appeared to be in deep, friendly conversation, with

This was and is a continuing trait of some Irish priests, best exemplified by an anecdote from the period of preparation (1938) for Sean Russell's bombing campaign against England.

At the time a reservoir was being built at Poulaphoucca, Co. Wicklow, and upwards of thirty young I.R.A. men were in the habit of stealing gelignite and angle irons (for testing the strength of the charges) from the site. One of the lads went to confession:

'I stole Father.' 'What did you steal my son?' 'Explosives Father.' 'For use in Ireland?' 'No Father—in England.' 'That's all right my son,' said the priest, who gave the young bomber absolution, told him to send along his colleagues to be absolved also and wound up by getting the O.C. of the group to carry the Eucharistic flag at the head of a procession held to mark the closing of a mission.

However the Civil War period was a rougher era and the bishops' pastoral took note of another grim factor then entering the war and urged the Republicans to take advantage of an amnesty which the government offered on October 3—because military courts were due to come into operation on October 15.

When the courts did begin functioning on November 17, they condemned seventy-seven men, including Childers and four leading members of the Courts' garrison who were executed as a reprisal after two pro-treaty deputies who had voted for the military courts were shot, one fatally. The executed men were Rory O'Connor, Liam Mellows, Richard Barrett and Joseph McKelvey. The executions of those leaders on December 8, two days after the Free State by the terms of the treaty officially came into existence, initiated a policy of reprisals whereby men who were already imprisoned were liable to execution if an

---

no sign of discord, disagreement or argument, just like two men discussing some point in a friendly fashion. They continued to talk until Father McMahon left Liam in the number one position at the sandbags . . .'

I.R.A. operation took place in the district in which they were held.

It was against this background of religious and military pressures that an executive meeting was held in the remote Nier Valley in Co. Waterford on March 10, which de Valera attended as the political leader of the Republican side. He voted for peace, but Liam Lynch stood out for a continuation of the struggle. Further meetings were held in April on the run near Mullinahone, Co. Tipperary, and in Dublin between which Liam Lynch was killed and Austin Stack captured.

At the Dublin meeting a special Army Council formed from the depleted executive and consisting of Barry, Liam Pilkington, Sean Hyde and Frank Aiken agreed with de Valera and the three members of the Republican cabinet who were not in prison (P. J. Ruthledge, M. P. Colivet and Donal O'Callaghan) to issue a proclamation calling a halt to hostilities. Frank Aiken succeeded Lynch and on April 30 issued an order calling on the I.R.A. to suspend 'all offensive operations' and on May 24 the Civil War came finally to an end with a 'cease fire and dump arms' order also signed by Aiken.

As far as the ending of partition was, or is, concerned, the Civil War was a total irrelevance—as even the briefest of chats with any Northern Unionist would show. The point is vividly demonstrated by my talk with Viscount Brookeborough, from 1943 until his retirement in 1963 the prime minister of that strange political entity that the Government of Ireland Act created in the north-east, like a political left-over from the Reformation.

Coincidentally, the day before I went north to see Brookeborough I was in Dublin for the funeral of Dunne and Sullivan, the killers of Sir Henry Wilson, whose remains were brought back to Ireland on July 6, 1967. A guard of honour of the contemporary I.R.A. marched openly on either side of the two coffins through the streets of Dublin. The guards were set-face, stern young men, moving to military commands and dressed in a strange 'uniform' of ordinary peaked caps and gloves. Police kept the crowds back as men who had been under sentence of death by the state which those police were guarding honoured their dead, some praying openly.

The Brookeboroughs live on a huge estate, Colebrook, near Brookeborough, in Co. Fermanagh. Outside the door stand two howitzers in memory of two relations of Brookeborough who were awarded posthumous Victoria Crosses in the First World War for gallantry at Ypres and at Givrenchy.

The relations and admirers of Dunne and Sullivan also remember Ypres. It was there that Sullivan lost a leg so that he could not flee after the shooting of Wilson, and Dunne stayed with him to save him from the enraged London mob, thereby ensuring his own execution also. At his trial, which was of course only a legal halt on the way to an inevitable execution, Dunne prepared a statement which said that they had 'fought for small nationalities . . . The same principles which led us to shed our blood on the battlefield of Europe led us to commit the act we are charged with.'

Lord Brookeborough and his wife said frankly that they considered Dunne and Sullivan to be murderers. Brookeborough had lost several relations in war for England, including two sons in the Second World War. 'I'm a Britisher,' he says, but he reminded me of the French General Massu of the O.A.S., both facially and physically and indeed in other ways too! He lived in almost feudal style at Brookeborough, pottering around in corduroys with a large clasp-knife dangling from his belt. In the wooded grounds around his mansion deer stalked through the trees, fat cattle grazed, and yards, barns and clusters of agricultural equipment, tended with nonchalant competence by innumerable workmen, combined to give a picture of a typical English demesne set down in an Irish countryside.

Lady Brookeborough, a woman of character rather than

beauty, made me welcome, offered me coffee and then gave up a chance to watch Wimbledon on television to sit down and attempt to put me right about loyal Ulster. The contrast between the Brookeboroughs and the I.R.A. men whom I had seen in Dublin the previous night could not have been more striking.

Lord Brookeborough told me that he first heard of the 1916 Rising in his family pew at the local church. Just back on leave from the war, his first reaction was shame. He felt embarrassed for the country, for his regiment and for those who had died in the war. At the time of the Rising his wife was having a baby in the Rotunda Hospital in Dublin and both were impressed at the manner in which the rebels paralysed the city. This made them determined to withstand any such rising in the North.

When Brookeborough returned in 1918 he decided that nothing serious was being done to put down the menace of Sinn Fein. The I.R.A. was becoming active locally and by the end of 1919 he had lost his faith in the efficacy of the R.I.C. as a police force. Demoralised R.I.C. men were being sent north as Sinn Fein and the I.R.A. took control of the South. Brookeborough felt that something had to be done. At Dublin Castle he saw Sir John Anderson and General McCreedy who told him that a force was to be established in the North, issued with whistles. Brookeborough believed that even more should be done and decided to form his own force and issue them with something more lethal than whistles.

Thus began the celebrated B-Special Corps. He organised it first in Brookeborough, from men who had been Ulster Volunteers and from former members of the British army, then moved throughout the six north-eastern counties building the force to the strength of the pre-First World War Ulster Volunteer Force. He and his men regarded Catholics as potential traitors and Sinn Feiners. The B-Specials were—then as now—the rock on which any mass movement by the I.R.A. in the North has inevitably foundered.

From the end of the Civil War until the present day a debate on the use of force has continued within the I.R.A. and the Republican movement generally. At some stages in the I.R.A.'s development the debate takes the form of Force *v*. Six Cos., or Force *v*. Free State; at other times it is Force *v*. England or Force *v*. Six Cos.; and sometimes it is Force *v*. a concentration on economic and social issues.

The use of force is a dilemma which the movement can never solve. The guns, the excitement and the secrecy attract new members thirsting for adventure. The guns go off and the authorities act. Take away the guns and the excitement and how do you offer a credible possibility of achieving the I.R.A.'s objectives and so attract new members? Even at the time of writing when the movement has, for some years, rejected the ending of partition as its main objective (speech by Cathal Goulding, reported in *United Irishman*, July, 1967) and committed itself instead to a radical social and economic policy somewhat to the left of Albania, it still finds it necessary, for recruiting purposes, to hold out the lure of the use of force to 'disrupt the existing state'. The ploy is automatically cutting it away from the significantly large Republican socialist element in the country who would support a constitutional movement, no matter how radical its policies. Thus it is in 1970, and thus it was in 1924 when Eamon de Valera emerged from the jail where he had spent the year following the end of the Civil War.

The best illustration of de Valera's attitude towards the treaty is contained in a letter of September 10, 1922 to Joseph McGarrity in which he said, 'If the Republicans stand aside and let the Treaty come into force acquiescence in it means the abandonment of National sovereignty [for which of course he had fought in 1916] . . . if the Repub-

licans do not stand aside . . . resistance means armed
opposition to what is undoubtedly the decision of the
majority of the people . . .'

It was a circle that could not be squared. On the one
hand his speeches and actions were, to the pro-treaty side,
at the worst outright i....ements to bloodshed and violence
and at the best were designed to wreck their efforts to make
the treaty work. On the other hand to the militant Republicans these speeches and attitudes, while they showed
that his heart lay in the right place, gave no indication
of where his head lay. Politically his concept of 'external
association'—an Irish Republic externally associated with
England in the same way as later led to Indian independence—was ahead of his time and found little acceptance.
The treaty was signed and he was forced to live with a
fait accompli.

De Valera, coming out to freedom under the tattered
banner of Sinn Fein, saw in the confused landscape con-
fronting him, little hope of implementing his own kind of
policies. On the other hand, having spent the Civil War
somewhat outside the military councils which had made
the running throughout the conflict (he had stipulated that
while he honoured his responsibility to stand by his comrades he was not to be regarded as a leader of the armed
wing) he was the most popular political leader on the
Republican side if not in the country. The war had claimed
the lives of Collins, Liam Lynch, Childers, Rory O'Connor,
Liam Mellows, Arthur Griffith and many others and despite their military defeat Republicans had done remarkably well in the general elections of August, 1923.

Roughly 15,000 Sinn Fein and I.R.A. prisoners had
been released from internment camps all over the country
by July 16, 1924, when the three most important Republican prisoners, de Valera, Austin Stack and Liam Deasy
were set free. In the six north-eastern counties, now beginning to settle down to the idea of partition, the I.R.A. were
smashed. The remnants that had survived the brutalities
of the preceding years had to contend with the B-Specials,

a large and well armed Royal Ulster Constabulary, the British army and the full force of the Protestant ascendancy controlling business and industry.

At Stormont, the Nationalist M.P.s were still boycotting that institution. In the South, the Republicans emerging from jail and internment camps had to face a largely hostile population also. Many people agreed with the bishops' pastorals condemning the Republicans, or at least Republican militants, which stated:

They have wrecked Ireland from end to end, burning and destroying national property of enormous value, breaking roads, bridges and railways, seeking by an incessant blockade to starve the people or bury them in social stagnation. They have caused more damage to Ireland in three months than could be laid to the charge of British rule in so many decades . . .

Formerly friendly houses shut their doors on I.R.A. men seeking shelter. Such jobs as were available were being swallowed up by demobilised Free State soldiers, and throughout the ranks of the I.R.A. there was much confusion and bitterness at their leaders, and particularly at their political leaders in Sinn Fein whom they felt had let them down, by opposing the treaty but offering no viable alternative. They could not understand how the pro-treatyites were able to defeat an I.R.A. which, prior to the truce, had been in control of the greater part of the country. Increasingly in the I.R.A. also there was a feeling that the political leaders had not been as intent on directing the struggle as they had been in making political capital out of their opponents. Many of the young men were simply waiting for the call, believing that the 'dump arms' order by Frank Aiken was a bluff, that the war was going to start again any moment and that this time they would win.

Part of their determination was based on the bitter experiences of the Civil War. In Kerry, in particular, terrible

things were done. Men were chained to mined barricades
and blown to pieces, interrogations were conducted with
the aid of a hammer and men went mad or were found to
be castrated. Bitter Civil War memories are one reason
why to this day Kerry is a fertile breeding ground for
the I.R.A.

To the Free State side any Republican killing was an
atrocity, no matter how justified such action may have
seemed to the Republicans. The pro-treaty side regarded
the anti-treaty forces as irregulars who had murderously
turned on their fellow Irishmen in defiance of the lawfully constituted state for which they had successfully and
with great sacrifice fought. Some Free State soldiers
reacted against the Republicans with a rigour born of this
attitude.

The Free State army intelligence department was believed to have been implicated in many of the killings. On
August 26, 1922, shortly after Collins was killed in an
ambush, three teenage youths were taken out of a lorry
and shot dead near Clondalkin; a week later a prominent
I.R.A. man called Banfield was killed in the same area,
and there were sufficient other such deaths as to embitter
the young I.R.A. men and make them wish for revenge.
Michael Fitzpatrick, who in the 1930s was to be one of
the most prominent members of the I.R.A., told me that
while being interrogated after capture in the Civil War at
Oriel House in Westland Row, the headquarters of the
Criminal Investigation Department, he was forced to walk
up and down a downstairs cell while shots were fired from
a .45 pistol at either side of his head. He had become so
desperate that he had decided to turn his head into the
path of a bullet, when the interrogation ceased. Another
life-long Republican, Joseph Clarke, a vice-president of
Sinn Fein at the time of writing, told me how his mous-
tache was ripped off during an interrogation, and that
while he was waiting to enter the room where this happened he saw another prisoner being taken out with his
entrails hanging out through his anus after a kicking.

Whether all these stories are true or not one can hardly vouch but the important thing is that they were believed, and used extensively for propaganda.

However, it is worth noting that unlike either the Russian or Spanish Civil Wars, the Irish affair differed in the degree of magnanimity shown by the victors towards the losers. There was no seizure of land or possessions for instance, and the losing side was left free to form political parties and to pursue professional or business interests uninterruptedly. On the I.R.A. side those who preferred to struggle on towards the Republic on leaving the jails or internment camps had first to answer the question—why had they left the jails or internment camps! All intending recruits were presented with a document in the name of Oglaigh na hEireann in which they were asked to state as follows:

1. Did you sign on any undertaking in order to obtain your release from Free State custody?
2. If so, give reasons why.

Those who signed out were either not allowed into the army, or if let in court-martialled and then rejected once they were found out. Selectivity was also enjoined in general order No. 21 issued by the chief of staff, Frank Aiken, on July 14, 1923, on the matter of recruits. This made three points:

1. No man would be permitted to join the ranks who was over 19 years of age on 12 July, 1923.
2. No recruit would be accepted without the express sanction of the battalion O.C. to whom full particulars must be forwarded.
3. Recruits when sanctioned by the battalion O.C. would be sworn in by the company O.C.

The I.R.A. was trying to exclude both faint hearts who might have been old enough to take part in the Civil War or War of Independence and had not, would-be spies and of course those who had committed the heinous crime of 'signing-out'. And despite the setbacks of the Civil War, jailings, internments and loss of life, the I.R.A. had sufficient strength by July, 1923 to hold a two-day meeting in the Elliot Hotel in Harcourt Street, Dublin. Here organisational plans were drawn up, and a draft constitution and rules agreed upon. At this meeting also it was decided to have nothing more to do with the I.R.B.

At this time the principal I.R.A. leaders were Frank Aiken, Andy Cooney, Maurice Twomey, Micky Carolan, Sean Russell, Jim Donovan, Sean Moylan, Sean Lemass, Tom Daly, Sean MacBride, Michael Price and Jim Killeen, who constituted the headquarters staff. Next in importance were prominent figures such as Peadar O'Donnell, George Gilmore, David Fitzgerald, Tom Maguire in Mayo, Ben Maguire (no relation) in Leitrim and Michael Fitzpatrick, all of whom were Civil War veterans. And there were other districts in the country that also provided recruiting grounds and sources of strength for the I.R.A.

I found in my interviewing that it was always safer to ascribe I.R.A. strength or influence to a particular leader, or to a local tradition, than to the formal organisational title held by a member of the organisation. The organisational blueprint that emanated from the July 12 executive meeting contained twenty-five closely typed pages, but in my experience the elaborate provisions it made for scouting, signalling, captains of right-half companies, captains of the left-half companies etc., existed only on paper, partially to impress young men. Whatever work was done in any given district depended on one good man.

As far as a social or economic policy was concerned the I.R.A. organisation at this stage was blank and provided only for a military organisation. The following extracts from the constitution are the most important ones:

(3) Its object shall be:

(*a*) To guard the honour, and maintain the independence of the Irish Republic.

(*b*) To protect the rights and liberties common to the people of IRELAND.

(*c*) To place its service at the disposal of an established Republican Government which faithfully upholds the above objects.

(4) CONTROL OF THE ARMY

The ARMY shall be controlled by an Executive of 16, which shall be appointed by a Committee of twenty-five elected as follows:—

Each Province elects five delegates.

Each Province nominates five further delegates, from whom the whole Convention will elect the remaining five. Any serving Volunteer to be eligible to act on the Executive.

This Executive shall have supreme control of the Army, and the Executive shall not itself, directly or indirectly, be subordinate to, or be controlled by any other body; subject to any alterations necessary to put into operation Section 3, subsection (*c*) above.

Such proposed alterations to be sanctioned by a General Convention.

(5) DUTIES AND POWERS OF EXECUTIVE

The duties of the Executive shall be to define policy for the Army. It shall have supreme control over the Army Council, and General Headquarters Staff. It shall not, however, have power to interfere with General Headquarters Staff in respect of purely Army matters such as Organisation, Training, method of conducting operations etc.

Ten shall form a quorum at meetings of the Executive.

(6) FINANCIAL POWERS

The Executive shall be responsible for the raising and safeguarding of funds for Army purposes.

(8) ARMY COUNCIL

The Executive shall appoint an Army Council of seven, of

T.I.R.A.   C which four shall be chosen from members of the Executive, and the remaining three may be appointed from outside the Executive. Four shall form a quorum at meetings of the Army Council. In the event of a vacancy occurring on the Council, it shall be filled by co-option, to be approved by the Executive.

(9) GENERAL HEADQUARTERS STAFF

The Executive shall appoint a Chief of Staff, who will appoint his Staff.

(10) GENERAL CONVENTION

A General Convention, representative of the whole Army, shall meet at least once in each twelve months, and shall elect a Committee to appoint an Executive as in Section 4, who shall hold office until the next General Convention. It shall also receive a report from the Chief of Staff, and a Financial statement from the Executive.

(14) GENERAL CONVENTION

The constitution of the General Convention shall be as follows:

    (a) All members of the Executive.

    (b) All members of the Army Council.

    (c) All members of the General Headquarters Staff.

    (d) All Divisional Commandants, and two other members of the Divisional Staff as elected by that Staff.

    (e) The delegates elected at the Brigade Convention.

(20) OATH

The oath of Allegiance to be taken by every member of the Army shall be as follows:

I .... do solemnly swear that to the best of my knowledge and ability I will support and defend the Irish Republic against all enemies, foreign and domestic, that I will bear true faith and allegiance to the same. I do further swear that I do not and shall not yield a voluntary support to any pretended Government, Authority, or Power within Ireland hostile or inimical to that Republic.

I take this obligation freely without any mental reservation or purpose of evasion—so help me God.*

The principal organisers of the I.R.A. chosen at the July meeting were Patrick McLogan, David Fitzgerald and James Killeen.

By April, 1924 the I.R.A. felt strong enough to express itself politically at least, and it was decided to support the Sinn Fein party. On April 28, a memo to this effect was issued to all volunteers urging 'every officer' to see 'that the men of his Unit not only join Sinn Fein Clubs, but that they work the clubs with the proper spirit of enthusiasm and along the straight lines of Republicanism. It is necessary to have a sympathetic civilian population. We must begin to develop it immediately and our starting off point is the Sinn Fein Clubs. We must join Sinn Fein Clubs.'

The sort of activity which the I.R.A. reorganisation and planning led to in the subsequent decade was not calculated to win 'sympathetic civilian population'. Here it is important to recognise the two ways in which I.R.A. activity has to be assessed: how the I.R.A. judged itself and how the public judged it. The I.R.A. did contain many a laughing cavalier, such as Frank Ryan, who saw nothing wrong in either a drink or a pretty face. But officially the organisation took itself with deadly seriousness, laying great emphasis on conventions, the holding of meetings, the keeping of records and on styles and titles. Was a man properly appointed or not? Was this the adjutant general's job or should the instruction come from the chief of staff? These questions mattered and I.R.A. policy was viewed as something sacrosanct.

Individual deviations from policy, or interpretations of it, were regarded by the many and implacable purists with the same severity shown by the Roman Curia to errant

* Over the years the Church's opposition to the I.R.A.'s being an oath-bound society led to the recruit being asked not to 'solemnly swear' but to make only a 'declaration' of loyalty to the I.R.A. This is the position at the time of writing.

theologians. And what I.R.A. policy came down to is evident in an agreement between the I.R.A. and the American Clann na Gael of September 15, 1926. Luke Dillon, secretary of the Clann, pledged to Dr Andrew Cooney, chief of staff of the I.R.A., that the Clann would give 'its undivided support, physically, morally and financially to Oglaigh na hEireann [Irish Volunteers] to secure by force of arms the absolute independence of Ireland'. This policy was, of course, easier to state than to implement. And even though the whole I.R.A. ethos was antipathetic to politicians, circumstances continually forced political debates upon the organisation and even sometimes forced it into positive attempts at political action.

The public was not aware of the time and energy which the I.R.A. devoted to planning and manoeuvring. But it was very much aware of the army's overt activities which followed from its policy of using physical force.

Some of these activities were directed by I.R.A. headquarters; others were not. One of these latter was the shooting of a British private, who with a party of other soldiers, women and children, was coming ashore on a tender from Spike Island, at Cobh, Co. Cork. This was motivated simply by anti-British feeling and was carried out by four I.R.A. men who had been on the I.R.A. side during the Civil War. Like many another incident it was their association with the old I.R.A. and access to guns rather than a deliberate policy decision which led to the killing.

There were other shootings too in 1924 such as that on May 6, when two guards were fired on by an I.R.A. man at Creag, Co. Tipperary, as he was about to be arrested. One of the guards died five months later, but the I.R.A. man escaped unscathed to America. The following year there were incidents such as the shooting of a man, Stephen Joyce, in Claremorris (as he was coming home from a dance) by armed men, presumably members of the I.R.A. Other incidents can be attributed to the I.R.A. with more certainty. On November 6 the Hill of Down railway station, Co. Westmeath, was taken over by a party of I.R.A. men under George Plunkett (a brother of the executed 1916 leader) to rescue Jim Killeen when the train arrived at the station. But the train had left five minutes earlier and Killeen went to court and to jail (he had been arrested for organising the I.R.A.). With eighteen other prisoners, he was rescued by an I.R.A. party under the leadership of George Gilmore on November 27.

An I.R.A. policy directive of 1925 concerned the showing of 'British Propaganda Films'. In Dublin, the Masterpiece Cinema was blown up after the film *Ypres* was shown, and in Galway the film *Zeebrugge* was seized and burned. Cinema managers were warned by the I.R.A. that if such films were shown they would be 'drastically dealt with'. And the year closed with a garda, Thomas Dowling, being 'drastically dealt with', by armed men who shot him dead at a graveyard in Fanore, Co. Clare, as he was coming home after patrol duty. As far as can be determined the shooting was in line with the general I.R.A. policy not to interfere with guards who did not take any particular interest in the I.R.A., but to discourage, and if necessary to shoot, those who did. (Surveillance of the I.R.A. was normally carried out by the armed Criminal Investigation Department.)

The I.R.A. paid dearly for issuing voluminous reports and directives. On July 30, 1925, police raided 68 Adelaide Road, Dublin, and in a secret room captured Michael Carolan and his secretary Margaret Clancy, and seized a vast pile of documents, publication of which as the trial proceeded (it opened on November 22) gave the public an embarrassing insight into the workings of the I.R.A. This fondness for paper work often amazed me as I attempted to research the subject. On the one hand I frequently met with evasions or refusals to give any information on the grounds that the I.R.A. was an oath-bound, secret organisation, or that somebody might be incriminated yet this same organisation churned out mimeographed documents in vast and incriminating quantities, inevitably to be found or seized by the authorities.

This urge to conceal and at the same time express oneself is a very Irish characteristic, and on June 20, 1925, it found a notable expression in the launching of an I.R.A. newspaper *An Phoblacht* under the editorship of Maurice Twomey. An article on its front page entitled 'Wolfe Tone and Ireland Today' was written by Frank Gallagher (who was later to become the first editor of the *Irish Press*). One would imagine that no secret society would dare sponsor a newspaper, which, when analysed by trained scrutineers in the secret service, would certainly yield important information as to changes in policy or personnel, but the I.R.A. apparently found this disadvantage outweighed by the tremendous influence, not alone on Republicans, but on left-wing young people, which the paper very shortly began to enjoy.

In 1926 the following, among other incidents, occurred:

June 2—Raid on sheriff's office, Dublin, by armed men. The jury list was seized, intimidation of jurors being a favourite I.R.A. tactic.

August 20—John Doyle, Seatown Place, Dundalk, was shot dead by a party of armed men.

November 14—A number of Garda stations were raided by I.R.A. men. A Sergeant Fitzsimons was killed in the course of a raid in Cork, and a guard was killed as a result of a raid on Hollyfort Station, Co. Tipperary. These raids resulted in considerable controversy when, following a number of arrests, allegations were made that the police had maltreated some of the prisoners. A sworn inquiry resulted in a number of police being severely reprimanded.

November 20—Crumlin Barracks in Dublin was attacked. A guard was wounded and the attackers driven off.

November 24—Knockanore Garda Barracks, Co. Waterford, was raided by armed men, who, after locking the guards in a cell, took away station records.

The same night Guard Hanly, Ballinakill, Leix, was

badly wounded by two cyclists whom he stopped because they had no lights.

A touch of anti-Semitism also showed in a series of armed raids on money lenders in Dublin, Limerick and other centres from July to October. The parties concerned, who were mainly Jewish, were threatened and all their books and records seized, the raiders in each case producing official authority from the I.R.A. Cars were stolen to carry out operations which were, to be fair, at least as much motivated by a desire to stamp out the practice of money-lending as to strike at Jews.

In 1927 there were the following incidents:

July 10—Murder of Kevin O'Higgins.

August 27—Detective Officer O'Donnell of Mallow was fired on by a wanted member of the I.R.A., named Con Healy (known as the 'One Eyed Gunner'). Healy was subsequently sentenced to five years' penal servitude for this offence.

There were innumerable arrests for I.R.A. activities during the year, illegal drilling being the most common offence.

In 1928 there were the following activities:

January 23—Three I.R.A. men fired on Robert Grace, the principal warder, Mountjoy Prison, North Circular Road, Dublin, after complaints had circulated in I.R.A. circles about ill-treatment of prisoners.

January 28—When Mr Sean Harling was entering his home, Woodpark Lodge, Dartry, Dublin, he was fired on by two men. He returned the fire and after an exchange of shots one of the attackers, a man named Coughlan, was wounded and died later. On February 15 the government appointed a tribunal which was satisfied that Harling did not fire until he had been fired at by Coughlan.

April 10—During a police search of a Sinn Fein office in Dawson Street, documents were found which led to a search of the home of Miss Florence McCarthy. Further documents were found which included a jury panel for the February sitting of the Central Criminal Court, and a

circular addressed to each member of the jury panel
signed 'Ghosts'. She was subsequently sentenced to six
months imprisonment.

The rest of this year was characterised by an increase
in the number of attempts to intimidate jurors, and by
incidents of a markedly anti-British character. The Grafton
Street, Dawson Street, Dame Street part of Dublin, a
predominantly Protestant area of fashionable business
premises, customarily displayed Union Jacks in shop
windows around Armistice Day or on occasions such as
royal birthdays. Throughout the year these were torn
down and destroyed by young I.R.A. men. The subsequent prosecutions frequently failed when an intimidated
jury feared to convict. British Legion and scouting halls
were also burned down throughout the year.

The pace of violence really stepped up in 1929 when
intimidation of jurors took the form of shooting them.

January 23—John White was shot in the stomach as
he stood at the doorway of his home at Terenure in Dublin.
He had served on the jury that tried Con Healy.

February 20—Albert Armstrong, an insurance inspector,
was shot dead while he was putting his car in his garage.
He had given evidence against I.R.A. men accused of
removing a Union Jack from his insurance company.

June 11—Detective Officer T. O'Sullivan was killed by
a trap mine at Tullycrine, Co. Clare. Detective O'Driscoll
of Knock Station had received an anonymous letter: 'I
found a box of ammunition and papers in a butt of hay
in the haggard. The times are so dangerous I was afraid
to keep it near the place. I threw it inside the ditch at
Lahiff Cross in Ardil's Meadow yesterday. I want you
to take it away. I do not want to get into trouble with
people around here. [Signed] Farmer.'

O'Driscoll found the box and carried it to Tullycrine.
There he met O'Sullivan and another guard. While
O'Sullivan was attempting to open the box it blew up,
killing him outright and badly wounding O'Driscoll.

November 8—The roof of the British ex-Servicemen's

Hall, Inchicore, was blown off by an explosion which shattered glass in several adjoining houses. This hall had previously been blown up on November 10, 1927.

December 11—Arms and an ammunition dump were found at the home of Sean Russell at Spring Garden Street, North Strand, Dublin. Russell was arrested and sentenced to three months' imprisonment.

Attacks on the police continued the following year though not on the same scale. The three following incidents in 1930 are worth mentioning:

July 27—A warder of Mountjoy Prison was chained to the railings of the 'Black Church', off Mountjoy Street, with a placard alleging ill-treatment of prisoners in Mountjoy pinned to him.

September 20—A member of the Garda Siochana was chained to railings in Drumcondra with an inscription: 'Informer Farrell arrests Republicans.'

November 23—Sergeant O'Regan, while on protection duty at the residence of the Ceann Comhairle (chairman of the Dail), Rathgar, Co. Dublin, was shot in the leg.

The year 1931 was notable for a tremendous upsurge in I.R.A. activity, for killings, shootings and for continual seizures of arms and explosives by the police, and by October it was obvious that the normal process of the law could no longer deal with the I.R.A. and a military tribunal was instituted. The shootings of jurymen and police witnesses made it almost impossible to get a verdict in an ordinary court, and the I.R.A. paper, *An Phoblacht*, was continually stoking the fires of revolt with statements such as the following for June 20: '*An Phoblacht* states that members of the C.I.D. should be treated as "social Pariahs" . . . that treatment must be extended to . . . Judges and District Justices, to uniformed police— to every individual who is a willing part of the machine by which our Irish patriots are being tortured.'

After a month in which several ammunition dumps were discovered by the police, Patrick Carroll of Inchicore, Dublin, was shot in Dublin by the I.R.A. as a police spy and the *coup de grâce* administered by a hand grenade which blew part of his head off. This occurred on January 30. A police superintendent named Curtin was shot dead in Tipperary, March 21, as he entered his house late at night.

April 5—a hundred members of I.R.A. were found drilling openly at Daingean, Offaly, under Sean McGuinness.

April 15—A campaign to boycott British goods began in Dublin and shopkeepers were intimidated.

April 23—While an I.R.A. party was drilling at Killakee, Co. Dublin, two students chanced by and were fired on by an I.R.A. man who thought they were policemen. Fortunately his cartridge was defective and the bullet merely wounded one student.

June 10—A large I.R.A. dump at Killakee, constructed by the Gilmores was discovered. It contained twenty-nine rifles, thirteen revolvers, four automatic pistols, one Lewis machine gun, three shotguns, three Very light pistols, bombs, explosives, 3,137 rounds of assorted ammunition, spare parts for firearms, documents, the head of King William of Orange whose statue had been blown up sometime earlier, and ironically in such surroundings the original of the Sinn Fein document addressed to the Versailles peace conference in 1919.

July 20—Killing of John Ryan at Oyle, Co. Tipperary. His body was found with a placard around his neck reading: 'Spies and Informers Beware. I.R.A.' Ryan had given evidence in a prosecution for illegal drilling. He received a threatening letter on April 29 purporting to come from the adjutant, South Tipperary brigade, I.R.A., stating that he had been found guilty of treachery and warning him that if he were found in the country after May 17 his life would be forfeited.

September 12—New and unoccupied Garda barracks at Kilreekle, Co. Galway, blown up.

September 13—Attempted murder or William McInerney, Kilrush. He was seriously wounded by revolver fire while examining a notice, 'Spies Beware', that had been posted on his hall door. McInerney had been very outspoken in his denunciation of the I.R.A. and of Republican activity generally.

Very early on in this appalling sequence of events it became clear to de Valera and other pragmatists such as Sean Lemass that militarily the Republican movement had neither arms nor the organisation to attempt a rising. They also saw that Sinn Fein, to which the I.R.A. gave allegiance, by its policy of refusing to recognise this Dublin parliament, was clearly isolating itself from the main stream of Irish political life despite the grandiloquent directives in the name of the Republican government from the Sinn Fein headquarters in Suffolk Street, Dublin.

Nevertheless to the hard-core I.R.A. militants any other course was a betrayal of the Republic. When it became publicly known at an I.R.A. convention on November 17, 1925, that discussions had taken place among leading Republican figures to find a more fruitful political and constitutional role, uproar broke out. Peadar O'Donnell secured an overwhelming majority for a resolution cutting away 'the army' from Sinn Fein, which more or less disappeared into a world of political make-believe. Subsequently the I.R.A. was to be a purely military organisation, thus frustrating the basic intention O'Donnell had had in proposing his resolution—an attempt not merely to cut away from Sinn Fein but to shake off the organisation's preoccupation with partition, the oath, and the second Dail, and to direct its energies into a leftward path of socialist Republicanism inspired equally by O'Donnell and Karl Marx. This was to aid in the formation of three other political organisations from within the womb of Republicanism: Saor Eire which lapsed without greatly influencing the movement one way or another; the Republican Congress which split the 'army' in half; and Fianna Fail which became the dominating political movement of Southern Ireland.

Three days after the I.R.A. convention passed O'Donnell's resolution the Ard Fheis of Sinn Fein itself was
held. In private session a resolution opposing the discussions that were taking place within Sinn Fein, along
the lines advocated by Lemass and others, was discussed.
The resolution was:

Owing to the insidious rumours that Republicans will enter
the Free State Parliament if the oath be removed, we call on
Sinn Fein to get a definite statement from the Government
[The 'Government' of the non-existent second Dail] that
they will adhere to the policy of Cathal Brugha, Erskine
Childers, and their fellow martyrs and enter only an Irish
Republican Parliament, for all Ireland.

De Valera, as president of Sinn Fein, held that no
declaration should be made which would appear to prevent the consideration of 'any honourable line of policy, or
to hamper any tendency towards the unification of the
Irish people'.

Finally the following resolution in the names of Coun-
tess Markievicz and Sean Lemass was passed by a majority:

That no change be made in the policy of Sinn Fein at this
Ard Fheis, but it is agreed that no subject of discussion is
barred from the whole organisation, or any part of it, with
the exception of the questions of the accepting of allegiance
to a foreign king and the partition of Ireland, and if at any
stage a change of policy is proposed an Ard Fheis must be
summoned to deal with the proposal.

But it was soon clear that major political developments
could not be influenced from outside the Dail. On November 25 the *Morning Post* published the findings of the
Boundary Commission showing that the border was to
remain as it had been since the treaty was signed.

This report, which caused a sensation in Ireland, requires some explanation. Following the royal signature of the constitution of the Irish Free State Act on December 5, 1922, the North, by provisions in the treaty, availed itself of its powers to opt out from under the rule of the Irish Free State by presenting an address to the king from both houses of the Northern parliament. The treaty provisions however had called for the setting up of a boundary commission, with a representative from each of the Irish governments under a British-nominated chairman. But the North refused to nominate a representative and the British nominated J. R. Fisher under the chairmanship of Judge Feetham of South Africa to negotiate with Dr Eoin McNeill, the South's minister of education, who immediately resigned his portfolio on publication of the *Morning Post*'s report. The South seethed with rage at the loss of expected portions of the Catholic areas of Tyrone and Fermanagh. Even those who were hostile to the Republicans in the Civil War for a moment contemplated renewing the struggle to get back the six north-eastern counties and Sir James Craig, the Northern prime minister, sternly warned that Ulster was prepared to fight against anyone who would take away 'the loved soil of Ulster from any of the loyalists who want to remain there'.

It had been wishful thinking on the part of supporters of the treaty to imagine that any such commission could have, or would have, altered the border in favour of the South and in the circumstances the Free State government had no option but to sign an agreement, on December 3, whereby the border stayed as it was. The Free State was freed from making various contributions to the United Kingdom's public debt and the payment of pensions to former members of the Royal Irish Constabulary. However it was not a popular settlement and told against Cumann na nGaedheal (the government) long afterwards.

The Ard Comhairle of the Sinn Fein executive agreed to call the extraordinary Ard Fheis provided for in the Markievicz-Lemass resolution on March 9. At this meeting de Valera asked Sinn Fein to accept the proposition that 'Once the admission oaths of the twenty-six and six county assemblies are removed, it becomes a question not of principle but of policy whether or not republican representatives should attend these assemblies'. It was also suggested that in the next general election candidates should be put forward who would 'assert their right to enter any assembly where the other electorate representatives meet for public business'. These proposals were rejected and de Valera resigned as president of Sinn Fein.

On May 16 in the La Scala Theatre, Dublin, he founded his own party Fianna Fail (the 'Warriors of Destiny'). The Fianna Fail attitude was that while the Free State Dail was not the legitimate parliament of the Republic, it would use it to achieve such a parliament. Members would assert their right to represent their constituents without being forced to take the oath. If the oath were to continue in being they would attempt to create a majority of representatives in the Republican interest, to meet outside the Dail and take over the administration of the country.

The I.R.A. met the new situation with a meeting at Peadar O'Donnell's house, in 39 Marlborough Road, Donnybrook, and decided on a programme for uniting Sinn Fein, I.R.A. and Fianna Fail. There was to be a three-party delegate conference with a panel of candidates to go forward at the forthcoming election with I.R.A. support. These candidates were to 'win a majority'. With this majority secured, they would meet outside the Free State parliament, agree on a government and 'restore the Republic peacefully'. The Republicans were to enter the Free State parliament and take over all the instruments of state. Restoring the Republic peacefully would entail repudiation of the treaty, of the boundary settlement, and all agreements with Great Britain. The I.R.A. was to get control of all arms in the Free State, and all enemy forces (that is the Free State Army) were to be withdrawn from Dublin, disarmed and demobilised 'to prevent clashing and overlapping'.

Sinn Fein agreed to this conference but stipulated that Fianna Fail must not 'enter any foreign controlled Parliament as a minority or majority, with or without an oath, or other formal declaration'. The national executive of Fianna Fail turned down these proposals unanimously.

Elections were held on June 23, 1927 and Fianna Fail won forty-four seats, but when the deputies presented themselves at the Dail they were met by the clerk of the Dail who told them that first they must comply with what he called a 'little formality'—the taking of the oath prescribed by Article 17 of the constitution. That blocked the line of approach to Dail Eireann, but de Valera announced that he was going to try another, also provided for by the constitution, which stipulated that a national referendum could be held on the oath question provided that 75,000 signatures were collected. Legal proceedings to test the constitutionality of Fianna Fail's being debarred from the Dail were also instituted but before either of these manoeuvres had a chance of succeeding a political murder occurred which changed the whole tenor of Irish politics.

Kevin O'Higgins, vice-president of the Executive Council, the cabinet formed by Cumann na nGaedheal, was murdered on his way to Mass on July 10. O'Higgins was the most able man in Irish parliamentary politics at the time. Apart from the reconstruction work which the Dail undertook after the Civil War, he had sustained the government throughout the war itself, and through many crises afterwards. He was a principal architect of the Statute of Westminster which came into being two years after his death and which de Valera was able to use to get rid of the oath. As often happens when a man of that calibre is killed, the shooting was not the result of a deep-laid plot, but the impetuous act of two young I.R.A. men acting unofficially and without authority from the movement. One of them had been chosen to play in a football match in the south-east of the country, and they escaped the police dragnet by driving to the game as though nothing had happened. They were never brought to justice although one of them was killed in cross-fire years afterwards when the I.R.A. unsuccessfully tried to execute one of its opponents.

The government replied to O'Higgins's murder by introducing three bills designed to bring stability to the country and Fianna Fail into the Dail. The public safety bill gave the authorities the most drastic powers; another required candidates at all future elections to make an oath-bound declaration, that if elected they would sit in the Dail and take the oath of allegiance. The third bill would have disqualified the election and vacated the seats of the Fianna Fail deputies who failed to take the oath. The bills did not have to become law. The day after they were introduced on August 11 de Valera and the Fianna Fail deputies took their seats.

De Valera addressed the clerk of the chamber in Irish as follows: 'I am not prepared to take the oath, I am not going to take an oath, I am prepared to put my name down on this book in order to get permission to go into the Dail, but it has no other significance.' Putting aside a Bible which lay on the table he said, 'You must remember I am taking no oath.'

Fianna Fail had lost for both political and emotional reasons for sounding militantly Republican. Speaking in the Dail on March 12, 1928 Sean Lemass, who had been 'minister for defence' in the underground Republican government in his Sinn Fein days, said: 'Fianna Fail is a *slightly* constitutional party. We are open to the definition of a constitutional party, but before anything we are a Republican party. We have adopted the method of political agitation to achieve our end because we believe, in the present circumstances, that method is best in the interests of the nation and of the Republican movement, and for no other reason. Five years ago the methods we adopted were not the methods we have adopted now. Five years ago we were on the defensive, and perhaps in time we may recoup our strength sufficiently to go on the offensive. Our object is to establish a Republican government in

Ireland. If that can be done by the present methods we have, we will be very pleased, but, if not, we would not confine ourselves to them.'

The following year on February 27, Sean T. O'Kelly referred to the Cumann na nGaedheal minister for defence as the 'so-called minister for defence', when speaking in the Dail, and on March 14 de Valera made one of the most important statements of all on the legitimacy of the state: He said:

I still hold that our right to be regarded as the legitimate Government of this country is faulty, that this House itself is faulty. You have secured a *de facto* position. Very well. There must be some body in charge to keep order in the community, and by virtue of your *de facto* position you are the only people who are in a position to do it. But as to whether you have come by that position legitimately or not, I say you have not come by that position legitimately. You brought off a *coup d'état* in the summer of 1922 . . .

If you are not getting the support from all sections of the community that is necessary for any Executive if it is going to dispense with a large police force, it is because there is a moral handicap in your case. We are all morally handicapped because of the circumstances in which the whole thing came about. The setting up of this State put a moral handicap on everyone of us here. We came in here because we thought that a practical rule could be evolved in which order could be maintained; and we said that it was necessary to have some assembly in which the representatives of the people by a majority vote should be able to decide national policy. As we were not able to get a majority to meet outside this House, we have to come here if there was to be a majority at all of the people's representatives in any one assembly . . .

As a practical rule, and not because there is anything sacred in it, I am prepared to accept majority rule as settling matters of national policy, and therefore as deciding who it is that shall be in charge of order . . .

I for one, when the flag of the Republic was run up against

an Executive that was bringing off a *coup d'état*, stood by the flag of the Republic, and I will do it again. As long as there was a hope of maintaining that Republic, either by force against those who were bringing off that *coup d'état* or after-wards, as long as there was an opportunity of getting the people of this country to vote again for the Republic, I stood for it.

My proposition that the representatives of the people should come in here and unify control so that we would have one Government and one Army was defeated, and for that reason I resigned. Those who continued on in that organisation which we have left can claim exactly the same continuity that we claimed up to 1925. They can do it . . .

You have achieved a certain *de facto* position, and the proper thing for you to do with those who do not agree that this State was established legitimately, and who believe that as a matter of fact there was a definite betrayal of everything that was aimed at from 1916 to 1922, is to give those people the opportunity of working, and without in any way for-swearing their views, to get the Irish people as a whole again behind them. They have the right to do it. You have no right to debar them from going to the Irish people and asking them to support the re-establishment, or if they so wish to put it, to support the continuance of the Republic . . .

The Executive have been trying to use force, and have been using it all the time. If they are going to meet force by force, then they cannot expect the co-operation of citizens who wish that there should not be force.

Of all this, the most important point is de Valera's pro-posal that those who continued in the I.R.A. could claim the same continuity that Fianna Fail had been claiming up to 1925. New I.R.A. men I spoke to from this period said that this statement gave it, the I.R.A., a particular stand-ing of responsibility in their eyes. Thus when President Cosgrave finally introduced the constitutional amendments setting up the Military Tribunal on October 14, 1931, de Valera replied to him the following day saying: 'These men are misguided, if you will, but they were brave men, anyhow, let us at least have for them the decent respect that we have for the brave.'

This sort of Fianna Fail utterance, of course, was given much wider circulation within the I.R.A. than were appeals to moderation like that of de Valera at the Fianna Fail convention on November 9, 1933, when he expressed disappointment at the Republican continuation in militancy despite the fact that he had abolished the oath.

However though the broad mass of I.R.A. supporters remained sympathetic to Fianna Fail while infuriating Cumann na nGaedheal constitutionalists they buttered no parsnips for the socialist-minded members of the I.R.A. Some, in particular, Peadar O'Donnell, David Fitzgerald and Michael Price, tried to harness the mutually antipathetic currents of force and constitutional socialism within the organisation after a great deal of debate with those who wanted to concentrate mainly on building the movement as a purely military organisation. And this of course says in a sense all that needs to be known of the strength and weakness of the movement, for although the organisation grew to the point of being a dangerous nuisance to law and order and of contributing significantly to the overthrow of the Cumann na nGaedheal government, it remained an organisation whose hour had passed and which refused to recognise this. Its espousal of physical force wrecked its political chances and it was so weak that when the crunch came and the constitutional government really exerted strength against the movement it did not have the broad-based national support to withstand the setback, even though the government itself was shortly to be defeated by Fianna Fail.

The I.R.A.'s 'politicals' however scored a temporary victory when an organisation of workers and working farmers was set up in May, 1931, following a decision of the I.R.A. convention of February, 1931. The chief organisers were David Fitzgerald, Peadar O'Donnell, Michael Price, Sean Russell and Michael Fitzpatrick. At a parade of the Dublin brigade, I.R.A., on June 7, Peadar O'Donnell said that the days of active service were over for the present and that the need for a Republican Workers' Party, working for a 'Peasants' Republic' and controlled jointly by peasants and workers, was very pressing.

The first congress was held in Dublin on September 26 and 27, 1931, with about 150 delegates present. The draft constitution contained the following proposals:

To abolish, without compensation, landlordism in lands, fisheries and minerals.

To establish a State monopoly in banking and credits.

To create a State monopoly in export and import services and to promote co-operative distribution.

To make the national wealth and credit available for the creation and fullest development of essential industries and mineral resources, through Industrial Workers' Co-operatives, under State direction and management, workers to regulate internal working conditions.

The names of the national executive of Saor Eire, as the party was called, were as follows: Sean McGuinness† (Mountjoy), (substitute, Fionan Walsh, Kerry), Sean Hayes (Clare), May Laverty† (Belfast), Helena Moloney, Sheila Dowling, Sheila Humphries†, D. McGinley, M. Fitzpatrick, Sean MacBride, M. Price†, Peadar O'Donnell†, David Fitzgerald (Dublin), M. Hallissey (Kerry), M. O'Donnell (Offaly), Patrick McCormack (Antrim), Tom Kenny (Galway), L. Brady (Leix), Nicholas Boran (Kilkenny), John Mulgrew† (Mayo), and Tom Maguire† (Westmeath). (The daggers denote those who also signed the manifesto of the Republican Congress.)

But there was a strong body of opinion which was unenthusiastic about the new movement. Maurice Twomey in particular was cautious, not alone about entering constitutional politics but also about the possibly damaging effects of any taint of Communism attaching to the movement. Twomey, a Corkman who became the outstanding influence on the I.R.A. after the resignation of Frank Aiken (whom he eventually succeeded as chief of staff)* remained a formative influence on the I.R.A. until the outbreak of the Second World War. A dedicated, right-wing Fenian, scrupulous in his religious observance, it is generally agreed in political circles that had he abandoned his republicanism to join Fianna Fail a cabinet post would have automatically been bestowed upon him. (Although often condemned by bishops and clergy, most I.R.A. men shared Twomey's strong Catholicism. Jack Brady who became an organiser with Jim Killeen told me that one of the hazards that he and others like him regularly encountered was identification by local police, who would immediately notice their strange faces when they attended Mass in some small country village. Yet Brady would never think of not going to Mass because of this.)

The 1932 army convention's support for Saor Eire was restricted to a not very enthusiastic resolution: 'That we approve of Saor Eire. That the activities of Saor Eire be confined to an effort to educate the people in the principles of Saor Eire without publicly organising it as Saor Eire.'

The caution of this wording also was vindicated in an incident which may be seen as a microcosm for the failure of Saor Eire. David Fitzgerald addressed a meeting in Co. Louth to explain Saor Eire policy to a farming audience—all of them sympathetic towards Republicanism. He was describing how Saor Eire would break up the landlords' holdings and distribute them to the landless when he was interrupted:

'Be Jasus then,' said the proud owner of 200 acres sitting in the front row, 'an you'll not take my land.'

Saor Eire received its national quietus when it was declared an unlawful association on October 20, 1931, along with the I.R.A. itself, Fianna Eireann, Cumann na mBan, Friends of Soviet Russia and a group of other Communist-sounding organisations. On the same day the Special

* Aiken was succeeded for a period by Dr Andy Cooney.

Powers Tribunal was set up consisting of five military officers. Introducing the bill which made this possible (Constitution Amendment No. 17) President Cosgrave said: 'The powers and machinery provided by this Bill are necessary not merely for this Government, but for any Government that may be in power if the will of the majority is to prevail.' (The will of the majority was shortly to prevail against Cosgrave, at least partially through the influence of the I.R.A. at whom his statement was aimed.)

The I.R.A.'s involvement in Fianna Fail's defeat of Cumann na nGaedheal took place in three ways: by working enthusiastically for Fianna Fail candidates at grass-root level, in the land annuities affair, and in the 'Release the Prisoners' campaign. Fianna Fail party campaigning was carried out by rank and file I.R.A. men. For the most part these men were united in outlook and social background with Fianna Fail supporters: small farmers, labouring men, tradesmen, people who in another country would be associated with a Labour Party. Though the scale and membership of the I.R.A. support (the best estimates place its membership on paper at this time as around 30,000) was considerably less than that of Fianna Fail it was an extremely valuable asset in an election campaign, being both energetic and vocal.

The I.R.A. seems to have extracted almost no concessions from Fianna Fail in return. Some prominent members grumbled at the policy of support. One, Michael Conway, told me how he had warned his colleagues against de Valera, saying: 'I'm telling ye that fella will be as bad as Cosgrave, he'll hang ye when he gets in, mark my words he'll hang ye.' Conway was close to being a true prophet: de Valera very nearly did have him hanged.

The second great I.R.A.-based issue from which Fianna Fail benefited was the 'Release the Prisoners Campaign', a loose-knit movement centring upon a number of Republican women: Madame Maude Gonne MacBride, Helena Moloney, Mrs Sheehey Skeffington and Madame Despard.

Madame MacBride was the widow of Major John Mac-Bride, the executed 1916 leader; Helena Moloney was a life-long socialist and trade unionist, sympathetic always to underdogs. Mrs Skeffington's husband had been murdered by a British officer in 1916, and Mrs Despard, a friend of Stafford Cripps and other British socialist leaders, donated a house in Eccles Street, Dublin to be used as a workers' college, only to have it set fire by a right-wing mob.

These ladies organised a 'Republican Prisoners' Dependents Fund' to alleviate hardships caused by the jailing of I.R.A. men. 'Release the Prisoners' is always an emotive cry in Ireland and public opinion was easily stirred by tales of prison hardships endured by idealistic Republicans. Some were genuine, the traditional Fenian defiance of prison regulations often bringing warders and Republicans into abrasive contact; some were self-inflicted, such as those of George Gilmore who refused to wear prison clothes, because of his political status and spent from October, 1931 to February, 1932 naked in a windowless cell. (By contrast his brother Charlie, who wanted to see for himself how poor George was getting along, told me that he spent the best part of an afternoon walking up and down outside Rathfarnham police station with blankets under his arm. Supposedly badly wanted by the police, he was trying to get himself arrested. He was, finally, after threatening to put a brick through the station window.) The issue of the prisoners played a considerable part in Fianna Fail's win. Actually it should have rebounded to the I.R.A.'s advantage but the movement failed to realise how sorely it was trying Cumann na nGaedheal. The setting up of the Military Tribunal had been a last desperate throw on the part of the administration, at its wits end to know how to combat the I.R.A.

Generally speaking the I.R.A., not recognising the state which set them up, did not recognise the courts. Any I.R.A. man, or woman, charged before a normal court generally refused to plead and announced that he 'refused to recognise the court'. However, the police, in order to place some curb on known I.R.A. men's activities, resorted to a tactic, known as the 'cat and mouse', of picking up suspects, holding them for a few days, releasing them and picking them up again shortly afterwards. But apart from the damaging publicity which this practice engendered some members of the I.R.A. shook Cumann na nGaedheal badly by retaliating in March, 1930, by claiming damages for wrongful arrest and false imprisonment.

The four men concerned, Patrick McKee, Charles O'Neill, John Sugrue and Donal O'Donoghue succeeded in the circuit court in winning damages of £100, £80, £40 and £100, respectively. We need not discuss the merits of the cases of the first three plaintiffs, but O'Donoghue was at the time on the I.R.A. Army Council, so his legal victory had considerable implications for the police and the Department of Justice. The success of these four was followed up in the courts by eight other I.R.A. suspects who if they did not recover anything worth having in the way of damages (£5 to £10 each) further underlined the government's almost complete inability to deal with the I.R.A. But curiously enough the I.R.A. did not appear to be aware of this near immunity and did not push its activities to the extent it might have.

Some members of the executive, however, either through natural bellicosity or an appreciation of the true situation, did push their luck pretty far. Frank Ryan, for instance, gave an interview to the *Daily Express* (published August 24, 1931) in which he not only justified the killings of Ryan, Carroll and Curtin, but claimed that the I.R.A. could act on an even wider scale. It was this speech, I understand, which led the Department of Justice to advise President Cosgrave to reinstate the Tribunal. Peadar O'Donnell addressed a parade of I.R.A. men (which the police had tried and failed to prevent) from nineteen counties on June 20 in which he said of the government: 'All the powers in their hands we must take into ours, and in the final phase we must meet force with force.'

In the event whatever 'powers' lay in the hands of the
I.R.A. were allowed to slip into the grasp of Fianna Fail.
There was friendly personal contact between some I.R.A.
men and Fianna Fail ministers such as Sean Moylan and
Oscar Traynor, but no formal alliance. The I.R.A. let the
political initiative drift away from it, apparently because,
in Peadar O'Donnell's phrase, the I.R.A. felt that its
cause would be best advanced by 'nipping at the heels
of Fianna Fail' to push the party along paths favoured by
the I.R.A. However the heels of one Eamon de Valera
were not for nipping at and he gratefully accepted the
present of the final weapon presented to him by the I.R.A.
—the land annuities campaign.

The land annuities dispute had its origin in a campaign
sponsored by Peadar O'Donnell, in his native Donegal.
He describes in his book, *There Will Be Another Day*,
how 'in late 1925 or early 1926' on the run from the
police he discovered that neighbours of his were being
served with summonses for non-payment of land annuities
which had accrued in the troubled times (roughly from
1916 onwards) and decided to help them. With the aid of
Colonel Maurice Moore, brother of George Moore the
novelist, O'Donnell organised a campaign to help people
hide their cattle so that they couldn't be seized by bailiffs,
and urging more people not to pay either arrears or any
annuities at all. The annuities were the sums which the
farmers paid to the Irish Land Commission, which in
turn passed the money over to the government for payment to the British national debt commissioners to meet
the loans raised for the purpose of buying out the landlords in the 1891-1909 period. After the treaty these
payments were made pursuant to the financial agreement of
February 12, 1923, which was signed by W. T. Cosgrave
and Major John W. Hills, the financial secretary to the
British Treasury, and to the Ultimate Financial Settlement, as it was called, of March 19, 1926, which was
signed by Ernest Blythe for Ireland and Winston Churchill for England. Between these payments and others cov-

ered by the two agreements specified for payments of pensions to former members of the Royal Irish Constabulary the total amount involved per year came to £5 million.

O'Donnel's Donegal agitation, which later spread to adjoining counties west of the Shannon, eventually petered out, but it generated sufficient support for Fianna Fail to take it up and make the retention of the land annuities by the Irish government seem a very attractive idea to small farmers in the 1932 election campaign.

All these factors and the fact that Cumann na nGaedheal had been in power for ten years ending in a period of economic slump helped to win the February election for Fianna Fail, and a sense of relief went through the I.R.A. when Cumann na nGaedheal was defeated. One man, now a prominent Dublin lawyer, said to me, 'I felt a tremendous release. It was a marvellous thing, we really hated those buggers, it was great to see them out.'

3 / THE TRIUMPH OF FIANNA FAIL

The defeat of Cumann na nGaedheal was not, however, to herald a new dawn for the I.R.A. In power de Valera immediately began taking steps to abolish the oath, and he released the prisoners from Arbour Hill Barracks on March 10, after he had formed his cabinet, amid scenes of great rejoicing in the streets of Dublin. Two days later *An Phoblacht*, which had been banned for the previous three months, appeared with an article by Maurice Twomey which said: 'Fianna Fail declares its intention to chop off some of the imperial tentacles; every such achievement is of value and will be welcomed. Notwithstanding such concessions, the Irish Republican Army must continue its work, and cannot escape its role as the vanguard of the freedom movement.'

Six days later on March 18 the Military Tribunal was suspended, and the orders which had declared the I.R.A. and Saor Eire to be unlawful were revoked. On

June 19 the I.R.A. marched in strength to Wolfe Tone's grave at Bodenstown where an oration was delivered by Sean Russell to a gathering estimated at over 15,000 members of the I.R.A. At a big demonstration to welcome the prisoners, held in College Green, Dublin, a few days after their release, one of the freed prisoners, Sean McGuinness, was reported as believing that 'The members of the defunct Executive Council were . . . a menace to society and the independence of Ireland, and it behoved all Republicans to unite and wipe out that menace at all costs.' (*Irish Times*, March 14.)

On October 15 and 22 *An Phoblacht* announced in successive issues that 'Free speech and the freedom of the press must be denied to traitors and treason mongers.' Speaking in Dublin at a public meeting two of the most prominent members of the I.R.A., Frank Ryan and Peadar O'Donnell, both spoke against allowing Cumann na nGaedheal speakers to be heard. Ryan said, 'No matter what anyone says to the contrary, while we have fists, hands and boots to use, and guns if necessary, we will not allow free speech to traitors.' O'Donnell said, 'The policeman who puts his head between Mr Cosgrave's head, and the hands of angry Irishmen, might as well keep his head at home.'

These were not cheering words for Cosgrave's supporters. Three days after McGuinness made his statement a convention of the Army Comrades Association was held to appoint a national executive. This body drew its membership from members of the army who had fought on the Free State side in the Civil War. Its aims were claimed to be benevolent, such as securing jobs in County Councils for out-of-work former Free State soldiers and its committee contained figures such as General Richard Mulcahy, and Dr Tom O'Higgins, a brother of the murdered Kevin O'Higgins.

Prior to Fianna Fail's taking office, rumours were rife that sections of the army and of the police would not allow this to happen. The rumours made the pre-election formation of the Army Comrades Association a highly suspect move to some Fianna Fail and I.R.A. supporters. This suspicion deepened after some Fianna Fail followers began to apply the I.R.A. policy of denying Cumann na nGaedheal speakers, in particular W. T. Cosgrave and Richard Mulcahy, a hearing at public meetings. The Army Comrades Association started to provide bodyguards to put down the bully-boys.

The I.R.A. and the Army Comrades Association also came into conflict when the idea of boycotting British goods, which was always flickering at the edges of I.R.A. planning, arose. A senior executive of Bass, the English brewing firm, made disparaging remarks about Ireland and a lorry load of Bass was destroyed in Dublin on December 14, 1932. Following this, the Dublin vintners appealed to the A.C.A. for protection and shipments of Bass were guarded by bodyguards of A.C.A. without further incident.

But the I.R.A. became involved with the A.C.A. most damagingly over the backlash of the land annuities campaign. On July 1, 1932, following its election pledges, the Fianna Fail government defaulted on the annuities due that day, and the British retaliated with a bill on July 11 allowing the government of the United Kingdom to recoup itself by imposing extra duties on imports from Ireland. The Irish struck again on July 23 with a similar bill, and what was known as the 'economic war' began. As Fianna Fail both reduced the amount of land annuities payable by the tenants, and at the same time funded arrears for three years, and sometimes longer, this was a highly popular policy with the small farmers.

The larger farmers, however, whose products were excluded from England by the tariff wall raised by the economic war, were incensed. A custom sprang up among the larger farmers of refusing to pay their land annuities, so that the Land Commission had to take legal proceedings in separate cases, involving thousands of defaulters, thereby clogging the courts. The government countered this move by passing the Land Act 1933 under which a warrant issued by the Land Commission took the place of legal proceedings, and over 400,000 of these warrants were lodged in twelve half-yearly periods, beginning in November/December, 1933, and ending in May/June, 1939, as a result of which a sum of over £2.5 million was levied or collected by the end of 1939.*

In the midst of this uproar a new complication arose on February 22, 1933. General O'Duffy had been dismissed from his post as commissioner of police by Fianna Fail. As Cumann na nGaedheal had been unable to hold meetings unscathed under a friendly police chief his going led many people on the Cumann na nGaedheal side to believe that they were in for an I.R.A.-Fianna Fail onslaught.

But although the Cumann na nGaedheal was not to know this the leadership of the I.R.A. and of Fianna Fail had already come to a parting of the way. Only four days before O'Duffy was dismissed the following directive was issued by the Army Council to the 'Commander of Each Independent Unit':

OGLAIGH NA hEIREANN
(Irish Republican Army)

ROINN; A/G   ARD OIFIG,
UIMHIR: BB 74   ATH CLIATH
                                         18adh Febhra, 1933

To:
The Commander of
Each Independent Unit

GENERAL ARMY CONVENTION, 1933

A chara,

The following statement from the Army Council will be read at each parade and Battalion Staff meeting called for the purpose of electing delegates to the Battalion Convention. Copies of the Army constitution are herewith enclosed.

---

* It would be impossible to chronicle all the deeds of violence, and acts of sabotage, which the 'no annuities' campaign inspired —in east Cork alone there were hundreds of such incidents.

1. In accordance with the constitution the Army Council had decided to convene the annual General Army Convention.

Briefly, the aim of the volunteer organisation is to assert the sovereignty and unity of the Republic of Ireland in which the ownership of the means of production, distribution and exchange will be vested in the Irish people. It will be the function of the forthcoming General Army Convention to consider how the task of achieving this object can be faced and to decide upon the policy of the Army.

2. The position of the Irish Republican Army from a military standpoint is dealt with in the Adjutant General's report which will be submitted to the General Army Convention. From this report it will be seen that the strength, training and discipline of the organisation have improved since the last convention. Whilst the strength of the organisation has shown a marked increase every year since 1925, the Army Council is of the opinion that the wide field for recruiting at the disposal of our forces has not been availed of.

In considering the policy of the Army, the General Army Convention will have to decide how the changes in the political situation, North and South, can best be utilised.

3. THE TWENTY-SIX COUNTIES: At the last Convention it was decided not to take any action which would actively impede the newly established Fianna Fail 'Government'. This decision governed to a great extent the policy of the Army Council, and every effort was made by the Council to avoid clashes. On the other hand, to put it mildly, not much assistance was given by the Fianna Fail 'Government' in carrying out this policy; the police and C.I.D. tried in many instances to provoke conflict. The Coercion legislation passed under the Cosgrave regime was not repealed—on the contrary in many cases it was actually used against Republicans, and thus we have witnessed the jailing of many of our comrades.

In dealing with England, the Fianna Fail 'Government' agreed to submit the question of the payment of tribute to arbitration. The payment of any tribute to England is an encroachment on the sovereignty of Ireland, which sovereignity is, and must remain, non-judicable. The oath of allegiance has been abolished, but the over-lordship of Britain was recognised by the appointment of a Governor General.

In its economic policy the Fianna Fail 'Government' has upheld and bolstered the capitalist system so that the economic war with England is being used for the advancement of both British and Irish capitalism within our shores.

Thus, these facts bring us to the realisation that the policy of the Fianna Fail Government is not directed towards the achievement of our aims.

4. It is the opinion of the Army Council that the policy of the Fianna Fail 'Government' is bound to lead to widespread dis-illusionment amongst a great proportion of its Republican supporters, and of the workers and working farmers. One of the principal tasks of the convention will be to decide whether such dis-illusionment can be availed of to assist in the achievement of the aims of the Irish Republican Army.

If it is considered that the tide of Republicanism arising from the dis-illusionment in the Fianna Fail policy can, and should be harnessed, the next consideration will be the means by which this should be done. Four means present themselves:

1. Through the medium of the Irish Republican Army alone.
2. By the re-organisation of Saor.
3. Through the medium of existing political organisations.
4. By the creation of a new organisation.

5. The next problem for consideration will be the policy of the Volunteer Organisation towards the Free State 'Government'. Since the last General Army Convention there has been no change in the attitude of the 'Government'. It claims that it is the legitimate government of the Twenty-six Counties, and that the Irish Republican Army is usurping its powers. In brief, it makes the same claims as regards the control of arms, and as regards its legitimacy as the Cosgrave 'Government'.

6. The proposed creation of a Volunteer Reserve Force*
as an auxiliary to the Free State Army will also require the
attention of the convention. It is the opinion of the Army
Council that the creation of this new appendage to the
Free State Army is aimed at diverting the activities of the
manhood of Ireland from the Revolutionary Movement,
and that its ultimate purpose will be to uphold the Treaty
and Constitution of the Free State. The Convention will
have to consider how best the threat of the creation of this
force can be met.

7. Since the last convention the Army Council has approved of the initiation of the Boycott British Campaign.
It is to be regretted that this campaign has not received the
support that might have been expected from the volunteer
organisation. It will be for the Convention to advise whether
this campaign shall be intensified or discontinued . . .

10. The Army Council must again draw the attention of
all ranks to the absolute importance of training, both in a
military and economic sense. It is vital that every member
of the Organisation has an intelligent conception of the task
to which the Army has pledged itself.

The influx of recruits to the Army further intensifies the
necessity for renewed efforts by unit commanders to raise
the standard of training and discipline to the highest
possible point.

The last General Army Convention decided:
THAT THE ARMY COUNCIL BE INSTRUCTED TO ESTABLISH AN
OFFICERS' TRAINING CAMP FOR THREE MONTHS, JUNE, JULY
AND AUGUST: THAT EACH UNIT BE COMPELLED TO SEND AT
LEAST TWO OFFICERS TO THE CAMP FOR ONE WEEK.

* This was a kind of territorial army which Fianna Fail was
setting up at this time. Recruiting opened on February 20, 1934,
and the volunteers were a frequent target for assaults by the
I.R.A. afterwards, particularly in Kerry. No loss of life was
ever involved, although volunteers were sometimes raided in their
homes, and their uniforms stolen. The uniforms were modelled
on those designed by Sir Roger Casement for the brigade which
he unsuccessfully attempted to raise among Irish prisoners of
war captured while fighting for England during the First World
War.

The Adjutant General's report shows how it was found almost impossible by General Headquarters to get units to provide suitable venues for these camps. The Army Council must express its regret at the lack of co-operation given by unit commanders to the General Headquarters Staff on this important matter.

11. The absolute necessity for the provision by units of financial support for the maintenance and equipment of the Army must again be emphasised. It is felt that while some units are worthy of every commendation, many others have made no efforts to fulfil the obligations undertaken by them in this respect.

Do chara,

D

_____

ADJUTANT GENERAL

The conditions of the time prevented Cumann na nGaedheal from trusting to Shakespeare's dictum that 'Two stars keep not their motion in the one orb', which in fact had begun to assert itself and continued to do so to the detriment of the stars of the I.R.A. Out of these conditions there arose a movement for whose creation the I.R.A. was largely responsible—the Blueshirts.

On July 20, 1933 an organisation known as the National Guard was formed from the Army Comrades Association to safeguard 'National interests and National culture'. Its director-general was General Eoin O'Duffy. At the suggestion of the secretary of the Army Comrades Association, Commandant Ned Cronin, it had adopted a blue shirt as uniform in April.

Its philosophy was militant from the start. The *United Irishman* of July 12, 1933, said, 'If a comrade is subjected because of his membership of the Association, to gross abuse his reply should be a swift blow or series of blows.' (The *United Irishman* was, at this time, the organ of Cumann na nGaedheal, edited by Ernest Blythe a former minister. The present day I.R.A. paper is also called the

T.I.R.A.   D

United Irishman.) By this time, *An Phoblacht* was coming
out in successive issues with demands for the nationalisation
of the banks and the breaking up of the larger farms but
Professor M. Tierney, one of the secretaries of the A.C.A.,
wrote in the *United Ireland* on December 13, 1933: 'The
corporate state must come in the end to Ireland as else-
where', and the other secretary, Professor James Hogan,
wrote a powerful series of articles attacking the I.R.A.
which were later reprinted in a widely sold pamphlet,
'Could Ireland Go Communist?'

Another correspondent in *United Ireland*, 'Oghnach',
suggested that the blue-shirt audiences should imitate the
Nazis when greeting their leaders and 'give three sudden
staccato bursts of mass cheering, each burst consisting of
one sharply ejected syllable . . . the word may be Heil
(Hail) pronounced sharply or it may be Hoch (Up)'. This
sort of thinking was like a red rag to a bull to the leftists
of the I.R.A. The spectacle of the bigger farmers, who
had not helped very greatly in the struggle for independence and were tainted with the brush of 'landlordism',
particularly in the Cork area, joining the no-rates campaign was also highly distasteful. These conflicting ideologies coupled with Civil War memories were enough to
set the I.R.A. against the Blueshirts in a weakening and
disastrous interlude for the I.R.A.

O'Duffy's first major effort as director-general of the
National Guard was timed for Sunday August 13, 1933—
a march of the National Guard to government buildings to
revive a ceremony of laying wreaths on the graves of
O'Higgins and Collins. Inside the Dail the idea of thousands of blue-shirted O'Duffy supporters bearing down
even on Sunday aroused Fianna Fail reactions. The government hastily set up what was known as the S-Branch, or
'Broy Harriers', called after Colonel Broy, the commissioner of police who had replaced O'Duffy. The S-Branch
was drawn from members of the Republican armed forces
during the Civil War and must have been the most hastily
organised police force in the world's history. One man,

Sergeant Willie Rowe, told me that he was asleep at midnight one Saturday evening and a knock came to his door. Somewhat fearfully he looked out the window—in those days midnight knocks could mean anything—to find not a hostile figure but a man who wanted him to come down immediately to Dublin Castle to be enrolled in a 'new police force they were founding'. One senior officer of the ordinary police force told me that he was on duty at a meeting of Cosgrave's in Dublin which was attacked by a number of Fianna Fail supporters and four I.R.A. companies who marched to the meeting in open formation. Many a head was broken and many a backside kicked at that meeting before Cosgrave was given a hearing through the efforts of the police and his own supporters. But to the officer's consternation a number of the I.R.A. attacking party were among the recruits who were admitted to the new force.

The Army Council of the I.R.A. decided to attack O'Duffy's marchers when they got as far as the Ballast Office at O'Connell Bridge, Dublin, a point where high buildings on either side make an ideal ambush site, and a headquarters to mastermind this operation was set up in Kevin Barry's old house in Fleet Street.* The I.R.A. also arranged to have armed men near every railway station and government building in Dublin. In addition, individual members of Fianna Fail armed themselves with a view to fighting off what seemed to all concerned like an attempt at a Mussolini-type coup. However on the very eve of the march the government revived the stringent public safety measures of the Cosgrave regime, which it had repealed on taking office, banned the parade and revived the Military Tribunal. O'Duffy called off the parade and changed the name of his now proscribed organisation to that of the Young Ireland Association.

* Barry, one of the youthful heroes hanged by the British during the Anglo-Irish struggle, gave his name to the ballad 'Kevin Barry' which is a favourite with nationalist Irish men and women of all shades of public opinion today.

For the moment O'Duffy's personality added a new and significant dimension to Irish politics. On September 8, 1933, Cumann na nGaedheal and a farming party known as the Centre Party united to form a new party, Fine Gael (Tribe of Gaels), under the leadership of William T. Cosgrave, and of James Dillon and Frank MacDermot of the Centre Party. These men were to be its parliamentary leaders, but its national organiser and leader was O'Duffy. Cosgrave, to the architects of the new merger, though a man of supreme integrity, did not appear to have the flamboyance and panache necessary to combat that of de Valera.

The Young Ireland Association was banned on December 8 following clashes between it and the I.R.A. The bulk of the I.R.A. leadership, Maurice Twomey and Sean MacBride in particular, deplored these futile fights. On January 17, 1934, a document was issued as a directive to I.R.A. company commanders stating that 'The present policy of the Army Council is that clashes between Volunteers and Imperialists are forbidden, and that conflicts are to be avoided.' This was largely ignored. Nor indeed did the government's actions during this time do a great deal to assuage opposition fears that Fianna Fail and the I.R.A. were closer than the public knew and that therefore Blueshirt militancy was necessary and justified.

The McGrory incident in particular caused a great deal of uneasiness. Mrs McGrory was fatally injured on the night of February 11, 1934, when the house of Joseph McGrory, Chapel Street, Dundalk, was blown up by a mine thrown through the front window. Two children also received serious injuries. Very little satisfaction was granted to either the public or the McGrory family over this outrage, which was in fact carried out by members of the local I.R.A. as an act of revenge. Joseph McGrory had given evidence against two members of the I.R.A. who were released by the Military Tribunal after the armed hold-up of a Blueshirt collector in Dundalk on January 9.

Thomas Lynch of Dunleer, Thomas Greene of Dundalk,

and four other members of the I.R.A. in the Dundalk area were brought before the Military Tribunal on March 19 on charges of refusing to account for their movements. Lynch was convicted of this and an additional charge of unlawful possession of ammunition, and was sentenced to six months, three months not to be enforced if he entered into recognisances (he was granted a 'free pardon' on September 27, 1935). On March 23, Richard Goss, James Finnigan and Matt McCrystal were sentenced to three months' imprisonment in default of entry into recognisances, and on May 3, Thomas Greene and Bernard Murphy were sentenced to six months' imprisonment, three months not to be enforced if they entered into recognisances. After release Finnigan left the I.R.A. and joined the Republican Congress group. Later he abandoned this organisation and operated on his own—as a battalion quartermaster in the I.R.A. he had had control of arms and ammunition and after leaving he refused to give them up to the I.R.A. On October 14, the I.R.A. kidnapped him and held him prisoner for a week before he escaped. Arms were discovered in Finnigan's possession on November 10 and he was arrested and brought before the Military Tribunal. On November 26 he was sent to prison for fifteen months. In July, 1935, while still serving this sentence, he was charged jointly with Richard Goss, Eamon Coffey, Thomas Walsh and Bernard Murphy, all of Dundalk, with the murder of Mrs McGrory. McCrystal was a state witness. This was the first murder trial before the Military Tribunal. On July 20, after a five-day hearing, all the accused were acquitted. (Goss was later executed in connection with a shooting incident in 1940.)

Before this, however, the country was swept with rumours concerning I.R.A. and Fianna Fail links when on February 16, speaking in the Dail, W. T. Cosgrave stated that a meeting of the I.R.A. had been held in 44, Parnell Square on February 11. On the same date he said police officers entered 5, Parnell Square, which was closed by order of the Military Tribunal. From here, he said, police officers kept number 44 under observation with field glasses. The meeting, he alleged, was to give instruction in the use and construction of a land mine to be exploded the following day. But the only explosion which took place the following day was in Dundalk, resulting in the death of Mrs McGrory. On February 21 the minister for justice, replying, said that all he was prepared to state to the house or to the people outside at that stage was that the police were satisfied that there was no relation between what happened in Dundalk and anything that took place in Dublin on the previous day.

Following the banning of the Young Ireland Association O'Duffy retaliated by founding the League of Youth six days later. Immediately an application was lodged in the high court seeking a declaration that the League was a lawful association, the object being to prevent the government's banning it. The hearing of this case dragged on for a number of years during which the Blueshirt movement wore itself out in a series of unconstitutional activities.

Whether the Blueshirts' shirt was a gesture of solidarity with shirted Fascist movements on the Continent, as the I.R.A. and Fianna Fail claimed, or whether it was adopted merely, as its originator claimed, to keep members from hitting each other in mistake for I.R.A. men at meetings, is a moot point. Certainly the movement was associated with the idea of the corporate state, then so fashionable with right-wing commentators. Certainly also its membership and support tended to be drawn from among the larger farmers and bigger businessmen, whereas that of the I.R.A. and Fianna Fail tended to come from the smaller farmers and the working classes.

Equally certainly however there had been a civil war and the I.R.A. and Fianna Fail members were breaking up Cumann na nGaedheal meetings. Both circumstances contributed to the speedy rise and fall of Blueshirtism. O'Duffy's personality was not suited to politics. His tactics included paying young lads to turn up in their blue shirts to rallies. As they also got their meals and free transport he both ensured large meetings and a correspondingly large strain on the organisation's resources. (The fee varied but some ex-Blueshirts told me they got ten shillings a meeting, a lot of money in those days.) He also boasted that the local government elections of July, 1934 would give Fine Gael a sweeping victory—Fianna Fail swept the boards. In August, he backed a motion at the Blueshirt congress which called on farmers to refuse to pay their rates until the economic war ended. He followed this up by declaring that Britain was fortifying her outposts in the six counties and the Free State, and if this meant war he, O'Duffy, would be in along with 'ninety-five per cent' of the Blueshirts. 'The other five per cent should give up their shirts.'

That was the end for the constitutionalists of the movement. Professor Hogan resigned from the Fine Gael on August 31 as a protest against 'the generally destructive leadership of its president'. On September 21 O'Duffy was pushed out of Fine Gael under pressure from its central council. He set up another League of Youth and subsequently a National Corporate Party, both unsuccessful. W. T. Cosgrave was elected president of Fine Gael and by the following September the League of Youth was amending its constitution 'to alter the dictatorial status which had been given to the office of Director-General'. By the following September the general was in Spain leading a group of ex-Blueshirts in Franco's army.

Tactically, it would have been far better for the I.R.A. either to have stayed aloof from the Blueshirts *versus* Fianna Fail struggle or else to join in on the side of the Blueshirts and Cumann na nGaedheal and attempt to disrupt the government, but the rank and file of the I.R.A., particularly in Cork under the leadership of Tom Barry, threw itself enthusiastically into the struggle. The following table gives an idea of the volume of incidents which the police were able to bring before the Tribunal:

Year	No. of days on which the Military Tribunal sat	No. of persons convicted by the Military Tribunal			
		I.R.A.	Blueshirts	Others	Total
1931	23	28	Nil	3	31
1932	23	17	Nil	2	19
1933	28	34	11	—	45
1934	110	102	349	—	451
1935	107	112	74	—	186
1936	43	129	Nil	—	129
1937	5	12	Nil	—	12
Total	339	434	434	5	873

Of the I.R.A. men and Blueshirts it is the Blueshirts who were sentenced to any lengthy period who are more to be pitied—the I.R.A. members at least emerged to find some sort of an organisation still in existence as a reminder of their sacrifice, but the speedy end of the Blueshirt movement meant that politically its members became nobody's children.

The elimination of the rightist Blueshirt movement should have led to a strengthening of the left. In fact the I.R.A.'s continuing and bedevilling debate on the use of force against some or all of three enemies—the Free State authorities, the Stormont government and the British —erupted again in such a way as to split the movement and leave Fianna Fail indisputedly the strongest force in Irish politics.

In a sense the Blueshirt upheaval and the I.R.A.'s pre-occupation with economic issues brought about the rupture, because in allying itself against the right the I.R.A. allowed itself to be driven further to the left than many of its members, Maurice Twomey in particular, thought either appropriate or prudent. Two incidents in particular alarmed the conservative element and brought matters to a head. These were the Gralton case and the Connolly House burning.

James Gralton of Effernagh, Co. Leitrim, a naturalised American citizen, had emigrated from Ireland to America in 1909. He returned in 1932 an avowed atheist and Communist, and became very active in propagating Communist doctrines. He was the owner of a dance hall in which he ran free dances to entice workers and young people to listen to his views. As the local clergy frowned on dances of any sort he drew large crowds and provoked corresponding resentment in clerical rightist circles. His dance hall was attacked and shots were fired into it. On February 9, 1933, he was served with a deportation order. He gave a personal undertaking to leave the country before March 4, but in the meantime he went on the run. As soon as he was caught he was arrested and deported.

The matter was taken up by the Revolutionary Workers Groups, as the Communist Party then styled itself, and by left-wing notabilities such as Mrs Sheehey Skeffington and Captain Jack White who had founded Connolly's Citizen Army, and a public campaign to 'Keep Gralton here' was launched.

In so far as the I.R.A. was concerned if Gralton had not existed Peadar O'Donnell and Frank Ryan would have been delighted to invent him, and *An Phoblacht* almost drowned out the *Workers Voice*, the Communist organ, in demanding the retention of Gralton. At a mass meeting in the Mansion House, Dublin, on February 27 to protest his expulsion a statement from the I.R.A. adjutant general was read saying that the army had already 'taken up the matter with the Army Unit in Leitrim and urged that everything possible be done to organise protests against the expulsion of James Gralton from his native land . . .'

What the statement did not say was that the Leitrim I.R.A. commandant, Sean O'Farrell, had advised against becoming involved with Gralton and allowed his men to stand neutral in the affair. Moreover Peadar O'Donnell had been pelted with mud and stones when he attempted to address a meeting in Drumsna, Co. Leitrim, and in fact while prominent left-wing I.R.A. men did attend the meeting the Army Council did not permit the adjutant general to deliver his statement in person and Michael Price and Frank Ryan were ordered not to speak either.

Gralton was caught and deported a few days later, but before the I.R.A. had had time to expunge the red hue he had imparted to their colours the Connolly House fracas blew up. As mentioned above Mrs Despard's house in Eccles Street was used as a workers' college by the left-wing I.R.A. It was also the headquarters of the Irish section of the Friends of Soviet Russia. Connolly House in Great Strand Street was the headquarters of the Irish Revolutionary Workers' Party. Both premises came under public scrutiny during February and March of 1933, largely because the Lenten lectures took note of the Gralton affair and the dangers of Communism generally. The preacher in the Jesuit church in Gardiner Street, not far from Eccles Street, was particularly strong on the issue.

Then a group of sodalists formed an organisation known as the St Patrick's Young Men's League which at first merely marched in the streets, occasionally stopping pedestrians in O'Connell Street to ask if they were wearing their scapulars! However on March 27 either this organisation, or a like-minded group attacked the houses in Eccles Street and Strand Street, causing some damage to fittings. Two nights later the mob looted and wrecked Connolly House before setting it on fire.

Charlie Gilmore, who had attempted to defend the place with a revolver, was arrested, charged with illegal possession of firearms and the attempted murder of a police officer. He conducted his own defence and was acquitted but the I.R.A. was deeply riven by the incident. He stated in court that he had had authority from the I.R.A. to bear arms in the defence of the Communist building. This was denied in an I.R.A. communiqué to the *Independent* on March 30. On April 1 however, the man who had given him permission to carry a weapon, his brother Harry, wrote contradicting this statement. Harry was court-martialled on Sunday April 9, but was acquitted on all counts even though he refused to sign a prepared letter to the press exonerating the I.R.A. of having dealings with Communists.

These two incidents imposed a severe strain on the I.R.A. To the right the movement was in danger of being ground between Communism and Fianna Fail. To the left the army soldiered to no purpose. In March, 1932 a 'Constitution and Government Programme for the Republic of Ireland' had been issued and the Army Council's manifesto for Easter 1933 said the I.R.A. believed that 'the reorganisation of Irish life demands the public ownership of the means of production, distribution and control' but neither 'constitution' nor 'programme' nor 'reorganisation' seemed to make any progress amid the welter of Blueshirtism, drilling and fisticuffs. What was needed, said the left, was a new political party. On March 17 and 18, 1934, a convention was held in Dublin to resolve the issue. It voted against the creation of a new political party. The margin was only one vote, that of Maurice Twomey, but Ryan, Price, Gilmore, O'Donnell, Fitzgerald and some of their supporters walked out of the convention and immediately set about trying to form a new movement without trying to win over their opponents. Offices were taken at 202, Pearse Street, later at 112, Marlborough Street, and on April 8 a conference was held at Athlone at which the new Republican Congress Party was launched, proclaiming itself 'So revolutionary that its achievement means the overthrow of all the existing political and economic machinery which at present holds this country and our people in subjection. Therefore our call is: Workers and working farmers unite on to the Workers Republic.'

The manifesto from which this extract is taken was printed in the national press and drew an immediate rejoinder from the Army Council, published in part in the national press, and in full in *An Phoblacht* on April 14. This said that 'in so far as the statement referred to is an attack on the present social and economic system, and an indictment of the policies of the Governments of the Six and Twenty-Six Counties, the Army Council is in complete agreement with it . . . this statement is merely repeating what has been stated over and over by the Army Council in its public pronouncements and through the columns of *An Phoblacht*.' But the Army Council went on to disown O'Donnell and Gilmore and said that 'This attack by Republicans can only assist the campaign of the Capitalist and Imperialist elements.'

The Army Council statement contained a passage which illustrates the very core of the hard-line, Fenian-cum-I.R.A. attitude towards constitutionalism: ' 'This Party will, in course of time, contest elections and enter the Free State Parliament. Inevitably it will follow the road which has been travelled by other constitutional Parties which, though setting out with good intentions, ended in failure. It is not very long ago since Fianna Fail leaders told us that they wanted to go into the Free State Parliament only for the purpose of smashing it up, but they now hold this institution and the whole Free State machine as sacred.'

The Army Council did not content itself with issuing this document, but continued to exert less public pressure on the Congress movement. Price, O'Donnell, Gilmore and Ryan were court-martialled *in absentia*, and expelled with ignominy—O'Donnell sending back word on hearing of the verdict that 'as he had been court-martialled in his absence, the sentence could be carried out in his absence also'.

However, Sheila Humphries, a prominent member of Cumann na mBan, and Eithne Coyle, another signatory, were shortly forced to withdraw from the new movement as a result of pressure from the I.R.A. There were other withdrawals at an early stage also. Three well-known members, Charles Reynolds, Seamus de Burca and George Leonard publicly recanted and reaffirmed their allegiance to G.H.Q. in a letter which appeared in *An Phoblacht* on April 21, 1934. 'We are satisfied,' they said, 'with the

Army Council's expression of agreement with the [Athlone] statement in reference to the attack on the present social and economic system.' The Army Council forbade I.R.A. men to have anything to do with the new movement under threat of dismissal and a few who disobeyed were in fact dismissed, but a much greater number—mostly in Dublin*—voluntarily resigned and went over to the Congress. Liam Kelly and Joseph Doyle were recruited in this way. Other active recruits were Norah Connolly O'Brien, a signatory of the Athlone manifesto; her brother, Roddy Connolly—both children of the executed 1916 leader James Connolly; Cora Hughes; and Frank Edwards, a Waterford school teacher who was later involved in a public controversy with his bishop following his dismissal, at the Bishop's instigation, for joining the Congress. All in all the effect of the Congress was to split the I.R.A. down the middle.

The Congress inaugurated its public campaign at a meeting in Rathfarnham on April 23, presided over by Liam Kelly, and on May 5, a newspaper, the *Republican Congress*, 'Organ of the Committees of Workers and Small Farmers working for the United Front against Fascism and for the Workers' Republic' made its first appearance.

Differences, however, built up within the Congress and came to light at a convention in Rathmines Town Hall on September 29 and 30. Michael Price differed from the majority of delegates on methodology and consequently was not elected to the executive. Price wanted the organisation to concentrate on strikes, resisting evictions, and the creation of a political organisation to contest municipal and Dail elections. O'Donnell, Ryan, Gilmore and others

---

* I was persistently given a figure of 4,000 for this defection, but I cannot estimate exactly either this or most other numerical claims for the I.R.A. Numbers of names on roll books did not in themselves give an exact picture of the numbers available to fight. However it can be safely assumed that the I.R.A., in the South alone, had upwards of 30,000 in its ranks at this time.

did not consider the time opportune for such a programme. They wished first to establish 'cells' in trade unions and to place their men in key positions in political organisations. Subsequently Price broke away from the Republican Congress and joined the 'Citizen Army'. (A sort of hangover from Connolly's 1916 army, which still kept itself within the Republican ethos, dimly hoping someday to achieve Connolly's goals.) Here again he opposed the majority, and in a short time he left that body. By 1936 his views had carried him on the platforms of the Irish Labour Party advocating the cause of the constitutional Labour Party.

At the end of 1934 the Republican Congress movement was in debt. George Gilmore had been sent to America to look for funds and meantime the Congress weekly was forced to suspend publication, flickering into life for an occasional issue as did the movement itself at times such as strikes when members came into conflict with police. There were activities such as those of January, 1935, when the Dublin chain, Bacon Shops Ltd, was strike-hit by Michael Fitzpatrick, a trade unionist who was also on the I.R.A. Army Council. The strike of the Dublin tram and bus workers in March, 1935, provided another basis for a united front with the I.R.A., as did agitations for the release of political prisoners, or events such as the I.R.A. Easter Week commemoration during which there were special contingents from the tramway strikers, the Workers' Union of Ireland, the Republican Congress, the Communist Party and the Unemployed Workers' Movement. At a May Day demonstration in College Green, the Republican Congress, the Communist Party of Ireland and the Unemployed Workers' Movement were represented. But relationships with the I.R.A. ruptured again at Bodenstown in June. The attitude of the I.R.A. was criticised in a leader in the June 29 issue of the *Republican Congress* which said:

From 1932 on it was clear the I.R.A. should rouse the

Republican population of Ireland into the new national advance.

Instead, Volunteers were sent out on silly attacks on neighbour lads of the same home circumstances who, in the absence of any lead from the I.R.A. were joining the Fianna Fail Reserve in the belief that it was to be used against the Fascists.

Instead of raising the economic war into an assertion of the nation's sovereignty, I.R.A. leaders tried to develop it into a squabble over Bass bottles in public-houses.

Instead of opening the road for a leftward movement. the I.R.A. leaders, to the cheers of such men as Professor Hogan, opened an attack on their own left-wing elements.

They took the same attitude as the Irish Hierarchy and the *Independent** towards the revolutionary workers within their ranks.

I.R.A. leaders refused to permit Northern workers to carry banners in 1934, and actually tore the banner—'United Irishmen of 1934'—carried by the Shankill contingent.

And in 1935 I.R.A. leaders ordered country units to attempt to smash up Republican Congress marchers.

But the shades were drawing in on the Republican Congress Movement.

Peadar O'Donnell announced the formation of an 'Active Service Unit' one hundred strong, on January 3, 1936. His proposals were:

The active service unit will meet once a week; full strength. It will be in four sections:
First Section will take on the task of penetrating the Fianna Fail Cumainn, I.R.A. units and Trade Union branches, with a view to developing demonstrations to reveal the strength of Republican feeling and to accelerate the independence ferment.
Second Section will organise the housing struggles and extend Tenant Leagues throughout the City.

* Which after the 1916 Rising carried a leading article calling for the punishment of the leaders.

Third Section will co-operate with the unemployed workers' movements, and also bring to general notice and support those small strikes that have become a feature of Dublin in these days when an injury to one is no longer the concern of all, and it will co-operate generally with strike committees.

Fourth Section will cater for the social, financial and educational side of the movement; will organise outings, collections and classes.

The 'Independence ferment' was far less than O'Donnell hoped. Early in 1936 the *Republican Congress* weekly was forced to suspend publication, and by the end of the year the Congress offices at 57, Middle Abbey Street had to be vacated, as there was no money to pay the rent. An attempt was made to revive the paper under the name of the *Irish People* (the name of the first Fenian paper edited by Charles Kickham in the 1860s). Like its predecessor, it was printed by Frank Ryan, at the Co-operative Press, St Anthony's Place, but only one number seems to have appeared, on February 29, 1936.

O'Donnell, Gilmore, Ryan, Roddy Connolly and Cora Hughes gamely continued their efforts, co-operating with the Communists, then under the leadership of Sean Murray, in connection with the visit to Dublin of the Scottish Communist, William Gallacher, M.P. in April, 1936. Gallacher attended the I.R.A. Easter Commemoration on April 12 as one of the Communist and Republican Congress contingent. The presence of this group—whose members displayed a red button in their coats—provoked a good deal of public hostility and the marchers were stoned by one section of the crowd. The next day a large crowd assembled in College Green and prevented the holding of a public meeting at which Gallacher had been announced as a speaker. Peadar O'Donnell had to be rescued from the mob by the police. The crowd, on breaking up, marched through the streets and demonstrated outside the headquarters of the Communist Party. Subsequently the Congress group had to abandon a number of other proposed meetings through fear of attack.

By November, 1936, the Republican Congress had practically ceased to exist, and the same may almost be said of the Communist Party of Ireland which was also in such financial difficulties that its organ, the *Workers' Voice*, ceased publication.

Meanwhile on the right the I.R.A. proper attempted to give itself a semi-constitutional role such as that of the Republican Congress. These efforts were not successful. In fact, its role in a bitter transport strike, which began in Dublin on March 3, 1935, led to widespread arrests. The government had placed army lorries on the streets to alleviate the distress caused by the strike, and on March 25 the Army Council issued the following manifesto:

> Oglaigh na hEireann,
> Ard Aifig, Atha Cliath,
> March 22nd, 1935.

Roinn: Army Council,
Uimhir: XD/61.

To the Joint Strike Committee,
Dublin Tram and Bus Workers.

A Chairde,

The Army Council has had under consideration the dispute between the Dublin transport workers and the Dublin United Tramways Company.

In the opinion of the Army Council, the situation is one in which more than the immediate causes of the dispute is involved. The action of the Free State Government in using the Free State Army for strike-breaking purposes, in the interest of a company to which the Government has given a monopoly, constitutes a definite challenge to all workers. That the complete transport system of Dublin should be at the mercy of a private monopoly is a matter affecting the welfare of all Dublin citizens.

The Army Council takes the view that the matters at

issue call for the intervention of all Republicans who stand
by the proclamation of Easter Week, wherein equal rights
and opportunities are guaranteed to all citizens.

The Army Council, realising the importance of the
principles involved, feels that the joint efforts of the Free
State Government and of the combine must be defeated.
To meet this attack, the organised support of all those who
stand for decent working and social conditions is necessary.
For these reasons, the Army Council hereby expresses its
willingness to assist the workers in their struggle.

Further, the Army Council is interested, as the governmental programme of the Irish Republican Army on the
question of transport provides:—

'Railways, canals, air and waterways, and all forms of public
inland transport shall be operated by a body set up by the
National Economic Council.'

The Army Council offers the services of the Army to assist
in mobilising the maximum support for the Dublin transport
workers in their struggle, and is prepared to send representatives to meet the Strike Committee for this purpose.

Is Sinne,
The Army Council,
Per............Secretary.

This statement alerted the government and on the following day, the houses of prominent members of the I.R.A.
and of the Republican Congress were raided by the police
and forty-four men were taken into custody. Some of
them, including Peadar O'Donnell, were released after
interrogation, but on April 24-29 the Military Tribunal
imposed the following sentences: Eighteen months' imprisonment on Con Lehane, solicitor (a member of the
Army Council at the time) for sedition, membership of an
unlawful association and refusing to give an account of
his movements; six months' imprisonment on Claude
O'Loughlin, Richard Batterbury, Leo Burdock, Thomas
Farrington, Patrick McElroy, Thomas Merrigan, Donal

O'Donoghue, James Hannigan, Andrew Walsh, John Farrington, Joseph Hendley, Sean Brunswick, James Cole, Michael Neary and Laurence Carwood, on charges of membership of unlawful associations, etc.; one month's imprisonment on John Nalty, William Scott and Michael Kelly for membership of an unlawful association, etc.

Sean MacBride, Maurice Twomey, Michael Fitzpatrick and Sean Russell went on the run, but Tom Barry, who had been arrested in Cork on March 26 on charges of seditious utterances at Tralee on January 6, was caught and got six months.

These setbacks promoted the growth of another burst of activity in favour of 'constitutional' advance, and at a convention held in Dublin on August 17 the agenda included proposals for contesting future elections and, in certain cases, recognising the courts. As usual those who believed in force objected strongly and there were threats of resignation. Nevertheless, another convention was held on September 21 and those present voted four to one to contest the next general election.

At a meeting at Barry's Hotel, Dublin on March 7, 1936, a new political party, Cumann Poblachta na hEireann, was formed. It was decided to try to have it both ways, by contesting parliamentary elections in the North and the South but stipulating that successful candidates would not take their seats. Maurice Twomey, who was lukewarm about the proposal, and Sean MacBride who was strongly for it, represented the I.R.A., and Republicans who abhorred Fianna Fail and Fine Gael and could see no sign of advancement in the nearly moribund Sinn Fein movement, also attended. Chief among these was the former chief of staff, Dr Andrew Cooney who had been particularly active in the I.R.A. in the 1920s; Dr James P. Brennan who was later to become active in Clann na Poblachta, a party Sean MacBride would lead; the Misses Fiona Plunkett, a sister of the executed 1916 leader; Florence McCarthy; Madge Daly of Limerick, sister of the widow of the executed 1916 leader Thomas Clarke, and Patrick MacLogan, the I.R.A. organiser who was at the time Nationalist M.P. for South Armagh. He was subsequently elected chairman of the new party.

However, the opposition, particularly in the Dublin brigade, to the proposal that the I.R.A. should have a political wing continued to be strong. A special convention was summoned in Dublin on May 19 at which the two most prominent I.R.A. men were again Sean MacBride and Maurice Twomey. MacBride proposed that Cumann Poblachta na hEireann should receive the active support of the I.R.A. but Twomey objected and pointed out that there was no difference between this proposal and the first Fianna Fail proposal. The discussion was heated and finally Twomey walked out of the meeting followed by the more prominent Dublin Brigade officers: Claude O'Loughlin, James Coulton and Kevin Lawless.

The meeting revealed both the typical I.R.A. man's Fenian distrust of constitutional politics, and his naïve belief that once he entered politics power was his for the taking. This view was not shared by the public as is shown by a table giving the votes secured by Republican Congress and Cumann Poblachta. The Communists put forward no candidates in this election but worked for the Republican Congress candidates. (The elections were held on June 30.)

Republican Congress

Name	Area	Votes	Total Poll
Frank Ryan	No. 2	418	32,517
George Gilmore	No. 3	730	32,617
Cumann Poblachta na hEireann			
J. McGrath	No. 1	675	21,519
A. Lynn	No. 2	482	32,517
M. Fitzpatrick	No. 3	720	32,617
S. Malin	No. 4	630	21,556
Madame Maude Gonne MacBride	No. 5	689	29,733

For a personal assessment of how people generally felt about the movement I turned to my friend and colleague Anthony Butler, author, art critic, raconteur and television personality, who was both involved and at the same time sufficiently detached to be authoritative. He gave me the following characteristically humorous reminiscence:

'The first idea I had of the existence of the I.R.A. came in 1927 when police invaded my school to arrest one of the teachers in connection with the shooting of Kevin O'Higgins. I was in a low primary grade and since we all hated the teacher involved—a sadistic brute—we were all on the side of law and order. Rumour spread that the arrest was only a fake to get him for his use of the cane. Mixed with this report was some mention of the I.R.A.s which we assumed was just a higher class than the ABCs. From that moment until the late 1940s the I.R.A. was a background to any thinking I might do on politics. It was the Mafia; it was truth; it was cruelty; it was justice —you didn't know what and this shifting assessment of their place in Irish life was one which most people shared.

'You couldn't escape the shadow of Republicanism and the I.R.A. in Dublin of the late 1930s. They weighed heavily on the nation; they were powerful and whatever the reality—menacing.

'The ebbing tide of revolution which was dying on the beaches of the new state had received some fresh impetus from the discontent generated by depressed economic conditions and the I.R.A. overlapped many other organisations in the labour field.

'In the great building strike of 1936 it played a large part even though the activities of its members were unofficial—this meant no more than an implied hand-washing by the Army: "Don't blame us if you're caught."

'While I was too cowardly—rather than too prudent— to involve myself with the I.R.A. I was like many others delighted to sniff the powder and vicariously enjoy the actions of others who were deeply involved, delighted to hang about the fringes of the movement and know people who were involved. One of my friends kept his private armoury in his cushions which didn't make for comfort or a peaceful mind, but he was an exciting person for a boy to know.

'The building strike went on for a long time and my father was involved in it so I, with little else to do at sixteen, took part as well. One feature of these days was the hunger march—the suffering artisans exposing their agonies to the people of Dublin. I marched with them but didn't last long.

'Plump, fresh-skinned and most definitely outside the classification of deprived citizen at least in appearance, I was poor propaganda material. But the whole thing introduced me to Paddy.

'Paddy was an I.R.A. hatchetman and executioner who, it was reputed, would shoot his own mother if the organisation demanded. Since she was faster on the draw than he was the reputation was purely theoretical. Through Paddy I was drawn into the Sunday morning discussion groups around the Nelson Pillar. Here a million plots were hatched although not one per cent ever reached fruition.

'Paddy would vanish now and then for a few days as the police made it a habit to pick him up no matter what happened through Republican activism. They always arrested him away from his home as it required siege tactics to take him in the bosom of his family and his mother was a deadly shot with a saucepan. Indeed until they learned to arrest him away from his home the political police tried as far as possible to take him on Fridays. It was much less dangerous to be hit by a fried kipper than to risk the scalding downpour of a stew outside the flesh-eating abstinence of that day.

'There was a vehicle builders strike on with the building strike and a number of "blackleg" workers were imported from England. Since this combined the national enemy with social justice Paddy offered himself and his "Peter the Painter" to the vehicle builders.

'Whether they accepted his offer or not I don't know but the decision was made to shoot the scabs. Knowing nothing of this I drifted into Paddy's small group one Sunday morning before the leader himself arrived. One of the faithful asked me if I was going to help Paddy the following morning and I said I was without being too sure what it was all about.

'When Paddy arrived I was an integrated if ignorant conspirator. The guarded language of the group, which stated nothing directly or concretely, contributed to keeping me in the dark.

'As arranged I turned up the next day outside the Northern Star Hotel in Amiens Street at 12.30. It was a hot steaming summer's day but Paddy and his two companions were ear-deep in trench coats that bulged in unexpected places as if they were carrying massive loads of scrap-iron. I wore an open-necked shirt, a sports coat and flannels and was the coolest man in every way amongst them. Paddy shook my hand and almost choked with emotion.

' "I didn't think you had the guts."

'Slightly puzzled I sat quietly on my bright new bicycle and discussed the weather, trying at the same time to work out what was involved. They didn't seem interested in chit-chat and kept looking up Amiens Street with fierce restlessness.

'An hour went by while I waited and talked and they displayed even greater apprehension and impatience. Finally we dispersed with Paddy thanking me profusely. I cycled away.

'It was a week or two before I found out Paddy's plans for that morning. A report in an evening newspaper told of the shooting in the leg of a British vehicle builder outside the Northern Star Hotel in Amiens Street. Paddy read it with a grin and nudged me.

' "Sorry, I couldn't ask you along for this one. Two of us was enough."

'He seemed a little ashamed of his neglect.

' "But don't worry, oul son. The next action is on I'll see you're in on it."

'The full horror of the event didn't strike me immediately but when it did I erupted in goose pimples. From that time on I kept clear of Paddy and put an end to my revolutionary career as an assassin.'

The year, 1936, that Butler abandoned his revolutionary career coincided with the government's coming to conclusions similar to his concerning the I.R.A. and for very similar reasons.

On April 29 and May 21 large-scale swoops on I.R.A. men in Cork and Dublin resulted in Twomey, most of the Dublin brigade and all the principal Cork I.R.A. men with the exception of Tom Barry (commanding officer Cork County), Tadgh Lynch (battalion adjutant), and Denis Griffin (County intelligence officer) being arrested. Sean Russell and Sean MacBride escaped the net but Donal O'Donoghue, who was then editing *An Phoblacht*, was arrested on July 8 in Co. Kerry. He went on hunger strike in Arbour Hill prison on July 11, remaining without food until August 7 when he was released.

The incidents that directed the government's attention to the I.R.A. varied from idiotic episodes like that which occurred on January 25 in the Masonic Hall at Tuckey Street, Cork, where a party of I.R.A. men struck a blow for Ireland by holding up the diners in the midst of a convivial occasion and smashing up plates and furniture, to incidents in which three lives were lost. The three deaths were those of Roderick More O'Farrell, who was fatally wounded on February 9, 1935; Vice-Admiral Henry Boyle Townsend Somerville, who was shot dead at 9.30 p.m. on March 24, 1936 as he stood at the door of his home at Castle-Townsend, Co. Cork; and John Egan, who on April 26, 1936 was shot dead in full view of everyone in Mitchell Street, Dungarvan, Co. Waterford.

The first two killings were not sanctioned by the Army Council but the death of Egan was as a result of an I.R.A. court-martial. It was probably never intended to kill More O'Farrell at all. This tragedy arose out of a rent agitation on the Sanderson estate in Co. Longford. Tenants were demanding a 50 per cent reduction in rent and the English agent, Captain Montague, was unable to collect any rents while the dispute continued. More O'Farrell, Senior, was appointed in his stead and the dispute simmered throughout 1934. On December 2, at a public meeting at Edgeworthstown, Co. Longford, official I.R.A. speakers, who had been formally invited by the Tenants Association to join in the agitation, made inflammatory speeches on the lines of: 'there must be plenty of pitchforks and boughs on the trees around Edgeworthstown but one strong bough should be left on a tree convenient to More O'Farrell's in case of need.' On February 9, 1935, a party of armed men raided the More O'Farrell house, outside Edgeworthstown, during a dinner party. More O'Farrell and his son strongly resisted the raiders' attempts to take away More O'Farrell* and several shots were fired, one of them striking young More O'Farrell who later died. Seven members of the I.R.A. were arrested and charged with murder at the Central Criminal Court in Dublin, but on December 10, 1935, before the evidence for the defence was taken, the jury brought in a verdict of not guilty.

When Frank MacDermot, speaking in the Dail on June 16, 1936, asked Minister for Justice Gerald Boland why the case had not been heard before the Military Tribunal, the minister replied that a certificate was not issued empowering the Tribunal to hear the case as the minister 'could not conscientiously state that the crime was committed for the purpose of interfering with the machinery of government, or the administration of justice'.

* I am informed that tarring and feathering, rather than shooting or hanging, was intended.

MacDermot was reflecting an opposition view that the Fianna Fail government and the I.R.A. were still in some form of collusion. This unease spread to the public, so that when I.R.A. trigger-happiness claimed two more lives Fianna Fail was driven, both by the necessity of upholding governmental authority and the need to show people where the government stood, to act forcefully against its former friends.

Admiral Somerville was shot dead because the Cork I.R.A., strongly anti-British and anti-Protestant, took violent exception to his giving references to young local men who wished to join the British navy. The shooting of an elderly man who had come unsuspectingly to the door of his home to answer a knock did more to alienate popular sympathy from the I.R.A. than any single act since the shooting of Kevin O'Higgins.

Then on April 26 came the Egan killing. Egan was an ordinary country lad, and his death horrified the countryside. He had been one of a party of five I.R.A. men arrested on July 12, 1935, for illegal drilling in Co. Waterford. On July 18 the commander of the West Waterford battalion of the I.R.A., William O'Donoghue, was arrested, and on July 30 received three months' imprisonment. He had been in charge of the drill session for which Egan and the others were arrested. At O'Donoghue's hearing Egan and two others were released, but the I.R.A. believed that Egan had earned their *nolle prosequi* by turning state's evidence, and that the other two men released with him were set free only as a sort of smoke screen. He was shot from a motor car (stolen earlier in the evening from the home of a district justice) and on May 14 four members of the I.R.A.—William O'Donoghue, John Tobin, Edmund Carraigan and Michael Conway—were arrested and charged with his murder.

Conway was sentenced to death but was released on May 4, 1938, his case having become in the meantime a *cause célèbre*. First, his counsel, Albert Wood and Art O'Connor, refused to appear before the Military Tribunal, saying that they would not act for him because they would not appear in any case before the Military Tribunal. Then his solicitors Messrs. Hogan & Lehane—Con Lehane being a former member of the Army Council, who had by then severed his connection with the army—sent the correspondence to the press. Only one paper, the *Mayo News*, printed it on July 18. After this, Conway's case proved a rallying point for I.R.A. publicists. 'Micksey', as he was called was one of the best-known I.R.A. men in Ireland at the time, and a classical example of a figure of menace to those outside the movement, and the epitome of decency, kindness, and sincerity to those within it. (He later became a monk.)

Twomey got three years from the Military Tribunal for membership of an unlawful organisation, on June 19, a day after the I.R.A. had been outlawed by an order from the executive council, after a two-day debate in the Dail. In the course of the debate the acting minister for justice, Gerald Boland, made the following significant statement concerning future government policy towards the I.R.A.: '. . . the fact that these murders have occurred . . . makes it clear that stern action must be taken against any organisation which claims to have the power of life and death over its members, or ex-members, or other citizens, or which claims that it is entitled to use force upon the community to compel obedience to its will. I now give definite notice to all concerned that the so-called Irish Republican Army, or any organisation which promotes or advocates the use of arms for the attainments of its object will not be tolerated . . .'

The next day he followed this up by saying, '. . . we smashed them [Blueshirts] and we are going to smash the others [the I.R.A.] . . . if there are people who know where arms are, and their sense of civic duty will not encourage them to tell where they are, then if any form of reward is necessary to induce them to do so, we will give it . . .'

The government also banned the Bodenstown meeting,

fixed for June 21. Trains and buses heading for the meeting were stopped, an aeroplane hovered overhead, and on the ground armed cars and police were grouped. One band of young Limerick I.R.A. men seized a lorry and attempted to make their way to Bodenstown but were arrested and sentenced to nine months by the Military Tribunal. And a young man, Sean Glynn, committed suicide in Arbour Hill prison on September 13. A subsequent commission of inquiry investigating his death found that imprisonment had so worked on his mind that he became depressed and took his own life.

4 / THE I.R.A.'S FOREIGN LINKS

The I.R.A. did not make any great impact on the outside world after the end of the Anglo-Irish war, and the outside world has never impinged very greatly on the I.R.A. There were some peripheral contacts with European countries, and improbably enough with Russia, but the only country to which the I.R.A. looked for assistance in any sustained manner was America, where large-scale emigration from Ireland following the great famine of the 1840s had created a powerful source of strength. Embittered Irishmen in America were approached by Irish leaders as diverse in their policies and appeal as Parnell, Redmond, de Valera and Sean Russell.

The I.R.A.'s contact with Europe was, on the other hand, principally through its left-wing members, such as David Fitzgerald or Peadar O'Donnell. Fitzgerald was a frequent visitor to Russia during the 1920s and the I.R.A. was officially represented at the World Congress of the Anti-Imperialist League in Brussels in 1927 by Frank Ryan and O'Donnell, and by Sean MacBride and Donal O'Donoghue at Frankfurt on Main in 1929. As a result of I.R.A. representations the Frankfurt congress (which met July 20-31) passed a resolution calling on 'the organised workers of Great Britain to withdraw the threat of war against Ireland and allow Ireland freely to organise her own life in accordance with working class ideals'.

The congress also pledged that the 'revolutionary organisations in Ireland' would receive the 'whole-hearted backing of the Congress' for their 'next attempt' to set up the desired state and elected an I.R.A. man called Magennis, who had been given two years hard labour for the possession of a revolver, as a member of the honorary praesidium of the congress. This was the most tangible result the I.R.A. deputation achieved.

Peadar O'Donnell and Sean Hayes introduced to Ireland an offshoot of the Third International with the formation of a branch of the European Peasants Committee which O'Donnell represented at the international congress of the movement in Berlin during March, 1930. However neither the I.R.A. nor the Communists thought much of each other. Police records of the 1930s show that two members of the British Communist Party who were deputed to visit Ireland during 1930 to study conditions on behalf of the Communist International reported that the Irish were 'too Mexican' to make good Communist revolutionaries. Presumably this means too volatile and unamenable to discipline. The Irish Catholic Republicans were certainly unmoved by appeals such as that of Peadar O'Donnell to 'think of the Army as the armed members of the toiling and working masses. The leadership must be that of a revolutionary working-class party whose membership may be all I.R.A., though the Army will be larger than the Party.'

First Saor Eire and then the Republican Congress failed to marry the class struggle to the I.R.A.'s efforts. In Irish circumstances such an outcome was inevitable as Stalin himself recognised when he had dealings with the I.R.A. not long after it had reorganised itself following the Civil War.

In the spring of 1925 I.R.A. headquarters considered seeking aid from Russia through 'Pa' Murray, a formidable figure during the war of independence and with extensive contacts in Russian circles in London. Through these he arranged for an I.R.A. delegation to be received in Moscow. The other militant Republican in the party was Sean Russell, with Gerald Boland sent by de Valera to hold a watching brief on behalf of the more constitution-ally minded section of the movement. The trio reached Germany and left Hamburg on June 27 with forged passports. (Ironically the outbreak of the Second World War would see Russell dying on a German submarine and Boland, as minister of justice in a government led by de Valera, distinguishing himself by the rigour with which he dealt with men who were still following Russell's leader-ship.)

At Leningrad the men were shown a variety of weapons —but 'Pa' was the only one who could use them! He has told me that his impression at the time was that the Russians simply did not have very much armament to give anyone, though this was not the reason which the Communists gave for refusing to help. After Leningrad they went to Moscow where Murray met Stalin. Stalin asked him what precautions he could guarantee against any weapons they might be given being seized by the Free Staters. He rocked Murray by producing a complete list of the amount of guns the government authorities had seized in Ireland to that date. In addition he wanted to know how many trained men the I.R.A. could guarantee to use the weapons. The interview lasted for about half an hour during which Stalin made it clear that he was worried that any weapons he might give to the I.R.A. would be discovered and used by Russia's enemies as a pretext for invasion. He thought that such a gift might particularly inflame the British.

All in all the interview and the visit were not successes. Stalin told Murray that, aboard the liner from Hamburg, the others had talked too much and that several people knew of their mission. Checking on this episode with Boland, he told me how they had met a friendly woman Communist 'who knew all about the Irish problem. She knew all about the Church and about our agricultural economy.' Whether or not the lady was a Cheka agent, the Russians do not seem to have been too impressed with the Irish revolutionaries. Boland told me that the first question he was asked on arrival was, 'How many bishops did you hang?' When he answered, 'None', his interrogator replied, 'Ah you people are not serious at all.'

This trip ended the I.R.A.'s chances, though not their hopes, of getting a large supply of armament from abroad. A trickle of Thompson guns with a significant history did continue to straggle in from New York. The guns were part of a consignment of 500 Thompson guns ordered from the Auto Ordnance Company, set up by Colonel Thompson in New York, on April 5, 1921. They were stored in a warehouse in the Bronx on La Fontaine Avenue, under the supervision of Lawrence DeLacy. DeLacy arranged to have them smuggled aboard the ship *East Side* for transhipment to Ireland on June 17. However on June 16 the consignment was discovered and seized as the *East Side* lay at her berth in Hoboken. The U.S. customs held on to the guns until September 14, 1925, when an order of discontinuance was issued allowing them to pass into the hands of Joseph McGarrity. This of course precluded their use in the Anglo-Irish war, but the I.R.A. did manage to smuggle some Thompson guns into Ireland during the war. On June 16, 1921, two of them were used to ambush a troop-train moving from Amiens Street to Kingsbridge—the first time Thompsons were used in warfare. (The ambush was carried out by a twelve-man party, led by Oscar Traynor, between Drumcondra Road and Botanic Road. The British admitted to three casualties, one of them serious.)

Eventually some of the American weapons found their way to Ireland, some in the personal luggage of a famous Kerry All-Ireland football team which visited America in 1927. Tom Barry told me that he had taken more ashore at Cork Harbour where he was an executive with the Port and Docks board. And Jim Killeen and Frank Driver recalled taking a lorry to Galway to pick up a consignment with Sean Russell. Killeen remembers the Galway episode vividly because two days after he and Russell had driven across Ireland with a lorry-load of illicit Thompsons he discovered that Russell had not taxed the lorry and that at any moment a vigilant policeman could have had them arrested.

The Russian episode convinced Murray, as it helped to convince other, more constitutional Republicans, that the I.R.A. had little future and he dropped out of the movement shortly after his return. By the end of 1925 the paths of the militants and of de Valera's followers had also diverged.

In America however the ground for Republican propaganda, though it shrank enormously after the end of the Anglo-Irish war, still continued fruitful as Murray could attest. Murray, who died at the end of 1968, was already an old man, interested in literature and history, when I first interviewed him in 1964. He told me of other incidents which he had taken part in during the war of independence before going on to talk of America.

For instance at one stage during the war while the conscription crisis was raging Cathal Brugha took him along with a party of volunteers who, if conscription had been introduced, were going to machine-gun the British government benches from the visitors gallery of the House of Commons. As the debate wore on member after member of the group lost his nerve, but Murray, whose special task was the assassination of Balfour, stayed on in London, although the delay was telling on him too. One day he learned that Balfour was to preside at Oxford at a university function that afternoon and to test his nerve he went to Oxford and accosted Balfour on the street under the pretext of seeking directions. Balfour courteously walked with him for about a hundred yards, during which Murray satisfied himself that he could have carried out his mission if he had to.

When we spoke of America we were sitting in his house

in Terenure waiting for a priest to call to hear his confession, because he had been unable to leave the house for some months following a car accident. He said to me that he had been in America and then said no more. I thought that his mind was dwelling on the priest's visit, and after a few moments silence ventured to prod him again.

'What were you doing there?'

There was a moment's silence and his kindly blue eyes flickered as though they had focused on something distasteful. Then he replied, 'Shootin' a poor divil!'

The man had been condemned to death as a traitor by the I.R.A. after a party of Volunteers was betrayed to Crown forces at Clonmult, Co. Cork. After they had surrendered they were tortured and then shot out of hand. The man had gone to America and it was not until after the signing of the truce that Collins got word of his whereabouts in New York. Murray and two comrades were sent to carry out the sentence, but when they got to New York they found that their quarry had changed his address. However by extraordinary ill-luck the unfortunate man turned up to watch the St Patrick's Day parade down Fifth Avenue, across the street from where Murray and his confederates were standing. With the aid of an Irish-American policeman who was on duty at the parade they traced him to his new lodgings and shot him dead, with a New York City police revolver. The killing went almost unnoticed and received only the most cursory investigation.

Sitting in his red-bricked respectability in suburban Dublin nearly fifty years later Murray sighed and said, 'I was sorry after. We heard later that the poor devil had been tortured to make him talk. We didn't know that at the time.'

Even today it is conceivable, though unlikely, that a modern I.R.A. party might receive the same assistance in New York, but it was not at all to be wondered at in the 1916-22 period. Current American statistics of the Irish

population in America estimate that there are twenty
million people born in Ireland or of Irish descent, living
there. The generation which lived around the time of
the Anglo-Irish war had comparatively recent memories of
crowding in ghettoes; persecutions by nativist groups such
as the Know Nothings; of grinding poverty and hostility
from the white Anglo-Saxon Protestants who denied them
employment; of discrimination in boarding houses and
sometimes in jobs with signs saying 'No Irish or colored
need apply'; and of an anguished parting from the country
they loved followed by a smelly, dangerous and often
deadly voyage to the States in conditions which have
branded the phrase 'coffin ships' into Irish folklore. Probably as many Irish died aboard these badly ventilated,
over-crowded ships and were buried at sea as were claimed
by every revolution from the time of Wolfe Tone to the
signing of the treaty with England in 1921.

The Irish relied heavily on the consolation of religion,
and took with them their own brand of ultramontane
Jansenistic Roman Catholicism. To many a hungry immigrant Irishman or woman the Church was the only life-
buoy in a sea of hostility. Thus today in America while
some Irish are organised in the service of the Democratic Party almost all Irish are organised in the service
of the American Catholic Church. An annual display such
as the St Patrick's Day Parade down Fifth Avenue is not
organised by Irishmen to draw attention to Ireland, or to
gain scholarships or industries for their native land, but
as a predominantly Catholic festival which is organised
with the approval of the archdiocese of New York.

Before 1922 the British were still in Ireland and it was
relatively easy to canalise both religious fervour and patriotic anti-British nationalism into organisations of some
power and significance. The combination of these emotions is caught exactly in an appeal which Joseph McGarrity issued in Philadelphia on June 4, 1914. Two days
earlier the Clann na Gael executive had met in New York
and set up a committee, headed by McGarrity, to attempt

to organise and equip a volunteer force for Ireland. In his appeal McGarrity implored nationalist-minded Irishmen to attend a meeting at 726, Spruce Street, on June 7: 'In the name of God, in the name of Tone's bleeding throat, in the name of Emmet's severed head, in the name of Fr. Murphy of '98, and in the countless dead, who died for Ireland, we ask you to be there.'

These emotions may seem quaint today but they helped to create the 1916 Rising and change the course of Irish history. And earlier John Redmond with his constitutional United Irish League of America, founded in 1901, used these emotions to get contributions which paid for the Irish Parliamentary Party's expenses in the elections of 1906 and 1910 and, until salaries were introduced for M.P.s, a large part of the ordinary living expenses of the Irish M.P.s.

In America as in Ireland the constitutional movement for Irish independence had to contend with the influence of the revolutionary movement of the I.R.B.'s American offshoot, Clann na Gael. It was the Clann which in 1907 sent Thomas Clarke back from New York to help revivify the I.R.B. in Ireland. Through men like John Devoy and Joseph McGarrity Clann money and policies passed into Ireland, and in 1916 helped to destroy the influence of Redmond in America as in Ireland. McGarrity also played an influential part in saving de Valera's life after the 1916 Rising. After de Valera's baptismal certificate was procured from St Agnes Church, New York, thus demonstrating his American birth, McGarrity got a lawyer friend, Francis Doyle, a prominent Irish American to use it to bring pressure to bear on President Wilson (through Joseph Tumulty) who in turn contacted the American ambassador in London who successfully entreated with the British cabinet not to execute de Valera.

The Irish in America, like the Irish at home, were a fractious lot and there was an obvious conflict of interest between the United Ireland League—the constitutionalists—and the Clann na Gael, the revolutionaries. John

Devoy founded a paper the *Gaelic American* in 1903 to combat the influence of Patrick Ford's *Irish World* which supported Redmond and parliamentarianism. The principal leaders of the Clann at this time were John Devoy, the old Fenian, Judge Daniel Cohalan, a Democratic politician of standing, and Joseph McGarrity. The Clann operated on a principle which was outlined by Cohalan that 'Ireland's true interest will be best served by a steady, resolute and progressive policy of organisation among our own people the world over and the cultivation of alliances with English enemies'.

The success of Clann propaganda may be gauged from the comment of the Irish-American *Chicago Citizen* of July, 1908—'There is not an Irishman in America today, in whose veins good red blood is flowing, who would not rejoice to hear that a German army was marching in triumph across England from Yarmouth to Milford Haven.' The 1916 Rising put the final seal on the decline of the United Ireland League which had been speedily going downhill since Redmond had pledged support to Britain in 1914.

The German ambassador to America, von Bernstorff, co-operated with the Clann through John Devoy in assisting Sir Roger Casement in his attempt to organise an Irish brigade from captured prisoners of war. Through Devoy again, Germany supplied arms for use in the Rising, but due to muddling over dates they did not arrive in time, and were scuttled off Cobh.

Following the Rising the Clann rode high in Irish-American affairs and attempted to force President Wilson to include Irish independence in the post-war peace settlement, for Wilson had made the point that the war was being fought for the freedom of small nations. Wilson, however, though not antipathetic towards the Irish as such, was bitterly at odds with Cohalan and also hesitated to offend Britain, needing England's support in launching the League of Nations. He held out against the Irish claim despite strong Irish-American pressure but on March 4, 1919, the House of Representatives in response to this influence voted 216 to 45 that the peace conference should favourably consider Ireland's claim to self-determination, and on June 6 the Senate voted 60 to 1 in favour of de Valera, Griffith and Count Plunkett being allowed to appear before the conference.

The Clann na Gael leaders, through the 'Friends of Irish Freedom', founded in 1916, had set up an Irish victory fund which by the end of 1920 had collected almost $900,000. Only $115,000 found its way to Ireland, but $750,000 was spent in attacking the League of Nations—'Britain's League'. Cohalan and Devoy joined forces with prominent domestic opponents of the League such as Henry Cabot Lodge and William Borah and they organised huge protest meetings against Wilson during his speaking tour in September, 1919, taking full-page advertisements in the newspapers along his route.

This was the position when de Valera arrived in the States in June, 1919. He stayed first at McGarrity's home in Philadelphia, and formed a strong personal friendship with him. Indeed the *Irish Republic*, produced in New York by a group of McGarrity associates, in September, 1940 said that it was McGarrity who persuaded de Valera to use the title 'President of the Irish Republic' instead of 'Priomh Aire', thus committing de Valera irrevocably to that title. Clann propagandists also allege that the title was one of the reasons why he split with Cohalan and Devoy. They, as I.R.B. supporters, recognised Collins, the head of the I.R.B. as automatically 'President of the Republic'.

But there were more cogent reasons for this disagreement. Devoy, an old man, was very much under the influence of the dynamic Cohalan, who, while passionately devoted to the cause of Irish freedom, felt that it was subordinate to the interests of America. Cohalan felt there inevitably could be a war between America and England, whose sponsorship of the League of Nations he saw as a part of a plot to overthrow America. To de Valera, whose interests were solely Irish, if Ireland won her freedom there was little difference in the view from Dublin if one looked on seas controlled by Britain or by America. To Devoy and Cohalan, looking down the Hudson the view was different. Wilson and his Democrats were blots on the landscape. De Valera realised he would have to act to take the Irish movement away from under Cohalan's nose.

In January, 1920, an Irish bond drive was launched, with Irish bond certificates sold on a guarantee of exchange for Irish Republican bonds after the Irish Republic was recognised. It is estimated that $5.5 million were subscribed, and of this de Valera made certain that $4 million were actually spent in Ireland. By November, 1920, de Valera was able to set up his own Irish-American Association, popularly known as 'Growl' because of the sound of the acronym A.A.R.I.—for American Association for the Recognition of the Irish Republic. This organisation soon became dominant in Irish-American affairs. Out of it arose a self-appointed commission, the American Commission on Conditions in Ireland, which reported the sufferings imposed on the Irish by the British (for the purposes of the report these sufferings, though basically genuine enough, were somewhat overdrawn) and an American Committee for Relief in Ireland was formed. This collected an additional $5 million to alleviate conditions in Ireland. The bulk of this probably went to aid the war effort.

De Valera, however, also aroused considerable controversy in Irish-American circles by attacking Cohalan and the *Gaelic American* and by appearing at the Republican Party's national convention against the wishes of Cohalan who also led a delegation there. The two groups made a bad impression with their quarrelling. Most of all he offended by an interview published in the *Westminster*

Gazette on February 6, 1920 (after his return) in which he proposed a solution for the Irish question similar to the association between Cuba and America.

Yet by the time de Valera slipped back to Ireland for Christmas of 1920 he had so mobilised American public opinion on the side of the Irish struggle that it became clear to the British that American funds and public opinion could continue to support the Irish for an indefinite period. There was also a very considerable body of sympathy for the Irish cause in England itself and both facts weighed heavily with the British cabinet when it called for a truce and entered the negotiations which culminated in the signing of the treaty and the British departure from the South of Ireland.

In America the withdrawal of the British was hailed as a great Irish victory. The subtleties of Home Rule, self-determination, dominion status, partition, government by devolution and all the rest of it largely escaped the vast bulk of those who supported the Irish independence movement. From 1921 it is true to say that the Americans as a nation switched off the Irish problem. She had got her independence, the British were gone. What more remained to be done?

For the Irish-American politicians most involved in the struggle the issue was not immediately clear either. For instance, McGarrity who was to spend nearly twenty years trying to wreck the treaty in fact welcomed it with an editorial in his *Irish Press* on December 10, 1920. He said, under the heading 'Irish Republic Triumphs': 'Ireland's sovereign Independence is acknowledged by the British Cabinet and their action is approved by Britain's King. This much is certain . . .' After castigating sections of the American press for their 'despicable' attempts to 'make it appear that the citizens of the Republic of Ireland are to give allegiance to King George', he went on to show that the 'supposed Oath' was merely a 'very clever juggling with words' to give as little hurt to the British ministers and 'the King's pride as possible'.

The difficult hurdle of the new state's title he took without a blink:

Many people will say that the name Republic has been dropped. No such thing has happened. Ireland is to be a Gaelic not an English nation, and at the first sitting of Dail Erin the Gaelic name for the recreated nation was adopted. That name is Saor-stat, pronounced Seer Sthath. If England prefers the correct English translation of the Gaelic term, which is Free State, instead of the Latin word Republic, Ireland should be quite happy that England has made such a choice.

He wound up by saying that 'putting aside all meaningless phrases if the Treaty made is approved and carried into effect, Ireland again becomes an independent sovereign nation among the nations'. The British, he said, would move out and the Irish take possession of their rightful heritage, boons for which he asked that 'every Irish heart be lifted up to his maker in gratitude'.

Michael Collins didn't go so far. He saw the treaty as not conferring full freedom, but 'freedom to achieve freedom', a 'stepping stone to the Republic'. Certainly de Valera didn't share McGarrity's view. He greeted the treaty's signing with a letter to the *Dublin Press*, co-signed by Brugha and Austin Stack, saying that the treaty was 'in violent conflict with the wishes of the Irish people'.

McGarrity soon swung back into line behind de Valera and a split paralleling the split in Ireland built up in the Clann. McGarrity sided completely with de Valera, Devoy with the upholders of the treaty (who gave him a state funeral through Dublin when he died in 1927). Clann na Gael split into two bodies: Clann na Gael, under Devoy, and the Clann na Gael Reorganised, or Clann na Gael and I.R.A. as it is better known, under McGarrity and Luke Dillon. This grouping remained imbued with the same sentiments as the I.R.A. in Ireland but McGarrity, though he became particularly bitter against Devoy, did not cool in his friendship with de Valera until the middle 1930s when de Valera began to jail I.R.A. men. (Once, however, de Valera entered the Dail in 1927 the Clann decided officially no longer to support Fianna Fail.)

After the Civil War Irish-American activities were mainly confined to the Clann. Broadly speaking New York City went to the Cohalan-Devoy section (as did a number of lesser centres throughout the country) but the principal Irish centres of Boston, Chicago, Cleveland, San Francisco, Philadelphia, Detroit and, in Canada, Ontario, all sided with McGarrity and his chief lieutenants, Luke Dillon, Connie Neenan, John Ryan and Major Enright.

McGarrity was born in 1874 near the village of Carrickmore in Co. Tyrone. He attended the local national school and worked on the family holding but at fourteen, during his parents' absence at Mass one Sunday morning, he ran away to Liverpool. About a year later a man in his lodgings who had bought a ticket to America had to return to Ireland on his mother's death. McGarrity, who had spent the previous nights praying to the Blessed Virgin for some way of getting to America himself, was able to buy the ticket from him for £2. He travelled in a black jersey and corduroy pants without any luggage. After about a day at sea a ship's officer began questioning him about his lack of luggage, but an American overhearing him asked, 'Has that boy got a ticket?' The officer replied, 'Yes,' 'Well then,' said the American, 'why don't you mind your own business? What right have you got to question him?' He and a group of Indians befriended the young McGarrity for the rest of the passage. The incident never left McGarrity's mind and confirmed him in his belief that America was a wonderful country.

He must have had extraordinary personality because another passenger, who arrived with him in New York, discovering that McGarrity had no money, gave him the fare to Philadelphia where McGarrity had a sister working in a hotel. Her first gesture of initiation into American society was to place a Derby hat on his head—which may have been why McGarrity always affected this type of headgear. He worked at the usual diversity of jobs which a young immigrant from Ireland at that period found himself lucky to get but being a teetotaller and enormously able and energetic, by the time he was twenty he owned a saloon in Philadelphia.

He brought his family to America and throughout his life continued the pattern of generosity he experienced on the boat. To give an example: at the time of the Irish independence controversy, McGarrity was driving a huge open touring car. Stopping one day at a street light he was surprised to find a passerby getting into the seat behind him without saying a word, and then after ten blocks tapping him on the shoulder and handing him a dime, thinking the car was a bus! Years later, during the Wall Street crash, McGarrity happened to meet this same man weeping in the small hours of the morning in Philadelphia station. He had lost his money, his wife was very ill and suicide seemed to be the only outlet. McGarrity gave him some thousands of dollars on the spot. No one knew of this until after McGarrity's funeral when the man turned up with almost three thousand dollars and told the story as he handed the money over to the relatives.

No one can say how much time, energy and money McGarrity expended on the Irish cause. The *Irish Press*, which he founded in Philadelphia in March, 1918 because the American government was inhibiting the circulation of the *Gaelic American* and the *Irish World* (the two existing Irish-American organs) is estimated to have cost him about two hundred thousand dollars, and his subsequent support for other independence groups must have cost at least as much.

It is a measure of the calibre of the man and of his friends that people were prepared to act on an equally generous scale with him. During 1929 the Clann na Gael leader, Major Michael Enright, hearing that McGarrity was in difficulties gave him his entire savings and had to go to work as a clerk in city hall, Chicago, as a result. Connie Neenan, another prominent Clann figure, who had mentioned McGarrity's difficulties to Enright said, 'I'm awful sorry that I came and asked you to get money for Joe.' Enright's reply was, 'Joe McGarrity wanted it and if it was ten times as much and I knew I was going to lose it I would still give it to him.' When the Irish Hospitals Sweepstakes began to prosper in America about 1934 McGarrity was appointed an agent, and he became relatively well-off again.

He had a literary bent as well, publishing three books of poetry and contributing to Irish culture and literature whenever he could. His concept of what constituted art was, however, strongly influenced by his political beliefs. During the 1911-12 tour of America by the Abbey Players the Clann's Anglophobia caused it to regard Yeats and the players as 'fellow agents of England' because they considered the Abbey's work 'stage Irish' and so of benefit to English propaganda about Ireland. McGarrity was very active in the attempts to get the company prosecuted in Philadelphia and after causing a disturbance at *The Playboy of the Western World*, wrote to his friend Patrick McCartan in Ireland: 'There was nothing in the play that would cause anyone who would witness it to have love or admiration for the people and the country represented in it. If the *Playboy* is art, to hell with art and those who create it.'

Luke Dillon, son of Co. Sligo parents who had emigrated to America from Leeds when he was six, was an Old Testament figure, stern, scrupulously honest, and undying in his hatred of England. Men went mad or died in prison conditions which he endured, to emerge in good physical and mental health. In prison he had refused the entreaties of Clann leaders such as McGarrity that he acknowledge his guilt and petition for mercy, sending out a letter that such a course would mean that, 'The rest of my life would not be worth such a surrender of principle.' He had been jailed for an attempt to blow up the locks of the Welland canal to prevent the Canadians sending troops to aid the British in the Boer War.

Dan Breen told me that he visited Dillon on his death bed, and that the dying man said to him, 'Dan, I've bombed the bastards and I'd bomb them again, but you have tasted their blood.' He had been active in dynamite plots in England during the winter of 1883-84, being responsible for, among other explosions, those at the Carlton Club and the House of Commons. Cornelius Neenan, who had emigrated to America from Cork, and who succeeded him as secretary of Clann na Gael after his death in 1929 took part in these also. Breen told me that when a beggar set up a pitch outside the rebuilt Carlton Club with a placard on his chest saying 'blinded by the Fenian outrages' Dillon asked that all Clann sympathisers passing through London give the man a half-crown. 'That's the way I'd like to see all the so-and-sos,' he said, according to Breen.

Other prominent Irish-Americans who continued in the Clann after the rifts and upheavals of 1921-23 were John Sullivan of Boston, Tom Pearse of Cincinnati, John Stanton of Cleveland, Jimmy McGee in New York and Harry McCarney in Philadelphia.

As with the I.R.A. in Ireland the same names recur over a period of decades. Those I have mentioned were men of above average ability, but they were deprived of strong public sympathy for getting the British out of Ireland and had many factors militating against the slightest chance of success. Moreover, the strong streak of sentimentality in Irish-American affairs tends to promote a situation in which Irish-Americans are swayed by what they would like to be true. They rarely apply themselves to finding out what the present situation is and how it differs from the land and problems of their youth. And if they were too young to remember Ireland or were born of Irish parents in America, they were subject both to parental memories and Irish-American education which, like that at home, had until very recently a strong anti-intellectual bias and an emphasis on inculcating devotion to the Roman Catholic Church.

The confusion, uncertainty and lack of initiative produced by this type of training predisposed most of those exposed to it towards accepting the *status quo* and the strong, simple certainties propounded on any issue from pulpit or platform. The day to day shifts in domestic Irish politics, the new allegiances, fresh groupings and new faces were a mystery to those in America who continued to send money and militant advice home to 'the boys'. They grew increasingly baffled and pained when the Irish refused their seemingly manifest duty of rising in wrath to drive the British out of 'Occupied Ireland'. McGarrity, for example, was so out of touch with the shifts in Irish politics that when Frank Aiken came to America in 1926 after the formation of Fianna Fail he was unaware that Aiken was no longer chief of staff of the I.R.A. and was shaken when Neenan, who had been back to Ireland, informed him. McGarrity complained in a letter to Aiken that 'America has been asked to give its support for the past three or four years to the Republicans at home, but I have failed to learn up to the present time just what the platform or the policy of the party is.' Americans would always be in the position of never knowing clearly what the 'platform or policy' was back in Ireland.

At the end of the Civil War on June 4, 1923 McGarrity had been receiving letters from de Valera, co-signed by Aiken as chief of staff, asking that McGarrity co-operate with 'Commandant General Moylan' whom Aiken and de Valera sent to America to build up support for the defeated Republicans. McGarrity does not seem to have appreciated the implications of another letter from de Valera, received a month later saying, '. . . the only hope for the future that I can now see is by *political* action. It would be a great mistake to imagine that the people were really in love with the Free State. With proper organisation we should be able to secure revision of the "Treaty" within four or five years. The main thing is not to let any time slip by in inactivity. If we could contest one seat in each constituency, we would have laid a solid foundation for the future. The trouble is the old one—money. Until we have made arrangements for the wounded and the army, we cannot use any of the money on hand for political purposes, even though the purpose is fundamental.' In the letter de Valera mentions that about $100,000 would be needed for the elections. This transfer of emphasis from physical force to political activity seems to have been lost on McGarrity who had rapturously accepted the now-to-be-revised treaty.

In a personal diary entitled 'Partial Records by Joseph McGarrity' (now in the home of his daughter, Mrs Elizabeth Defoe of Philadelphia who kindly allowed me to see it) one can trace a growing disillusionment with Fianna Fail. He could not understand why de Valera should jail I.R.A. men and other prominent Irish-American figures were similarly bewildered. In June, 1935, the leaders of all the most prominent Irish-American organisations issued an appeal to coincide with the Bodenstown procession, asking Fianna Fail and the I.R.A. to unite. The pamphlet, called 'Republicans Must Unite', is addressed to 'Members of Fianna Fail and of The I.R.A.'.

Extracts from it show the lack of understanding among Irish-Americans about domestic Irish politics. Under the heading 'Who Wants More Civil War', the appeal says:

This year there are again rival pilgrimages to the grave of Tone—Tone who died for a United Irish Republic.

The rival processions occur because the Fianna Fail Government and the I.R.A. are practically at war. So serious is the danger of Civil War that LEADING SUPPORTERS OF FIANNA FAIL AND OF THE I.R.A. IN U.S.A. HAVE COME TOGETHER AND HAVE ISSUED AN APPEAL FOR UNITY AMONG ALL IRISH REPUBLICANS.

TO UNITE THE IRISH PEOPLE WAS THE AIM OF TONE. WHY

CANNOT WE UNITE TO-DAY? OUR COMRADES IN THE U.S.A.
HAVE SET US AN EXAMPLE; LET US FOLLOW IT!

Irish Republicans in America view with grave concern
the present developments which, if allowed to continue,
will lead to hostility between Republican sections in Ireland.
We believe that Ireland has reached the critical stage when the
Republican enthusiasm of the people can be used to re-
establish the Republic or may be dissipated in civil strife.

In this serious situation, we urge the Irish people to
insist that representatives of all Republican thought in
Ireland must meet in conference to find a means of recon-
ciling their various differences, uniting on unswerving
principle, presenting a solid front to the common enemy
and re-establish the independence of the country as a
Republic. Signed:

JOHN J. REILLY, National Chairman, American Association
for the Recognition of the Irish Republic.

JOE MCGARRITY, representing Clann na Gael of America.

JAMES BRADY, Sec., Federation of Societies for Irish Independence.

SEAN HAYES, Chairman, Associated Irish Societies of New
York.

JOHN STAUNTON, Chairman, Irish Societies of State of Ohio.

CON MOUNIHAN, Chairman, Irish Societies, Boston, Mass.

PAT HEGARTY, Chairman, United Irishmen of Springfield,
Mass.

M. J. MULLANE, Chairman, Irishmen of Butte, Montana.

M. J. MCGING, Chairman, Associated Irish Societies of
Chicago.

M. H. ENRIGHT, Colonel, Clann na Gael Guards of Chicago.

ROBERT MONTEITH, Captain, Casement Brigade.

GERALD O'REILLY, representing Congress Supporting Groups
of U.S.

This appeal completely misjudges the tone and temper
of the Irish electorate at the time. There was no danger
of civil war. But the signatures on the appeal show how
widespread was the feeling among Irish-Americans that
the I.R.A. and Fianna Fail were somehow the same organ-

isation having a family quarrel. In fact, they were two mutually antipathetic political organisations with different goals, or rather very different views about how to achieve the same goals of getting the British out and reuniting the country. In a way one can see in this sort of exchange a microcosm of the American bafflement in dealing with the shifts of Cypriot or South Vietnamese politics. If only they could all get together and do the right thing! (Curiously, on another analogy between Vietnam and the Clann na Gael the Clann is known to its members by the code name of V.C.!)

The constitution of the V.C., adopted at a Clann convention in Philadelphia at which the nearly moribund body was revived in 1946, contains the following:

ARTICLE 1.
Section 1

This organisation shall be known as the V.C., it shall be non-sectarian and shall not interfere in American Party politics.

Section 2.

Its objects are: *First*—To aid the people of Ireland in maintaining their complete national independence under a republican form of government with full civil and religious liberty guaranteed to all its inhabitants. *Second*—To foster and encourage a study of the language, literature, history, music, laws and traditions of Ireland at home and abroad. The Gaelic language shall be used at all public and private functions whenever feasible. *Third*—To foster a spirit of friendship between the Republicans of the U.S. and Ireland.

But the real flavour of the organisation comes across in the initiation ceremonies, a mixture of cloak-and-dagger I.R.B.-I.R.A., Masons and Elks type ritual appealing both to the conspiratorial-minded and to those who like the mystery, miracle and authority of the Church.

The initiation ceremonies are laid down as follows:

Perfect silence should prevail during initiation. Nothing else should occupy the attention of the meeting.

The Warden will see that the Camp is not disturbed during the ceremony, and that every member shall avoid any needless movement or word. At such time a whisper may disturb a candidate or an officer, and mar the impressiveness of the ceremony. Each member shall endeavour to make the ceremony what it is designed to be—solemn and impressive.

S.G. [Senior Guard]—'Conductor, proceed to the anteroom and ascertain if there are any candidates in waiting.'

When the Conductor reports the names, addresses, etc., of the candidates, the S.G. asks:

S.G.—'Recording Secretary, have these candidates been duly elected?'

The Recording Secretary reports, giving data of election in each case.

S.G.—'Conductor, proceed to the ante-room and interrogate the candidates.'

The Conductor then retires and asks the candidates the following questions in their proper order:

Conductor—'State your name, age, birth-place and occupation.'

Conductor—'Do you believe in Ireland's right to be a separate and independent nation?'

Conductor—'As the Irish Republic is established, are you willing to sustain it by all means?'

Conductor—'Understanding, as you do, that the object of this Organisation is the freedom of Ireland and the elevation of the Irish race, are you willing to bind yourself by a solemn obligation to aid in carrying out that object and to obey the laws of this Order?'

Conductor—'Are you now, or have you ever been, a member of an organisation having for its object the freedom of Ireland?'

The Conductor having ascertained that the candidate has answered all questions satisfactorily to the Camp will return to the ante-room and collect the initiation fee. If any candidate admits being now, or having ever been a member of this or any similar organisation or if any of the answers should be unsatisfactory, or should call for special action, the Camp may act as may be required by the Constitution. If the answers are satisfactory, the S.G. will say:

S.G.—'Conductor, prepare the candidates and present them for initiation.'

The S.G. will detail a sufficient number of brothers to act as escort to the candidates. The Conductor will then take his sword and retire to the ante-room. The Conductor will then give three knocks at the door as a signal for his assistants to retire, one assistant conductor being selected for each candidate, who shall take a position on the right of the candidate. The Conductor will direct the march and place himself at the head of the escort. At the entrance door he will give three distinct knocks with his sword. The Sentinel will at once open the door and the escort will pass inside with the candidates, after which the Sentinel will close the door. When the escort has advanced three paces into the room the Sentinel will abruptly and in a clear voice say to the Conductor:

Sentinel—'Halt! Who comes there?'

(Escort halts.)

Conductor—'Friends who desire to unite with us in the cause of Ireland.'

Sentinel (to S.G.)—'Shall I permit these friends to proceed?'

S.G.—'Advance.'

Conductor—'Forward, march.'

The Conductor will lead the escort and candidates to within three paces of the S.G., making a circuit of the centre table and will command:

Conductor—'Halt!'

The candidates will be aligned by the assistants facing the S.G.

Conductor (to S.G.)—'Sir, I present these candidates for final examination.'

S.G.—'Friends, you have come to us seeking the privilege of membership. That privilege is denied to unworthy men and granted only to those who can stand the test of a strict examination as to character and patriotism. We are engaged in a holy cause that can be served only by men of courage, devotion and loyalty. We are banded together to free the land of our fathers from English rule and to sustain the Republic of Ireland as now established. We admit no man to our ranks who is not fully in sympathy with this object. Every man in our Order has taken a solemn oath binding himself to aid in accomplishing it. It is an oath which does not conflict with any duty you owe to God, to your country, your neighbour or yourself and which no true Irishman can condemn. It must be taken before you can be admitted to our Order. You have already signified your willingness to take our obligation, but we give you, even now, the privilege of withdrawing if you so desire. Answer honestly and freely, are you willing to take this oath?'

If the answer be satisfactory the S.G. will say:

S.G.—'Conduct the candidates to the proper office for obligation.'

The Conductor and his assistants will then march the candidates to the J.G. [Junior Guard] and align them facing the J.G.'s chair.

Conductor—'Hold up your right hands.'

(S.G. gives two raps.)

The J.G. then administers the obligation, speaking clearly and distinctly, dividing the sentences into short clauses, so that the candidates may have no difficulty in repeating the words after him. He will not tell the candidates to kiss the book, the Ritual not being for that purpose, and the uplifted right hand being sufficient.

OBLIGATION

I (name), do solemnly swear that I will labour while life is left me to put an end to English rule in Ireland and to sustain the Republic now established on Irish soil and to elevate the position of the Irish race everywhere.

That I will obey and respect the Constitution and Laws of the V.C. and all orders coming from the proper authority.

That I will never reveal its secrets to anyone not entitled to know them, even if my connection with the Organisation should cease from any cause whatever.

That I will foster a spirit of Unity and Brotherly Love among Irish Nationalists.

That I do not now belong, and never will belong, to any organisation opposed to the principles or policy of the V.C.

And finally I swear that I take this oath without any mental reservation whatever, and that I will keep it in letter and spirit until death. So Help Me, God.

All Present—'We are all witnesses to the obligation you have taken.'

Conductor—'Keep it as you love Ireland and value your honor as a man.'

J.G.—'Conduct the brothers to the S.G.'

(One rap.)

On arriving at the S.G.'s chair the Conductor will align the new brothers and say:

Conductor—'S.G., I present these brothers for final instructions.'

S.G. (Shaking hands with each of the new brothers)— 'Brothers, I greet you and welcome you to our ranks in the name of Ireland.'

The name of the Organisation is the V.C. Its local sub-divisions, or branches, are styled Camps, and each Camp is known by a number.

The Republican Congress break-away in Ireland was reflected in a similar split in America under Gerald O'Reilly who took most of the left-wing support with him. Then de Valera introduced a pension scheme for I.R.A. men who had taken part in the Civil War, and as many of these had emigrated to America after the war (where they supported the Clann) their acceptance of the pension cut them off from revolutionary activity against the government that was paying the money, and further weakened the Clann. And there were natural American disunities. For instance during 1930 the Clann split down the middle over the opening of a speak-easy to raise funds. One club, the James Connolly Club, led by James O'Mahoney, opposed the scheme and both the club and some individual members of other clubs broke away.

The greatest single weakening factor, however, was the spread of the Irish Sweepstakes movement to America. This took some of the ablest executive brains, as well as rank and file, out of the Clann organisation. Joe McGrath, principal founder of the sweep was astute enough to see the possibility of the old I.R.A. arms and letter smuggling network as a machine for smuggling illegal lottery tickets back to Dublin, and many Clann na Gaelite members devoted themselves more to ticket-pushing than to revolution. Other Irish Americans also supported the sweepstake enthusiastically, distributing tickets throughout the United States, sending counterfoils and money to the counterfeit addresses in Ireland or on the Continent, to be passed on to the sweep headquarters in Dublin. They behaved with that enterprising abandon that the Irish display when they can defy authority and make money at the same time.

Both the vigilance of the postal services and the enterprise of the Irish were well demonstrated on one occasion when a sweep agent, called Irwin, a steward on a Cunard liner, was arrested at Pier 16 and taken with his counterfoils and remittances to a neighbouring precinct station for the night before facing fines and confiscations in the morning. The fine was not serious, heavy though it was, because the sweep would remit this money to him, but the loss of the counterfoils meant that there could be a lack of trust on the part of subscribers. However, the following morning after being fined and losing his counterfoils and the money he had collected, Irwin walked out of the court whistling. All through the night while he was in custody the entire precinct staff, most of whom were Irish (and those who were not knew better than to protest) had laboured to fill in duplicate counterfoils made out on police stationery. These were duly sent to Dublin and accepted by the sweep authorities as being valid counterfoils under the circumstances.

All this meant of course that there was very little time left in Clann circles for fomenting revolution in Ireland.

Harry Short, who was present at the hall on 125th Street when Sean Russell announced, for the first time in America, his scheme for a bombing campaign in England, reckoned there were only forty people present.

5 / THE BOMBING CAMPAIGN

Sean Russell's path to New York apparently began when he met Joseph McGarrity in Ireland in 1929. McGarrity's business had temporarily collapsed. He had been expelled from the New York Stock Exchange but a subsequent inquiry cleared his name, fixing the responsibility on his partner, a man named Kenny and restoring McGarrity to his seat. McGarrity had gone to Bolivia but returned to New York within months, full of plans for development in South America. When these met with no response from his associates he went to Ireland and there became friendly with Russell.

McGarrity's visit helped to create further dissension within the movement. On what might be called the 'physical force wing' there were two plans for action. One was Tom Barry's scheme for seizing a northern town, as the Dublin post office was seized in 1916, holding out for as long as possible and then falling back on the border at, say, Armagh, to rouse the people behind them. The scheme, known as the 'Barry Plan', was widely discussed but never became official army policy.

Unfortunately Russell's plan did. McGarrity had a friend approach a young German chemist in Cleveland who was an expert on explosives, and after talking to the chemist, became convinced that small, easily concealed and easily disposed of explosives with a high destructive content if let off in busy English cities would be the best method of freeing 'occupied Ireland'. Russell had seen too much of civil war in Ireland to want to embroil North against South on the lines of the Barry Plan and, moreover, he did not want to destroy Irish property or to take Irish lives if he could help it. To Russell, as Britain was, in his view, maintaining partition, Britain was the logical place to carry on the war.

The scheme was of course impracticable with the weakened I.R.A. and its position following the governmental crack-down, but it was the very weakness of the I.R.A. which enabled Russell to come to the top. The Blueshirt-I.R.A. struggle took itself off to Spain at the end of 1936. Frank Ryan left from Dun Laoghaire (a borough of Dublin) on November 11 with a group of Republican Congress supporters, notably Frank Edwards and Christie Walsh, and O'Duffy's men began setting off two days later from Dublin. For the I.R.A. this meant a renewal of internal controversy as MacBride, Fitzpatrick and Mac-Logan tried to persuade their followers from going after Ryan, who was appealing to both socialist inclinations and the desire for 'action'. Russell was offering a possibility of 'action' nearer home and against a more familiar enemy than the forces in Spain. Moreover McGarrity continued to lend him moral and financial support. Probably as much as 80 per cent of the money required for the campaign was supplied by him and he grew more determined in his support as de Valera took an increasingly stiff line with the I.R.A.

In McGarrity's diary for August, 1936 are references to meetings with Russell, by then quartermaster-general of the I.R.A.; to Maurice Twomey's arrest by de Valera's 'Free State' police; to Micksey Conway's being charged with murder, and to reports of 'brutalities' against I.R.A. prisoners. He describes with sadness the sentences meted out to I.R.A. men who came from Republican families prominent in the time of the Anglo-Irish struggle. (Sean McSwiney, a brother of Terence McSwiney who died on hunger strike, and Sean Og MacCurtain, a son of the murdered mayor of Cork, were at that time before the Military Tribunal.) After noting that in the North the Craigavon government was also cracking down on the I.R.A. McGarrity writes, 'Craigavon and de Valera at least agree on one thing and that is that all those known to be Republicans must be jailed or hanged.' This was not in fact de Valera's attitude as he demonstrated during the period of his constitutional innovations. These included removing the governor general, on December 11, 1936; enacting a new constitution by referendum on June 1, 1937, abolishing the senate's power of veto and altering its nature in an attempt to give it a 'vocational' character—which failed as the electoral colleges which put forward the senatorial nominees do so on party lines; and changing the name of the state from the Irish Free State to Ireland, or, in Irish, Eire.

In the midst of these changes de Valera set up a cabinet committee, on December 15, 1936, to make recommendations concerning the release of prisoners sentenced by the Military Tribunal. On the day this committee was announced an I.R.A. convention in Dublin, meeting not altogether in secret as police records of the time show, proposed that battalion commanders be given greater powers to deal with 'deserters' and those showing hostility to the I.R.A. This was the sort of thing which caused young Egan's death, for which Micksey Conway had been sentenced, but despite this Conway was one of those whom the Dail committee freed.

The case of the young Limerick man, Sean Glynn, who committed suicide in Arbour Hill prison after the proscribing of the Bodenstown procession affected McGarrity powerfully. He describes the I.R.A. prisoners being 'so unmercifully treated in prison that young Glynn was found hanging dead in a cell in Arbour Hill Prison, Dublin . . . This was the last straw for me. I had already spoken at a public meeting of the Clann in the Town Hall, New York, in protest at the jailings and prison tortures.' He went on to note that he had given an interview to the *Philadelphia Ledger* protesting the 'Free State Government policy and that of the Craig Government'.

Although he was still in touch with de Valera and

growing increasingly friendly with Russell, McGarrity laboured under the old American difficulty of being out of touch. He was surprised to find that Sean Russell had had an interview with de Valera, in April, 1935, to talk over the possibilities of 'co-operation', as McGarrity termed it, between the I.R.A. and de Valera. De Valera's version of this 'co-operation' was that Russell and the I.R.A. would turn in their arms and disband. According to McGarrity's diary, Russell reminded de Valera of his statement after the Civil War about Republicans hiding arms and munitions—not to part with them 'until the country was independent'. This Russell said the I.R.A. was willing to do. According to the diary: 'Russell asked, or rather promised co-operation with the Fianna Fail party in every way for a period of five years from that date if Dev would promise to declare a Republic for all Ireland at the end of the final year period. Dev refused to agree to that saying "You want it both ways".'

McGarrity notes that he had been in Dublin during December, 1935 and on a visit to de Valera's house had a long talk about changes de Valera was proposing in the Free State constitution. But he had not been aware that de Valera had been in contact with the I.R.A. McGarrity wrote that 'Russell believes Dev has taken orders from Anthony Eden to suppress the I.R.A. in anticipation of some promised concession being fulfilled by England; there is no proof of this.'

An entry in the McGarrity diary for October 31, 1936, gives evidence of his naïvety in Irish affairs. He had arranged to send J. O'Hara Harte of the Society of Friends to Ireland to seek peace between the I.R.A. and the Free State Government, and the I.R.A. and the Craig regime in the six counties. McGarrity wrote: 'Have arranged a plan. $1,000 already provided for expense of the mission, balance of 1,000 will be ready by the time the mission is ready to sail—God grant it success.' McGarrity adds, 'de Valera has according to reports published his long looked for constitution for his Free State. Not a word about United and Independent Ireland, Six Counties forgotten—shame on Dev and his party.'

O'Hara Harte sailed from New York for Ireland on November 18, and a month later a baffled O'Hara Harte sent a cable from London recounting his interview with de Valera. He had told de Valera that the I.R.A. had signed a statement that they were willing to negotiate outstanding differences. Harte was amazed, McGarrity wrote, when the president said, 'he would not enter into any negotiations. Not only would he not meet the I.R.A. as a body or as individual persons but he would not accept my service as a mediator.'

So, mad though the British bombing campaign may seem to us, it must have appeared logical to men in Ireland in 1936 who thought it possible that de Valera, Craigavon and the I.R.A. (illegal on both sides of the border) should sit down together to arrange for the unification of the country under the chairmanship of an unknown Irish-American Quaker.

In America Russell first publicly announced his plan in early August, 1936, to a handful of Clann supporters. In an interview, with the *Daily Mirror* on August 14, Russell made a number of amazing claims:

You know, of course, that de Valera has betrayed the trust of the Irish nation by becoming the tool of Great Britain.

Instead of fighting, as he promised, for the Republic of Ireland, he has been content to allow her to be a nation subject to a foreign King.

Republican forces are awaiting an opportune moment to fight with all their might for the nation's freedom.

When the moment will come I do not know. It may come when the British become embroiled in a European conflict. But our plan of campaign is ready.

As de Valera knows only too well, we have splendid military forces in Ireland, with cleverly hidden arsenals.

Then, over in England, where we shall also take the offensive, we have another secret army of Irishmen, who meet quietly, for drill and target practice.

We have also quantities of ammunition and other war material in England.

Our Air Force may be small, but it is reasonably efficient.

When hostilities start we shall certainly send planes to bomb England.

It is a very definite plan in our scheme for an offensive.

Admiral Somerville was recruiting for the British Navy, and we won't tolerate a foreign Power recruiting for its navy or army.

I plainly warn the British people not to interfere with Ireland.

Russell's statement was pure propaganda. (There was a scheme in New York Clann na Gael circles at the time to fly an aeroplane across the Atlantic, bomb the British House of Commons, and then crash land on the coast of France, because there would not be enough petrol left to recross the Atlantic. There was not the slightest hope of laying hands on such an aeroplane, and the scheme never got beyond the level of discussion.) It is doubtful if Russell even had any title to make propaganda for the I.R.A. at home. Tom Barry wanted to have Russell court-martialled over the loss of two Thompson machine guns. He had no faith in Russell's plans nor had Sean MacBride who took particular exception to his involvement with the O'Hara Harte mission. But Russell directed his appeal at the younger men and with their help carried the day.

Some time during March, 1938, the die was cast at a meeting in Dublin. (Eoin MacNamee, a principal spokesman on Russell's behalf, Michael Fitzpatrick, then chief of staff and who presided at the meeting, and Sean O'Broin who stood guard at the door taking credentials were unable to tell me the exact date and place of the meeting.) Earlier on the morning of the meeting an unofficial convention was held in the home of Mairtin O'Cadain to plan strategy. MacNamee went to this meeting with the names of twelve Russell supporters from whom an Executive was to be picked.

These were, Jack McNeela, Tony D'Arcy (both of whom were to die on hunger strike), Victor Fagg, who, interestingly enough, is a Protestant from Westmeath, Charlie Dolan, John Tully, Jimmie Traynor, John James Kelly, George Plunkett, Ted Moore, Ned Kerrigan, Johnny O'Connor and Larry Grogan. Grogan was one of those who later signed the declaration of war on England, served on Lord Halifax. MacNamee also had a letter from Russell explaining his position. This was read by Maurice Twomey. The convention was a tense affair, run on military lines, each man giving his name and rank to Sean O'Broin who called it out from the entrance while the applicant stood to attention before being admitted.

The anti-Russell section was armed—one of the few times at which arms were carried at an army convention. Joseph McGarrity was present although he was a member of the Clann, not of the I.R.A. Russell himself was not present. In his opponents' view he was no longer in the I.R.A. through his refusal to take direction from the then executive. Barry proposed that as there were sufficient arms in Dublin to arm the Dublin brigade the I.R.A. should march on the North that very night, but the Russell scheme was carried at the end of an all-night sitting. Russell sensed the difficulties that had arisen and felt they should strike a blow at the earliest moment.

The fatal result was that the bombing party chosen to go to England was only half-trained in the use of explosives and hence some of the fatalities to the bombers and to innocent English bystanders. The destruction of property was all Russell aimed at, but badly made bombs in inexperienced hands went off at the wrong times with disastrous results. Russell possibly thought that more efficient explosives would be coming from America. MacNamee remembers passing Park Lane Hotel with him one afternoon and being asked by Russell, 'would he like to be able to blow that up with a pen?' MacNamee said, 'Certainly, but how?', pointing out that it was made of reinforced concrete. Russell smiled and went on to impress Mac-Namee with the sort of advanced methods of warfare to be placed at their disposal. (These were apparently pen bombs, mentioned to me by members of Clann na Gael as being talked about in America during the 1930s but they either proved impractical or could not be got out of the country for they never figured in the campaign.)

The campaign was appallingly ill-conceived. MacNamee told me that there was, as far as he was aware, only one Thompson gun and possibly six revolvers doing the rounds of the London units of the I.R.A. at the time. There was an Irish Republican Defence Committee, an open organisation which raised funds and carried out propaganda and Cumann na mBan, the women's auxiliary group which did somewhat similar work, but in terms of military power the I.R.A. scarcely functioned. In August, 1937, MacNamee, intelligence officer of the London battalion, returned to Ireland for a holiday and learned of the projected bombing campaign and of the differences concerning its merits. MacNamee, a Co. Tyrone man, supported the idea because he understood that it was to be accompanied by an attack on the North.

At the time, apart from its military weaknesses, the London I.R.A. was split into various factions. Jack Lynch, the officer commanding Britain, was arrested during Mac-Namee's visit to Ireland and Jimmy Joe Reynolds was appointed in his place. Reynolds, later to be blown up in a faulty mine explosion at Clady, Co. Donegal, made one of his first steps on being appointed O.C. the dismissal of all the battalion staff. The result was that officers from G.H.Q. in Dublin came over to set up the inevitable courts of inquiries. The row, a foolish affair involving Cumann na mBan women's gossip, was patched up and on MacNamee's recommendation London in 1938 was split into various companies with defined spheres of influence. During this period prominent Dublin I.R.A. officers such as Seamus Malin, Mairtin O'Cadain, Maurice Twomey and Thomas MacCurtain spoke in London.

From October on groups of handpicked I.R.A. men were brought back from England to be trained in Dublin and to return and spread their knowledge. The classes consisted largely of instruction in bomb-making and were held mainly in a hall known as The Green Lounge in St Stephen's Green. Other venues were also used around Dublin, one of the most important being Killiney Castle in Killiney. (Today in the summer amiable English tourists visit it unaware of the castle's history. Occasionally the words 'Up the I.R.A.' appear in large whitewash letters on the gates but these are speedily obliterated before they arouse any questions among the English visitors. In the 1938-49 period the castle was owned by a Dublin civil servant who was violently anti-British and, when the castle was commandeered on the outbreak of the Second World War by the military for use as a billet, he used to emerge from the basement which he retained for his own use, to run up the tricolour on the flag pole whenever a German victory was announced!)

The principal instructors in bomb-making were Patrick McGrath, who was later executed for the shooting of a policeman in Dublin, and Jim O'Donovan, Russell's former colleague in the war against the British. O'Donovan had come out of retirement at Russell's request to train a new generation of young Irishmen, a decision which was to cause him considerable loss. He was a member of a semi-state body, the Electricity Supply Board, in a comfortable position at the time and when the campaign misfired he lost his job and spent the war years interned in the Curragh. It was O'Donovan who drew up the 'S-plan', the official blue-print for the campaign, which called for the destruction of obvious military targets such as communications centres, B.B.C. transmitters, aerodromes, bridges and military installations.

Twelve handpicked volunteers crossed over to England

during Christmas week 1938 and went to five centres: Walsh and O'Kennedy to Glasgow; Eoin MacNamee, Charlie Casey and S. McGuinness to London; Rory Campbell and Patrick Fleming to Manchester; Joe Deighan, G. Quigley, and M. Cleary to Liverpool; and Jackie Kearns and J. Fuller to Birmingham.

On December 8 Russell announced an event that he hoped would give respectability and authority to the campaign. This was the taking over by the I.R.A. of the authority of the 'Government of the Republic of Ireland' from the 'Executive Council of Dail Eireann'. This meant that those who had recognised the second Dail as the *de jure* government of Ireland now recognised the Army Council (and Sean Russell as its head) as the legitimate rulers of Ireland. The announcement was printed on page one of the *Wolfe Tone Weekly*.

The people of Ireland were largely unaware of this transfer, but after it Russell could claim, as de Valera had said, that the authority of the Dail lay outside that assembly, that he now had this authority for his actions. Yet on the day the notice was published, an abortive effort was made, without his authority, to blow up the Nelson Pillar. Peadar O'Flaherty, believed to be Russell's right-hand man, planned the explosion for a Saturday evening, when the streets would normally be full of people. To avoid fatalities, he planned to set the explosives, withdraw and notify the police, giving them time to cordon off the area. Joseph Deighan told me that he and the other members of the group actually walked down through O'Connell Street (from An Stad in Upper Frederick Street where most I.R.A. men stayed) with wads of gelignite on them, liable to be blown up at any moment by a jostling passer-by, but quite prepared to carry out the task. Arriving at the pillar they found that O'Flaherty had forgotten that it closed earlier on Saturdays in winter. When Russell heard of this harebrained scheme, he was furious and sacked O'Flaherty on the spot, but his control of the organisation was so loose that he could not prevent

O'Flaherty signing the declaration of war on England which the I.R.A. issued a month later.

When the chosen twelve arrived in England they found organisation so lax that they had great difficulty in finding dumps for the explosives. Russell had excellent contacts in the customs service and in shipping circles and he managed to get the stuff into England. But once there it was no easy matter for young Irishmen living in 'digs' to find dumps for hundredweights of potassium chloride, sulphuric acid and iron oxide. Some willing friends who stored material knowing nothing about the campaign itself or what they were storing found their business gone, their families broken up and themselves behind prison bars after the campaign began and Scotland Yard began to round up suspects. One man who stored some stuff for Eoin MacNamee knew so little about him that he told the police that his name was McKenna. When the bombs started to go off he realised the position and in his desperation dug holes in the garden and covered them in. However, the police raided him before he had properly obliterated all traces and he got seven years hard labour.

A fact which cannot be too strongly stressed is the innocence, or if one wishes the ignorance, of the volunteers with whom the 'operations officers' in the various cities worked. Most were young men who, having left school around the age of twelve, emigrated to labouring jobs and had not the slightest resentment against England.

Paddy McNeela was a typical recruit. His brother Jack was to die on hunger strike and was at the time the principal I.R.A. officer in England. Paddy came from Ballycroy, Co. Mayo, where his memories were of the fiddler coming into the village, playing in one or two houses for a fortnight and taking up a collection at the end of the week, maybe getting thirty shillings in twopences for his work. Some overriding laws governed upbringing in Paddy's day. The Rosary was said every night; Mass was attended in all weathers though it meant a four-mile walk. At Christmas the average stipend to a priest was ten shillings, almost a week's wages. A wedding cost perhaps thirty or forty pounds but it was one great day out in everyone's lives and the money had to be found. The priest's authority was near absolute.* Paddy remembers a parish priest going to a house and burning what he called 'bad books'. In nearby Spiddal a cross was erected to poteen stills which were publicly burned by the famous Redemptorist priest, Father Conneally. Sermons were of the order 'two men will die in this parish' if mixed dancing or poteen drinking were not given up immediately. Growing up, Paddy and his companions firmly believed that the priest could, if he wished, 'put horns on you'.

Understandably, coming from this background, Paddy was far from mechanically minded. He remembers one drill session at which a hand grenade was thrown and failed to explode. Another young man picked it up, tested it with his teeth and said, 'Hm, it's alright, it should have gone off.' They tossed it around for some moments until their horrified instructor took it from them and threw it away, whereupon it duly exploded. When Paddy emigrated to England he was completely lost in London, but in a village in one of the Home Counties he found a life more like the one he had left and got on famously with the people. He remembers he found them very backward and simple.

* A 'station' in Kerry gave the following anecdote to the nation. A 'station' consists of Mass and communion followed by a large breakfast in a house, not a church. The custom, which dates from the penal days, is now dying out in Ireland except in the more remote areas, but at Paddy's time it flourished. A priest, who arrived at the house on a fine hunter, placed his umbrella in the kitchen, still open as he wished to dry it. Two of the menfolk of the place, not having seen him arrive were trying unsuccessfully to push it out the narrow doorway when the priest returned for it. They watched in amazement as he folded it with a flick of his thumb, and then Pat turned to Mick as the priest galloped off and said, 'Dey has de Power. Didn't I tell you dey has de Power?'

'They'd listen to everything I'd tell them and take it in, jokes and all.'

When he was asked to take part in the bombing campaign, he no more associated those simple villagers with going to war for the Republic and the end of partition, than he claimed to have any knowledge of the rights or wrongs of the issues involved.

Paddy was lucky enough to escape detection but a more experienced colleague, J. F. Reegan from Cork, back from the Spanish Civil War and its hardships (the common diet was a few drops of olive oil in water, and a handful of grapes; with bread, meat, milk or coffee almost unknown) crossed to England and was captured, probably through an informer, and sentenced to twelve years' hard labour.

A leading contemporary Irish journalist, then just a homesick boy from Derry, was recruited when he went into Mooneys in the Strand in London where he hoped to pick up some Irish company. A man he knew slightly from his boyhood came up to him at the bar and spoke. Learning that the bombing campaign was being planned, he offered his services, was enrolled and began mixing 'Paxo', as the explosive was known, in his landlady's saucepans. The National Gallery in Trafalgar Square was to be his first target but his superior officer, a plumber, decided that there were too many tiles in it and that it wouldn't burn. Meanwhile his landlady, discovering the white substance, very sensibly flushed it down the lavatory.

MacNamee, who lived in Roseleen Road, Fulham, used to test balloons in his fireplace, timing how long it would take for the acid to eat through the rubber and ignite the iron oxide. Once he went out while waiting for the acid to take affect, and came back to find that the landlady had cleared out the fireplace, balloons, iron oxide and all. She warned him that two yardsmen in a local scrap-dealing business, whom he had prosecuted for stealing his bicycle, knew him to be an I.R.A. man and were going to get him locked up. MacNamee immediately quit the digs The police called to pick him up that night.

Michael McInerney, now political correspondent of the *Irish Times*, disposed of some half ton of explosives down his landlady's lavatory after he learned what his Irish friends intended to do with the stuff that they had asked him to store.

Not all landladies were sympathetic although most of the young I.R.A. men of course stayed with established Republicans who had been in Britain for some years—which, however, made it easy for the police to pick them up. Then the I.R.A. habit of keeping documents, writing out receipts, and leaving incriminating evidence lying around terminated many a promising arsonist's career. There was also the problem of accents. A group of young I.R.A. men from west Cork or Mayo going into a shop for an alarm clock, to be used as a timing device for a bomb, would give a cheery greeting to the assistant such as, 'Tell us daughter would ye be after havin' a few alarm clocks there?' They would be told, 'Certainly sir, do you mind waiting for a moment?' and would obligingly stay on the premises while the assistant went to telephone Scotland Yard.

Nevertheless some of the operation officers in the campaign did show considerable expertise in eluding the police. Joe Deighan told me that even though he was well-known in Liverpool as an I.R.A. suspect at least, if not something more active, and was continually shadowed, he was nevertheless able to set off a number of successful detonations—carrying his bombs in what looked like a lunch box on his knee in crowded public transport! (Public transport was frequently used by the I.R.A. Where a taxi driver might remember one fare, a bus conductor would not. It is a miracle that this did not lead to some really ghastly accidents. A jolting tram or bus is not the best conveyance for gelignite.)

It should also be pointed out that had the I.R.A. made

more use of women it might have done better because women were less likely to be seized by the police. I met one lady who had emptied several cinemas on different occasions by letting off tear-gas bombs. She could have easily destroyed substantial installations.

The bombing campaign began formally on January 12, 1939, with an ultimatum to the British prime minister, the government in Northern Ireland, the British foreign secretary, Hitler, Mussolini, and anyone else whom the I.R.A. thought would be moved by such a document. It said:

I have the honour to inform you that the Government of the Irish Republic, having as its first duty towards the people the establishment and maintenance of peace and order, herewith demand the withdrawal of all British armed forces stationed in Ireland. These forces are an active incitement to turmoil and civil strife not only in being a symbol of hostile occupation but in their effect and potentialities as an invading army.

It is secondly the duty of the Government to establish relations of friendship between the Irish and all other peoples. We must insist on the withdrawal of British troops from our country and a declaration from your Government renouncing all claims to interfere in our domestic policy.

The letter declared that neither the government of the Irish Republic nor the Irish people were actuated by any feelings of hostility towards England but warned:

We shall regret if this fundamental feeling is ignored and we are compelled to intervene actively in the military and commercial life of your country as your Government are now intervening in ours.

The Government of the Irish Republic believe that a period of four days is sufficient for your Government to signify its intention in the matter of the military evacuation

and for the issue of your declaration of abdication in respect
of our country. Our Government reserve the right of
appropriate action without further notice if on the expira-
tion of the period of grace these conditions remain unful-
filled.

(Signed) Patrick Fleming

Four days later on finding that neither the British nor the
Orangemen seemed disposed to meet its wishes the I.R.A.
issued another declaration. It was written by McGarrity*
and said:

On the twenty-third day of April in the year 1916 in the
city of Dublin, seven men, who were representative in spirit
and outlook and purpose of the Irish nation that had never
yielded to nor accepted the British conquest, set their
humble and almost unknown names to the foregoing document that has passed into history, making the names of the
seven signatories immortal.

Those signatures were sealed with the blood of the
immortal seven, and of many others who followed them into
one of the most gallant fights in the history of the world;
and the Irish nation rose from shame to honour, from
humiliation to pride, from slavery to freedom.

Three years later (on January 21, 1919), the Republic
proclaimed in Easter week 1916 was ratified and formally
established by the elected representatives of all Ireland and
a solemn declaration of independence sent out to the nations
of the world.

To combat that declaration and to prevent the proclamation of the Republic of Ireland from becoming effective, the
Armed Forces of the English enemy made war upon the
people of this country. They were met by the Irish Republican Army, and challenged and resisted so stubbornly that
after two years of bloody warfare the English were forced

* McGarrity is now dead, but present day I.R.A. documents
are still signed with his name, showing the continuation of his
influence.

to ask for a truce with a view to settlement by negotiation.

Unfortunately, because men were foolish enough to treat with an armed enemy within their gates, the English won the peace. Weakness and treachery caused a resumption of the war and the old English tactics of "Divide and Conquer" were exploited to the fullest extent. Partition was introduced, the country divided into two parts with two separate parliaments subject to and controlled by the British Government from London. The Armed Forces of England still occupy six of our counties in the North and reserve the right "in time of war or strained relations" to re-occupy the ports which they have just evacuated in the Southern part of Ireland. Ireland is still tied, as she has been for centuries past, to take part in England's wars. In the Six Counties, a large number of Republican soldiers are held prisoners by England. Further weakness on the part of some of our people, broken faith and make believe have postponed the enthronement of the living Republic, but the proclamation of Easter week and the Declaration of Independence stand and must stand forever. No man, no matter how far he has fallen away from his national faith, has dared to repudiate them. They constitute the rallying centre for the unbought manhood of Ireland in the fight that must be made to make them effective and to redeem the nation's self-respect that was abandoned by a section of our people in 1922.

The time has come to make that fight. There is no need to re-declare the Republic of Ireland, now or in the future. There is no need to re-affirm the Declaration of Irish Independence. But the hour has come for the supreme effort to make both effective. So in the name of the unconquered dead and of the faithful living, we pledge ourselves to that task.

We call upon England to withdraw her armed forces, her civilian officials and institutions, and representatives of all kinds from every part of Ireland, as an essential preliminary to arrangements for peace and friendship between the two countries; and we call upon the people of all Ireland, at home and in exile, to assist us in the effort we are about to make in God's name, to compel that evacuation and to enthrone the Republic of Ireland.

> Signed on behalf of
> The Republican Government and the Army
> Council of Oglaigh na hEireann
> (Irish Republican Army)

Stephen Hayes	Patrick Fleming
Peadar O'Flaherty	George Plunkett
Laurence Grogan	Sean Russell

The ultimatum had been greeted with derision or disbelief, but the declaration of war was followed by explosions one of which immediately showed the futility of Russell's aim of conducting such a campaign without losing any life. A twenty-seven-year-old fish porter, Albert Ross, was killed on his way to work in Manchester when a bomb went off in a street main.

In London there were three explosions at electricity plants and throughout the north and the midlands other power units, gas and electricity mains, were damaged. On July 26 a young Scotsman, standing in the left-luggage office at King's Cross station, was killed in an explosion that severely injured his wife and fourteen other people.

On Friday August 25 the worst incident of all occurred. Five people were killed, including an old man of eighty-one, and a schoolboy of fifteen, twelve very badly injured and forty more less seriously hurt in an explosion at 2.30 p.m. in the thoroughfare Broadgate in Coventry. Two I.R.A. men were executed for this, one of them, Peter Barnes, being at least morally innocent. He had been involved in buying flour bags for the mixing and carrying of explosives (though he didn't know where these were to go off). The man who actually cycled into the street with a bomb in the carrier and parked the bicycle outside Astley's Shop, was a psycopath, who at the time of writing, is still receiving treatment.

During the next fifteen months bombs went off in

letter boxes, lavatories, telephone boxes, railway cloak-
rooms, cinemas, post offices and business premises of all
sorts. Sometimes cinemas were emptied by tear gas.

Curiously enough it was the Irish government that first
passed laws directed at the I.R.A. The British had of
course been rounding up I.R.A. agents by the score but
it was in Dublin that the Offences against the State Act
was passed on June 14, setting up military tribunals
(special criminal courts composed of army officers) and
stating:

Every person who usurps or unlawfully exercises any function of Government whether by setting up, maintaining or
taking part in any way in a body of persons purporting to be
a Government or by any other action or conduct whatsoever
shall be guilty of felony and shall be liable in a conviction
thereof to suffer penal servitude for a term not exceeding
ten years or to imprisonment for a term not exceeding two
years.

The act also gave the government power to issue a suppression order against anybody who 'raises or maintains a
military or armed force'. The following day the I.R.A.
was declared an unlawful organisation and police and
military clashed with the Republicans in a riot when the
I.R.A. tried to make the annual pilgrimage to Bodenstown.
Incredibly enough, in London after several explosions the
previous day, some two hundred Irishmen marched
through the centre of the city in honour of Wolfe Tone,
carrying banners demanding the release of I.R.A. prisoners
in the custody of Scotland Yard—their procession guarded
by British police.

This tolerance wore thin. On July 24 when Home
Secretary Sir Samuel Hoare introduced the Prevention
of Violence (Temporary Provisions) Bill in the House
of Commons, he told the House that sixty-six members of
the I.R.A. had been convicted, and that 1,500 sticks of
gelignite, 1,000 detonators, tons of potassium chlorate, a

quantity of ferrous oxide, seven gallons of sulphuric acid, and four hundredweight of aluminium powder had been seized. By then there had been 127 terrorist attacks, fifty-seven in London.

Sir Samuel said the government had been informed that the I.R.A. campaign was 'being closely watched and actively stimulated by foreign organisations'. With the darkening face of Europe the House was not disposed to question whether the foreign organisations meant Clann na Gael or Nazis. Four days later the bill became law. It gave the home secretary powers to issue expulsion orders against suspected persons living in England and to issue prohibition orders against suspects wishing to enter the country. In emergencies, search warrants were to be issued by police officers not below the rank of superintendent and the police could arrest and detain suspects for five days without warrants. There might have been some opposition to these drastic provisions for Arthur Greenwood, the Labour M.P., said that while the opposition recognised the need for stronger powers, it regretted that the government should have quite so much authority. But on July 26 further explosions occurred at the left-luggage offices at King's Cross and Victoria stations. At King's Cross the Scottish doctor, Dr Campbell, lost both his legs in the explosion.

Speaking in the Seanad on the same day de Valera said, 'No one can have any doubt as to the result of the campaign in England, and no one can think that this government has any sympathy with it.' He appealed to those carrying on the campaign, asking them how they could hope to reach a decision by these means. He believed that a number of them were animated by high ideals, but that they were misreading Irish history and making no allowance for changed circumstances.

Although the horror of Coventry had not yet come there was by then no hope of the I.R.A.'s 'having a decision' from the campaign. Failure and disorganisation had done their work. Thus, after his near escape in

London Eoin MacNamee had gone to the Leamington Spa and Stratford areas. With only a bicycle he could transport very little explosive and he asked for a car, but there was no money to spare. During mid-Lent in Coventry, MacNamee was told to report to G.H.Q. in Dublin. Here he found Sean Fuller, one of the Birmingham operations officers, who said that opinion within the movement was now swinging against Russell. Mairtin O'Cadain, in whose house the plot to install Russell was given its final polish, was by now very anti-Russell. Nor was there any sign of the promised campaign against the North. This depressed MacNamee, now that most of his friends in London were captured.

He attended a meeting of G.H.Q. staff with Larry Grogan, Stephen Hayes, Micksey Conway, Sean Russell, Michael Traynor and Sean Fuller. Russell, depressed and waspish, asked MacNamee what he was doing there and wanted to know why he had not told the people in London where the dumps were. Confusion on the whereabouts of the explosives had led to MacNamee's recall to Dublin. He explained that he had told I.R.A. officers in authority where the dumps were, but that these men were now all behind bars, and that in any case he would always restrict the spread of such knowledge because he believed in secrecy. To which Russell replied, rather oddly for a conspirator, 'you're trying to create an air of mystery'.

Russell next criticised Fuller's handling of operations, and Fuller, as chagrined as MacNamee, did not return to the campaign. He dropped out of the I.R.A. after his arrest later in a round-up by the Irish police. MacNamee went back to England with Michael Traynor via Rosslare. Keeping apart on the boat, they separated on docking to give MacNamee an opportunity of checking on the ammunition dumps.

When MacNamee met Leo Duigan, now officer commanding London, he found most of the 'stuff' had been disposed of. Checking a yard owned by a Jack Healy he learned that the explosive materials had been seized by Scotland Yard, and that Healy had been given ten years' penal servitude at the Central Criminal Court. Meeting his contact with Russell at Regent's Park he told him what had happened and advised against any intensification of the campaign because during that month (March) the cases of captured I.R.A. men were being heard at the Old Bailey and he felt it would prejudice them to have any further bombings for the time being. The contact disregarded this and said that continuation of the campaign would show the I.R.A. meant business. MacNamee knew how some of the prisoners were being treated and asked Russell to see that at least their dependants were cared for as cases of near starvation occurred when bread-winners were suddenly hurled into jail for storing a sack of white powder in a closet.

Ill treatment of I.R.A. men in jail was by no means infrequent. Sometimes it occurred through the defiant attitude of the prisoners. Sometimes an episode such as the Coventry explosion prejudiced warders and police against the I.R.A. One big row in Dartmoor broke out after the Coventry explosion and eleven I.R.A. men were so badly beaten up that they had to be treated in hospital. After this, the I.R.A. prisoners in Dartmoor had to drill and work separately from the other prisoners. However, neither MacNamee's counselling, nor that of like-minded members of the movement had any effect.

When MacNamee returned to Dublin after checking on the dumps in London, he found that Russell, though depressed, had no intention of calling off the campaign. In fact he set out for America on April 8, shortly after receiving MacNamee's report, to publicise the campaign there and raise funds for it. But though he attracted enormous publicity in America, by the end of 1939 the campaign was dead. Only about a dozen incidents occurred in 1940, the last recorded one being in March when an unexploded bomb was found in a litter bin at Grosvenor Place. Another bomb that was not found went off at Westminster City Council refuse depot after the bin had been tipped into the heap. The most serious explosion of 1940, on February 22, was in a bus litter bin in Oxford Street, which seriously injured seven people. This can be seen as a kind of futile postscript to the hanging of Barnes and Frank Richards (alias McCormick) on February 7 for their part in the Coventry explosion.

This hanging aroused a wave of bitterness against England in Ireland. Emotional scenes recalled the height of the 'troubles' and every public body and the legislature itself pleaded for clemency for the condemned men. They have since passed into an only slightly lesser place in the martyrology of Ireland as have Dunne and Sullivan, the men who shot Sir Henry Wilson.

In English law, both Barnes and McCormick were guilty under the rule of 'Common Purpose' whereby if two or more persons agree to commit a dangerous felony, resulting in a death, all the persons in the combination or conspiracy are guilty of murder. Before being sentenced Richards said to the judge, 'My Lord, before you pass sentence of death, I wish to thank sincerely the gentlemen who have defended me during my trial and I wish to state that the part I took in these explosions since I came to England I have done for a just cause. As a soldier of the Irish Republican Army I am not afraid to die, as I am doing it for a just cause. I say in conclusion, God bless Ireland and God bless the men who have fought and died for it. Thank you, my lord.' Barnes said, 'I would like to say as I am going before my God, as I am condemned to death, I am innocent, and later I am sure it will all come out that I had neither hand, act, nor part in it. That is all I have to say.'

By English law Barnes's possession of a receipt for a flour bag and suitcases used in the incident, and a letter to a friend in the Republican movement in Dublin, made him an accessory. So far as intent to kill or complicity in the actual deed is concerned, Peter Barnes was innocent. Barnes was not in Coventry while the bomb was being prepared, and not there when it went off. The tragedy of

Peter Barnes typifies the tragedy of all the confused, well-meaning, idealistic, uneducated young men who joined the I.R.A. without realising what they were letting themselves in for.

At thirty-two he gave up his job with Offaly County Council and went to an industrial England in 1939, while England was on the verge of a war with Germany, to free his country of 'British domination'. He probably never visited the North in his life, and had no inkling of the complexity of the Protestant-Catholic relationships. He paid for his idealism with his life on an English scaffold.

6 / YEARS OF DISASTER

In Ireland the effect of the bombing campaign on the I.R.A. and on public opinion was to make a bad situation worse. The Offences Against the State Act, which allowed for imprisonment and detention without trial, became law on June 14, 1939. A few days later the I.R.A. was declared an unlawful organisation and the Bodenstown march was proscribed. The army was called out and the I.R.A. made no effort to defy the ban. Then on August 22 the special military court* for which the Offences Against the State Act allowed was proclaimed and from then until the end of the war the operation of the court was to cast a gloomy shadow over the I.R.A.

The international situation resulted in a declaration of emergency on September 2, whereby the government, both Dail and Seanad, resolved 'that arising out of the armed conflict now taking place in Europe, a national emergency exists affecting the vital interests of the State'. The Emergency Powers Bill was enacted the following day. From then on the government had control of supplies, tillage, transort, censorship, military matters and, of course, all measures to be taken against the I.R.A. To emphasise this

* The court's members were Colonel Bennett, Colonel McKenna, Major Joyce, Major Whelan, Major Tuite.

hard line Gerald Boland became minister for justice on September 8.

The government also reorganised the Special Branch, although it was hardly the instrument upon which a government might depend for its internal security during wartime. The reorganised branch was headed by Chief-Superintendent Patrick Carroll, Chief-Superintendent Sean Gantly and Chief-Superintendent Michael Weymes. Its most colourful member, one Michael Gill a sergeant, at the outbreak of the war, was speedily promoted to chief-superintendent, through his talent for catching I.R.A. members. More than any other figure of the war, he was regarded as Nemesis by the I.R.A. and was feared and hated.

On the military side, the Director of Military Intelligence at the outbreak of the war was Colonel Liam Archer. He was succeeded by Colonel Dan Bryan with a formidable team, Lieutenant Colonel Joe Guilfoyle and Major Florrie O'Donoghue (who had both gained experience against the British under Collins) and Dr Richard Hayes, who later became director of the National Library. He was a cipher expert who trained himself to master every German code.

Junior officers who served under these men have all distinguished themselves in civilian life. Norman Hewitt became a top travel agent, Con McGovern an airline manager for an American company, and Douglas Gageby, one of Ireland's best journalists, founded the *Evening Press* and later became editor of the *Irish Times*. This team, with more experience, education, energy and resources than the I.R.A. soon proved itself more than a match for both the I.R.A. and the spies whom the Nazis sent to Ireland. (They were sent, in part, to take advantage of the existence of the I.R.A.) The poor resources of the I.R.A. had been demonstrated the previous year when in November at Clady, Co. Tyrone, three I.R.A. men were killed when a faulty mine went off.

The three were James Joseph 'Jimmy Joe' Reynolds, one

of the six men charged with the murder of Roderick
More O'Farrell in Longford in 1935 (he was acquitted
after the second trial) and also one of the prime movers
in the British bombing campaign, John J. Kelly from
Donegal, and Charlie McCaffrey from Tyrone. They
had been making a mine to destroy some customs posts
along the border. Blowing up customs huts had always
been a favourite I.R.A. tactic and a number had gone up
in 1937 in protest against a visit by King George VI and
Queen Elizabeth. (This gave rise to the I.R.A. ballad 'A
Bonfire on the Border'.) The 1938 explosions were intended to start Russell's northern campaign, to reproduce
in Ireland the kind of onslaught made in England.

Tarlach O'hUid, who visited Charlie McCaffrey in
hospital where he lingered for two days before dying of
his injuries, remembers that McCaffrey, who never fully
recovered consciousness, kept repeating over and over
again, 'Stand back John Joe there's a wee thing wrong.'
Clearly the bomb was inexpertly made. Children sleeping
in the house where it was made had to be dug out from
the debris, mercifully unhurt. Patrick Kelly, a brother of
the dead man who was not in the I.R.A., had allowed his
brother to use his cottage. He, his wife and daughter
were flung across an adjoining room but escaped serious
injury. A neighbour who had been saying the Rosary at
the time of the blast said that it was her prayers that
saved the family.

A number of customs huts that did go up were destroyed by bombs placed in attaché cases handed to bus
conductors, carriage paid, with addresses to non-existent
people. The cases were then deposited in the customs hut
awaiting 'callers'. It was intended that the cases should
explode after the customs' officials had gone home. One
time, a driver, Peter Lony of the Erne Bus Company,
was given a case addressed to a Miss Eileen Douglas,
Lisnascigh, c/o Clontivran Customs House. Like any rural
bus driver in Ireland he made it his business to see that
Miss Douglas got her case and took it on the bus from

the customs hut where he found there was no Miss Eileen
Douglas there for it. After inquiries for the non-existent
lady he and his conductor took the case in the front of a
crowded bus back to the Clontivran post and left it there
to await Miss Douglas's arrival. Happily the hut was still
open. (When it was shut the normal procedure was for
the driver to take the case home with him and deliver it
again in the morning.) A few hours later the case exploded
and parts of the hut were found a mile away.

Police activity in the North naturally increased after
these explosions and deaths, and on December 22 the
R.U.C. made a big swoop in Belfast, putting thirty-four
I.R.A. men behind bars. Their arrest, which ruined any
chance of a northern campaign getting off the ground, was
accompanied by a statement from Sir Dawson Bates, the
Northern Ireland minister for home affairs saying, 'The
fact having come to the knowledge of the police that plans
have been prepared by the Irish Republican Army for
attacks upon persons occupying prominent positions and
upon Government and other property during that Christmas and New Year period, the Government decided . . .
there was no alternative other than to arrest and intern
well-known leaders and prominent members of this illegal
organisation.'

In the South imprisonments after the English campaign
had brought less established figures to the top of the
I.R.A., in particular Stephen Hayes. Hayes, from Co.
Wexford, an amiable ex-footballer, fond of a drink, and
an official in the County Council, had been appointed
adjutant-general by Russell in October, 1938. Before
leaving for America in April, 1939, Russell had him
promoted to chief of staff during his own absence. This
appointment was never ratified in the normal fashion by an
Army Council meeting. Hayes did not insist on regular
meetings of the Army Council, and there were differences
of opinion as to the proper course in the disasters which
were occurring. Cork and Kerry I.R.A. split from the main
body, and from each other, and the North began to look

more to Belfast than Dublin for direction. In the South, Michael Traynor, Tony D'Arcy, Jack McNeela and Don Adams, all new faces on the Army Council, were thinking of guerrilla raids on the North from southern bases. All were disillusioned with the routine of parades and confusion which existed in the South and realised that there was very little hope of overthrowing the southern state. Then sometime before Christmas 1939, Tom Doyle, a civil servant in the Department of Defence, presented an audacious scheme for raiding the Magazine Fort in Phoenix Park, Dublin, where the bulk of the Irish army's ammunition was stored. This idea appealed to Traynor and the others because, while they had a considerable number of guns stored around the country,* ammunition was in very short supply. Prior to Doyle's approach, Traynor had switched his emphasis from bomb making to guerrilla warfare, so the raid, although it involved fantastic risks, fell into their general scheme. An Army Council meeting, in the unlikely setting of the home of a Radio Eireann musician in Booterstown, Co. Dublin, decided to go ahead with the raid.

It began about half-past eight in the evening of December 23, 1939, and continued for two hours. The I.R.A. immobilised the entire garrison (an officer, two N.C.O.s and ten men armed with rifles and a Lewis gun) and got away with 1,084,000 rounds of ammunition in thirteen lorries. Entrance to the inner gate of the fort was gained when a military policeman left this open to answer a ring at the outer gate. There he met a man in civilian clothes who said he had a parcel for the officer in charge. The military policeman opened the gate for him and was promptly held up.

In a way, conditions in the Fort symbolised the attitude of the country as a whole to the threat of war. Accord-

*Ballykinlar army camp in the North of Ireland was raided so often and so many Tommies stationed there were convicted of selling rifles to the I.R.A. that it became known in I.R.A. circles as 'the Stores'.

ing to standing orders the inner gate should have been locked behind the military policeman, but in practice this was never done and Doyle knew of the laxity prevailing throughout the Fort. The policeman and the sentry on duty were captured with equal ease; the rest of the garrison was sitting around a fire in the guardroom when the I.R.A. burst in. Heads rolled in the upper echelons of the army for the unpreparedness that left the country virtually defenceless.

Stung by the I.R.A.'s audacity the government reacted with a ruthless speed and efficiency which showed results almost immediately. All army and police leave was cancelled, roads were blocked, cars and lorries had to pass checkpoints and money was liberally spent by intelligence agents. Beginning on St Stephen's Day, the ammunition was gradually recovered. Only about one lorry load got away to the Cooley mountain district of Co. Louth, where some incredible feats of endurance were performed by a farmer who made repeated journeys up the side of a precipitous mountain, carrying bucket loads of bullets.

'The arms were almost dragged out of me,' he told me years later.

On January 4 the Dail met in emergency session and by eighty-two votes to nine passed a measure allowing the government to set up detention camps at the Curragh headquarters of the regular army. Henceforward the I.R.A. men knew that, if captured, they might be thrown into the Curragh and left there until the government felt it was safe to let them out. This disturbed more people than those in the I.R.A.

Apart from the nose-tweaking of the Magazine Fort raid, the government faced an ever growing number of unconstitutional activities by the I.R.A., legal challenges, and constitutional threats on its political front.

On October 22, 1939, a gelignite bomb had been exploded at the outer wall of Mountjoy Jail in an unsuccessful attempt to release four I.R.A. prisoners: Paddy Mc-

Grath, Willy McGuinness, Peadar O'Flaherty and Laurence Grogan. About the same time, the Killiney Castle bomb-making factory was discovered and machine guns, revolvers and large quantities of paxo were seized. On November 18, Amiens Street post office, in Dublin, was held up and £5,000 taken. Five days later the National Bank in Clonliffe Road was raided and £200 taken. In the wake of these doings the legal difficulty presented itself.

On December 1, Mr Justice Gavan Duffy, in the case of a *habeas corpus* application for Seamus Burke of Mayo, who was interned in Arbour Hill Jail, held that part six of the Offences Against the State Act 1939, was in conflict with the constitution and therefore invalid. He found that the minister's power, under the act, to order the detention of a person when he was 'satisfied' that it was necessary to do so was the assumption by a minister of the executive branch of powers reserved by the constitution to the judiciary. He consequently ordered Burke released. While an appeal to the Supreme Court was immediately entered this decision raised the question whether the other I.R.A prisoners in Arbour Hill should be set free. After a private debate to decide whether new legislation should be introduced, or whether the prisoners should be freed, the government released fifty-three I.R.A. men from Arbour Hill on December 2. On the same day a bread van was held up on the North Strand in Dublin, and nearly £500 was taken. The driver was badly beaten up

December saw the sentencing of Barnes and McCormick, which had a powerful effect on Republican sentiment in Ireland, and the issuing of a circular from the Irish Republican Publicity Bureau to users of the Northern and Ulster Banks advising them to transfer their accounts to southern based banks, because 'those banks with headquarters in Belfast are considered to be operating against the best interests of national economic freedom'. Then came the Magazine Fort raid itself, the seizure on December 29 of an I.R.A. pirate radio station in a Dublin suburb and the fatal shooting of a policeman in Cork on January

3 as he attempted to arrest an I.R.A. man Thomas MacCurtain.

The government took parliamentary action following Mr Justice Duffy's decision. On January 5 the Emergency Powers (Amendment) Act, 1940, was passed, giving the government the right to intern Irish citizens without trial. in the same way as aliens could be interned without trial during the war which then existed. Because the emergency powers acts were passed pursuant to the resolution relating to the Second World War their constitutionality could not be challenged; the Offences Against the State Act, having been passed before the war began, was subject to judicial review. When part six of this act was declared repugnant to the constitution the government decided to carry out future internments under the Emergency Powers Act of 1939, as amended by the act of January 5 enabling it to intern Irish citizens. Such internments could not be challenged in the courts as the acts were not subject to judicial review.

All this legal manoeuvring aroused some serious misgivings on the part of responsible people. President Douglas Hyde, for the first time since the constitution came into force on December 29, 1937, convened a meeting of the Council of State* to advise him whether the act should be referred to the Supreme Court (under article 26 of the constitution) for a decision as to its constitutionality. After consultation he decided to do so. Even though both houses of parliament had passed the bill it could not become law until he signed it, and this he would not do until he heard the court's decision. On February 9 the court declared the bill to be valid in rela-

---

* It consisted of the prime minister, the deputy prime minister, the chief justice, the president of the High Court, the chairman of Dail Eireann, the chairman of the Seanad, the attorney general, Deputy William T. Cosgrave, Deputy James M. Dillon, Senator Robert P. Farnan, Senator John Keane, Deputy General Richard Mulcahy, Deputy William Norton, Senator Michael Tierney.

tion to the constitution and it was duly signed and became law.

The next day the I.R.A. again raided the Ballykinlar camp and got away with 100 rifles. This was an irrelevant episode as the I.R.A. did not have bullets of the calibre required for the stolen rifles. The raid was inspired by a false idea within the I.R.A. as to the strength of republican sympathy throughout the country. This false idea developed partially from reasons which have already been suggested and partially from what seemed to be tangible evidence that the public was swinging towards republicanism—albeit of a constitutional sort.

In Dublin at this time there was much talk of a new political movement which was believed to be a challenge to the government and was popularly reported to be ready to take over the government on some form of corporative basis. This movement, which came to be known as Coras na Poblachta (System of Republicans), did in fact contain the nucleus of a party. Eight years later it formed the core of a coalition which introduced some new ideas into Irish politics and which took power from Fianna Fail. In the early months of 1940, however, its leaders were not capable of such a feat nor were the times right for a change.

The principal figures in Coras na Poblachta were Simon Donnelly, who had fought in Boland's Mill under de Valera in 1916, Sean Fitzpatrick, another War of Independence man, Con Lehane, who had lately left the I.R.A., Sean Gibbons, Tom O'Rourke, Sean Dowling, one of Rory O'Connor's principal lieutenants in the Civil War days, Colonel Roger McCorley, one of the principal I.R.A. leaders in Belfast who during the Anglo-Irish war had taken the Free State side in the Civil War, Frank Thornton, one of Michael Collins's top intelligence officers, Roger McHugh, a lecturer in English at University College, Dublin (and now professor there), Captain Martin Bell and Peter O'Connor.

Coras na Poblachta sought the formal declaration of a

republic. Though it realised that its writ would run only in the twenty-six counties, it would claim that the jurisdiction extended over the six counties. Nobody bothered too much about how this writ could be enforced, either on a wartime England, or a wartime North of Ireland. In fact this declaration of a Republic was made eight years later by the coalition which ousted Fianna Fail. Its language policy required the use of the Irish learned at school, with Irish street signs, shop signs and government documents and bank notes. This policy was followed by successive governments. Coras na Poblachta also proposed to introduce national service, for educational purposes, to ensure that everyone understood his responsibilities.

The basic economic principle of the Coras na Poblachta founders was the statutory right to employment and a living wage. In other economic fields the party's thinking was strictly republican in the I.R.A. sense. It proposed breaking the link with British currency, the nationalisation of banks and the making of people employed in banks into civil servants.

Free education for all children over primary age was proposed as a right, as was a university education when feasible. This last proposal has become Irish governmental policy only since the mid-1960s, although another of the party's ideas, the introduction of children's allowances, was taken up by Fianna Fail three years after Coras na Poblachta was dissolved. Dissolution occurred because people tended to discuss the party rather than join it. Indeed some of the Coras leaders themselves, notably Frank Thornton, felt that duty lay in joining some of the forces then springing up to defend the country.

The I.R.A., meanwhile, elated with its upsurge, the psychological effects of the Magazine Fort raid and an undue reliance on the sympathy during the Barnes-McCormick hangings, persevered with plans for an attack on the North and a meeting was arranged in the Meath Hotel in Parnell Square, Dublin. The normal procedure for such a meeting was for delegates to visit a nearby hotel for directions, making their way unobtrusively in ones and twos to the chosen venue. But in this case each person was told to go direct to the hotel, and vigilant Special Branch men on duty at railway stations and bus depots realised that prominent I.R.A. men from Mayo, Donegal, Tyrone, Sligo, Galway, Belfast, Roscommon, Leitrim and other parts of the country were in Dublin, converging on the Meath. In a police raid everyone was captured. Knowing nothing of Traynor's, Dom Adams' and Paddy McNeela's plans the authorities thought the meeting was merely a gathering of I.R.A. men and sentences ranged only from three to six months.

Even so, these imprisonments began a grim chapter in the history of the I.R.A. In Mountjoy, prisoners were treated as ordinary criminals and there was continual agitation for political treatment. After the influx of new prisoners it was decided in February to back these demands by hunger striking. On March 1, Jack McNeela and Jack Plunkett, both of whom had been seized with the ill-fated pirate transmitter in December, were due to appear before the Special Criminal Court in Collins Barrack, Dublin. It was decided to prevent their being taken to the court. The prisoners barricaded themselves in D-wing (which also contained the execution chamber), using their beds, tables and anything else they could get, and armed themselves with the legs of tables and chairs. Some very savage fighting broke out when the warders, augmented by members of the Special Branch, stormed the barricades.

Cornered, the prisoners fought fiercely and the police were not too particular how they subdued them. Traynor remembers seeing D'Arcy standing with his hands up after surrendering, when a policeman brought down his baton across his head. On the other hand, Seamus Byrne, who had also been arrested in the transmitter swoop, recalls how a big sergeant approached him with a baton in one hand, and stuck out his hand to say, 'Musha is that yourself Mr Byrne?' He remembered him from his ap-

pearances as a solicitor in court. The two of them retired
to an empty cell and smoked until things quietened down
—after hoses had been turned on the prisoners. (Hosing
is an effective form of riot control. It not only knocks down
the protester but takes his breath away, leaving him
chilled, shaken and unfit for further activity. With men
who had been on hunger strike for four days this was a
harrowing ordeal.)

Hunger-striking is a double-edged weapon. It damages
the striker physically almost as much as it increases his
moral stature among his sympathisers. Until February,
1940 I.R.A. hunger strikers had generally carried the day
against the government, understandably in a country that
had won its independence partly from deaths on hunger
strikes during 1916-21 of men such as Terence McSwiney
and Thomas Ashe. Fianna Fail had come under considerable pressure afterwards—both from those who wanted the
prisoners let out, and from those who wished to have
them kept in.

Within the six-month period before the Mountjoy strike,
an I.R.A. internee in Arbour Hill Military Jail, Charles
McCarthy of Cork (on hunger strike from September 16
to October 12) was released. On the same day Con
Lehane* went on a hunger and thirst strike. His case was
raised in the Dail on October 19 by the Labour leader
Deputy William Norton. Lehane abandoned the strike two
days later and was subsequently released.

The government had also been pressed into showing
clemency towards a group of other Cork men, Jeremiah
Daly, Richard McCarthy and John Lynch, who had gone
on strike despite the government statement of October 31
'. . . that as arrest and detention in accordance with the
powers conferred by Parliament are the only means available for the maintenance of public order and security
they cannot permit the State authorities to be deprived of
these means through the policy of hunger strike. The pris-

* He had left the I.R.A. and was furious at being caught in
one of the many I.R.A. sweeps of the time.

oners on hunger strike will, accordingly, not be released.'

Each of the strikers was told of this decision formally and individually. But on November 8 the Labour Party called on the government to release all prisoners on hunger strike. The next day de Valera defended the government's action but when Jeremiah Daly abandoned his hunger strike on the 11th he was released three days later, and Lynch and McCarthy, who had been removed to St Bricin's Military Hospital, were also released after treatment.

Above all there had been the case of Patrick McGrath the chief operations officer who had been severely wounded in the fight against the British, during which he had been an outstanding figure. His case was considered to be sufficiently important for the Government Information Bureau to issue a statement to the effect that a government order had been obtained for his removal on November 15 to Jervis Street Hospital from Mountjoy Prison, where he had been on hunger strike from October 23. He left hospital on December 4 and a *nolle prosequi* was entered in his case before the Special Criminal Court on December 7. His spell at liberty was not to be very long—he was executed the following year for shooting two policemen.

The sort of dilemma that these cases had presented to the government is well illustrated by the following passage from the debate in the Seanad on the Offences Against the State (Amendment) Bill, 1940.

Mr MacDermot: Might I ask the Minister one question? He said that he intended to intern these people. Does he intend to continue to hold them if they go on hunger-strike?

Mr Boland: I certainly hope so.

Mr Fitzgerald: Say 'Yes' or 'No'.

Mr Boland: The intention certainly is to hold them, hunger-strike or no hunger-strike because things have gone too far altogether.

Mr Fitzgerald: The last Senator who spoke here mentioned that the Taoiseach said: 'All Parties now know where they are', and he commends the action of the Government in releasing the hunger-strikers. How does the statement of the Taoiseach yesterday, that all Parties now know where they are, fit in? He went into the Dail and he stopped the operations of the Dail, departed from the whole procedure there, to give a public assurance that there would be no release for the hunger-strikers, and then he released them. Yesterday he gave us an assurance that the Government are going to take their responsibilities seriously and see that any means that may be necessary will be used to put down this criminal organisation. He may tomorrow change his mind, just as he did with regard to the hunger-strikers. How are we to know where we stand, and how are any Parties to know where they stand.

Mr Boland: As regards the question of vacillation and letting out the hunger-strikers, I do not want to run away from that either. I admit that, on the surface, it looks bad. It looks like weakness and it may be very hard to justify making a statement and going back on it. But there are all sorts of considerations. We have got to deal with a very delicate problem and members of a Government have to listen to cases made by responsible members of the Oireachtas who come to them and put up propositions. These propositions were not made in public, but I may mention a matter that was put to me. I am breaking no confidence because I shall mention no names.

A prominent member of the Opposition said to me in private—I mention no names and I hope I am breaking no confidence; this was a man who had taken very strong action against these people—that, in his view, we were not entitled to let these people die on hunger-strike because, due to our attitude and general policy towards these people in the past, they were entitled to believe that if they went on hunger-strike, we would let them out. He said:

'You did not make this announcement before they went on hunger-strike and I believe you are bound not to let them die.' Things like that had to be borne in mind, but I can assure this House that we are not going to let people take the law into their own hands and that we shall not be prevented from detaining them if we are satisfied they must be detained. Our patience has certainly been tried. Our policy of conciliation has got perhaps an over-trial; I think that is on the credit side, and I wish to pay a tribute to Senator Tierney for having said so much—that it was well worth while to have tried it. We tried that *ad nauseam*. We may have gone too far, but that has got to stop. There is no question of ruthlessness or rigour, but I am sure that there is going to be insistence that everybody in this country will obey the law.

A hunger strike begun shortly after Boland's declaration was obviously coming at a moment of peak determination on the government's part to resist such pressure and the seven men who rejected their food on February 25 realised this but were determined to die if necessary in order to achieve their aim.

The strikers were Thomas MacCurtain, Thomas Grogan, John Lyons, Michael Traynor, Tony D'Arcy, John McNeela and John Plunkett. Their principal demand was that they be allowed to walk around the jail freely without being confined to their cells at four o'clock each evening. They also sought to have John Dwyer and Nicholas Doherty, each serving five years' penal servitude in Mountjoy, transferred to military custody.

Doherty was convicted of being in possession of a rifle and ammunition taken from the Magazine Fort. He and Lyons went on hunger strike on February 25 but took food on March 6. Dwyer had been sentenced for having attempted to induce members of the defence forces to disclose information concerning Baldonnell Aerodrome. On March 1, John McNeela was sentenced to two years' imprisonment and John Plunkett to eighteen months' imprisonment on a charge of 'conspiracy to usurp a function of Government' (running a pirate radio). They were transferred to Arbour Hill and were removed to St Bricin's Hospital on March 27. Tony D'Arcy and Michael Traynor were sentenced to three months' imprisonment on March

5 for refusing to answer questions about the Meath Hotel case. They were transferred to Arbour Hill and were removed to St Bricin's Hospital on March 27. D'Arcy died on April 16 and McNeela on April 19.

Thomas MacCurtain, a son of a lord mayor of Cork who had been killed by the Black and Tans, had been in the I.R.A. since boyhood and was continually involved in its activities. He was awaiting trial for the murder of Detective Officer Roche and was removed from Mountjoy to St Bricin's on April 6. Thomas Grogan, awaiting trial in connection with the raid on Magazine Fort, was removed on April 1 from Mountjoy to St Bricin's suffering from pleurisy. On April 19, the day of McNeela's death, the hunger strike at St Bricin's was abandoned.

Michael Traynor recalled the strike for me without horror or bitterness.

'There were two nice doctors in the ward, one was Fianna Fail and one was Fine Gael. The Fianna Fail man was very embarrassed but the Fine Gael man was all in favour of us. Each evening we'd take it in turn to tell each other in great detail about the best meals we'd ever had or what the best meal we could ever hope to have would be like.

'The old bedboard had been done away with by Fianna Fail and our beds were fibre mattresses with a spring upon an iron bed. After a while, we had to have all our joints bandaged because they were only skin and bone and bedsores or gangrene would have set in easily.

'After a bit, I remember, I couldn't even turn in the bed without help. We had to be rubbed down each day with olive oil to prevent the bedsores. I could smell death off myself, a sickly nauseating stench. We would have died except that we drank a great deal of water each day.

'But our other appetites went, and we concentrated on saving our energies and our lives to beat the strike. I'd been on two hunger strikes before in Crumlin Road [Belfast's jail] but these were only canter strikes—this was a real galloping strike. Tony D'Arcy died first, he called out, "Jack, Jack, Jack McNeela, I'm dying." McNeela was in the bed opposite to D'Arcy and he insisted on getting out to go to his friend. I pleaded with him not to. There was no one in the ward at the time. The armed guard was outside a locked door. After the orderlies got the door open they lifted McNeela back to bed but he died two days later. Then we got word from Stephen Hayes telling us that all we had struck for was granted and that we were to call off the strike.'

Their first meal was two poached eggs on toast, tea, milk and sugar, followed by a dose of hydrochloric acid to replace their lost digestive juices. The acid treatment continued for a week and after every meal the prisoners could see the blankets rising round their distended stomachs.

The prisoners' euphoria after the strike was short-lived because they did not get what they had struck for, and they were served either with internment orders or with notification of their prison sentences. This was stunning for Grogan who got fourteen years for his part in the Magazine Fort raid.

MacCurtain was one who survived to become a leader of the I.R.A. campaign of 1956-62. The Roche case, for which he was to be tried, began when in the course of a scuffle a shot was fired as Roche and detectives tried to take MacCurtain into custody in Cork on January 3, 1940. Roche was fatally wounded, dying the next morning. This case aroused tremendous interest in Ireland because of MacCurtain's background. He was sentenced to death by the special Criminal Court on June 13, and the execution was fixed for July 5. But after an application for *habeas corpus* the execution was postponed for a week. The Supreme Court dismissed the appeal and the country seethed with controversy. MacCurtain's father had fought alongside many members of the present Fianna Fail for a thirty-two-county Republic and while everyone accepted that the I.R.A. and Fianna Fail travelled on parallel lines up to the point where the use of force was sanctioned, MacCurtain's case was seen as a test to whether Fianna Fail was prepared to kill to prevent force being used. It seemed certain that MacCurtain would die, but on July 10 a government statement declared: 'The President, acting on the advice of the government, has commuted the sentence of death on Thomas MacCurtain to penal servitude for life.' No one in Ireland outside the small circle from the government of that day knows the truth of what happened, but it is authoritatively supposed that a sister of Cathal Brugha's widow, the Reverend Mother of a convent in Armagh, interceded with Cardinal MacRory to have a last talk with de Valera, and that this final appeal decided him.

The hunger strikers' ordeal naturally excited much controversy throughout the country but government censorship restricted newspaper comment and coverage of the event. D'Arcy's death for instance was recorded in a short single column story on page eight of the *Irish Independent*. It was wartime and most people realised that episodes such as the Magazine Fort raid would jeopardise Ireland's claim to neutrality during the war. At the inquests on the dead men only relatives were allowed to attend. Sean MacBride appeared for the next of kin in both cases.

The verdict on D'Arcy was 'died of inanition, secondary to cardiac failure while on hunger strike'. This was the first time a coroner's jury had sat on a hunger-strike case since the death of Thomas Ashe, and the jury ordered a rider that, 'Immediate action should be taken with regard to the five men at present on hunger strike and in a serious condition. We desire to express our sincerest sympathy with the widow, relatives and friends of the late Anthony D'Arcy in their bereavement.' Most people in the country would have had sympathy with that rider but when McNeela died and the hunger strike was called off, the death of a bishop, Dr Hugh McSharry at the age of eighty-nine, was the main-page lead in the *Irish*

Independent with a hundred and four lines of type. The end of the strike and the death of Jack McNeela rated only twenty-five. The *Irish Times* gave it a slightly bigger show but on a left-hand, inside page, and the *Irish Press* also played it down.

The inquest on McNeela on April 22 aroused some controversy because a Carmelite priest, the Rev. John J. O'Hare gave evidence that he had seen the prisoners on the day of McNeela's death, and that as a result of his conveying instructions to them from I.R.A. headquarters, the strike was called off. He said the strike could have been called off three weeks earlier and both lives saved, if de Valera and Boland had allowed him to visit the prisoners. He gave evidence of meeting with the prisoners to substantiate his claims. As he had already spoken at the D'Arcy inquest, making somewhat similar statements, Boland felt constrained to go into the box during the McNeela hearing and make a statement which in effect denied the allegations. This exposed him to a scorching cross-examination from Sean MacBride.

However, any sympathy the I.R.A. might have hoped to gain by the martyrdom of D'Arcy and McNeela was speedily dissipated by the tottering organisation's subsequent tactics. In retaliation for the deaths, a mine was exploded in the laneway off the Lower Castle Yard in Dublin Castle, headquarters of the Special Branch, injuring a number of guards and the castle's housekeeper (part of the castle and the Chapel Royal are open to the public) and two policemen were shot at in the streets of Dublin. Public sympathy for the I.R.A. dwindled.

The two detective officers who were taking mails from Pearse Street sorting depot to the Department of External Affairs were attacked in Holles Street by a group of I.R.A. men, armed with Thompson guns. The mails were thought to contain despatches for Sir John Maffey, the British representative. Both policemen, Detective Officers McSweeney and Shanahan were immediately promoted to the rank of sergeant and the government offered rewards of up to £5,000 for information leading to the arrest and conviction of the persons who took part in the attack. (These were never claimed.)

The following day, after visiting the wounded men in hospital, de Valera, who had hitherto allowed Boland to make most of the stern public utterances concerning the I.R.A., went on the air from Radio Eireann to personally issue a statement:

'This moment, when small nations throughout Europe are devoting all their effort to strengthening national unity in order the better to defend their independence, is a moment that a group in this country has chosen to attempt to destroy our organised life.'

He referred to the 'dastardly attack made on two gallant policemen and the exploding of the time bomb in the headquarters of Dublin Castle'. He said, 'Were these deeds allowed to continue, Civil War would be the inevitable consequence and such a weakening of our strength as to make our country an easy prey to any invader.' He warned that no such situation would be permitted to develop and said to those 'now planning new crimes against the nation that they would not be allowed to continue their policy of sabotage. They have set the law at defiance, the law will be enforced against them. If the present law is not sufficient, it will be strengthened; and in the last resort, if no other law will suffice, then the Government will invoke the ultimate law—the safety of the people.'

He was backed up the next day by the leader of the Fine Gael party, W. T. Cosgrave, who speaking on a motion to issue a writ for a by-election in West Galway, announced that having heard the de Valera broadcast his party would not contest the Galway by-election. This election was for a seat formerly held by a government deputy, but Cosgrave went further and announced that neither would Fine Gael move a writ for a by-election in Co. Kilkenny where a seat formerly held by a Fine Gael deputy* was now vacant. He said that Fine Gael had

* This seat was later won by my father.

decided that a contest 'would not be in the interest of the country . . . if by any chance there was a marked reduction in the support accorded to the Government, it might be interpreted that that lack of support was due to the action which the Government, in recent months, had taken in connection with order in the State.' Fine Gael was 'particularly anxious that those engaged in unlawful activities . . . should realise that their activities should cease definitely once and for all and that there should be at least this much unanimity in the country that every citizen who respected his country would do his utmost to ensure that that sort of activity would cease.'

This inter-party co-operation was taken a step further and almost completely ruled out any prospects of I.R.A. recruitment of new members for the war years. An all-party defence conference was formed on May 28 and this body organised and propagandised to such effect that the prevailing spirit of patriotism was canalised within six months into the setting up of a Local Security Force of 133,000 men, drawn from towns, villages and baronies throughout the country.

Nevertheless between May and the following August upward of twenty incidents involving I.R.A. men with the police occurred. Arms dumps were seized; German spies hoping to make contact with the I.R.A. were captured; an I.R.A. man died after shots were fired at men digging a tunnel from Lapp's private asylum in College Road, Cork, in the direction of the Cork Jail which had recently been converted into a military detention centre.

Micksey Conway came into the news again. He had been on the run for some months and was captured at Harold's Cross Greyhound Track, after resisting arrest and being shot in the leg. Then on the morning of August 16 three detectives raiding No. 98a, Rathgar Road, Dublin, were fired on. Detective Officer Hyland was killed instantly, the other two detectives, McKeown and Brady being so severely wounded that McKeown died the following day in the Meath Hospital. On learning of the shootings the government immediately deleted from the Emergency Powers Act the right of appeal from findings of the Military Tribunal. That court was given a new brief under legislation which came into force on August 16. It was charged with the 'imposition and the carrying out of the sentence of death, and no appeal shall lie in respect of such conviction or sentence'.

Patrick McGrath and Thomas Harte, who were captured in the raid, were brought before the Military Court the following day. They were remanded until August 20 when they were found guilty of the murder of Hyland and sentenced to death by shooting. Sean MacBride defended them and appealed to the High Court and then to the Supreme Court, where after a three-day hearing (September 2, 3, 4) the appeal was again rejected. McGrath and Harte were duly executed by shooting in Mountjoy Prison at 6.45 p.m. on September 6.

It might be noted here that the trigger happiness of both police and I.R.A. should be examined in the light of the prevailing circumstances. Nerves were strained to breaking point as a programme of searches and raids was carried out in the most intensive fashion at all hours of the day and night on the homes and haunts of suspected I.R.A. men. Members of the Special Branch and of the I.R.A. frequently came into verbal conflict and both sides began to develop personal grudges and fears as to what might happen if one should fall into the hands of the other. Public opinion had also so swung away from the I.R.A. and behind the government that when on September 8 a communication similar to that circulated by the Cork I.R.A. on the execution of Barnes and McCormick was issued to cinema managers ordering them to close their cinemas as a mark of respect 'to the memory of Major-General Patrick McGrath and Thomas Harte, officers of the Irish Republican Army, who were murdered in Mountjoy on Friday', none of the cinemas closed—although all had shut for Barnes and McCormick. No incidents occurred, but to be on the safe side the police rounded up some forty-four I.R.A. suspects. Then on November 5 an event took place which stiffened the government's resolve to resist all pressures whether internal or external.

Speaking in the House of Commons on the U-boat sinkings in the Atlantic approaches to Britain, Churchill referred to Britain's being barred from using the south and west of Ireland to refuel her aircraft and flotillas. This, he said, was 'a heavy and invidious burden which Britain should never have to shoulder'. He suggested that if Britain could use Lough Swilly and Berehaven the whole situation could be changed.

De Valera replied two days later saying, 'There can be no question of handing over these ports so long as this State remains neutral.' He added that any attempt to bring pressure on the Irish government by any of the belligerents could only lead to bloodshed, and that so long as his government stayed in power it intended to defend its rights to the ports and to every other part of Irish territory. The following day two I.R.A. men were arrested in Dublin, after an exchange of shots, and given fourteen years each. On November 14, the police scotched a plan to raid a number of Dublin banks when they made a series of arrests which uncovered the plans of the banks.

As a result of the continuing decline of I.R.A. fortunes the belief became current in I.R.A. circles that the growing toll of arrests and set-backs was not so much a result of either bad I.R.A. planning or good police work, but of treachery within the movement. Where the I.R.A. was able to establish to its satisfaction that its code of honour had been infringed the punishment was drastic. For instance, on November 20 John Quinn, a lorry driver from Dundalk who had given evidence for the state after he had been arrested collecting ammunition for the I.R.A., was shot in the right thigh and in the left arm in reprisal.

To a group of I.R.A. men in Belfast, whom death and jailings had now brought to the top of the movement, it appeared that something more sinister lay behind the happenings in the South. Sean McCaughey, Liam Rice, Charles MacGlade, Liam Burke and later Pearse Kelly and Eoin MacNamee in particular, began to believe that there was a traitor at the very top of the organisation— Chief of Staff Stephen Hayes. The idea apparently originated with McCaughey who, like the other young men, was reared in the North and had very little contact with, or knowledge of, the South. Whatever reasons he had for becoming suspicious of Hayes in the first place died with him but investigations over a period of months led his colleagues to the conclusion that McCaughey was right. They decided that Hayes should be arrested, charged with his 'treason' and, if and when he admitted his treachery, executed.

Hayes knew nothing of their suspicions and arriving in Dublin for a routine meeting on June 30, 1941 he was immediately kidnapped. Then began a nightmare lasting almost two months during which, in Hayes's own words, he was both 'thunderstruck and gunstruck'. His captors took him and his brother-in-law, Lawrence De Lacy also of Enniscorthy, Co. Wexford (the man who had been instrumental in smuggling arms in conjunction with Joe McGarrity during the Troubles), to an isolated cottage in the Wicklow Mountains owned by Roger McHugh, a Coras na Poblachta founder and a Republican sympathiser though not a member of the I.R.A. or a party to the Hayes kidnapping. Prior to being taken to this cottage, Hayes was taken to the Cooley Mountains in Co. Louth, and then, after De Lacy had escaped from the Wicklow cottage, he was force marched to the Wicklow hills and down through Templeogue and Terenure to a house at Castlewood Avenue, owned by a friend of Pearse Kelly's aunt, a Mrs MacEoin, again a Republican sympathiser though not a member of the I.R.A.

There are two versions of what occurred during this period, that of Hayes and that of the I.R.A. It is not possible to say which is correct at this stage, without access to closely guarded Department of Justice files if, indeed, even these contain any information. It is possible to say, however, that the episode almost certainly caused two deaths and quite certainly wrecked the I.R.A. for the time being.

The I.R.A. version of the sequence of events is as follows. Immediately following Hayes's arrest a provisional Army Council was formed. Eoin MacNamee was brought down from Belfast to serve on it with McCaughey, MacGlade, Sean Harrington who later served for a month or two as chief of staff, Jack Lynch, Tom Mullally, Stephen Rynne, Andy Skelton and Joe Atkinson. It was an unusually large council because of the importance of the affair and the necessity of getting a broad measure of agreement within the organisation on a course of action. The I.R.A. says that Hayes was continually interrogated but not tortured or harmed in any way. Pearse Kelly told me that a light dog-chain was fixed to his legs but that he was not otherwise harmed and that it was arranged that after his court-martial Hayes would be examined by a doctor, a member of a well-known Dublin family, who could then testify that Hayes had not been ill-treated.

Hayes was court-martialled on July 23. The court-martial consisted, according to his recollection, of McCaughey, Pearse Kelly and two I.R.A. men called McCarthy and Farrell, from Cork and Galway respectively. Also present were MacGlade, Liam Rice and Liam Burke. Pearse Kelly acted as official note-taker and procedural expert (because he had worked in a solicitor's office and as a reporter).

Sean McCaughey as prosecutor put the following two charges to Hayes:

1. That you, Stephen Hayes, conspired with 'The Irish Free State Government' to obstruct the policy and impede the progress of the Irish Republican Army.
2. That you, Stephen Hayes, are guilty of treachery for having deliberately forwarded information of a secret and

confidential nature concerning the activities of the Irish Republican Army to a hostile body, to wit, the 'Irish Free State Government'.

The court-martial, which lasted from 9.00 p.m. to 7.00 a.m. found Hayes guilty on both counts and sentenced him to death for being, as an official I.R.A. 'Special Communiqué' stated, 'a party to the most heinous conspiracy of crime in Irish history'. The I.R.A. version adds that Hayes, after the verdict was announced, expressed a wish to write a confession.

The 'Special Communiqué' says that Hayes did this 'with the hope that it will undo some of the harm and injury I did to Oglaigh na hEireann [Irish Republican Army] through my co-operation with them [Free State government personnel].

'I decided on making this confession after I was made aware of the verdict of the court-martial. I further affirm that this confession of facts is the truth, the whole truth, and nothing but the truth, and has been made voluntarily by me.'

Pearse Kelly's recollection is that he and McCaughey were in a house rented by the I.R.A. in Gaeltacht Park, Whitehall and used as a temporary headquarters, when Liam Rice arrived and said, 'He's prepared to talk.' McCaughey and Kelly were surprised as they had been trying to collect additional evidence with which to confront Hayes, with a view to clearing up unexplained mysteries about some recent arrests.

McCaughey, Kelly, Rice and MacGlade then went to Castlewood Avenue and asked Hayes if he was prepared to talk. According to Kelly he replied, 'I might as well.' The next problem was, what form would his confession take, a question and answer or a straight handwritten account from Hayes himself? The latter course was agreed to and Kelly got rolls of the type of parchment used in solicitors' offices for Hayes to use. The writing took until September 8.

It had been decided to shoot Hayes on the morning of the all-Ireland football final later in the month. However, on the morning of September 8, Wright had gone to bed leaving Burke writing a letter in the same room as Hayes. Burke was called to the door by Mrs MacEoin and Hayes noticed that Burke had left his revolver and holster hanging on the mantelpiece. He grabbed the revolver, flung himself out of the window and shuffled down Castlewood Avenue, his legs still shackled, into the busy suburban shopping centre of Rathmines and through the bewildered shoppers to the Rathmines Garda station where he gave himself up.

Hayes's versions of what happened are quite different from that of the I.R.A. One is contained in a statement he wrote with the aid of a barrister, Eoin O'Mahony, on March 18, 1949, in which he gives a point by point refutation of all the statements in the confession and describes how he was tortured and starved. This written statement amplifies the evidence he gave during the trial of McCaughey before the Special Criminal Court.

Both statements say that he was captured at gun-point and taken to various places of detention where he was beaten, starved, continually urged to admit that he was a traitor and forced to write a confession admitting all the allegations put to him. In court he stated that he had partially met their demands by admitting some of the charges after beatings, threats of being shot or of being tied up and beaten to death. He said that he had finally decided to write a full confession when, after his courtmartial, McCaughey threatened to hang him from a hook on a wall and to leave him there to die if he refused to meet their demands completely. He was prevented from sleeping for twenty-four hours and in this state of terror and fatigue, he finally gave in and began to write a confession of over 150 pages.

In the handwritten statement which he gave me, Hayes says that he purposely dragged out the confession to gain time. This statement says that the confession 'took over a

month to write during which time I was being subjected
to torture . . . Starvation diet, head beaten. All left side.
Chained to bed at night. Tied to bed. Rope and chain
fetters day and night. The substance of the confession was
dictated by McCaughey.'

Hayes told me that he was beaten with a rifle butt all
along the left arm so that it swelled up horribly. A broom
handle was also used. His right side, he said, was spared
so that he could write. He claimed that he never offered
to write any confession and that the partial ones which
he was forced to make before the trial were used in
evidence against him. These, he said, were dictated by
McCaughey and others. He denied completely that he
was a traitor.

Hayes blamed the whole episode on the atmosphere of
suspicion at the time. 'A man called Murphy by one
group would be known as Smith to another, which could
make his doing suspect if he were found out by the first
group. That sort of thing.

'The Irish are rebels not revolutionaries,' he said. 'After
the Magazine Fort raid, there was great debate about what
we should do next. I favoured a coup, taking over the Dail,
capturing the heads of the Government. There was no
hope at all during the war of getting a man, let alone a
bomb, across to England so the campaign there was finished. The atmosphere was very tense. George Plunkett
had an idea that he would take four or five fellows down
O'Connell Street, and if anyone stopped them they'd
pull on them.

'The Army couldn't march anywhere. Our strength was
overrated, we'd no arms. In my county of Wexford, for
instance, there were about twenty rifles and two Thompson guns. The recruiting grounds of the ordinary young
fellows growing up in the country was closed to us because
of the Local Defence Forces organised by the Government
which took all the manpower. So the "Army" was back
to the pre-bombing campaign stage of trying to build
itself up to a point where we could "talk as equals" to

Germany when they won the war. The main thing, as I saw it, was to try and keep the organisation intact and we were sending fellows round the country to try and organise things.

'We had a good bit of support at the time. Even though people would vote Fianna Fail they would keep stuff in the house for us or do a turn for us. But we obviously hadn't a hope of doing very much. I only took over from Russell when he went to America because there was no one else and Russell begged me to do it. I remember, before he went away, he took me up to George Plunkett's house to try to get him to persuade Peadar O'Flaherty not to sign the Declaration of War on England because everyone was annoyed with him for trying to blow up the pillar. But we had to let him sign it in the end.

'That shows you how things were even then, and you can imagine what they were like when the Free Staters started to round us up and everybody got jittery. Russell had been saying that the people would fall in behind the I.R.A. when the campaign broke out and that the Government wouldn't take any action against us. He put too much faith into an organisation that wasn't there. You can imagine how everyone got more and more suspicious and nervy. McGrath had no authority to carry a gun, for instance, but with the executions and deaths and hunger strike, no one was too eager to check before they fired on someone. Everything was going wrong and I suppose these fellows wanted a scape-goat. I don't think that McCaughey was the full shilling anyway.'

Hayes's own written statement was drawn up to circulate among Republicans to exonerate him but this plan fell through. The statement ends:

I am prepared to swear an oath that I never entered into any conspiracy with the Free State Government, through Dr James Ryan, T.D., Minister for Agriculture, Thomas Deirg, T.D., Minister for Education, Senator Chris. Byrne or Lawrence De Lacy, to wreck the Irish Republican Army.

Further, I would like to affirm an oath, that I made no confession voluntarily.

Stephen Hayes

This comes at the end of a lengthy refutation of the I.R.A.'s 'Special Communique'. In all, it deals with fifty-one points made in the communique. Checking Hayes's statement against that of the I.R.A., any informed Irish person can see at a glance that, if one must make a choice, Hayes's document is much more likely to be accurate. Hayes, according to his confession, was supposed to have acted for the government so that Russell would be confined in America and the British bombing campaign go off half-cock. The Coventry bomb explosion was supposed to have been done to discredit the I.R.A. Hayes is supposed to have carried out the Magazine Fort raid at the suggestion of the government; to have deliberately timed useless explosions in England at the time of the Barnes and McCormick appeals so that the two men would be condemned in the outbreak of public indignation; to have connived at the assassination of Sean Russell by British secret agents in Gibraltar; to have arranged the murder of an innocent victim, Michael Devereaux of Wexford. for which an I.R.A. man George Plant was subsequently executed; to have carried out the Dublin Castle explosion at the express wishes of the government and to have further attempted to discredit the I.R.A. by arranging a number of bank raids as a result of which a young man called Richard Goss was arrested on July 18, 1941, and executed in Portlaoighise Prison on August 9.

These allegations do not merit a detailed serious consideration. On the Magazine Fort raid charge, for instance, it is only necessary to remember the period when it took place, and to ask what government in the world would allow an underground organisation deliberately to come and make off with all its ammunition. Such analysis shows that the statements in the I.R.A. communique are false and were obtained by force. It does not shed any light on whether Hayes was a traitor but if he was the government took a very strange method of rewarding him. On June 19, 1942, the Special Criminal Court gave him five years penal servitude for 'maintenance of an illegal force'. A similar sentence was handed out to a member of the Special Branch, James Crofton, who had been mentioned in the confession as being a link with Hayes through whom the government passed instructions.

Crofton was arrested for trying to get a Nazi spy, Herman Goertz, out of Kerry in a fishing boat from Fenit on the Dingle Peninsula.

During the time Hayes was being held, McCaughey was approached to say that the life of Richard Goss, an I.R.A. man accused of shooting at military and police, might be saved if Hayes were set free. McCaughey refused this plea. Goss was executed at Portlaoighise Prison.

Hayes's escape upset the I.R.A. It came at a time of great tribulation. McCaughey had been arrested a few days earlier as he sat on a tram en route to the house where Hayes was writing his 'confession'. Immediately after the escape Burke left Castlewood Avenue to tell Kelly what had happened and Rice stayed behind to warn any I.R.A. men who might call to make themselves scarce. Rice was standing on the footpath watching for Kelly when a police car from Rathmines drew up. He fired on Detective Officer Dinny O'Brien. O'Brien and his colleagues fired back and Rice was badly wounded in the lung.

In this atmosphere, a meeting was held in Mountjoy Square to decide what to do next, and by whatever yardstick one judges the matter an incredibly bad decision was taken. It was decided to publish Hayes's confession and Dr Lombard Murphy, chairman of the board of directors of the Irish Independent Newspapers Ltd, was contacted and asked if he would publish the Hayes confessions.

The idea was ludicrous. The policy of the *Independent* was right-wing, pro-clerical and anti-I.R.A. It was wartime and all papers were subject to censorship. Dr Murphy turned down the proposal at once and the I.R.A. decided to issue the document itself. Pearse Kelly and a number of helpers used a copy of *Thom's Directory*, which gave the addresses of Dail deputies, senators, bishops and other dignatories among whom they circulated the 'Special Communique' with disastrous results.

The vast majority of I.R.A. members had been quite unaware of Hayes's kidnapping, and this confession of deceit and treachery dismayed them. Tarlach O'hUid summed up the general reaction saying: 'As far as I was concerned the confession meant the end of the I.R.A. for me. There I was in Derry Jail, already fed up to the back teeth with my comrades, and with the circumstances which had led me there, and this thing came. To me it meant that either Hayes was a traitor, in which case the I.R.A. was a lousy organisation for having such a man at the top, or else he was innocent, in which case the I.R.A. was a doubly lousy organisation to extract such a document from him. Either way I was finished.' (Incidentally O'hUid, despite this, refused to sign out of Derry Jail, and stayed there for the remainder of the war, being in fact one of the very last prisoners to be released.)

Apart from all this the publication of Hayes's 'confession' brought tragedy. It described how Michael Devereaux of Wexford, a battalion officer, was allegedly framed on government instructions. The I.R.A., believing he had given away dumps and information leading to the capture of some of his colleagues, had him court-martialled *in absentia*, found him guilty and ordered him to be shot. The I.R.A. communique said that the sentence was carried out by the divisional O.C. of the Wexford area. Within forty-eight hours of the communique being issued detectives were on their way to the area. Masquerading as I.R.A. emissaries from G.H.Q. they persuaded a local I.R.A. man, who could not read and accepted their credentials, to lead them to a cave on the Knockmealdown

Mountains where Devereaux had been shot and his body buried. Whether Devereaux was framed and shot in error, or whether he was innocent but shot through misunderstandings, or whether he was, indeed, a traitor, the publication of his fate was more than indiscreet. It was clear that the man's former colleagues might be in jeopardy

The finding of Devereaux's body opened one of the most distressing chapters in Irish legal history. After widespread police inquiries two I.R.A. men, Joseph O'Connor and George Plant, were charged with Devereaux's murder. Two former I.R.A. men, Patrick Davern and Michael Walshe, gave evidence against them. However, during the trial they withdrew their statements and the prosecution case collapsed. It was an open secret that I.R.A. pressure had been put on the two witnesses. Pearse Kelly told me that he met the two in jail and found them greatly disturbed. Being simple men, they had not realised their statements could incriminate former comrades. He advised them that they could retract their statements and destroy the prosecution's case. One may guess at what other pressures were brought to bear.

The government met this situation with a manipulation of the legal code, countering the I.R.A.'s tactics by issuing an Emergency Powers Order on December 30, 1941. This order dealt with the law relating to the admissibility of evidence before the Special Military Court. It provided that whether the offence was committed before the making of the order or not, 'It was proved that a statement relevant to the charge was made by any person including the accused and that such statement . . . was made voluntarily, lawfully . . . taken down in writing and was acknowledged by the person who made it, then at any stage of the trial the prosecution may read such a statement as evidence and may cross-examine the person who made it.'

The powers of the court concerning such a statement were that it could act on the statement against the accused and that an application to read a statement could be made even though the person who made it was not present at the trial, or was dead, or was present at the trial even though he did not give evidence. The order further provided that if a military court considered it proper on any occasion during a trial that it should not be bound by any rule of evidence, whether of military or common law, then the court should not be bound by such rule.

Under this order Plant was put on trial again with the two I.R.A. men who had rescinded their confessions, Davern and Walshe. All three were sentenced to death. The last two sentences were commuted but Plant was executed in Portlaoighise Prison on March 5, 1942.

Plant bore his sentence philosophically. He told one of the prison orderlies that 'those who live by the gun die by the gun.' Sean MacBride told me that of all the trials in which he took part during the war, he found that of Plant the most harrowing.

'He was a particularly nice fellow and seemed to have no fear. The night before his execution he sat up reading, completely composed all night, and went to his death wearing his best suit.'

After the Hayes affair, the I.R.A. in the South was smashed although it refused to admit it. Pearse Kelly became chief of staff after MacGlade was picked up within days of McCaughey being caught, and tried to resuscitate the movement. The Brugha family, Helena Molony, the businessman Lucas and Brian O'hUiginn worked with him to draw up a social and economic programme on which the I.R.A. could work.

In addition to all the setbacks the I.R.A. had little money. At the beginning of the war, police who were investigating the possible consequences of a visit to Ireland by Joseph McGarrity (he left on August 14) swooped on a house, 16, Rathmines Park, Dublin, on September 9, arrested the four I.R.A. men in the house and seized a quantity of ammunition, some I.R.A. documents and $8,265. Both Eoin MacNamee and Hugh McAteer told me that during the war bank raids were necessary to pay I.R.A. debts and to get enough money to continue operations. And certainly the treatment of the deportees who were sent from England as a result of the I.R.A. bombing campaign points to an acute lack of funds.

Clearing centres were set up to help the flood of deportees who arrived from England. But a letter from the deportees' committee shows how little money was available

Deportees' Committee, 41 Parnell Square, Dublin
14/8/1940

A chara,

We enclose P.O. for ten shillings. We regret to state that this fund is now completely exhausted, and except money is forthcoming from an unexpected source you cannot expect any remittance next week, or will you, we're afraid, any further remittance from this committee.

We extremely regret the necessity for sending this notice to you, but we have exhausted every source known to us. If, in the future, we see any prospect of getting further help for you, we shall communicate with you.

Yours sincerely,

L. Kearns MacWhinney   Agnes McCullough
Una de Staic   Helena Molony

No further help was forthcoming although Kelly pressed on and spoke to Eoin O'Duffy to see what help could be expected from the Italians or Germans. These activities succeeded only in placing him behind bars when he called on Herman Goertz, the German spy living in Dublin, to warn him that the police were looking for him. They were looking for Kelly too, and after arresting Goertz a few hours before Kelly's call, seized Kelly himself when he knocked on the door of Goertz's hide-out in Clontarf.

7 / THE I.R.A. IN THE NORTH

Whether Hayes was a traitor or not, it is certain that the I.R.A. men who went to the South to assess his guilt or innocence were from backgrounds so different from his (and those of the average Southern I.R.A. man) as to make understanding between the two groups a very difficult business at the best of times, and almost an impossibility in the tension and suspicion of war. These differences in tone and background are basic not only to an understanding of the I.R.A. but to the whole partition issue. First, most prominent I.R.A. men in the North are Catholics and thus they are in an inferior social, political and economic position. Catholics drifted into the I.R.A. in great numbers. Protestants if they were militantly minded (and in the North in the 1920s and 1930s it was difficult not to be so), joined the B-Specials. So there was an armed 'them and us' situation. The Royal Ulster Constabulary was of course open to Catholics, but Catholics never showed much enthusiasm for it. Though one-third of the force was expected to be Catholic at its inception only about 12 per cent ever became so, and if one looks at the careers of some I.R.A. men one can understand why.

One of the most prominent I.R.A. men in Belfast after the end of the Civil War was Jimmy Steele, now a baker's roundsman. Jimmy, who spent most of his life in prison, literally devoted his life to the I.R.A. He and his wife had only one week's holiday together before the end of the 1956-62 campaign in twenty-five years of marriage. Steele was reared in the famous Queen Street area of Belfast. Queen Street runs parallel to York Street, adjoining the dockland area. Queen Street is Catholic, York Street Protestant, and between these two main arteries run a series of smaller intersections with names like Frederick Street, Lancaster Street, Great George's Street, Little George's Street, Henry Street, Cecil Street, Grove Street and Earl Street. At times of civil commotion, notably in 1932 and 1935, these were little more than shooting ranges. When disorder began anyone crossing those intersecting streets took the risk of being hit by a Catholic bullet coming down or a Protestant one coming up. So began the tunnelling through garden walls, and through the actual houses themselves, so that shoppers wanting to pass along one of these little death traps could walk the entire street without being fired on. But it meant little comfort or privacy in the lives of those who occupied these houses. In those circumstances, one did not have to ask, 'Why did you become an I.R.A. man?' of Steele. For a lad with his spirit and courage, there were few other courses open.

Much the same applied in the case of Michael Traynor, a man with a national reputation in the movement since the 1930s. He grew up in a mixed area of Protestants and Catholics and remembers regular bombings and shootings in the early 1920s. He recalled how as a small boy during the Anglo-Irish war in 1920 he and two friends went to see the naked bodies of three I.R.A. men found with crosses cut into their foreheads and insteps.

'There were small black holes in their heads,' he said. 'I remember they were found in Dan O'Neill's loanin [a Belfast term for a boreen or lane] in the Whiterock Road area. They had been shot as a reprisal for the deaths of three auxiliaries. I remember the MacMahon murder,* we didn't think that especially brutal for the time. I remember we thought that throwing hand grenades into the bedroom of two elderly sisters on St Patrick's night in Thompson Street was far worse because there was an awful job cleaning up afterwards with feathers and bits of bedding and pieces of flesh all splashed around the room. That was done by the B-Specials.'

The youthful Traynor and his family regarded the B-Specials as being outside the law. They seemed able to

---

* This was committed by the 'Murder Gang' which, on March 23, 1922, broke into the home and shot male members of the MacMahon family and a man employed by them. The reprisal came on May 19. I.R.A. men went to a cooperage in Little Patrick Street, Belfast, and asked the coopers, 'Who are the Mickies here?' The Protestants pointed out the 'Mickies' (as the Catholics were known) whereupon the Protestants were lined up against a wall and five of them shot, three fatally.

shoot anyone they wished and to get away with it. During the Anglo-Irish war there were sound reasons for Traynor's opinion of this group's immunity, and very sound reasons also for fearing another organisation known as the 'Murder Gang'. This flourished in Belfast during the period, carrying out assassinations and reprisal raids on Catholic strongholds. The gang was composed of former British soldiers, members of the U.V.F., and some sprinkling of R.I.C. men and B-Specials. Its members would set out from their cars and tenders in stockinged feet, with blacking on their faces to raid Catholic areas after dark. In the poor Belfast street lighting these marauders created terror among Catholics, as they loomed up out of the darkness to shoot a passer-by dead on the street or to hurl a hand grenade through a window, escaping like phantoms. Their tactics were eventually met by a simple strategy worked out between the civilian population and the I.R.A.

A custom known as the 'murder yell' sprang up. Anyone seeing a member of the gang gave a long, drawn-out, high-pitched keening yell of 'M - u - r - derr - eh' which was taken up by the entire district. Colonel Roger McCorley told me that this sound, with the banging of dust-bin lids, pots and pans, was the most eerie he had ever heard. On hearing it, McCorley and his I.R.A. patrols would hasten to the spot, guiding each other with red-tinted flashlights. When the shooting stopped and the invaders were driven off, the keening died away. The flashlights would be switched to green for 'all clear'. The memory of those terrible days survives today in a street ballad:

> Oh, she got up and rattled her bin,
> For the Specials were a-coming in,
> Tiddy-fal-la, Tiddy-fal-la.
> Oh, she got up and rattled her bin,
> For the Specials were a-coming in,
> Tiddy-fa-la, Tiddy-fa-la.

Such a legacy of fear and hatred can still erupt. Two Protestant gunmen marched out one night in 1966, so moved by the songs and ceremonies with which the South was commemorating the 1916 Rebellion that they determined to kill I.R.A. men. They didn't find any, but they shot up some Catholic barmen, killing one of them. Such bigotry and tension lay behind the rioting and destruction which the world learned of during the fearful days of August 1969.

The principal I.R.A. leader to emerge from Derry, the second city of the North, after the 'Troubles' was Hugh McAteer, who became chief of staff in 1941 for a time. His family had been nationalists for generations. One of his great grandfathers was a 'reader'—a man who read *The Nation*, Thomas Davis's paper of the 1840s to neighbours at Ceili houses. *The Nation* cost sixpence, which in 1845-48 was a day's pay, and the fact that it should be so readily bought shows the strength of the nationalist tradition in the Derry area. Derry is, of course, a classical example of gerrymandering and discrimination. Today not even the most bigoted Unionist could deny that a Catholic majority in this city is unjustly denied its civil rights by a Protestant minority. That is why the civil rights movement had such a success in the area, making the world's headlines after an R.U.C. baton charge on October 5, 1968. Led by a Protestant, Ivan Cooper, and a Catholic, John Hume, it cut across sectarian barriers to the tune of 'We Shall Overcome' and demanded, not Catholic power, but civil rights and justice for all in the name of the city's nobler traditions.

All the boys in McAteer's area joined the Fianna, the boy Republican's scout movement, as children in happier areas would join the Cubs, to become scouts later. McAteer remembers police surrounding them in a field as they drilled in 1928 and firing over their heads. Experiences like these, schooling by the Christian Brothers, attendance at Gaelic League classes (then controlled by the I.R.A.), readership of *An Phoblacht*, inevitably turned him to the

I.R.A. Such social philosophy as he and his friends felt was expressed in trade unionism, or in discussions about the land war. To the young men of McAteer's youth it was a toss-up whether they joined the I.R.A. or became missionaries. Religious fervour and Republicanism were completely entwined.

'Independence was nearly as strong in our minds as religion,' said McAteer.

'We would go out unthinkingly after Mass at 11.00 a.m. and we'd walk fourteen miles for our copy of *An Phob-lacht*.'

He was a member of the St Vincent de Paul charitable organisation at this time, but it did not occur to him or his friends to apply St Vincent de Paul's social principle to his Republicanism. Independence, separatism, getting the British out, these were their goals. Success in these objectives would end the conditions they saw around them. The average house had concrete floors downstairs and there was little furniture or firing. But everywhere were numbers of children turning green with malnutrition. Were it not for the Christian Brothers, who dosed the children with cod liver oil daily, many of these children would not have survived the hungry 1930s. Some of them were known as 'half timers', being half-time at school and half-time at work, generally four-hour stints at each, and all under the age of twelve. McAteer formally joined the I.R.A. at Easter 1933. He remembers celebrating Fianna Fail's election victory that year by smashing windows. He and his friends had worked in Donegal as Fianna Fail election supporters.

In the countryside, for a young Catholic the differences were of degree rather than kind. Joe Deighan came from South Armagh outside Newry, a predominantly Catholic centre, not far from the border, and close to the Gap of the North through which (from the days of the Fianna legends) the men of Ulster sallied forth to attack the tribes of Leinster. It is a small farming area where memories of the 'Troubles' were much in mind. No

Catholic in that area would join the British army although relationships between Catholic and Protestants were good. There was little hardship though in nearby Newry hunger was common among the Catholics, particularly in the 1920s and 1930s. Growing up, however, young Deighan realised there were more differences between him and the Protestants than the blue gates and blue cartwheels with which the Protestants adorned their property.

The sons of Protestant neighbours could get jobs in their own country but he couldn't. And in 1931, this fact, coupled with the songs about Emmet, Parnell and the stories of Fenians that he heard as a child, drove him to join the local I.R.A. at seventeen. They met in the mountains to drill in barrack-ground style unsuited to guerrilla warfare. There were a few revolvers, an occasional rifle, but anything larger, such as a Thompson gun, was as rare as plum cake in Oliver Twist's orphanage. Local people turned a blind eye to their activities and would hide them in times of trouble. At election times the young I.R.A. lads would back the Nationalist candidates in whatever way they could.

Deighan's first sentence was six months in Crumlin Road for 'promoting sedition'. In those years, constitutional politics in Northern Ireland for a nationalist-minded Catholic, like young Deighan, offered only frustration and disillusionment, or, if caught trying to lick the system by unconstitutional methods, jail. The Council for Civil Liberties issued a report on the Northern situation in 1936 which said:

Firstly, that through the operation of the Special Powers Act contempt has been begotten for the representative institutions of government.

Secondly, that through the use of Special Powers, individual liberty is no longer protected by law, but is at the disposition of the Executive. This abrogation of the rule of law has been so practised as to bring the freedom of the subject into contempt.

Thirdly, that the Northern Government has used Special Powers towards securing the domination of one particular political faction and, at the same time, towards curtailing the lawful activities of its opponents . . . The Government's policy is thus driving its opponents into the way of extremists.

Fourthly, that the Northern Irish Government, despite its assurances that Special Powers are intended for use only against law-breakers, has frequently employed them against innocent and law-abiding people, often in humble circumstances, whose injuries, inflicted without cause or justification, have gone unrecompensed and disregarded.

This report was issued after the 1935 riots when there had been eleven murders, two attempted murders, 574 cases of criminal injuries, 133 cases of arson and 367 cases of malicious damage. Westminster had refused an official inquiry saying 'the matter was one which came solely within the jurisdiction of the Northern Ireland Government', when pressed by Catholic spokesmen such as T. J. Campbell, Cardinal MacRory and Bishop Mageean.

From the start, Stormont did not seem to be a seat of either justice or permanence to Catholic nationalists, who were split themselves between Sinn Fein and the Irish Parliamentary Party. In the early days of the Northern parliament the parliamentary faction, led by 'Wee Joe' Devlin, was paramount, but both sides boycotted the new institution, expecting the Boundary Commission to carve up Ulster and so make the new state unworkable.

After the commission's findings, 'Wee Joe' realised that the border was there to stay and took his seat. By 1927 he was the leader of a ten-man opposition, but unable to influence Northern affairs to any extent. One of the Unionists' first actions had been to abolish proportional representation in local government elections and to rearrange constituencies to give control to Unionists. In 1929 proportional representation was abolished in parliamentary elections also, wiping out independents and leaving a Protestant government firmly entrenched by a majority of three to one over a Catholic opposition. Schooling was also firmly established on a denominational basis (by the Education Act of 1923 and subsequent amendments to it in 1925 and 1930) thus perpetuating the ghetto mentality on both sides.

The I.R.A. began to make inroads into the opposition support after the 1933 election, when de Valera was elected for South Down. He did not take his seat but his victory gave the Republicans an idea for an election strategy. They put up candidates for the 1935 Westminster elections, and to avoid splitting the vote the Nationalists stood down. The Sinn Fein philosophy overcame the traditions of the old Irish Parliamentary Party, but not that of the Unionists, and the ill-conceived strategy cost the Nationalists seats in West Belfast, Armagh and Down. It also reintroduced abstentionism to the Northern political scene, and by the outbreak of war in 1939 only T. J. Campbell, who had succeeded Devlin as leader of the opposition, attended Stormont with any regularity. Catholic mistrust of Stormont was such that when Campbell accepted a judgeship from the government, this champion of the Catholic cause was dubbed 'Judas' Campbell by those he had striven to serve.

They were bad, bitter times. The rank-and-file of Protestant and Catholic followers heard declarations from Sir Basil Brooke that Catholics were disloyal and should not be employed, and from Cardinal MacRory that the Protestant Church was not part of the true Church of Christ.

It was their Northern Catholic birth which inevitably turned two of the most prominent I.R.A. men of the Hayes era towards Republicanism. Eoin MacNamee and Pearse Kelly were born in Co. Tyrone, Kelly in the town of Dungannon and MacNamee in the district of Broughdearg. MacNamee's wild, mountainous, poverty stricken area had turned against the I.R.A. by the time he reached his teens, because around Tyrone and south Derry, the I.R.A. had lent themselves to a clerically-inspired anti-poteen campaign, smashing stills and pouring away the liquid which had been an impoverished people's only means of keeping out cold and reality. That the I.R.A. had survived at all was attributable to the traditions of the county, the home of the O'Neills and also the birthplace of Joseph McGarrity, and the fact that the Catholic majority was discriminated against by the Protestants through control of political power at Stormont and of local government bodies allocating houses and state jobs throughout the province.

MacNamee remembers being confused in his early days in the I.R.A. because the local I.R.A. were all Catholics, whereas in his early reading about the freedom movements of 1798 and 1805 there were copious references to Protestants. He could not grasp what had happened in the meantime. Nor could he reconcile the fact that local I.R.A. men saw no difficulty in shouting 'Up Dev' and 'Up the I.R.A.' in the same breath. Even as a boy of sixteen this slogan struck MacNamee as containing within it a certain paradox. However, the rebel streak was strong in him and he overcame these confusions and his distaste of the local I.R.A. who were rowdy and given to drink. He moved out of his own parish to the neighbouring Greencastle parish and joined a more orderly and responsible company. At that time in 1934-35, little was happening. After six or nine months he, like the young Deegan, emigrated to England and found his way to London where, at the age of seventeen, he became interested in socialism. He found his way into the Republican Congress, which was then active in London, principally under Michael Kelly, Charlie Donnelly (who was killed in Spain fighting for the Republicans), Sean Mulgrew and Tommy Paton. Eventually after the bombing campaign he returned to become ultimately head of the I.R.A. in the North.

Pearse Kelly joined the I.R.A. in Dungannon in late

1939 or early 1940. He was one of a group who had been to school together, attended Irish classes and shared a common Catholic nationalist 'Irish Ireland' outlook. War's outbreak saw troops billeted in the town, and the thoughts of fighting the British became more immediate. Kelly remembers, 'We thought the movement had reached very sad days when the people we saw in it locally were I.R.A. men.' They considered starting a movement of their own, but because of its tradition they decided to join the I.R.A. *en bloc*. They formed a company and absorbed those present. It was a good example of how the I.R.A. exists as a tradition rather than as a cohesive movement. Shortly before joining Kelly, who was a junior reporter at the time, attended a court at which he saw Eoin MacNamee for the first time. He remembers him as being 'a solid indestructible man who seemed to have a rock-like tenacity'. MacNamee got six months after a hearing which apparently interested him as much as it did the flies on the wall.

It was after this case that Kelly joined the I.R.A. Kelly's area was apparently better armed than MacNamee's because he remembers Thompsons and rifles being used for training around Esker Lough and at his father's and grandfather's farms around the Dungannon area. His first active engagement was against the British when it was proposed that a hall in the Catholic part of the town be used as a billet. The local population regarded this as a slight because an Orange Hall in the Protestant part would have done just as well. Accordingly Kelly and his friends burned down the hall and ended the attempt to billet troops in the Catholic area.

Kelly, a very rigid and upright man, also established a Republican police in the Dungannon area, with a view to keeping the some fifty or so I.R.A. men under his command busy, and at the same time curbing a spate of petty hooliganism and larceny which had broken out in the area. Kelly's police rounded up those concerned in the hooliganism and took them to Edendork outside Dun-

gannon and beat them up. The hooliganism stopped and
the I.R.A. stock soared.

As a result of these activities Kelly was brought to
Belfast where the principal leaders, Sean McCaughey,
Liam Rice and Charlie MacGlade, were just beginning
to get suspicious about events in the South and Stephen
Hayes. They began to pay frequent visits to the South,
thereby paving the way for MacNamee, McCaughey and
Kelly to rise in the movement.

In Belfast Kelly was involved in a major I.R.A. coup.
An I.R.A. sympathiser, Fergus Kelly, who worked for a
chemist in Armagh, had been standing behind his counter
when a group of, as he described them, 'British brass hats'
came in, made some purchases and went off leaving a
long, official-looking envelope on the counter. Opening it
he found that it contained various documents which turned
out to be the new code, complete with key, for British
troops in Northern Ireland. It was due to come into
operation in seven days.

Fergus Kelly immediately made an exact copy of
everything in the envelope, and then called on Pearse
Kelly with the result. They restored the envelope, and
when the officers returned the next day they were met in
the shop with courtesy, blandness and duplicity. 'Had
they found anything?' the officers asked. 'Well what?'
asked Fergus. 'An envelope?' 'Ah yes! There was an
envelope somewhere.' Then after much searching, 'Would
this be it?' and the envelope was taken down from a shelf
where it had been shoved casually between two jars of
medicine. Some very relieved British officers went off not
knowing that the code had been cracked. It duly went
into operation and was frequently broken by the I.R.A.,
although this did not add much to I.R.A. effectiveness.

Shortly after Kelly's arrival in Belfast two I.R.A. men
got drunk and raced up the Falls Road in a stolen car
firing shots, one of which wounded a girl. Two innocent
I.R.A. men were pulled in by the R.U.C. Kelly ordered

an investigation of I.R.A. men and issued a statement. After describing the events this ended:

At a Courtmartial, James Murphy, ('Spotter') 7, Garnet St, was found guilty of (1) having taken part in the stealing of the car, (2) being in illegal possession of a Revolver the property of the Q.M.G., Oglaigh na hEireann, (3) endangering the life of Mary Teer by indiscriminate use of Revolver, while under the influence of drink. Accused was dismissed from the Army with ignominy and deported from Belfast.

Terence Donegan, 30, Milan St, was also ordered to leave Belfast, and the remaining three defendants [passengers in the car] were also punished by order of the Courtmartial. The sentences on all five have now been carried out.

Following the promulgation of the Sentences by the Courtmartial the Northern Command Staff made the appended announcement:—

'In view of the alarming frequency of incidents of this nature, and the fact that they are popularly attributed to Oglaigh na hEeireann, we desire to issue a stern warning of our determination in future to take drastic measures to stamp out ruthlessly all such attempts to bring Oglaigh na hEireann into disrepute, and we are confident that we shall have the earnest support and co-operation of every loyal citizen of the Republic in our efforts to ensure the efficient administration of justice.'

Signed for and on behalf of the
Northern Command Staff.
Dated this 5th day of July, 1941.

This statement was accepted by the R.U.C. and the two I.R.A. men who had been arrested were released. Had a similar statement been issued by Protestant extremists in the Shankill Road area the R.U.C. would probably have accepted it also. In both areas it was the Protestants and the Catholics who reigned supreme, never the R.U.C. or the government of Northern Ireland.

This denominational solidarity dated back to the days

of the famine, when a census in Belfast showed that the population of the city was 35 per cent Catholic, the majority living along the line of today's Falls Road in western Belfast. Unfortunately, in the near vicinity, attracted by the same hopes of getting work that had brought in the Catholics, were the working-class Protestants who lived along the Shankill Road parallel to the Falls. The two sections were frequently in savage conflict because of economics, religion and political allegiances. Around July 12 each year the Shankill people come out in a blaze of bunting to honour King Billy, commemorate the Battle of the Boyne and swear fealty to the union with Britain. Lady's Day, August 15, was traditionally a time of Catholic fervour, though it was not so extreme.

While Catholic sympathy with the I.R.A. was heartening to its leaders, they knew that the influences that drove Catholics into the I.R.A. were also driving Protestant and Catholic apart to such an extent that the I.R.A. must inevitably be lost between them. To present themselves as armed Catholics on the Northern scene would gain no Protestant support, and without this a thirty-two county republic was impossible.

Accordingly the I.R.A. made two major efforts during the 1930s to bridge the religious divide. One attempt was defeated by the Protestants, the other by internal dissension in the I.R.A. itself. The opportunity for the first attempt came during the outdoor relief riots which disfigured Belfast in 1932. These arose over a governmental proposal to cut the rate of outdoor relief as an austerity measure, and it temporarily united both the Protestant and Catholic poor in common outrage.

The Army Council tried to take advantage of this feeling by issuing an 'address from the Army Council of the Irish Republican Army' to the 'men and women of the Orange Order' to coincide with the July celebrations:

Fellow Countrymen and Women,
  It is a long call from the ranks of the Irish Republican

Army to the marching throngs that hold the 12th July Celebrations in North East Ulster. Across the space we have sometimes exchanged shots, or missiles or hard words, but never forgetting that on occasions our ancestors have stood shoulder to shoulder. Some day we will again exchange ideas and then the distance which now separates us will shorten. For we of the Irish Republican Army believe that inevitably the small farmers and wage-earners in the Six County area will make common cause with those of the rest of Ireland, for the common good of the mass of the people in a Free United Irish Republic. Such a conviction is forming itself in an ever increasing number of minds in North East Ulster.

Working-farmers and Wage-earners of North East Ulster! You surely must see that your future is bound up with the mass of the people in the remainder of Ireland. To preserve yourselves from extinction, you and they must combine and go forward to the attainment of A Free Irish Nation within which life and living will be organised and controlled by you to serve your needs and thus end the present economic and social injustices for ever. *The industrial capacity, and training of you industrial workers, of North East Ulster ensure for you a leading influence and place in the economy and life of a Free Irish Nation.*

EXPLOITATION OF RELIGIOUS PREJUDICES

To prejudice you it is emphasised that we of the Irish Republican Army and the mass of Republicans are mainly Catholic, and that your religious beliefs would not be respected in a free Ireland! It is quite true we are mainly Catholics, but in Southern Ireland the same political and economical interests and voices that tell you we are Catholics, tell the Catholic population of the South that we are Anti-God fanatics, and yearning for an opportunity to make war on the religion to which the majority of us belong!

The fact is we are quite unaware of religious distinctions within our Movement. *We guarantee you, you will guarantee us, and we will both guarantee all full freedom of conscience*

and religious worship in the Ireland we are to set free.
This is the simple truth, and just now when Imperial interests are attempting to conceal themselves behind the mad
fury of religious strife, you and we should combine to
make certain that no such escape should be provided them.

Do you not find yourselves queued shoulder to shoulder
outside the Unemployed Exchanges waiting for the 'Dole',
that crumb which the exploiters throw to the exploited of
different religions? In these vital matters your religion or
your membership of the Orange Order counts for little, nor
does Catholicism to the unemployed and starving Catholics
in Southern Ireland.

*The fact is that the religious feelings of the masses of
both Orangemen and Catholics are played on and exploited
by the Imperialists and Capitalists the more surely to enslave
them.*

THE VICTORY OF THE BOYNE!

You celebrate the victory of the Boyne. This battle was a
victory for the alliance of the then Pope and William of
Orange; strange alliance for you to celebrate; strange victory
for Catholics to resist! History has been muddled to hide
the occasions when your forefathers and ours made common
cause, and passions are stirred to manufacture antagonisms.
If William of Orange and His Holiness could achieve an
alliance, there is hope that 'NO SURRENDER' may come from
a throng which also roars 'UP THE REPUBLIC'.

Your stock were the founders and inspiration, and North
East Ulster the cradle, of the modern Revolutionary Movement for National Independence and Economic Freedom.
Your illustrious ancestors and co-religionists, The United
Irishmen, by their gallant struggle in 1798 set aflame the
ideals of Republicanism which never since have been
extinguished. We ask that you should join us to achieve
their ideals—National Freedom and religious toleration.

The offer of friendship went further than that appeal
according to rumours surviving from the period. One

member of the Army Council told me flatly that these were not rumours—'We put guns into the hands of Orangemen for use against the B-Specials,' he averred. When I attempted to check the truth of this story with Lord Brookeborough he was thunderstruck. 'You shatter me,' he said and his wife and he shook their heads in disbelief.

But the old sectarianism of Belfast reasserted itself during rioting throughout October, 1932. Republicans said that this was deliberately fomented by some members of the R.U.C. in baton charging and firing on Catholics. This is not impossible. In those bad times there was strong Protestant feeling on which the I.R.A. with its emotional appeals could never get a purchase.

The Ulster Protestant League, founded in 1931, adjured its members 'neither to talk nor walk with, neither to buy nor sell, borrow nor lend, take nor give, or have any dealings at all with them, nor for employers to employ them, nor employee to work with them'. The 'them' of course were Catholics and the League habitually paraded through Belfast with bands and banners flying, lambasting the government for being 'soft' on Roman Catholics, just as Paisley's followers did prior to the 1969 riots, calling for the resignation of the minister of home affairs. All this began to have an effect on Protestant support for the government and government spokesmen were driven to show their reliability to the Unionist cause by extremist replies. In his July address, Lord Craigavon made the first of his statements about Protestantism and government in the North—still quoted by long-memoried Nationalists. He said, 'Ours is a Protestant government and I am an Orangeman' and by July, 1934, he had escalated this to 'we are a Protestant parliament and a Protestant State . . . I am an Orangeman first and a member of parliament afterwards.'

Efforts to create unity still, however, continued. The *Republican Congress*, organ of the breakaway I.R.A. section led by Gilmore, Ryan and O'Donnell, had carried in its issue for June 2, 1934, a triumphant page-one headline proclaiming a 'United front between Orange and Green' following the formation of *one* James Connolly Club for unemployed Protestant and Catholic workers.

Small though this beginning was, it was nevertheless a highly significant step forward, and it was arranged that a sizeable contingent from the Shankill Road would march later on June 17 to Bodenstown with banners bearing inscriptions such as 'Wolfe Tone Commemoration, 1934 Shankill Rd, Belfast Branch. Break the connection with capitalism', 'Connolly's message our ideal', 'James Connolly Club, Belfast, United Irishmen of 1934'. However, when the United Irishmen of the North reached the assembly field at Sallins en route to the graveyard of the founder of the United Irishmen of all Ireland they found the disunited Irishmen of the South waiting for them. A group of Tipperary I.R.A. men, led by a redoubtable figure called Matty Ryan, attacked the Congress group in an attempt to seize the Congress banners which had been proscribed by the Twomey-Fitzpatrick section of the I.R.A. The attempt failed as the two groups clashed to the accompaniment of 'Up Tipp' and 'Come on the Shankill Road'. Eventually the battered Belfast men marched on to Wolfe Tone's grave where further scuffles broke out in which the only lasting damage was to the United Orange-Green front.

Such were the efforts which the Catholic I.R.A. made to woo the Protestants. On the Protestant side another tradition existed which, properly cultivated, should have been more promising. This was the liberal Presbyterian strain of Wolfe Tone exemplified by Rev. W. Montgomery who, though worsted by Cooke, helped to give Northern Protestantism that more attractive vein which never quite dies out, even at moments of extreme religio-politico fervour. Thus during the Home Rule crisis of 1912 one of the sponsors of the plan which brought Winston Churchill to speak in favour of Home Rule in Belfast on February 8 of that year, was the Rev. James

1. Members of the Third Western Division of the I.R.A. in Sligo, May, 1922. (*Belfast Telegraph*)

2. An I.R.A. patrol on the border of Donegal and Tyrone, May, 1922. (*Belfast Telegraph*)

3. Hugh McAteer at the time of his escape from a Belfast jail in January 1943. (see chapter 7)

4. A group of I.R.A. men tunnelled out of a Derry jail in March, 1943 and fled across the border in a truck. They were picked up by Southern soldiers and interned. This photograph of their arrest was taken by a woman who stood unnoticed behind a hedge. (see chapter 7)

5. The Lisnaskea barracks of the Royal Ulster Constabulary after the I.R.A. raid in December, 1956. (*Irish Times*)

6. The customs post at Killeen, on the Belfast-Dublin road, wrecked in a raid in April, 1958. (*Irish Times*)

7. A radio transmitter, small arms, automatic pistols and other military equipment seized in a police raid on a house in Harcourt Terrace, Dublin, April, 1958. (*Irish Times*)

8. Irish-American 'Minute Men' picket the British consulate in New York in April, 1958. They were protesting against the trial of two men from Co. Tyrone for taking part in the booby-trap murder of Royal Ulster Constabulary Sergeant Arthur Ovens. (*Irish Times*)

9. This denial by the I.R.A. of responsibility for the Longford raid is highly significant: these raids, carried out by Joseph Christle's men, led the government to reopen the Curragh internment camp. The esteem in which Joseph McGarrity (see chapters 4 and 5) is still held by the I.R.A. is shown by the fact that this and other I.R.A. documents are signed over his name although he died in August, 1940. (*Belfast Telegraph*)

10. A bus, belonging to the Royal Ulster Transport Authority, burned by the I.R.A. in December, 1961. (*Belfast Telegraph*)

11. Police tackle an I.R.A. demonstrator in January, 1966 at a protest against trials arising from incidents which occurred during Princess Margaret's visit to Ireland. (*Irish Times*)

12. Nelson's Pillar, Dublin, after the explosion which wrecked it in March, 1966. (*Irish Press*)

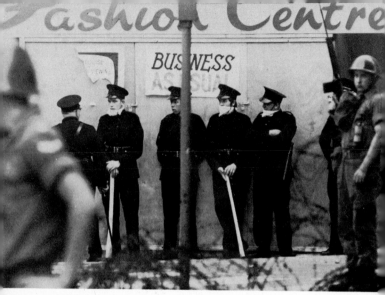

13. B-Specials in Derry in 1969. The handkerchiefs are for protection against gas. (*Irish Press*)

14. A member of the Royal Ulster Constabulary in Derry in 1969. (*Irish Press*)

15. A citizen of Derry defies a baton charge in 1969. (*Irish Press*)

Armour of Ballymoney, a man whose memory is justifiably revered in the annals of Northern liberalism. There were Protestant subscribers to this tradition active on the Republican side during the Anglo-Irish war and it was still alive in 1939-40 both in constitutional and unconstitutional politics.

Constitutionally there was the Irish Union Movement, founded by Denis Ireland, a Presbyterian who later became a senator in the Dublin parliament through Sean Mac-Bride's influence. This movement also attracted a considerable amount of liberal Protestant support in the North because of its programme of better relationship with the South, a programme which stemmed from Wolfe Tone's writings. However, on September 10, 1942, it was discovered during an R.U.C. raid on I.R.A. men that some of them, in particular one John S. Graham, had been active in the movement. As the Orangemen had always regarded Denis Ireland as a traitor and renegade because of his all-Ireland view, the I.R.A. men's arrest afforded an opportunity to detain and interrogate members of the Irish Union. This spread the suspicion that it was an I.R.A. hot-bed. Not surprisingly the movement collapsed. (Graham and some of the other liberal Protestants, who constituted one of the best I.R.A. companies in Belfast, had joined the Union, not for purposes of infiltration but through the same tradition that brought them into the I.R.A.: an interest in socialism, Wolfe Tone's writings, the Irish language and the Gaelic League. This group figured in a major crisis within the Belfast I.R.A.)

Despite all the speeches and slogans, the martyrs, commemorations and appeals to tradition the average young I.R.A. man's existence consisted largely of skulking around fields or back streets, holding drill sessions with obsolete weapons in disused halls and talking about 'action' that practically never came. The action that did occur was usually disastrous. In particular there were the two raids on the armoury at Campbell's College which resulted in

the celebrated Crown Entry* raid by the R.U.C. in the
midst of an I.R.A. court-martial. The R.U.C. swoop
settled some very big I.R.A. fish, including Jim Killeen,
Michael Traynor and Tony MacLaverty, O.C. of the
Belfast battalion, who was being court-martialled at the
time. This was not for any misdemeanour but because he
had issued instructions to some of the I.R.A. men who
were caught in the armoury raids, allowing them to
recognise the courts so that they had a chance of making
a defence.

Increased wartime pressures on the I.R.A. made communication between Dublin and Belfast more difficult,
and some Northerners began to think that a self-contained
Northern unit was desirable. The principal architect of this
idea was Charles MacGlade, a Belfast printer, and so
'Northern Command' came into being. The command in
fact embraced seven counties, the six counties of Ulster
proper and Co. Donegal. Eoin MacNamee, who later
became its head first heard of this unit in June, 1939,
after his return from the bombing campaign in England.
The formation of this command meant that the I.R.A.
in the South was led from Dublin, in the North from
Belfast, in England from God knows where and that
each group carried on more or less independently of
each other.†

Although it was widely discussed in I.R.A. circles,
Northern Command's level of organisation may be judged
from the fact that there were supposed to be two battalions
in Co. Tyrone, Eoin MacNamee's native county, but
when he began to organise there weren't twenty members

* An 'entry' in Belfast is a narrow lane, or entry, for passers-by
from one street to another.

† This picture of a lack of communication is not exaggerated.
Pearse Kelly, one of the first people I interviewed for this book,
compared my lack of knowledge on starting my research to his
incomprehension about Dublin's affairs when the Hayes investigation first took him to the South.

in the whole county. But such was the spirit of the volunteers and MacNamee's expertise in training, that he remembers being able to set up fairly good battalions in both east and west Tyrone within six weeks. Their armaments, however, consisted only of a few weapons left over from 1922.

It is worth following MacNamee's career as it impinged on most aspects of I.R.A. activity. He was captured on June 11, 1939, charged with being a member of the I.R.A. and sentenced to six months in Crumlin Road Jail. After serving his time he told the authorities that he was going to Newry to give them the impression he was going to cross the border. He was issued with a Newry ticket, but on leaving the prison he was met by a girl, and placed in a 'pound loney' area of the Falls Road used as an I.R.A. barracks. He remembers young men with guns and batons setting out on all sorts of military excursions. Everyone in the house was courteous to him but he soon discovered that he was under a form of house arrest! The Command had apparently decided to suspend him for illegal organising in Tyrone. When this news leaked out a mutiny took place in Tyrone. Then a communication arrived ordering MacNamee to return home. Part of this silly row lay in the fact that there is a traditional Tyrone versus Belfast animus somewhat akin to that existing between Cork and Dublin. However, since he was to be reinstated without trouble, the row blew over and Eoin returned to find himself a hero in Co. Tyrone.

He also found that there was little a hero could do apart from organising parades and training camps, but he was then appointed Adjutant General West Tyrone and about April, 1940, he went on the run. He remembers that four or five other prominent Tyrone men had to do the same, so there were a number of full-time organisers working throughout Tyrone. (The adjoining Donegal, though partially in the Free State area, was much more difficult to organise because it did not have the abrasive reality of Union Jacks, British uniforms, gerrymandering

and discrimination before it.) About this time he met Sean
McCaughey for the first time. McCaughey was O.C. of
the Northern Command, which had a headquarters in Carrickmore, near Joe McGarrity's old homestead. All seemed
to be going well now, but the course of I.R.A. ways never
run smooth. With the exception of MacNamee all the full-
time organisers in Tyrone were captured in a gun battle
with the R.U.C. at Carrickmore.*

Eoin then moved up to become brigade O.C., reorganising the brigade staff to cover gaps left by the
arrests, and despite these had the brigade whipped into a
pretty effective unit by the autumn of 1940. It was at
this stage that the issue of the Belfast battalion courts-
martial blew up. For some time past volunteers had complained that battalion officers had been beating them up.
There was at the time a strong Fascist influence in Belfast
I.R.A. circles. An occasional I.R.A. man affected the
Bersaglieri cap of Mussolini's crack troops and Fascist
techniques, such as beatings with batons and doses of
castor oil were frequently employed by what was known
as the 'belt and boot brigade'.

Looking at newspapers of the time one will sometimes
come across small paragraphs about young men being
beaten up by unidentified passers-by. These incidents
were the ones that came to the surface; others did not, and
some were pretty savage. A favourite I.R.A. punishment
of the time for serious dereliction of duty was wounding
a man in the leg, or in both legs for more serious cases,
with a revolver shot. Frank Morris of Convoy, Co. Done-

* They were Arthur Kearney, Jim Brogan, Pat McCallan and
Jim Kirk. Another prominent I.R.A. man, Dan McMahon,
was captured and left in his own home on the night of the raid
under the guard of an R.U.C. man while the rest of the party
went to surround the men at Carrickmore. However, when the
R.U.C. man guarding McMahon heard the shooting at nearby
Carrickmore he went to the door to see what was happening.
What he couldn't see happening was Dan McMahon making
his escape through the back door!

gal, one of the few reliable men whom Eoin had been able to recruit to the I.R.A. in the county, told me that his first noteworthy I.R.A. action was to attend a court-martial at which the sentence on a suspected informer was wounding in both legs. This was later reduced to wounding in one leg only, but the sentence was duly carried out.

Those who sanctioned these punishments felt that volunteers needed fear to keep them in line, whereas other prominent leaders, in particular Jimmy Steele, disagreed violently. To Steele, membership of the I.R.A. was an honour and privilege, and this fact alone enjoined a high standard of conduct. He first heard of these activities in Crumlin Road Jail, and began taking statements from incoming volunteers so that on his release he had a complete dossier. With this he had the entire battalion staff court-martialled in a little hall in a 'loney' off the Falls. It was a strange business and while it was being held Belfast was like an armed camp, with armoured cars, ordinary police cars and foot patrols four and five strong on every side of the street in the area. Evidently the R.U.C. had word of some impending I.R.A. activity, but didn't know what it was to be.

The outcome of the court-martial was that a number of officers were reduced to the ranks. This curbed the 'belt and boot' faction for some time, but the issue arose again when the command staff was arrested in the Hayes affair.

All that prevented serious trouble then was the fact that McCaughey's case was before the courts in Dublin. Everyone felt that any outbreak of shooting would prejudice a verdict. McCaughey was sentenced to death but was reprieved and sent to Portlaoighise Jail. It is thought that his reprieve came through the intercession of Cardinal MacRory. The I.R.A. did make overtures to the Church on his behalf; MacNamee went to see the Bishop of Down and Connor, Dr Mageean, who was generally regarded in Nationalist circles as a Republican sympathiser, but he offered no encouragement. But perhaps the

bishop took another line in private with the cardinal
because McCaughey's reprieve was quite unexpected. On
the other hand, although the government was incensed at
the Hayes confession and the embarrassment it caused,
McCaughey had not been captured bearing arms, or as a
result of any affray that had cost life. So, even in wartime,
his execution would have aroused violent reaction. (The
I.R.A. had made preparations so that if he had been
executed, a prominent intelligence officer from the Gardai
who had been decoyed to Belfast, ostensibly to meet Eoin
MacNamee, would have been ambushed and shot.)

After the reprieve, MacNamee and Hugh McAteer
found that in the wake of the Hayes affair the activities
of the 'belt and boot' brigade resumed and their own
leadership was challenged. So, one night in November,
1941, MacNamee mobilised the Protestant company, led
by John Graham. They drafted in a squad of men from
county brigades and left a man on the Falls Road to tell
Graham that, if they did not return very shortly, he and
McAteer were to be followed into a house on the Falls
Road where the battalion was meeting—with guns blazing
if necessary.

MacNamee and McAteer were both armed and their
appearance at the battalion meeting caused alarm. Eoin
told the senior officer present that if the battalion failed
to co-operate with the command, he would be shot. In a
tense atmosphere, a member of the battalion staff, Patsy
Hicks, one of its strongest figures, stammered out, 'I've
seen these things before. I'm taking orders from the command O.C.' Hicks was known to have seen some stern
affairs, so his reaction deflated the balloon of defiance
at once. The atmosphere grew more cordial as allegiance
was reaffirmed and everybody settled down to discuss
future plans. Meantime, the Protestant squad, whom
MacNamee had forgotten, rushed into the room prepared
to shoot. Seeing MacNamee unharmed, they too calmed
down and the incident ended peaceably.

After the Hayes affair it was clear that the I.R.A. had no immediate role in the South and a series of provincial conventions were set in train to decide future policy. MacNamee took over the one in Connacht; Sean McCool, who had succeeded Pearse Kelly as chief of staff, that of Munster; Hugh McAteer that of Ulster, and Frank Driver the Leinster gathering. Out of these conventions some degree of reorganisation took place with a view to transferring activities across the border and beginning a campaign exclusively in the North. About 20,000 rounds of the Magazine Fort ammunition, .303 calibre bullets for rifles, had found its way into MacNamee's custody in Tyrone, and between this and a quantity of arms still existing in various dumps throughout the South, it was felt that the I.R.A. was still relatively well-organised in the North. Against a backdrop of strong Catholic support, it could strike a reasonably effective blow against the administration.

But as with the English campaign the first blows were struck by the Southern authorities against the I.R.A. MacNamee, who was attending Skerry's College in St Stephen's Green, Dublin, under the name of Diamond, ostensibly to learn Morse code, but in reality to provide a cover for his presence in Dublin, was picked up in Brandon Road as he walked towards a dump in the Drimnagh area of Dublin. Within a few weeks Sean McCool joined him in the Curragh.

However, the defiant and resilient Northerners pressed ahead with their plans for a campaign which was finally agreed to at a Northern Command convention held on March 25, 1942, in Belfast. The funds for the campaign were obtained by a raid on the Academy Street Civil Defence Headquarters, which netted about £4,200—a payroll for civil defence workers throughout the North. The I.R.A. was in debt at the time to landladies who had put up men on the run and part of the Academy Street money went to paying these bills. The rest went on buying information* from police sources, on the provision of medical attention for wounded men, for printing Tarlach O'hUid's newspaper, the *Republican News*, running radio transmitters and buying ammunition or guns from British soldiers. It would have been better if no guns had been obtained for the campaign. Three I.R.A. men died as a result, one by hanging, two by shooting on the streets of Belfast, and five members of the R.U.C. and of the special constabulary lost their lives.

Constable Thomas James Forbes, a married man with four children, was the first policeman to be shot in the North for ten years when he and a group of other police were fired on in Dungannon on April 4, 1942. Constable William Mackey survived with fractured ribs because a bullet, aimed at his heart, struck a button in his coat. The following day Constable Patrick Murphy was shot dead in Cashmere Road, Belfast. A group of young I.R.A. men involved in this shooting, all of them under nineteen, retreated to Cawnpore Street, where they made their way into a house. Here they were arrested by four of Murphy's comrades, whom they could easily have killed as they came up the stairs, but did not. All six were sentenced to death for the murder of the policeman, and this sparked off the greatest agitation initiated by I.R.A. action during the whole of the war.

In Dublin Sean MacBride set up a reprieve committee and acted as its secretary. No fewer than 207,000 signatures were collected, and huge meetings were addressed by such diverse speakers as Denis Ireland of the Irish Union, Jim Larkin, the trade unionist, and past and present Republicans of every shade and hue, including members of Fianna Fail. The agitation spread outside Ireland. Secretary of State Cordell Hull took up the matter after being pressed by the Irish minister to Washington,

---

* Before being picked up MacNamee had established contacts with intelligence personnel in the Southern army who, he told me, showed him their reports before passing them on to their superiors.

Robert Brennan. The execution of six I.R.A. men for the death of one would have jeopardised Fianna Fail's effort to keep order, to say nothing of the effect in the North.

Hull also saw Anthony Eden in Washington and put pressure on Lord Halifax, the British ambassador. In London the American ambassador, John Winant, made representations. In Dublin the American ambassador, David Gray, said that 'some measure of clemency is probably expedient. The British and Canadian representatives here hold the same opinion. Hanging six for one would shock public opinion.' However, Gray took a poor view of all the pressure for reprieves, and in a letter dated August 27, 1942, to de Valera wrote:

Those of us who like yourself have attempted and are attempting by diplomatic means to procure a measure of clemency for these young men, find ourselves embarrassed by the pressure exerted here upon the Northern Government. As you know, governments, especially in war time, do not like to be coerced and fear that clemency exercised under pressure will be interpreted as weakness.

I am afraid that if we fail, the originators of the pressure campaign will have a heavy responsibility. I appreciate your sincere desire to keep this agitation within reasonable bounds and your considerable success in this direction, but repeat what I said in our recent talk—that, except for yourself and a few others, Ireland does not seem to appreciate what the war means, the gravity of the situation and the danger of rocking the boat at such a time.

Yours sincerely,

David Gray.

Irish sentiment in America was less sensitive than Gray's and influential congressmen such as the majority leader Senator McCormick, and many others urged the State Department to intervene.

The agitation was largely successful. Five of the six were reprieved, only Thomas Williams being hanged on September 2. It is believed in Belfast that the British cabinet favoured hanging all six, to deter the I.R.A. from activity for the rest of the war, but that Cardinal MacRory from Armagh approached Cardinal Hinsley, who was friendly with Brendan Bracken, Churchill's wartime minister for information. Bracken, an Irishman himself, could claim superior local knowledge and his word probably carried exceptional weight.

Williams's hanging was a frightful business that could have occurred only in Belfast. On the night before his death, Catholics kept vigil outside the jail saying the Rosary, while an Orange mob jeered them, shouting obscenities about Williams and singing Orange ballads.

Before his execution Williams wrote the following letter to McAteer:

Hugh, a Cara,

Just a note to let you know how my comrades and I are getting along. I do not expect an answer as your answer to Joe serves us all in that respect.

I am proud to know that you are our leader. My comrades and I are sure that you will use your utmost powers to free our dear, beloved country. And bring about the reestablishment of the Republic and its constitution.

It is beyond the powers of my humble intellect, to describe the pride of my comrades, in knowing that they are going to follow, in the footsteps of those who have given their lives to Ireland and the Republic. To describe the courage and coolness shown when sentenced to death. As Joe has previously stated to you. Our sorrow is not being able to attack the court and the 'Northern' Junta. But now you know the reason.

My God, can we tell you and our comrades who will carry on the fight, can we tell you of the gladness and joy that is in our hearts. To know that the Irish people are again united, aye, and well may England quake, Irelands awake, Irelands awake. After 20 yrs of slumber our nation will once again strike, Please God, at the despoilers who have infringed the nation's liberty, freedom and murdered her sons, her daughters, who have given us a foreign tongue;

shall please God, strike and strike hard and make the tyrants go on their knees for mercy and forgiveness.

But shall we make the mistake of '21, no, no, tis men like you and your staff will see to it. That no farcical so-called Treaty shall in anyway be signed by a bunch of weak-kneed and willed Irishmen. Better that the waves of the mighty oceans sweep over Erin than take and divide our nation, murder her true sons again. Better would be that heavens would open and send fire to destroy Erin, than to accept another Treaty like it.

In writing this, dear Hugh, do not think that I am saying it to you or the gallant soldiers of Oglaigh na hEireann, it is from my heart that it comes to the weak-willed and ignorant Irish men who may put any trust in England. My only regret is now I will not be with you in the fight and last stage of Ireland's battle for freedom. But with the help of God and His Blessed Mother we may be in heaven looking down upon our dear, beloved, tortured, crucified Erin, and look with pride on the men and women who will carry on the battle until victory.

Well dear Hugh I'll close with the message to Oglaigh na hEireann, 'To carry on, no matter what odds are against you, to carry on no matter what torments are inflicted on you. The road to freedom is paved with suffering, hardships and torture, carry on my gallant and brave comrades until that certain day.'

> Your comrade in Ireland's cause,
> Lieut. Tom Williams,
> 'C' Coy. Belfast Brigade,
> Oglaigh na hEireann.

For days before and after Williams's execution, tension hung over Belfast, particularly in Nationalist quarters. Two days before Williams was hanged, one of Hugh McAteer's principal lieutenants Gerry O'Callaghan was shot dead when the R.U.C. raided a dump at Hannahstown outside Belfast. O'Callaghan was moving arms to a safer place, for use in avenging Williams's death. Demonstrations took place in Dublin against business premises that refused to close and riots broke out throughout the city. In the North the reaction was grimmer—although the condemned man himself had sent a letter to his comrades asking that no reprisals be taken for his death. Within an hour of his execution police patrols were being fired on. At Clady, Co. Tyrone, Constable James Laird and Special Constable Samuel Hamilton were shot dead on September 5. In Belfast on the same day a shooting took place in Abbercorn Street, when an R.U.C. man and a boy of sixteen were wounded. And of four I.R.A. men arrested under arms in Belfast on the same day, two were sixteen and one seventeen years old.

The wave of bombing and shootings finally led to a curfew in Nationalist areas of west Belfast. From October 10 no movement was permitted on the streets between 8.30 p.m. and 6.00 a.m. On the first day of the curfew a battle broke out outside Donegal Pass police barracks after a bomb was thrown there. Special Constable James Lyons was fatally wounded and a number of other police and passers-by received lesser injuries. All these incidents affected the nerves of Belfast people, but the campaign petered out with the enforcement of the curfew, although a shooting on October 1, 1943 claimed the life of Constable Patrick McCarthy, shot dead during a payroll raid on Clonard Mill at Odessa Street off the Falls Road.

The I.R.A. had intended to bring a number of other police officials and warders to their Maker but these plans misfired. One of the most celebrated policemen Northern Ireland has ever produced is District Inspector James Fanning, who was a particular scourge of the I.R.A. He was cycling to work one morning when a car passed him and a Chicago-style assassination was attempted. He was shot off his bicycle, and he described to me how he lay on the pavement with 'a feeling of cold and surprise. I felt the sting of the bullets, but no pain, just terrible cold.' The car carrying his would-be killers passed so close that he could see the men in it, handkerchiefs round their faces, as they fired through the windows at him. The bullets struck the pavement near his head and around his body. His wounds were so bad that when he was picked up blood ran out through the eyelets of his shoes, but he recovered after a lengthy stay in hospital and returned to duty.

He was not long back at work when one of those responsible for shooting at him (both I.R.A. and R.U.C. very often had a shrewd idea of what transpired in the enemy's camp without always being in a position to do anything about it) sought a permit to go to England. Fanning duly issued one, but could not resist asking the man if 'he was not ashamed of what he had done'. His assailant replied, 'Oh now Mr Fanning I don't want to talk about that at all.' In the circumstances, Fanning regarded his attitude as being entirely understandable, if reprehensible, and there the exchange closed.

All these incidents made the I.R.A. seem a formidable force to the public, but in fact, as in the South, the reality was quite otherwise. A week after the hanging of Williams, on September 10, the publicity headquarters of Northern Command was raided and the owner of the house, Sean Dynan, John Graham, the O.C. of the Belfast battalion, and David Fleming from Kerry were captured along with a complete issue of the I.R.A. paper the *Republican News*. This last loss was remedied by the efforts of McAteer, Gerry O'Reilly and others who sat up during the night producing a further 6,000 copies which duly were distributed.

Then on October 6 McAteer and O'Reilly were themselves captured. They had been decoyed to the home of a boyhood friend of McAteer's who was then a member of the R.U.C. and who had, by chance, bumped into McAteer earlier in the week and promised him some worthwhile information if McAteer would call to his home. The life of this young man hung by a very slender thread thereafter, but McAteer refused to have him executed as he could easily have done either later in the war or after it. (However, the man's father's undertaking business fell off and he went bankrupt as a result of an unofficial boycott against him.) After his capture McAteer received a fifteen-year sentence and was sent to Crumlin Road Jail, from which he immediately planned to escape.

The walls of the jail are more than three feet thick, the windows are barred and thick glass is set into steel frames. A twenty-foot wall surrounds the front garden overlooked by warders' quarters and the administrative offices and, during the war, this wall was patrolled by armed guards. If a prisoner did succeed in getting so far he then had to run past the windows of the warders' cottages outside the walls. Normally there was also a police patrol on Crumlin Road itself, a busy artery in the heart of Belfast. However, a trapdoor was discovered in the ceiling of the lavatory which led to an attic under the slates of the jail roof. McAteer, Paddy Donnelly, the prisoners' leader, Jimmy Steele and Edward Maguire decided to escape together. Ladders were made from sheets torn lengthwise in halves and the halves then sewn together end to end and bound with waxen cords. A hook was made from a brass bed end to catch the top of the wall and bandages were wrapped around it so that it would catch in the barbed wire with which the wall was protected.

On the morning of January 15, 1943, the four received permission to go to the lavatory and, standing on a table which was later removed by their friends, hauled themselves up into the attic, replacing the trapdoor underneath them. Once in the attic, they smashed their way out on to the roof. Incredibly, no one heard the noise of the breaking slates. They reached the wall without mishap, here to discover that the jointed stick which they had made to hoist the hook on to the wall was too short. Maguire stood on McAteer's shoulders in an attempt to hoist the hook on, but fell off. He and McAteer began squabbling as to whose fault this was when Donnelly intervened to say specifically, 'I think, lads, ye should finish this conversation on the other side of the wall!'

They eventually got over the wall safely, McAteer alone being injured with torn ligaments in his ankle and a badly reefed hand from the barbed wire. In the gloom of the January morning no one noticed them mingling with the crowds and, despite the fact that they were wearing prison clothes, Belfast's wartime shabbiness afforded them protection in this regard also. A £3,000 reward was immediately posted for the capture of any or all of the four, but Maguire and Donnelly stayed free to the end of the war, Steele lasted until May, and McAteer was not picked up until the following November.

The escape gave the I.R.A. a brief injection of life and McAteer and Steele figured in two spectacular exploits during their freedom. The first of these was the Derry Jail escape which was being prepared before McAteer's and Steele's exploit. The ground floor cells of Derry Jail were floored with wood, beneath which was nothing but clay. A group of prisoners—Liam Graham, Eddie Steele, John McGreevy and James O'Hagan—began to tunnel under the floor of Liam Graham's cell and, working for over five months, they and their prison comrades managed to sink a shaft extending twenty feet straight down and turning sharply to extend out under the roadway outside the jail and up into the coal hole of the Logue family in Harding Street. The clay was dumped into lavatories and twice the sewers clogged as a result, but although the sewers were laid bare and the clay discovered, the authorities apparently never connected its presence with an escape bid. The larger boulders which the diggers encountered were hidden under the floorboards of other ground floor cells. Once the escape nearly ended in tragedy when a tunnel collapse buried Graham, but he was dug out before he suffocated.

The escape was timed for March 21 and the day before this Steele hired a truck in Belfast and drove to Derry. En route the driver stopped at an R.U.C. barracks to

deliver a message which gave Steele a nasty scare. While
the driver was inside, for all Steele knew giving the game
away, he had the unnerving experience of sitting on a
level with a poster announcing a £3,000 reward for the
capture of Hugh McAteer, James Steele, Paddy Donnelly
or Edward Maguire who had feloniously broken out of
Crumlin Road Jail. Nobody in the barracks connected the
driver's helper with the photograph on the poster and the
driver went on blithely to Derry where, to his horror,
Steele produced a revolver and informed him of what
lay ahead.

Twenty-one prisoners made their escape through
Graham's tunnel, while outside the door one of the in-
mates played the bagpipes to cover the noise of their
departure. The last prisoner to shoulder his way to
escape was Brendan O'Boyle (who got clean away and
remained at liberty throughout the war in Dublin only
to die tragically later). Fifteen prisoners piled into the
truck and made their way over the border where they were
picked up by the Southern army and lodged in the
Curragh for the duration of the war. Unknown to the army
patrol which held up the truck, a woman with a camera
was standing behind a hedge when this happened and took
a photograph of the incident.

This escape created a fantastic impact on Nationalist
sentiment, coming on top of the Crumlin Road breakout.
The I.R.A. leaders began casting round for some similar
exploit to impress public opinion and raise morale within the I.R.A. without, at the same time, endangering life.
A young volunteer suggesting holding up either a picture
house or a dance hall for the purpose of making a demonstration while volunteers guarded the doorways. Steele and
McAteer were highly enthusiastic, but to avoid loose talk
they told the volunteer that his idea was impractical. They
themselves decided that the following Easter they would
take over a place of public amusement. The Broadway
Cinema not far from the Falls Road was selected as the
target and on Holy Saturday afternoon, sixteen volunteers

set off, two at a time, to converge on the cinema. The manager and projectionist were held up while armed volunteers guarded every exit and entrance. A slide was then flashed on the screen:

This cinema has been commandeered by the Irish Republican Army for the purpose of holding an Easter Commemoration for the dead who died for Ireland.

Jimmy Steele then read the 1916 Proclamation from the stage and Hugh McAteer read a statement of I.R.A. policy for the coming year. The proceedings closed with the observance of a one minute's silence for the dead and the raiders got away safely. Statements were issued to all the newspapers and Lord Haw-Haw included the incident in his broadcast from Berlin that evening.

While these exploits raised the stock of the I.R.A. enormously among its sympathisers they had the opposite effect on their enemies, particularly among prison warders. Up to the time when the war began to swing against the Germans, warders in Belfast generally treated the I.R.A. prisoners with some deference, but when it became apparent that the allies were likely to win, the I.R.A. came in for sterner treatment, and jail escapes marked a turning point in warder-I.R.A. relationships. Hitherto, the hundred or so Republican prisoners in Belfast Jail had tried various methods to secure political treatment. These included not doing the prescribed prison work and going on hunger strike, and though they failed to gain their objective a kind of unofficial political status was accorded the prisoners. After the Crumlin Road escape, however, prison regulations were sternly enforced, and cell searches and bread-and-water diets became commonplace. One result of these tactics was that the prisoners sent out word asking their comrades to shoot a particularly bullying warder, but the most popular warder in the prison was killed by mistake.

The prisoners then resorted to the 'strip strike'. John

Graham and David Fleming had argued against a hunger strike, because it either weakened prisoners irretrievably or had to be carried through to the death. So a strip strike started in mid June, 1943. Twenty-two prisoners* in Belfast Jail took off their prison clothes and the authorities retaliated by taking every other article from their cells, including their handkerchiefs. Bedding and blankets were not restored until 8.30 each evening. Towels were taken after the morning wash and no reading material was permitted other than religious books. Cells were thus left empty apart from the prisoner himself, the frame of his iron bed, his sanitary vessel and a carafe of water for the whole day.

An account of what the strip strike was like, was written by Seamus Steele in a journal he produced in 1954, *Resurgent Ulster*:

The prison bell goes at 7 o'clock. You awaken with a start. No nice slow leisurely wakening here but before the last clang you are wide awake. The cold bare walls stare back at you and you realise that you have another long day to spend naked. You ponder how long it is until you will see that bed again—13 hours—780 minutes—46,800 seconds and you have to live thru' every second. But you have a half hour yet for the warders do not come until 7.30. How you treasure that last half hour. The old lumpy fibre mattress, the army blankets, and the hard worsted sheets feel like down. For soon you hear the clang of the keys and the rush of feet. The warders have arrived. They are laughing and joking and full of the ordinary joys of

* James Brogan, Tyrone; Frank Morris, Tyrone; David Fleming, Kerry; John McMahon, Portadown; Ned Tennyson, Portadown; Sean Gallagher, Derry; P. Heggarty, Derry; John Graham, Belfast; Joe Cahill, Belfast; Dan McAlister, Belfast; Gerry Adams, Belfast; James Hannon, Belfast; Joe Myles, Belfast; R. Dempsey, Belfast; H. O'Hara, Belfast; S. McParland, Belfast; P. Corrigan, Belfast; Charles McCotter, Belfast; T. Morley, Belfast; W. Doyle, Belfast; J. McCusker, and Seamus 'Jimmy' Steele, Belfast.

life. You wonder if the fight is really worth while. But this passes very quickly and you get the courage to at least last another day. The slops are removed and the door is banged in your face again. You still have another minute or two and you get back into bed again. When the bed is removed you stand naked in your cold bare cell.

At eight o'clock the breakfast arrives. This consists of one pint of tea, eight ounces of bread, and half an ounce of margarine. Your table and chair have been removed so you take your treasure to the old bedstead. You try to eat it slowly as you know it will do you more good and it will last longer, but the hunger is so great that you eat it very quickly. Any stray crumbs are quickly retrieved. You drink the tea and all is finished and you are nearly as hungry as ever. It will be four and a half hours before you get any more.

Now the day has really begun. You hear the prisoners going out to work. How you envy them their warm clothes. They are happy people. Nevertheless the fight must go on. The day must be spent. You begin the parade again. Eight paces up, one at the turn, and eight paces back again. You begin this parade and people wonder what is the matter with you. Perhaps you make a football out of an old pair of socks and try to get the blood to circulate. You think on how cold it is even though it is the month of June. What will it be like in January? You put this out of your head at once. The sun is shining outside but this does not reach your cell. What is that? A knock on the wall and then a knock on the pipes. It is the signal that your next door neighbour wants to speak to you. You listen at the door and all is quiet. You get your enamel mug and use it as a kind of telephone on the pipes. Perhaps there is some news. But no! Your pal is finding it hard also and you try to encourage him. Stick it a little longer and there is no knowing what will happen. Suddenly the spy-hole is opened and an un-friendly eye looks in and gives a sharp order to get off the pipes. Even this small luxury is denied us. Well, on it must go. You begin the parade again or perhaps read a few pages of the Bible. You read but you do not take any-thing in. There is such a vast difference between what you read and the position you are in. Perhaps if you read the part on Job you get a little comfort. He has done his suffering for God, you are suffering for a principle. It helps a lot if you offer it to God too.

It is usual for them to search your cell. What do they expect to get in your empty tomb? Perhaps a small butt of a cigarette that you managed to get. At any rate everything is gone through, even at times your hair and beard. You will have a beard by this time for you are not allowed a razor. Perhaps if they did the death of Tone could be re-enacted. You cannot see this beard for your mirror has also been removed.

The dinner arrives and you are just ravenous. This consists of one pint of soup, two ounces meat, one ounce vegetables and about three small potatoes. If one potato is bad it is a calamity. There is no use asking for another one for you will in all probability get another bad one and draw down the enmity of a warder on your defenceless shoulders. Well, you eat everything—potatoes, skins—every scrap, no matter how unpalatable it is it fills an empty space. It is now only twelve o'clock and you think it is only four and a half hours from the morning, that is another eight and a half hours to go until you get into that bed again. You lie on the cold bedstead and try to rest for you have been on the constant move since the morning trying to keep warmth in your body. You are so cold that you begin the whole parade again. Perhaps you have a visit from the prison chaplain. You are delighted to see him and at the same time feel embarrassed and ashamed. You do not like to detain him too long as he has to visit all the other fighters and perhaps some of the other prisoners as well. He has a very difficult job. You can see the light of sympathy in his eyes and at the same time he gives you to understand that he thinks you are striking your head against a stone wall. Perhaps you are too. You are in the grip of a mighty machine. What is the use? Others fought against it for years. Some went to an early grave, while others went mad. What was to be your fate? Nevertheless you must not let your comrades down. We are all in this to the end.

At two o'clock the noise starts again. The other prisoners go out to work and you have simply nothing to do. In these circumstances a man realises how incomplete he is on his own and how much a social creature he really is. How content you would be doing anything! Even the hateful monotonous task of sewing mail bags that you were doing before the strike began. Perhaps you climb on the back of your bed and look out of your window. There is very little to be seen. Perhaps some hapless creatures marching around a ring in the courtyard awaiting trial. Perhaps some of your own comrades who will get the same kind of a trial that you got and a savage sentence. If you are caught it will almost certainly mean a report followed by a sentence of 'bread and water'. They cannot confine you any closer but your diet will be reduced to a total of eight ounces of bread and one pound of potatoes per day. These morsels make you feel more hungry than if you get nothing at all.

At four o'clock the prisoners return from the shops and the tea arrives which consists of the same as the morning with one pint of porridge and half a pint of milk. This has to keep you going till eight o'clock the next morning. You could eat it at once and still be hungry but you must keep a little for later in the evening. Even though there is still four hours left you have the day's back broken. You have done nine hours and every hour you do leaves one more down and one less to do. If you get a chance now you try to get something from the prisoner next to you. This is done by using a string, which you had concealed, and a weight. Perhaps you have a few booklets to exchange that will while away the monotony of the evening. If you are caught it will mean punishment but it is worth the risk. Look at the satisfaction you get if you succeed. Even if it is only a small thing you have a feeling that you have beaten them.

Perhaps the prisoner below you who is in sympathy with your ideals sends you some of his food on the line. His own food is little enough and if he is caught it will mean punishment for him but he knows you are fighting his fight too. The time is passing but will 8.30 never come? At long last you hear the rattle of the keys. How welcome

is that sound now. They start at the top. Will they never
reach your length? The door opens and you get your bed.
You are under the clothes in a few minutes. You are asleep
in a few more. It does seem a pity to go to sleep as you
don't find the time until that awful bell goes again.

Conditions seem to have been even colder than they
would have been in winter for in prison the heating is
switched off during the summer and the stone cells had
no way of heating up. The strike was called off after about
three months to allow John Graham to get treatment for
a badly swollen knee.

McAteer was recaptured on November 21 as he was
coming out of St Paul's Church, and with his capture the
era of the I.R.A. as a significant fighting force in Belfast
came to an end. In jail, prisoners still asserted their
demands for political treatment by going on hunger strike,
but outside, police pressure and the war itself combined
to destroy the organisation. Protestants and Catholics who
huddled together in air raid shelters during the Belfast
bombings never had quite the same bitter animosity towards each other after the war. And the introduction by
the British Labour government of the welfare state to
the North (despite the votes of twelve Tory candidates
from the North against these innovations) damped down
rebellious feelings. Henceforward, Northern Catholics
began to seek an end to gerrymandering and discrimination in housing and jobs, rather than a reunion of the
country under a Dublin parliament. When the I.R.A.
campaign broke out in 1956, it was obvious even to I.R.A.
leaders in Dublin, who had grown up in the meantime,
that Belfast was not a suitable theatre for operations. The
city remained calm despite events along the border.

Ground between the Military Court and the Curragh, the I.R.A. men in the South shared similar experiences to those of the North with street shootings, individual acts of heroism, executions and defiance of prison regulations. While the provincial conferences were being held and the Northern campaign plans were being laid, it became obvious that the prime need to carry out such plans was the provision of some reliable men. Sean McCool sent word from the Curragh for a number of selected personnel to 'sign out'—that is, to give undertakings of good behaviour for the future.

Two of these were Seamus 'Rocky' Burns and Harry White. Burns was killed in a gun battle with the R.U.C. in Belfast on June 2, 1944. Even though he had 'signed out' under orders, such was the rigidity of the traditional Republican sentiment to 'signing out', or recognising courts, that several Belfast Republicans refused to attend his funeral because he had 'signed out'.

White, a plumber by trade, had been active in the bombing campaign in England before his internment. After his release he went on the run and escaped police surveillance until one evening in November, 1942, when he and a comrade, Maurice O'Neill from Kerry, were holed up in a house in Donnycarney, Dublin, and a party of Special Branch men made a lightning raid.

Shooting followed and Detective Officer Mordant was killed. White made a break and succeeded in getting out the back, across a number of adjoining gardens and walls until finally, hurling himself over a wall leading to a railway embankment, he fell sixteen feet into a dense thicket of briars. He lay there for two days with a gunshot wound in the leg while around him the police combed the area. Eventually, covered in mud and blood, he made his way to a bus-stop, boarded a bus, dismounted in crowded O'Connell Street in the heart of Dublin, and walked to a refuge in the Summerhill area of Dublin, where he learned that there was a price of £5,000 on the head of one Harry White, alias Anderson.

A few days later, Maurice O'Neill was executed in Mountjoy Prison for Mordant's murder. His execution provoked particularly widespread protests as he was a popular figure in his native Kerry, but the government, desperately trying to preserve its neutrality, was adamant. An iron-gloved approach to the I.R.A. was the order of the day with vigorous raids and interrogations. As a result relations between individual I.R.A. men and the Special Branch became understandably strained, and the I.R.A., in its shattered and disorganised condition, came to regard the Special Branch as a greater enemy than the British Crown.

On September 9, 1942, Detective Sergeant Denis O'Brien, one of the most prominent Special Branch detectives and a brother of Sean Lemass's secretary, was shot dead as he left his home in Ballyboden, Rathfarnham, Co. Dublin to go to work. The shooting greatly increased public feeling against the I.R.A., particularly as the murder was carried out almost in view of his wife. As she held her dying husband she watched his assailants cycling past.

A number of I.R.A. men were charged at various times in connection with this killing, but only one was executed for it—Charles Kerins, twenty-six, of Kerry on December 1, 1944. At the end of his trial the president of the Military Court delayed sentence until later in the day to allow Kerins, if he wished, to make an application whereby he might have avoided the capital sentence. When the court resumed Kerins said:

'You could have adjourned it for six years as far as I'm concerned, as my attitude towards this Court will always be the same.'

He thus deprived himself of the right to give evidence, to face cross-examination or to call witnesses.

The Special Branch was equally tense when dealing

with I.R.A. men, and in such an atmosphere guns blazed on both sides in cases where a prisoner would normally have gone quietly. The best one can say of a shooting on July 4, 1943, in Mount Street when a young I.R.A. man, Jacky Griffith, was machine-gunned off his bicycle by the Special Branch, is that it was the last fatal shooting in the South of Ireland between police and I.R.A. from that day to this.

Through all this period, Harry White managed to stay free, remaining on the run for five years and surviving some remarkable adventures. Once he had the audacity to attend a public meeting in O'Connell Street, Dublin, to protest the hanging of Thomas Williams. Mrs Kathleen Clarke, widow of the 1916 leader Thomas Clarke, made a fiery speech threatening that if it took place, there would be a march on the border. As Mrs Clarke was a Fianna Fail senator and a former lord mayor of Dublin, White became enraged at what he considered hypocritical rabble-rousing and he called out, 'What about George Plant?' He was nearly lynched by Fianna Fail supporters but managed to get away. He later took a lorry-load of men in full daylight across the border, hoping to capture a British officer, any British officer, in reprisal for Williams's death.

Later that month he was attending a wedding in Bally-jamesduff, Co. Cavan, when police surrounded the house, shots were fired and the bride's brother, Patrick Dermody, was shot dead in a gun battle which also took the life of a guard. This affray provoked great bitterness, from police and public at the death of the policeman and, in I.R.A. circles, over Dermody's death. Dermody was so powerful in border areas that he held regular courts at which he settled land disputes and other squabbles. White managed to shoot his way out of this trap also and did not see the inside of a jail again until 1946 when he was picked up in Derry and handed over to the Gardai by the R.U.C.

I.R.A. apologists say that White was handed over because the R.U.C. hoped that the Southern 'death court' would condemn him to death. However Sean MacBride persuaded the court of the fact that while the bullet which killed Detective Officer Mordant was fired from White's gun he was entitled to defend himself as the raiding police had not identified themselves before opening fire. The court held that this was not murder, but excessive use of force by White when resisting unlawful arrest and it found him guilty of manslaughter. O'Neill had been tried and executed on the charge that he had murdered Mordant on the date in question. But it is clear from the evidence that White and O'Neill were separated at the time the fatal shot was fired and it is at least arguable that O'Neill knew nothing about it.

The years in the Curragh left their mark on those who remained in the camp after White and Burns. Most men, on leaving the internment camp, were so unable to deal with ordinary life that it took upwards of six months before any of them could screw up their courage to do normal things such as signing on at the Labour Exchange to draw unemployment benefit or applying for jobs. Even to cross the road was a terrible effort, the traffic, thin enough after the war, seemed fantastic after the years in the Curragh. The difference in women's fashion frightened them and added to the general air of unfamiliarity. After years in confinement with adult men, children seemed fragile and small-scale. Most remained Republican in sympathy but had no means of solving the border problem. Some were broken and turned to drink or developed nervous breakdowns.

Strangely enough, only one case of homosexuality in the Curragh has ever been mentioned to me. There was a great deal of horseplay. Sometimes the clothes were stripped off an internee by his friends, and he was left to run naked through the camp on a winter's day, but the overwhelming majority of prisoners made a deliberate effort not to allow sex to unbalance them. Between almost frenzied bouts of football or other athletic activity and hours spent making medals, baskets, leatherwork and so on, sexual frustration was largely exorcised. But dissension, the principal bugbear of Republicans, remained.

Pearse Kelly, who was camp O.C. during the greater part of his five years internment, described his first impressions of the Curragh in a prison record which he was kind enough to give me:

It was December with the usual dismal rain. The car stopped at a big, barricaded gate just above the camp and one of my escorts remarked 'Well, you'll have plenty of time to hibernate down here. This isn't a health resort at any time, but it's at its worst now so you know what's in store for you.'

From my elevated position I had a panoramic view of the camp, a conglomeration of long low wooden huts erected in military lines, behind a quadruple fence of barbed wire and completely surrounded by a deep trench, evidently designed to prevent tunnelling. I was conscious of a slight shiver of apprehension as I took in the dead, drab look of the place.

After being searched and stripped, I was given a dilapidated mattress and a pillow with four old army blankets. The compound gate was unlocked to allow me in and I entered to find no sign of life apart from a Military Policeman who directed me to Hut 314.

When I entered the hut, I stood aghast. For a moment I couldn't make out what was happening. The rise and fall of the babble of voices that filled the turbid air, stilled momentarily as attention centred on the newcomer. Almost at once the din broke out again with men shouting at each other across the hut with voices raised to be heard above the general bedlam. A scene of apparent disorder met my eyes, all I could discern was a litter of beds with lines of discarded clothing hanging from the rafters and men, some squatting in silence on their beds, others huddled up in their blankets. Thirty men lived and slept in this hut and out of the forty in the compound there were sixteen similarly occupied, almost 500 internees.

Heating was supplied by small turf stoves and the walls and window-frames were of such inferior quality that, in bad weather, rain seeped through.

Before Kelly's arrival, the camp had been going through a particularly bad phase. On December 14, 1940, there had been an outbreak of rioting resulting in several bad injuries and one death. The cause was the ugly, brooding, hothouse atmosphere created by close surveillance, internment, frustration and a feeling among the internees that some stand had to be made.

The internees considered the food in the Curragh to be 'lousy bad', as Michael Traynor put it. It probably was, but it was the same food as army privates received, and when on December 14 the army's butter ration was reduced by a quarter this reduction was also extended to the internees' diet. It was the last straw. Peadar O'Flaherty, the prisoners' leader, lined them all up and gave a stirring address.

'Are we men or mice?' he asked, and gave the order to set fire to a prison hut.

Unfortunately, the fire spread to a number of other huts and six of them were destroyed with a great quantity of beds and bedding. And then, during investigations, it was discovered that the internees had been tunnelling for the whole summer and had almost reached the barbed wire.

Fierce fighting began when the military and military police went to put out the fires. Two internees and two members of the army were badly injured and taken to hospital. The internees were rounded up in the open, where they spent the day until being herded into two huts, one of them with a concrete floor. Being December this came to be known as the icebox. Throughout the night there was desultory shooting around the huts as trigger-happy military police fired at shadows. Inside the huts the internees were apprehensive that someone was going to be shot. For two days after the incident the men were kept in these two huts, only a cookhouse detail being allowed out to collect food and bring it back. Several of the internees had diarrhoea and dysentery, but the only sanitary facilities in the huts were buckets which provided an added dimension of unpleasantness.

The prisoners then refused to be counted and an armed guard had to be sent to the huts to check them. Only when it was certain that no escapes had occurred were the prisoners allowed to go to the dining hall. They lined up outside their huts facing a party of armed military police, nerves on both sides at breaking point. The military had been attacked during the fire with wooden trestle boards, iron trestle bars, broom handles and pieces of piping and fittings, and had replied with gun butts and rifle shots. In this instance the prisoners had no intention of rushing the armed party, but as their numbers swelled coming out of the huts, about fifty internees came to within ten yards of the armed party. Shooting broke out, one internee, Bernard Casey, of Co. Longford, being fatally wounded and another, Walter Mitchell, escaping with a bullet that lodged between the heel and the sole of his shoe.

Following this, a period of nearly two weeks of extreme tension ensued in the camp. The prisoners were penned into the icebox at night, hearing stray shots outside and fearing that something worse might occur. One night, a strong force of military police surrounded the camp and took selected leaders, among them Michael Traynor, to what was known as 'the glasshouse', a wing of the camp with a double row of cells under a high glass roof. Here, Traynor says, a fortnight of sheer horror followed. Jittery military policemen ran along iron stairs at night to quell suspected outbreaks. Beatings and kickings were more frequent than halfpence.

Readers who have seen Brendan Behan's play *Borstal Boy* will get an insight into the kind of fears that political prisoners engender in their captors. Traynor remembers his period here as a time of 'diabolical treatment'. Outside the camp, Sean MacBride tried to have the case of Bernard Casey brought into the open and debated publicly to focus attention on the appalling conditions in the camp, but this attempt failed. When those who were held to be the ringleaders of the disturbances were identified, they were brought before a military court and sentenced—to their great delight. Traynor, although he got five years, regarded being away from the military police 'as if I was in heaven'. They used the condemned cell in Mountjoy as a recreational centre and, with plenty of food parcels from outside, it was a relatively pleasant interlude for a man who had begun the year with a fifty-day hunger strike.

After Kelly's arrival things improved, *vis-à-vis* the authorities. But for a time, among the internees, they got worse. Basically the trouble stemmed from the unnatural atmosphere of the place and the divisions between the Dublin and Belfast wings of the I.R.A. But trouble also flared up over issues such as prisoners collecting their own coal, rather than having it delivered to the huts by the authorities; the reading of the Stephen Hayes's 'confession'; and varying political views, Fascism versus Communism, or the issue of whether, in the event of an invasion, the internees should offer to sign out and fight in the hitherto hated Free State army, in a common defence of their homeland.

When Kelly arrived, the camp O.C. was Liam Leddy from Cork and he continued as such for some months until Kelly, Eoin MacNamee and Tom Cullimore decided that the only way to establish morale was by electing a new camp council. This trio made the Hayes 'confession' widely known throughout the camp although some prisoners were already aware of it. Joe Deighan, for instance, told me he had seen the 'confession' before Kelly showed up, but the publicity given to it by the trio led to their ostracism by the Leddy wing and they were 'sent to Coventry'. However, about 150 prisoners eventually came over to their side and by the end of the war, all the internees were on the Kelly side. For a time, relationships between the two wings were extremely bad. Any man caught talking to a member of the opposite camp was disdained by his own side and considered not to be a true Republican at all. But the position gradually eased over the years as the Kelly wing began to win concessions from the authority such as an ending of the physical punishment by the P.A.s,* an increase in the fuel allowance and facilities for hobbies and camp concerts. The Gaelic Athletic Association secretary, Padraig O'Caoimh, himself an old I.R.A. man, sent in a set of footballs and medals that were keenly played for, and the prisoners got such control of their own affairs that one Christmas they acquired all the equipment and ingredients to manufacture a successful run of poteen. 'Gaelteachts', peopled entirely by Irish-speaking internees, were set up and Mairtin O'Cadain ran highly successful language classes. Other prisoners who had more education than their fellows also gave tutorials in their own special subjects and many a young country lad, who had left school at twelve, emerged from the Curragh with a far better education than he could possibly have acquired any other way.

The even tenor of the prisoners' ways was threatened principally by the activities of Niall Verschoyle Gould, a devoted Communist who had been on the fringes of the Republican Congress movement and active in organising strikes in Dublin. Gould formed the centre of a coterie of other Republican Communists, in particular Michael O'Riordan, Johnny Power and Dermot Walshe. These three had fought in the Spanish Civil War, and they elected Gould as their tutor in Russian.

Gould did not confine his activities to teaching Russian.

* Military policemen, Poli Airim in Irish, P.A.s for short. Prisoners in the Curragh complained to me that in the early days of the Curragh it was not unusual for prisoners found guilty of some breach of camp regulations to be forced to run a gauntlet of P.A.s armed with batons which they used to strike at the victim's limbs, their heads being protected by the mattress and blankets which they were forced to carry on their way to the 'glasshouse' for a sojourn on bread and water.

As the central premise of Irish Catholicism was traditionally, before the Vatican Council II, an unthinking acceptance of authority, his clever dialectical approach undermined several fervent young Catholic internees. They were unaware of the Church's association with Britain in the enactment of the Act of Union and the subsequent quashing throughout the nineteenth century of every manifestation of Irish nationalism. He also undermined their faith in their nationalist gods, pointing out how John Mitchel had fought in the American Civil War on the side of the South and slavery, and he was well on the way to distracting the camp's attention from British oppression and/or de Valera, to that of the class struggle, when Kelly decided to take some action.

A message was smuggled out to the Bishop of Kildare and Leighlin, in whose diocese the camp was located, telling him that the morals of the camp were being perverted by a notorious Communist who was undermining the teachings of the Church and making the Curragh a hotbed of sedition and Marxism. Within three days Gould was removed from the camp and deposited in Mountjoy Jail. (To be a Communist in Ireland requires unusual self-control and discipline. While the tolerance of the people would rarely condone violence to a self-confessed Communist, such a declaration, even now, would inhibit his career in most fields, certainly in teaching.)*

In all some two thousand internees passed through the camp. The sort of men they were and the problems they faced are illustrated in this concluding passage from

* Gould apparently taught his beliefs to his son. In 1957, years after the Curragh and the war, family estates in Longford came before the courts for a decision as to what should become of them. Evidence was given that a lawyer acting for the court had gone to Moscow and found Gould Jr working as a labourer digging a trench across a Moscow side street. The boy had refused to take any interest in his inheritance or to give any directions as to what should be done with it. The money was duly lodged in the court.

Kelly's camp memoirs describing the advice given to him by an old friend who had left the camp.

He urged me to get away out to the country where I would really appreciate freedom as he had done. The barbed wire had no terror for him then, he actually came to have a sort of regard for it when he found he could fondle it without being molested.

'Don't mind,' he added, 'if you find yourself talking to the animals in the fields. These were the first things I made friends with when I came home, for if the animal doesn't like you it walks away, and you know at once where you stand. One feels nearer to Heaven too, to stand on a hillside of a sunny evening in the harvest, and as far as the eye can carry to watch the corn and crops and grasses with their glorious hues and they waving in the breeze and the sun dancing on them. As to the people, 'tis little I can say about them, for even yet I can't fit in no matter where I go, and I hate crowds. Back of it all, I am at times conscious of a deep yearning for my old friends of Tintown.'

The last sad act of the I.R.A. drama of the 1940s was a strip strike in Portlaoighise Prison. In the Curragh, Arbour Hill or Mountjoy jails, the Republican prisoners were allowed to wear their own clothes. But on transfer to Portlaoighise they had to wear convict uniform. When Sean McCaughey arrived there, in September, 1941, like the men who had gone before him he refused to wear these clothes.

From then until the middle of 1943, he and the others were kept in solitary confinement. They were not even allowed out to the lavatory and the confinement was made doubly rigorous by having an empty cell on either side of them. In 1943, their conditions were relaxed somewhat. They were allowed out of their cells into a larger cell together for an hour in the morning and the afternoon and they were also permitted a paper per week and a letter per month. By refusing to wear the convict clothes, the prisoners had set themselves in defiance of the prison authorities, so very little else was done to make their stay there enjoyable. McCaughey was allowed no visitors during the four and three-quarter years he was in Portlaoighise Jail.

Like the others, he spent all this time naked except for his prison blanket. Finally on April 19, 1946, he went on hunger strike for release though it is alleged by his comrades that it was well understood by the prison authorities and by the government that he would have come off the strike if he had been removed to the Curragh. Whatever the truth of this, the early days of his hunger strike produced no result and five days later he went on thirst strike too. Seventeen days later Sean McCaughey died with his body in a condition better imagined than described. Patrick McLogan, who saw the body after death, said that McCaughey's tongue had shrunken 'to the size of a threepenny bit'.

The inquest was held in the prison and the deputy coroner refused to allow Sean MacBride, counsel for the next of kin, to cross-examine the governor. The following passage occurred during MacBride's cross-examination of the prison doctor:

Mr MacBride: Are you aware that during the four and a half years he was here he was never out in the fresh air or sunlight?

Dr Duane: As far as I am aware he was not.

Mr MacBride: Would I be right in saying that up to twelve or eighteen months ago he was kept in solitary confinement and not allowed to speak or associate with any other persons?

Dr Duane: That is right.

Mr MacBride: Would you treat a dog in that fashion?

Mr McLoughlin: That is not a proper question.

Mr MacBride: If you had a dog would you treat it in that fashion?

Dr Duane (after a pause replied): No.

Mr MacBride: Did you have to attend the prisoner for a nervous breakdown?

Dr Duane: He suffered from a nervous condition for a time.

Mr MacBride: By reason of solitary confinement?

Dr Duane: I don't know.

Replying to his own counsel, Major Barrows, the prison governor, said of McCaughey:

He refused to wear prison clothes, and a man could not go out in the air without clothes, from the health point of view. Decency forbade it, and apart from that, his health would not stand it. You cannot have a naked man walking about a prison.

The jury's verdict was:

That the conditions existing in the prison were not all that could be desired according to the evidence furnished; but there was no reflection on the Governor, Medical Officer or Staff intended.

So ended the Stephen Hayes affair. The only man who could really say what prompted his suspicions of the former chief of staff is dead. If the affair had not brought McCaughey southward he might have survived the war, though, given his temperament, he might have been killed in a police battle, been executed or died during one of the jail strikes.

The plight of the other prisoners in the jail, such as Thomas MacCurtain, Michael Traynor, Liam Rice and Harry White, led to support for the new party which grew up around Sean MacBride in those years and which put Fianna Fail out of office in 1948. Just as Fianna Fail had come to power in 1932 to the echoes of 'Release the Prisoners', the same call sounded against them in 1948. One of the first acts of the new minister for justice, General Sean MacEoin, who, as a member of the I.R.A. had been sentenced to death by the British, was to 'release the prisoners'.

No facet of I.R.A. activities aroused so much distrust and alarm, at home and abroad, as did the organisation's links, real or imagined, with the Nazis. These must, however, be assessed against the background of Irish neutrality.

On September 5, 1939, Winston Churchill wrote to the First Sea Lord and other top figures in the Admiralty demanding a 'vigilant watch' on the I.R.A. in Ireland. He reasoned that 'if they throw bombs in London why should they not supply fuel to U-boats?' The I.R.A. of course did not have any U-boat fuel, nor did anyone else in Southern Ireland. But the mere existence of the I.R.A. made such a threat worth guarding against.

Churchill, moreover, was infuriated that in 1938 de Valera had negotiated both a satisfactory settlement of the economic war and an end to British rights, under the Anglo-Irish treaty of 1921, to what were known as the 'treaty ports'. Without control of these Irish neutrality would not have been possible. The ports were Berehaven and Cobh, both near the major southern port of Cork, and, to the north, Lough Swilly in Co. Donegal. From Lough Swilly the approaches to the Mersey and the Clyde could have been more easily guarded by British warships than from Derry, and from Cobh and Berehaven destroyers could have foraged westwards after the U-boats and linked up with incoming convoys far out to sea. Without them, such operations had to start from British bases such as Lamlash, Pembroke Dock or Falmouth, thereby reducing the British range of action by approximately four hundred miles.

Discussing a London *Times* comment on the 1938 agreement which said that 'The agreement releases the government of the United Kingdom from the . . . onerous and delicate task of defending the fortified harbours of Cork, Berehaven and Lough Swilly in the event of war',

Churchill snarled in his memoirs: 'Further releases might have been obtained by handing over Gibraltar to Spain and Malta to Italy. Neither touched the existence of our population more directly.' And during a victory broadcast on May 13, 1945, Churchill vented his irritation with de Valera in public, saying:

Owing to the action of the Dublin government . . . the approaches which the southern Irish ports and airfields could so easily have guarded were closed by the hostile aircraft and U-boats.

This was indeed a deadly moment in our life, and if it had not been for the loyalty and friendship of Northern Ireland, we should have been forced to come to close quarters with Mr de Valera, or perish for ever from the earth. However, with a restraint and poise to which, I say, history will find few parallels, His Majesty's Government never laid a violent hand upon them, though at times it would have been quite easy and quite natural . . .

Throughout the war British opinion continued to be puzzled by the Irish position, much as if Wales had opted for neutrality after several hundred years of association with Britain. The British had reluctantly approved de Valera's constitution in 1937 and the abolishment of the office of governor-general, but nevertheless did not concede Ireland's right to have an ambassador accredited to her. The governor-general was not replaced for three years, and then only in ambiguous fashion: Sir John Maffey, who was actually retired at the time, was appointed British representative in Eire in November, 1939. Britain still saw Ireland as belonging to the British Commonwealth, but Sir John could not be appointed as a high commissioner because the Irish did not recognise the Commonwealth, as Whitehall did not recognise the new Irish state. He was therefore designated a representative though with diplomatic status. In London, the Irish representative, John Dulanty, continued as he had since 1930 as high commissioner for Ireland.

Irish neutrality as regards Britain had been prepared for by de Valera as far back as May 29, 1935, when, in a debate in the Dail, he said: 'Our territory will never be permitted to be used as a base for attack upon Britain.' He reiterated this stand on April 25, 1938, when signing the London agreements whereby he regained the treaty ports. He was equally farsighted where Germany was concerned. Through Joseph Walsh, secretary to the Department of External Affairs, he had informed the German ambassador, Dr Edward Hempel, on August 26, 1937, that Ireland wished to stay neutral in any war, and would do so unless attacked first, perhaps by bombing. (Even at that early stage the Irish government seemed to be more aware of the potential of the Luftwaffe than did England.) Walsh also played the Irish-American card adroitly at a lunch with Hempel, pointing out that the Irish-Americans would set their faces against any Anglo-Irish tie-up, and would do what they could to make Britain pause before attempting to invade Ireland.

Hempel explained this position to Berlin and on August 29 the German Foreign Ministry telegraphed him:

In conformity with the previous friendly relations between the two countries the German government will refrain from all hostile activity towards Irish territory and will respect Ireland's integrity provided that for her part Ireland will observe strict neutrality towards Germany. In the event of war against England the German government will do its utmost to reduce to a minimum the resulting unavoidable disadvantages for Ireland and Irish trade. Germany is entirely clear as to the difficulties facing Ireland in consequence of her geographical position.

The Germans were not being altruistic about this. If the British *had* tried to take over Ireland, Germany would not have been in a position to prevent her. Also, as Paul Leverkuehn in *German Military Intelligence* shows, a central and crippling problem bedevilled Nazi-I.R.A. affairs. Apart from bad luck, spies being captured immediately on arrival and the I.R.A. being 'riven with enmity', German military intelligence found itself continually at loggerheads with diplomats who effectively stymied all its schemes because of the doctrine that 'military plans should play second fiddle to political decisions'.

The American position was simple. As Professor Bob Stewart, now dean of the Fletcher School of Diplomacy at Tufts University, Boston, and wartime member of the State Department section dealing with Irish affairs, put it to me, 'I sure wanted Ireland in that war.' To this end the ambassador to Ireland, David Gray, a relation of Roosevelt and a wealthy man but not a career diplomat, exercised a great deal of enthusiasm and energy, but little diplomacy, and as a result was virtually *persona non grata* with the Irish government towards the end of the war. This was a pity because he was a man who genuinely loved Ireland, but as he said, 'I had a job to do.'

The mind boggles at the way he sometimes went about his job. In one of his telegrams to the secretary of state (January 7, 1941) we find him saying that he had told de Valera that 'he had capitalised on hatred of Great Britain for political reasons and so must take some responsibility for the existing popular state of mind'. Later he describes another interview with de Valera, saying:

'He began to talk about his rights. I told him that . . . the only right that he and myself enjoyed was to believe in our religion, and be burned for it if need be. Every other right depended upon force to maintain it and that he was steering a very dangerous course if he thought otherwise. He called my views the greatest exponent of force he had ever met and made it clear that it was a case of facing reality. Curious, but almost friendly, I grow fond of Mr de Valera as we argue!'

De Valera's determination to maintain neutrality seems to have checked this friendship and Gray, after an interview with de Valera in April, when, he says, 'de Valera flushed angrily and shouted that it was impertinent to question the statements of a head of state', reported:

I think the effect of a stiff attitude will be sobering. It is the only way to impress him that there are realities closing in upon him. He always outmanoeuvred Chamberlain. I no longer hope to get anything from him by generosity and conciliation. He must be made to realize that it is possible that a situation is approaching in which if it be essential to survival his ports will be seized with the approval of the liberal sentiment of the world, that he will have only the choice of fighting on the side of Great Britain or Germany.

Gray later learned that de Valera told an opposition leader that Gray had misrepresented Ireland to the secretary of state and that if the situation were not so tense, and Gray not a friend of the president, de Valera would have asked for his recall.

Apart from all this, formal American policy frequently put the Irish national temperature up, particularly over the delays in supplying American ships to Ireland. Only two were made available. Then there was the unwillingness of the Americans to let Ireland have munitions and war supplies so long as she stayed neutral, the issue of conscription in Northern Ireland and the landing of American troops in the North. There was also the Americans' belief that the Japanese embassy in Dublin was filled with Japanese spies. In fact it contained four Japanese nationalists who behaved with diplomatic decorum. The German embassy was also supposed to be a centre for transmission of information to Berlin, though the only broadcasts from the embassy occurred at the beginning of the war and consisted of weather reports for the Luftwaffe. These had ceased by 1942, as Hempel's wartime dispatches make quite clear. Even so the British and the Americans refused to believe they had ceased.

The conscription issue and the American landing were the most important episodes, raising the possibility of loss of life if the British tried to enforce conscription on Catholics in the North or the Americans attempted to cross the border. The conscription problem made the last fortnight of May, 1941 a time of acute crisis. Southern Ireland and the Northern minority were inflamed at the proposal apparently motivated by the bombings in Belfast and the fact that very few volunteers were coming forward in the North. Even the pro-British Gray was aghast and on May 24 he cabled the secretary of state:

Opposition leaders yesterday informed me that conscription without a conscientious objector's escape clause for minority Catholic nationalists will constitute a major irretrievable and probably fatal political blunder at this time and play directly into de Valera's hands with grave possibilities for American interests. They predict draft riots, the escape of draft dodgers to Southern Ireland who will be acclaimed as hero martyrs by three-quarters of the population and the fomenting of trouble by Republicans and Fifth Columnists. The clearest headed leader predicts that de Valera will seize the opportunity to escape from economic and political realities by proclaiming himself the leader of the oppressed minority and with the blessings of the Cardinal will rouse anti-British feeling and call a Holy War. I think it a very likely prediction. All classes of opinion here unite in condemning the move as calamitous. It appears to be a repetition of the same fatal blunder made during the last war. The weak and failing Ulster Government is probably seeking to sustain itself by provoking a crisis. Unless Great Britain is prepared from a military point of view to seize the whole country it appears to be madness. So little can be gained and so much lost.

Eighty thousand Irish volunteers in the British army will be disaffected, there will be no material number of Nationalist conscripts, a government, a popular majority and an army inclined to be friendly to Great Britain rather than to the Axis will become definitely hostile, possibly giving active aid to Germany and most important of all the pro-British opposition will be helpless and the opportunity for dividing the country on the question of the ports will be lost for the duration. The effect on Irish-American opinion at this juncture is not for me to estimate. This is a grave situation.

In London American Ambassador Winant saw Churchill and Eden in lengthy sessions. A stern message from de Valera warned the British against imposing conscription on Irishmen. The London meetings ended with Churchill's agreeing that Winant send the following dispatch to Hull:

The Ulster Government has weakened considerably over the weekend and in consequence the Cabinet is inclined to the view it would be more trouble than it's worth to go through with conscription. No immediate decision will be taken and in the meantime the less made of the affair the better.

That ended the proposal. My information from Unionist circles is that Northern Prime Minister Andrews had drawn back leaving Churchill with no option but to call off the attempt. Andrews apparently took the R.U.C.'s estimate of the situation more seriously than did the hard-liners in the cabinet, notably Sir Basil Brooke, later Lord Brookeborough.

Relationships with the Americans were strained again when American combat troops armed with heavy artillery landed in the North on January 26. De Valera protested against the violation of the sovereignty which the twenty-six counties claimed over the six, and most of the civilian population feared that the landings were a prelude to an invasion of the South.

Time put an end to these apprehensions and the unofficial co-operation which the Irish extended to the allies helped considerably to improve relationships. British flyers who crashed in Ireland were speedily put on the mail boat back to England or, if their planes were still serviceable, these were refuelled and returned. Many an R.A.F. man got back to England this way with a cockpit load of butter, eggs and steak. His Luftwaffe counterpart ended up in the Curragh internment camp for the duration of the war. The Germans protested about this but de Valera had accepted the American argument that any allied plane forced to land in Ireland was clearly on a non-operational mission, whereas any German plane being so far from home was obviously operational. To return the flyer to Germany would be to infringe neutrality.

Sometimes it was necessary to intern British flyers for the sake of appearances, but they managed to escape as a matter of routine. In contrast, the Germans were held behind bars until the end of the war. And when America's General Jacob L. Devers crash-landed in Ireland late in 1943 with a briefcase full of allied invasion plans concerning Operation Overlord (the D-Day code name) he was not subjected even to the pretence of internment. He was driven to the border in an official car and handed over to the Americans within a few hours of landing, his plans and his identity intact.

Also around the time of D-Day, it became known in Dublin that the Irish officials were 'worried by the overcrowding in the Curragh, because of all the interned British airmen. There were so many of them that they were beginning to affect the health of the Germans.' A new camp was opened for these internees at Gormanstown in Co. Meath to the north of Dublin, and the internees were driven off by lorry. The lorries were stopped on the way and the internees, all badly needed flyers, were put into a fleet of waiting cars and driven to the border! The Irish government also allowed the Royal Observer Corps to set up plane spotting posts around the Irish coast. A British radio transmitter operating from a van went unremarked by the Irish authorities who took part in regular staff talks with the British army heads on the same basis of mutual trust and co-operation that the Irish Secret Service continually co-operated as a matter of routine with that of Britain.

But despite all these gestures of goodwill, Irish neutrality remained balanced against a precarious background of changing international conditions and every I.R.A. action threatened it. The Irish government's position would have been swept away overnight had the Nazi-I.R.A. links led to any serious trouble for the British. That they did not may be attributable to a number of factors: the efficiency of the Irish security forces, the ignorance of the Nazis about Irish affairs, German inter-departmental warfare and above all the disorganised nature of the I.R.A. itself.

Sean Russell's departure to America had been disastrous for his bombing campaign in England and for the I.R.A. at home. In Detroit on June 6, 1939, it became disastrous for him also in a manner which brought him into the arms of the Nazis, and to an extraordinary death. He was arrested by the Detroit police, apparently as a precautionary measure, because King George and Queen Elizabeth were at the time just across the border in Canada. The subject was raised in the House of Representatives by Congressmen Sweeney of Ohio and Mac-Granery of Pennsylvania, who called it 'a very stupid blunder on the part of our Government which demonstrated British influence in the U.S.'. Russell was released on bail after McGarrity had put up a $5,000 bond and some seventy members of congress had threatened to boycott the royal visit.

A temporary bonanza of publicity boomeranged on Russell when he was served with an expulsion order to quit America by September 10. He went on the run, but although he managed to stay hidden under the Clann na Gael cloak, reduced wartime shipping prevented him from getting a boat to Ireland. One chance remained. On January 24, 1940, the German Foreign Office in Berlin received a telegram from the German consul-general in Genoa asking 'whether the German Government would be prepared to provide transport to Ireland for Sean Russell, Chief of Staff of the I.R.A., who unknown to the American Government is still in New York. If this is possible, he will make his way here by a new direct line from New York under an alias.'

Russell's arrival in Berlin from Genoa is recorded in the War Diary of May 3. Ambassador Hempel's objections to becoming involved with Russell were over-ridden by the opinion of Wermann, the under-secretary of state, who in a memorandum dated February 10, 1940, pointed out that basically Fianna Fail and the I.R.A. wanted the same thing, the reunification of the country, and that their only difference lay in their choice of methods. Wermann thought that 'by reason of their militant attitude towards England, the I.R.A. is Germany's natural ally'.

An attempt to place Russell in contact with a German agent, Captain Herman Goertz, who was setting out for Ireland at that time, misfired because Goertz had taken off from Fritzlar airfield in the early hours of May 5, just a short time before Russell arrived at the airfield to brief him. Russell was then enrolled in a course at Legel Laboratory in, as the Abwehr Diary notes, 'the use of sabotage materials'. It was while attending his bomb-making class that he was reunited with an old friend—Frank Ryan, the Republican Congress leader who had been captured by Franco's forces during the Spanish Civil War.

Ryan, an acting brigadier in the Lincoln Washington Brigade, had been captured in the late summer of 1938 by a group of Italian troops. This fact saved his life as the Italians hoped that they would be able to exchange him for one of their own officers. Had the Spaniards captured him he would have been treated like every other captured member of the brigade and shot. The Italians failed to make an exchange but by the time they had turned Ryan over to Franco's troops some months had elapsed. In the meantime a group of American journalists, who had been allowed to speak to prisoners, discovered Ryan's presence and wrote about him. In Ireland people of all political persuasion signed petitions for his release. Somewhat pathetically I.R.A. slogans—'Release Frank Ryan or else'—appeared. Ireland had adopted a policy of non-intervention in the Spanish conflict and had an ambassador in Madrid but de Valera telegrammed Franco asking him to spare Ryan. No one in Ireland knew whether the telegram had any effect until after nine months Leslie Barry, Tom Barry's wife, and a sister of Michael Price, one of the principal figures in the Irish Red Cross, discovered his whereabouts through the agency of the Red Cross.

During this time Ryan lived in a cell with eighteen other condemned prisoners. Every morning nine of the eighteen were taken out and shot and their places filled by another nine. Ryan never knew which morning was to be his turn. All he could do was scratch his name on a comb which he hoped to be able to throw through the cell window of prisoners who had not been condemned and in this way leave behind some record of his fate. He had been wounded in the fighting and his slight deafness had become marked. In the terrifying isolation caused by deafness, imprisonment and language barriers, the arrival of Leslie Barry's first food parcel must have seemed like a message from heaven.

At the end of the Spanish war de Valera arranged through Leopold Kerney, the Irish ambassador in Madrid, for a Spanish lawyer for Ryan, and de Valera saw to it that the expenses of defending his former enemy were defrayed by the Irish state. Ryan's sentence was commuted to life imprisonment, and he was granted the further concession of a monthly visit from his lawyer, Señor Champourcin, and the right to receive food parcels. Meanwhile in Germany Dr Jupp Hoven and Helmut Clissmann,* who during their student days in Ireland had been friends of Ryan (a photograph of Ryan with Clissmann and Hoven appeared on the front page of *An Phoblacht* during Ryan's editorship), supported his case. Hoven officially notified the Abwehr that in his judgement the release of Ryan under German auspices would create a good impression in Ireland and would also place Ryan

* Clissmann became a businessman in Ireland and married an Irish girl.

at Germany's disposal. His idea was eventually taken up. The Nazis approached the Spanish police authorities and Ryan's lawyer contacted the Irish ambassador, who in turn got in touch with his government. All parties agreed to Ryan's release, and he was handed over to German custody at Irun-Hendaye on July 15, 1940. He was emaciated and haggard and almost completely deaf. The Nazis drove him to Paris and took him to eat at the Tour d'Argent where Kurt Haller, section leader in Abwehr (II) Office I West in Berlin, remembers that he was 'completely flabbergasted by the whole thing and thought he was dreaming'.

When Russell and Ryan were introduced, according to Haller they 'embraced one another like brothers who had not seen each other for many years'. Russell immediately agreed to take Ryan with him back to Ireland on 'Operation Dove' a loosely defined mission which left Russell free to take any action he saw fit in Ireland. It was finally sanctioned at a meeting on August 5 of Foreign Minister Ribbentrop, Admiral Canaris, Lieutenant Colonel Lahousen, the Abwehr head and Dr Veesenmayer, in charge of Irish affairs at the Foreign Office, who introduced Russell to Ribbentrop.

Ribbentrop was offensive to Russell saying flatly that he doubted whether Russell was a genuine agent or indeed, if he were Russell at all. Apparently he disliked the Irish as a race. Despite this arrogance the Nazis thought enough of the Russell-Ryan mission to place a U-boat at their disposal, and it sailed from Wilhelmshaven on August 8, captained by Commander Von Stockhausen.

Neither Russell nor the U-boat ever reached Ireland. On August 14 Sean Russell died in Frank Ryan's arms, when they were some one hundred miles west of Galway. He had been taken ill with agonising pains in the stomach shortly after leaving and these got progressively worse. There was no doctor aboard, only a medical student as an orderly. Ryan persuaded this man to give Russell a purgative thinking that he was suffering from constipa-

tion. But it appears from the medical reports submitted
to German doctors by Ryan, the orderly, the captain and
the second in command of the U-boat, that Russell died
from perforated ulcers.

He was buried at sea with full military honours, wrapped
in a German flag. Not knowing what his mission was
intended to be nor what conditions were like in Ireland,
Ryan returned with the submarine to Germany. He
never saw Ireland again. His last days were pathetic. On
January 15 he suffered some sort of a stroke, and his
condition deteriorated progressively. It was wartime, the
hospitals were full of wounded, there was very little food,
and the aerial bombardment grew heavier and heavier.
As he was so deaf that he could not be left alone at night
because he couldn't hear the sirens, he had to sit at cafes
with a cup of coffee so that people could warn him when
the sirens sounded. His friends and contacts in the German
establishment were gradually transferred from Berlin.
An Irish friend, Francis Stuart, the writer, who was
lecturing at Berlin University, comforted him as best he
could, occasionally taking him out for a drive to one of the
Havel lakes to spend a day on the beach, and Stuart also
attempted to get the Irish chargé d'affaires to arrange a
passage for Ryan back to Ireland. But Ryan's health had
deteriorated so badly that he was unable to travel. In
January, 1944 he was taken to a sanitorium at Dresden
Loschwitz. He died on June 10, after a period of agony
during which his breathing was so painful that he had to
be placed sitting in an armchair with the back of another
before him so that he could rest his head on his arms
before speaking. He was buried in the Dresden Loschwitz
cemetery. A wooden cross giving his name as Francis
Richard appears above the grave with his date of birth
and of death inscribed on it.

Apart from the Russell-Ryan affairs the Nazis made a
number of attempts to win over the I.R.A.

Oscar C. Phaus, journalist and founder of the German

Bund, returned from America to Germany on December 2, 1938, and was approached by the Abwehr and asked to establish links with the I.R.A. in Ireland. The Abwehr knew little about the I.R.A. beyond the fact that if it carried out bombing attacks in England it must be a potential German ally. Phaus landed in Ireland on February 3 and tried to contact the I.R.A. by approaching General Eoin O'Duffy, the former Blueshirt leader. If O'Duffy, on meeting a Nazi agent, did not actually put him in touch with the I.R.A. he at least made no attempt to have him arrested. Within a matter of days Phaus had established contact and was driven by Maurice Twomey to meet members of the Army Council.

Various stories circulate about this meeting, one of them being that Phaus thought that he was going to have to shoot his way out, so unfriendly did the atmosphere become and so disbelieving was the attitude of those whom he met. A telegram from Germany, in reply to one which had been sent immediately upon his arrival at the meeting, confirmed his identity. The story seems a bit unlikely but, at all events, from then onwards Seamus O'Donovan became the principal Nazi link with the I.R.A. and later in the month visited Phaus in Hamburg with a memorandum for the Abwehr setting out the I.R.A.'s policies and the strength of its equipment. Nothing was decided about sending equipment to the I.R.A. but discussions took place about Nazi policy in the event of war between Germany and England.

O'Donovan again visited Germany in April and in August, 1939, the third journey very nearly being the I.R.A.'s final contact with the Nazis. A row with the German customs infuriated O'Donovan. The Abwehr spent so much time trying to mollify him that it was only after he had left that the Abwehr realised it had arranged courier routes for messages and money, come to agreements on wireless transmissions and on possible arms and other supplies, but had forgotten to give O'Donovan the code word for the wireless exchange which would be needed to arrange these things. A few days after the outbreak of war a code phrase—'House of Parliament'—was devised and sent to London via a Breton, Paul Moise, working for the Breton underground movement Breiz Atao.

It was not until October 29 that the first message to Germany was received from O'Donovan's transmitter. It asked about arms, but the Abwehr could not help as the message had not indicated any likely supply routes. (This transmitter was the one which the police seized on December 29 in the raid on Ashgrove House which captured D'Arcy and MacNeela.) Very little of value passed over the transmitters either from Berlin or Dublin. The I.R.A. never did succeed in setting up a supply route, nor did it respond to the German requests to cease operations against de Valera and concentrate instead on military installations in Britain and the North. Indeed one of the messages which the Irish sent the Germans told of a direct rejection of advice—the report of the I.R.A. raid on the Magazine Fort.

One can be reasonably certain about the valueless nature of the I.R.A.'s messages to Germany. Major Florence O'Donaghue and Colonel Dan Bryan, the leading figures in the Irish Secret Service during the war, both told me I.R.A. transmissions were worthless. I also spoke to one of the chief broadcasters and scriptwriters connected with this transmitter—Seamus Byrne, a solicitor and playwright whom I had known since boyhood. (He was one of the four men arrested when the police raided the house.) I spoke too to the chief broadcaster from the transmitter which the I.R.A. operated from Northern Ireland, Tarlach O'hUid, now a journalist. From the statements of all it appears virtually certain that the transmitters' main use was for the dissemination of internal propaganda to give an impression of a strength on the part of the I.R.A., which it did not really possess. In fact the discussion which the Southern radio occasioned worried German Ambassador Hempel so much that he telegraphed a strong warning to his foreign office about rumours circulating in Dublin concerning the I.R.A.-German link-ups. Hempel felt that if the Germans were to be seen helping the I.R.A. this would prejudice them in the eyes of both Irish and English—the Irish because there was a widespread antipathy towards Germany on religious grounds and the British because it might give them an excuse to breach Irish neutrality. Hempel's advice was not taken but the Germans would have saved life and money if they had listened to him.

The most important German spy in Ireland was Captain Herman Goertz who parachuted from a Heinkel on May 5, 1940, landing in County Meath near Summerhill and then managing to remain free for nineteen months. Some Irish army officers, who were not exactly pro-Nazi but were willing to make the war an opportunity for doing something about the partition issue, met Goertz. They decided against collaboration with him because of their contempt for I.R.A. security and their distrust of its military powers. There were also some nationalists, and others who had some influence with the government through language circles such as the Gaelic League, who were disposed to assist Goertz in his mission of creating difficulties for the British in the North. But here again his involvement with the I.R.A. stymied him.

He expressed a very low opinion of the movement in a series of articles, published posthumously in the *Irish Times* in August, 1947. (Goertz had poisoned himself the previous May rather than face deportation back to Germany.) He wrote:

The I.R.A. had become an underground movement in its own national sphere, heavily suppressed by men who knew all their methods. Inside the I.R.A. nobody knew what game was really played, not even their leader. Their internal means of communication were as primitive as boys playing police and brigands. They got no further than the open message in

the sock of a girl. And what messages! There was no code—
they did not want to learn the most simple code, they
preferred to sacrifice their men and women. They had not
a single wireless operator; they made no attempt to learn
messages discipline; their military training was nil. I once
said to one of them whom I admired for his personal
qualities: 'You know how to die for Ireland, but of how to
fight for it you have not the slightest idea.' In spite of the
fine qualities of individual I.R.A. men, as a body I considered them worthless.

From the start the I.R.A. had meant trouble for Goertz
who, upon landing, had marched seventy miles to Laragh,
Co. Wicklow, and the home of Mrs Iseult Stuart, wife of
a man who had befriended him in Berlin and a sister of
Sean MacBride. Mrs Stuart gave him hospitality and
brought him clothing, but a few days later, contact with
the I.R.A. having been effected, he went, on I.R.A. advice,
to the home in Templeogue of Stephen Carroll Held, a
businessman whose father was a naturalised German. On
May 23 Held's house was raided by police who missed
Goertz, but seized his transmitter and some $20,000 in
notes. This seizure alarmed the government more than
any development since the Magazine Fort raid. Five days
later the all-party National Defence Council was formed
and on June 3 400 I.R.A. suspects were rounded up and
interned in the Curragh.

The money which Goertz had suggests that the Germans
thought highly of him. In his articles he describes sending
money to a transmitting station in the North and makes
other references to helping the I.R.A. financially. But it is
very difficult to discover just what became of these sums.
I.R.A. leaders such as MacNamee, Kelly and McAteer
impressed me as being among the most honest men I have
ever met, and they all assured me that it was necessary to
stage dangerous bank robberies in order to pay I.R.A.
debts. Nor did the equipment of the rank and file ever
indicate any degree of affluence. Goertz's money seems to

have vanished into that murky limbo of espionage where nothing flourishes but crookedness, mediocrity and betrayal.

Reading his articles, and knowing that the man who wrote them committed suicide, one could not help feeling sorry for Goertz. He describes how all his efforts to get back to Germany failed, either because of police vigilance or treachery. A plan to get him away by boat from Fenit, Co. Kerry, in February, 1941 was scotched when the Irish authorities picked up his I.R.A. collaborators, and a British patrol boat waited just outside the three mile limit. He actually got away from Brittas Bay in Co. Wicklow but his engine broke down and he had to return. He tried again in September while German planes circled overhead but, he wrote, 'again my boat failed. It was extremely hard on me to stand on a broad field near the sea and watch those friendly aircraft overhead.'

Assessing the I.R.A. and Goertz's role, Veesemayer, of the Irish Section in the Abwehr, in a lengthy report which he made on November 24, 1941, on a number of telegrams which Hempel had got from Dublin concerning the Hayes affair, said of Goertz: 'His communications are mostly one sided and therefore of a relatively valueless nature . . . both the Irish and the English police are informed as to his whereabouts . . . the value of his activity in Ireland has sunk to nil.'

The only spy other than Goertz to remain at liberty for any length of time was Ernest Weber-Drohl a former strong man in a circus. He was sixty-one when he appeared in the Dublin District Court on April 24, 1940, charged with entering Ireland illegally. He convinced the court that he was, as he described himself, 'Atlas the Strong', that he had come to Ireland to look up two missing children by a sweetheart whom he had loved and lived with in Ireland in 1907 and that he landed in Ireland in a small boat from a tramp steamer which had taken him from Antwerp. The boat, he claimed, had overturned and he had to swim for his life, losing in the process his passport, marriage certificate, pipes and letters. Weber-Drohl went on to say that a sailor who had come with him from the tramp steamer in the little boat had assisted him in righting it, and that the sailor had then made his way safely back to the steamer.

The strong-man story was a nicely blended mixture of fact and fiction: the sailor had made his way back in the little boat but not to a steamer. He had come from a German U-boat that approached the Irish coast. In a rough sea, the little boat had overturned and a wireless transmitter, which Weber-Drohl was supposed to hand over to the I.R.A. to replace the one seized in Rathmines, fell overboard. He had left Wilhelmshaven aboard U-boat U37, on January 28, 1940, so prior to his appearance in court he seems to have spent at least a month at liberty in Ireland. During this period he saw Jim O'Donovan and handed over money and code words to be used when another transmitter was found. This is about all Weber-Drohl achieved because three days after his acquittal the Secret Service picked him up.

The other German spies were caught almost on landing. One, Karl Anderson was arrested in Kingsbridge Station in Dublin on June 13, 1940, the day after landing in Kerry, and three others were picked up in July. These three agents were called Tributh, Gaertner and Obed, and they had landed in Baltimore Bay on July 18, with an incredible story of courageous seafaring behind them, having sailed from Brest in a yacht, the *Soizic*, rigged like a Breton fishing boat. The yacht had been commandeered for the voyage by a famous German yachtsman, Christian Nissen. They had passed close to British warships on a number of occasions in their thirty-six foot craft before landing—and almost instant capture. Obed was an Indian, and three foreigners on a Cork road in wartime asking how to get to Dublin quite naturally attracted attention and they were arrested. None, of course, had made any contact with the I.R.A.

After 1941 the only German agent to make contact with Republican circles (and that only tangentially) was Gunther Schuetz, who made a spectacular escape from Mountjoy Jail in Dublin on February 28, 1942, after manufacturing a rope and grappling hook from some copper wire to scale the walls. He had earlier used some of the money given to him on departure from Amsterdam to buy women's clothes, allegedly for his fiancée, and dressed as a becoming young woman he made his way to the home of Kathleen Brugha (Cathal Brugha's widow) which was a centre of underground activity. Both Mrs Brugha and her daughter Noinin were active Republicans (Noinin afterwards married Seon O'Broin, one of the leaders of the raid on the Magazine Fort) and the police were actually coming to arrest her when they found Schuetz, who was using the name of Marschner. In the interval since his escape he had been put in contact with the I.R.A. and it had been arranged that a boat would be provided to take him from Dingle to Germany. However, on March 30, the day he was to go, the skipper of the boat, Charlie McGuinness, three men who were to act as crew, and the dining car attendant on the Belfast-Dublin train who was an I.R.A. courier were all arrested.

Churchill's fears about the possibility of an I.R.A.-Nazi tie-up proved groundless throughout the war. Eamon de Valera had wanted his country to be neutral and neutral it stayed, in one of the greatest diplomatic feats of the Second World War.

10 / REPUBLIC AND REPUBLICANS: I

The extraordinary doggedness of the Republican tradition persisting, despite many disasters, through the generations cannot be overlooked. Even with the disappearance of the border there would be some Republicans somewhere who would still claim to be the lawful inheritors of Ireland's revolutionary traditions, entitled to shed blood for what they believed a historically justified cause.

This sentiment was articulated on behalf of the Irish language by Diarmaid O Donnchadha* when he said:

It is charged that we pay more heed to the words of dead heroes than we do to living leaders. We accept that charge as a compliment . . . Comparison between the statements of aim of living leaders and the writings and speeches of dead heroes is the only way to be certain that the living pursue the aims of the dead. We want to make sure, to echo the words of Pearse, that they are preaching the same gospel rather than perhaps a saner and a wiser gospel.

This 'gospel of continuity' was in part responsible for the outburst of activity that took place after the Second World War. The campaign of border raids during 1956-62 was in some ways the most costly of all post-1921 I.R.A. activity. It occurred after the portcullis of years had been dropped on the events of the 1940s so that the bulk of those taking part knew of the leaders of other days only by hearsay—if at all.

And this is one of the extraordinary features of the I.R.A.: the manner in which the tradition of continuity exists side by side with a blank ignorance of earlier events and personalities. It goes far to explain the I.R.A. ethos, touching as it does on questions of Irish education generally, the I.R.A.'s own educative process or indoctrination, and the religio-politico nature of the division of the country, all of which combine so that the young I.R.A. man knows only as much about his country and Republicanism as the I.R.A. lets him know. Before turning to the 1956-62 phase of activity it is necessary to examine these forces.

It must first be understood that 'a Republican' or 'the Republic' in I.R.A. terms do not mean the same thing as

* Page 3, *The Case for the Defence; answers, based on facts and logic, to charges against the Irish Revival.*

they would, say, to a student of Plato, Rousseau or Jefferson.* A Republican is not merely a man who sees Ireland as one nation, a geographical and cultural unit, and who objects to that nation being partitioned and to the spectacle of the flag and troops of another country giving daily evidence of that partition. There are such men, of course, but let us see how the question, 'What exactly is a Republican?', is answered in a pamphlet issued to commemorate the death of Austin Stack on April 27, 1929.

Stack was condemned to death for his part in the 1916 Rising, but his sentence was commuted to penal servitude. He underwent many subsequent terms of imprisonment, and some incredible hunger strikes and other adventures, such as the smashing up of Belfast Jail in November, 1918, when he was commandant of the prisoners there. He held various ministries in the underground Republican government, and during the Civil War itself was deputy chief of staff to Frank Aiken. He is venerated by his contemporaries as the very model of a perfect Republican.

The name Republican in Ireland, as used amongst Republicans, bears no political meaning. It stands for the devout lover of his country, trying with might and main for his country's Freedom.

Such a man cannot be a slave. And if not a slave in heart or in act, he cannot be guilty of the slave vices. No coercion can breed these in the freeman.

Fittingly, the question, What is a Republican? fails to be answered in our memorial number for Austin Stack, a man who bore and dared and suffered, remaining through it all and at the worst, the captain of his own soul . . . What then was Austin Stack, Republican?

A great lover of his country. A man without a crooked

---

* We may also discount the definition of an I.R.A. prisoner in Derry Jail who rose in disgust in the dining hall one Christmas Day, on being served with a herring, to proclaim as he held the offending object between finger and thumb, 'Any man who would eat these is no Republican.'

twist in him. One who thought straight, acted straight, walked the straight road unflinchingly and expected of others that they should walk it with him, as simply as he did himself. No man could say or write of him: 'He had to do it.' That plea of the slave was not his. His duty, as conscience and love dictated, he did. The force of England, of the English Slave State, might try coercion, as they tried it many times. It made no difference. He went his way, suffered their will, and stood his ground doggedly, smiling now and again. His determination out-stood theirs, because it had a deeper foundation and a higher aim. Compromise, submission, the slave marks, did not and could not exist for him as touching himself, or the Cause for which he worked and fought, lived and died.

Fifty years after 1916 another Republican, Joe Christle, who himself took up arms in the 1950s, wrote an essay defining a Republic as he saw it. Christle split from the main body of the I.R.A. during his period of activity, but the sentiments contained in his essay would be acceptable to most members of the I.R.A. both past and present.

THE LIVING REPUBLIC!

The great purity of the Republic, the sublimity even of its object—the guarantee of equal rights and equal opportunities is precisely that which makes our force and our weakness. Our force, because it gives us the ascendancy of truth over imposture and the rights of public interest over private interest. Our weakness, because it rallies against us all the vicious; all those who in their hearts meditate the robbery of the people, all those who having robbed them seek impunity, all those who have rejected equality as a personal calamity and above all, those who embrace politics as a family trade and the nation as a prey.

It must not be forgotten that the desecrating voice of the establishment raged equally loud in denouncing Pearse in 1916 as it did in denouncing South in 1956. In Ireland the voice of the establishment has been and still is the voice of criminals and here crime massacres innocence to reign. If now no man is led out blindfold to be executed in an Irish prison yard, it is because no man rebels against the criminals in power.

In this situation the first maxim of policy for the Republic should be to conduct the people by reason and the enemies of the people by strength . . .

Let us commune with them who declared the right of the people of Ireland to the ownership of Ireland with equal rights and equal opportunities for all citizens. The men who faced the firing squads of the establishment gave testimony to the truth of what had been declared and gave the lie to every Judas who would betray them.

The people can be relied upon to rally to the Republican Ideal when Republicans themselves rally to the Ideal . . . equal rights and equal opportunities. It was for this the Republic was proclaimed and for this alone is there any meaning to Republic.

But the establishment will be heard to shout 'Oh No! Republic means Democracy and this formula is guarded by the Ballot-Box.' That is a deceit and this deceit founded the Free State and was used by clever men to cloak the surrender of 1922 as a stepping stone to the Republic. These clever men were heard to say that 'the people fought for the right to vote.' In other words the people fought for the right to choose their masters. But this is blatantly deceitful for the Founders of the Republic wrote—the people shall be master; the people who wept in Gethsemane and who died naked on the Cross.

The Republic is not a formula to be dispensed at Ballot boxes once in every five years. It is the way of life. It is not that some are chosen to be masters for this would be 'Beggars change horseback but the lash goes on'; it is, that all have admitted the reality of equality . . .

[The Republic] could not tolerate education based on privilege because in the Republic there can be no privilege . . . the Republic would encourage the fullest expression by writers, poets and artists [and] could not have troops of an alien enemy occupying part of the national territory . . .

We should with strength seek to destroy the establishment but not after destroying it seek wantonly to kill its agents for to do so would be to violate the honour of the Republic.

What made men join a movement dedicated to the establishment of such an ideal Republic? Family and environmental influences played a large part, as the careers of two of the I.R.A.'s outstanding figures show.

Sean O'Broin, one of the leaders of the Magazine Fort raid, comes from Kerry where the Civil War took a grisly turn. At Ballyseedy Republican prisoners were chained together and set to dismantle a mined barricade so that they were blown to pieces. Cathal Brugha's son Ruari, a successful businessman and Fianna Fail senator gave me this statement:

'I joined the I.R.A. at sixteen while I was still at school. It was the result of the environment in which I grew up. My father had been killed fighting in 1922 for the ideals of Easter Week, founded on a love of Ireland and its people, and an angry determination to save the nation from being completely smothered by English influences. In the struggle that followed 1916 against England, people had to endure many things. Hard decisions had to be made. Young men had been sent to their deaths in bitter fighting all over the country. Spies and informers had been executed but the leaders in this conflict were not fighting for military victory alone. The real struggle was for the mind and soul of a once proud nation, and now, at the end of it all, they were asked to swear allegiance to a foreign king and to acknowledge the right of the former enemy to keep troops in Ireland. These symbols of domination contrasted so violently with the inspiring vision of a free and independent Ireland that they were utterly unacceptable. This, I believe, is why my father made his sacrifice.

'Naturally, the atmosphere of my home was not only Republican and anti-treaty but also anti-Free State and generally derogatory of politics and politicians. I think my decision to join the I.R.A. was inevitable because, with my upbringing and background, it would have been shirking a duty not to do so. In any case, for the very young, there was an element of excitement in it. Raids, arrests, secret parades, arms classes and the occasional public parade, which were a challenge to authority, helped to make it attractive. You felt you were part of something and had a sense of identity with the high ideals of the past.

'I.R.A. policy, as I understood it, was confused. It was taken for granted that one joined the I.R.A. to get an all-Ireland Republic of which Ireland had been cheated by England with the aid of some Irish politicians. I learned that the Free State was a British dominion created by an English act of Parliament; that there was a governor-general appointed by the king of England; that we were British subjects; that Ireland was partitioned by Britain and kept that way by British troops against the will of the majority of the people. I was led to believe that the ideals of anyone who went into politics (i.e. Leinster House) would be undermined or weakened; that he would become pro-British and that it was an act of treason to the Republic to acknowledge the state or the government. This was the type of doctrine one heard or read about in *An Phoblacht*.

'The things that stand out in my mind now as being significant did not seem so then. There was an instruction to the rank and file of the volunteers [I.R.A.] to refuse to recognise the courts if charged with political offences. The theory of the *de jure* authority of the second Dail was used to justify the existence of an armed force. This theory rested on the fact that the second Dail had not been properly dissolved and that those who had refused to enter the Free State Dail retained the *de jure* authority of the second Dail. That argument was supported by reference to a statement [by de Valera] made in Leinster House that "the real authority lies outside this House". I think that the idea of the continuing authority of the second Dail had considerable influence on some of us at that time. This theory was being upheld despite successive governments being elected under a free franchise. We became the victims of an illusion that could never become a reality. It prevented constructive thought about the country and how best to serve it. But for a young person to turn his back on this teaching would have been seen as an abandonment of principle.

'To some, in that atmosphere, to do so would have been as impossible as changing one's religion. As a result, normal judgement could not be exercised and such political steps as the removal of the governor-general and the oath of allegiance, the introduction of the Irish Nationality and Citizenship Act, the recovery of the occupied ports, the new constitution with a president elected by the people—all of which were milestones in our development towards political independence and which would have been welcomed in 1922, were regarded by extreme Republicans as political stunts.

'I had resolved from the beginning to avoid gunfighting involving Irishmen because I rejected the idea of civil war. Many of the things which happened during the 1930s caused me to have misgivings. There were indiscriminate actions and shootings which were not consistent with the aims of the movement. Those in charge seemed unable to cope. All this led me to think critically and therefore independently and prevented me from becoming too deeply involved.

'As I see it now, the dilemma facing the leaders arose from their complete acceptance of the theory that force was the only way to achieve their aims. They felt committed to this policy partly through loyalty to those who had already lost their lives and also because of a deep distrust and dislike of political methods. Any deviation from the accepted principle appeared to them to be an abandonment of the struggle for Irish freedom and unity. This prevented them from considering other means.

'It is easy to criticise that campaign [Russell's against

England]. However unrealistic and ill-advised that policy may have been it is true that some brave young Irishmen, acting in good faith, took part in it for the sake of their country. They carried out extremely difficult tasks in the most dangerous conditions. They suffered ill-treatment and long terms in British jails. Some of them never fully recovered from their experiences. Their sacrifices must appear on the credit side somewhere.

'In the autumn of 1940, I was interned. In the Curragh I was struck by a curious situation. Irish soldiers were guarding alike I.R.A. and British and German internees in separate internment camps. I realised that Irish neutrality was a token of our sovereignty. I found it difficult to resent the government which had interned me because, in their view, I was not prepared to acknowledge their right to maintain order and defend the freedom of this part of Ireland. An unusual aspect of this situation was that many of us, certainly I myself, could have secured release simply by giving an undertaking. But this was what one could not do. It is one thing for a free man to declare his attitude of his own free will. It is quite a different thing for a detained political prisoner to do so in order to get out. And so many hundreds of men and some women (in Mountjoy Jail) remained in prison away from their families rather than "sign out" and lose their independence of mind and self-respect. As a result, many of them suffered torment—torn between responsibility for their dependants and loyalty to a cause.

'There is an interesting aspect of the later prison situation that is not generally known. During the invasion scare, sentenced I.R.A. prisoners in Arbour Hill detention barracks decided that, if there was a British invasion of the twenty-six counties, they would volunteer for service in the Irish army. This may not seem peculiar today, but for them it would have meant putting on the uniform of the former Free State army with its memories of deaths, executions and civil war.

'Circumstances had brought them into a cul-de-sac;

they had been taught no way of serving their country
except by arms and sacrifice. These were some of the best
elements in the nation. The stream of idealism that runs
in every generation was at that time partly diverted, as it
were, into the desert. They could have helped to supply
some of the patriotism together with the dynamism
essential in national politics. They sought nothing for
themselves; they only wished to serve their country.

'It was obvious to me that the twenty-six counties were
politically free and that the sort of activity in which the
I.R.A. had been engaged had not helped to end partition.
The six counties is a largely planned area with all the ills
that such areas possess wherever they exist in the world.
There will be extremes of political differences and loyalties
there for a long time. There is gerrymandering because
of vested interests and because of inculcated mistrust and
fear among the descendants of planter stock. We need to
understand that the division in Ireland arises out of its
tragic history and may not be quickly resolved.'

Another famous name in I.R.A. history is that of
Micksey Conway who, at the time of writing, is Brother
Maolmuire in the Cistercian community at Collon, Co.
Meath. The formidable figure of the 1930s is no more.
He is a low-sized, greying man with sincerity and decency
radiating from blue, kindly eyes, from his weather-beaten,
disciplined face and his warm, strong handshake. He was
only a boy of twelve during the Civil War but he remembers incidents such as soldiers coming to Tipperary town
and firing over the heads of looters who had taken butter
from shop windows and were trampling it into the street.*

He told me he was first attracted to the I.R.A. by the
dedication and religious fervour he saw in its leaders. It

* Tipperary, a rebel county, the home of Charles Kickham
the Fenian writer, had its share of bitter Civil War memories,
executions and divided families. One court-martial of two men
who had betrayed I.R.A. volunteers to Free State soldiers
thereby causing their deaths, was guarded by a brother of one
of the two accused, and subsequently executed, men.

matched his own religious feelings and made him see the
I.R.A. as something noble and pure. This dedication was
to lead him into some pretty desperate situations. The
Egan shooting for instance led to his death sentence, but
when he was finally reprieved, he told me, he was dis-
appointed. He had become resigned to the thought of
death for imprisonment meant constant supervision by
warders who sat beside him even while he slept, lest he
attempt to strangle himself. This seemed a far worse
fate than death in a cause he felt to be intrinsically good.*

Conway joined the Cistercians in 1951. When I met him
seventeen years later he had been to Dublin only twice in
the meantime. His normal daily routine was to get up at
4.15 and work all day, returning to bed at 8.30 p.m.—
which he found trying in summer. He was very hopeful of
the reforms and the renewal of the Church set in train
by Vatican II. Driving back to Dublin after interviewing
him, my abiding impression was that it would be difficult
to meet a more sincere man.

The sort of influences playing on the idealistic mind of
young I.R.A. volunteers may be gauged from some typical
Republican publications from the Civil War to the
present day.

In an issue of a broadsheet, *The Fenian*, dated September 13 '7th year of the Republic', probably edited by
Erskine Childers whose influence on Republican polemics

---

* This is a common attitude towards loss of life in religious
I.R.A. men. Oscar Traynor, who commanded the Dublin brigade
in the Anglo-Irish war, and had to initiate and sanction some
pretty stern actions, told how one morning in Wicklow Street he
met a man on his way to Mass in Clarendon Street Church and
it emerged that the man was also going to receive communion,
'But,' asked Traynor, 'weren't you the man who carried out
——last night? I've just bought a paper and it says he was
killed outright?' 'Yes,' replied the gunman, 'of course I am,
what's that got to do with it? That execution was sanctioned by
the legal government of Ireland. I was only doing my duty.'
With that he went off to receive communion.

T.I.R.A.   K has lasted until our day, one can trace the same threads of bitterness, high-mindedness, dedication and contempt for the institutions of the state other than those stemming from the mystical 'second Dail'. *The Fenian* always referred to the Free State as 'the Slave State' and defined its attitude thus:

In answer to some correspondents we wish to say that it is not our intention to devote space daily to the reports of the proceedings of the so-called 'Parliament' now sitting in the very appropriate premises of the Royal Dublin Society. The only parliament entitled to legislate and govern in this country is Dail Eireann, The Parliament of the Irish Republic. The Kildare Street debating club is not the Dail. It therefore is entitled to no respect or obedience from the Irish people. The only use of interest its proceedings have for us is to afford us a certain amount of amusement, or of insight into the minds of the men who have endeavoured to sell their birthright for a mess of English pottage.

Another Republican apologist, Frank Gallagher, in a pamphlet 'By What Authority?' published in London during the Civil War, defined the Republican position in a manner which would stand today for many Republicans:

Before the Treaty was signed, Civil War in Ireland was impossible. What made it possible?

For five terrible years the nation had remained united on three great principles:

1. The existence of the Republic founded in Easter Week, and confirmed by national plebiscite in 1918;

2. The sanctity of our national independence declared by the Sovereign National Assembly in January, 1919; and

3. The territorial integrity of Ireland, which had outlasted history itself.

The Treaty violated these three fundamental principles, destroying the Republic, surrendering our national independence, partitioning our ancient nation.

The significance of the Government of Ireland Act meant nothing.

The question of the oath was responsible for voluminous literature in its own right. One of the more notable pamphlets, 'The Oath of Allegiance and All that It Implies', by 'Skellig' (J. J. O'Kelly, a member of Sinn Fein's first Dail, and a noted propagandist on the Republican side) devoted most of its animadversions on the oath to 'The Lustful Henry the Eighth's' machinations, and traced those supporting (in 1925) the Free State back to the days of Henry. Throughout the pamphlet references to the debauchery of the royal line made it clear that anybody subscribing to the contemporary oath of allegiance was, if not quite incestuous, homosexual and degenerate, at least very lacking in patriotism.

Lest there be any religious scruples in the minds of I.R.A. men there was also a pamphlet entitled 'False Pastors' by Columban na Banban, who was very likely Father O'Flanagan, former vice-president of Sinn Fein, which said that the Irish bishops had the right and duty to lay down a code of behaviour for the faithful—except when they were in error. That the Irish bishops were very much in error we learn here:

It is charged that through a long course of years they have been false to this nation; that they have time and again encouraged the enemy of our people; that they have blessed those amongst ourselves who stood for the compromise of our national principles and honour, and cursed the men who were ready to fight and die to win our liberty and independence. It is charged against them that when at last in 1921 victory seemed at hand, they sided with the men who betrayed the nation; and that then, encroaching on the purely temporal, prostituting their spiritual power and profaning the most sacred things, they conspired with a domestic enemy, the most terrible our people have ever known; and that they condoned by their criminal silence the perpetration of savage and inhuman deeds. It is charged against them that they are the principal cause of the blackest crimes which stain our history, not that they were the actual perpetrators, but because, by reason of their position and influence, the part they played makes them more responsible and guilty than the actual criminals.

The constitution of the I.R.A., published by the Republican Information Bureau in June, 1932, contains a passage explaining how it is that on one hand the I.R.A. might hold secret drill sessions, be bound by oaths and passwords, and on the other, drill openly, and publish newspapers and pamphlets:

It is well to emphasise here that the Irish Republican Army is not, and never has been, what is termed a 'Secret Society'. Its existence, constitution and policy are openly declared. Secrecy as to its activities is only maintained to safeguard it from attack. The policy of the Irish Republican Army is published and proclaimed in writing and speech as openly as circumstances permit.

The justification of having an army at all reads:

Until the Republic of Ireland is freed from foreign aggression and can function freely, the necessity for the Irish Republican Army will continue. Only to a Government of the Republic can the Army give allegiance. Should the time arrive when its services will be no longer necessary to defend the nation's sovereignty, it will disband.

The flexibility of this last principle is demonstrated by the fact that in June, 1969, when armed attacks on the North had clearly failed, the I.R.A. had turned itself to defending 'the nation's sovereignty' by burning down the homes of Germans who had bought land in Ireland.

Republican theology has always been subject to this kind of interpretation. One of Peadar O'Donnell's pamphlets, 'For Or Against The Ranchers?' printed by the *Mayo News* in Westport shortly after the outbreak of the economic war, tells small farmers that:

This rancher-based cattle trade versus tillage fight now is primarily a fight on the national issue. The ranchers are not fighting against exclusion from the British market; . . . It is in their role as Imperialists that the ranchers and big farmers are warring now, and it is in their role as Nationalists that the mass of the Irish people must overwhelm them. Any leadership that does not take its stand on the full Separatist platform must, therefore, fall short of the needs of the situation.

Young men reading *An Phoblacht* would find sentiments akin to those of O'Donnell. Its editorial for March 26, 1932, contained the following:

The enemy of Irish Independence, British Imperialism, is still entrenched and active. Its immediate aim will be to stir up conflict, seeking to drive a wedge into any movement that aims at its undoing. British Imperialism stands for the maintenance of the present Social and Economic system; it is for all National organisations accordingly to fight any influences that tend to foster internal strife, mobilising en masse against the common enemy. The Treaty was imposed by force; its alternative ruthless war: it is unnatural and immoral. Partition, its changeling, is a degrading abomination, foisted upon us by the foreigner. To undo both is our obvious duty.

The *Irish Workers' Voice*, official organ of the Irish Communist Party endorsed this line in its publications. The Communist Party's inaugural meeting was held on June 4 and 5, 1933, in Dublin, where Sean Murray, the great figure in the Irish Communist Party in the 1930s, said that 'the manifesto was to be issued to the working men of Ireland, to all fellow fighters for national freedom. The delegates here today from the four corners of Ireland are living proof that a society of United Irishmen can be formed in this twentieth century.'
The *Wolfe Tone Weekly*, which began under the editorship of Brian O'Higgins in September, 1937, though not

as popular as *An Phoblacht*, was a journal of some influence until its end in September, 1939. Brian O'hUiginn (the Irish version of his name by which he was generally known) was a member of the first Dail. As a polemicist he lacked the grace and social content of Peadar O'Donnell, tending more towards Gaelic revivalism than socialism. The *Wolfe Tone Weekly* was however well edited and laid out, better than either *An Phoblacht* or the *Republican Congress*.* O'hUiginn's first editorial set the tone for the two years of his paper's existence:

What we believe in our hearts . . . of the heritage we have received from the unconquered and breathless dead. When we think of the many men who, in the full vigour and glory of their manhood, lay down their lives without a murmur of complaint or regret, we must ask ourselves this question— for what did they die? And if we are honest we must answer in their own words, spoken with their dying breath —they died for the full and complete and untrammelled freedom of all Ireland, of every sod of Ireland. They did not die for a prosperous so-called 'Free State', nor did they die for a cosmopolitan Republic. They died endeavouring, in the words of Wolfe Tone, 'to break the connection with England, the never-failing source of all our political evils.' They died endeavouring to make the Sovereign Republic of all Ireland, in the inspired words of Padraig Pearse, 'Not free merely, but Gaelic as well; not Gaelic merely, but free as well.'

Since 1916 the most important influence on all sections of Republican thought has been Padraig Pearse. Pearse's writings† derive their strength from the manner in which

---

* O'hUiginn also produced tastefully designed Celtic art work. My father, who politically could hardly have differed more from him, would never allow any Christmas cards to be bought by our family other than those produced by O'hUiginn.

† Many of them, particularly a series entitled 'Tracts for the Times', showed a markedly socialist content, a preoccupation with death, a conviction, that all must end in sadness. This

they express the ideal of Irish separatism—'Ireland Free is Ireland Gaelic, Ireland Gaelic is Ireland Free'—and from the themes of self-sacrifice and communion with the dead, which are common both in the Irish missionary tradition and in the typical Republican attitude towards serving Ireland.

'Patriotism,' he wrote, 'is in large part a memory of heroic dead men and a striving to accomplish some task left unfinished by them.' (This later appeared on a memorial programme issued by the I.R.A. at Easter 1968.)

The way in which Pearse mixed revolution and religion was particularly powerful. His statement on 'freedom and the sword' embodies teachings learned by every Irish Catholic schoolchild of his time:

'One of the sins against Faith is presumption which is defined as: "A foolish expectation of salvation without making use of the necessary means to obtain it." Surely it is a sin against national faith to expect national freedom without accepting the necessary means to win and keep it. And I know of no other way than the way of the sword: History records no other, reason and experience suggest no other.'

This quotation appears on the title-page of a document on I.R.A. policy published in June, 1932 by the Republican Publicity Bureau. It is interesting to contrast it with an entry in the diary of Fergal O'Hanlon, nineteen, who was killed in the Brookeborough raid on New Year's Eve, 1957. Across two pages recording Easter Sunday and

---

theme cropped up in short stories like 'Eoineen na nEan' (Eoineen of the Birds), 'Bridget of the Sorrows', in 'Isogain', in his poem 'The Mother' with the statement, 'I do not grudge thee Lord my two strong sons' (both Pearse and his brother Willie died before firing squads) and in his celebrated statement on the outbreak of the First World War. This trend towards morbidity may have been heightened by the death of his sweetheart, Elaine Nicholls, who was drowned off Great Blasket Island, off the coast of Kerry, while giving another girl a swimming lesson in 1909.

Monday 1956, Fergal wrote, 'I know of no way by which freedom can be obtained and when obtained maintained, except by armed men.'

The *Wolfe Tone Weekly* includes articles signed 'A Catholic Priest' on the 'Morality of Revolt', declaring that if one were revolting in the interests of the principles contained in the leading articles, one was not breaking the laws of God or man. The late Sean Dunne, a Labour deputy who spent the war years interned in the Curragh for his youthful Republicanism, described this mentality to me as being that of a '- - with a .45 wrapped in Rosary beads'. Earlier the *Weekly*, in a panel set in heavy black type that appeared in the issue of April 16, 1938, under the heading '1916', said, 'the men who took part in the Easter Week Rising were Irish in heart and soul, and their prayers were said on Irish Horn Rosary Beads. Do those who commemorate them follow their example?'

A poem in the *Wolfe Tone Weekly*, on September 11, 1937, from Jimmy Steele, at the time serving seven years, shows again how religion and Republicanism mingled.

A Prison Prayer

O, Sacred Heart of Jesus we pray to Thee today,
To aid our suffering Motherland
Upon her bloodstained way.
For loyalty to serve her,
For strength to set her free,
O, Sacred Heart of Jesus!
We send our prayer to Thee.

O, Sacred Heart of Jesus!
Look down on us today,
Make us strong and fearless soldiers,
Ever ready for the fray.
'Gainst Thine and Ireland's enemies,
Wherever they may be,
O, Sacred Heart of Jesus!
We put our trust in Thee.

Another poem in the *Wolfe Tone Weekly*, in January, 1938, was reprinted in many other Republican journals in Ireland and America. Entitled 'Who is Ireland's Enemy?', it included these stanzas:

Who is Ireland's enemy?
Not Germany, nor Spain,
Not Russia, France nor Austria;
They forged for her no chain,
Nor quenched her hearths,
Nor razed her homes,
Nor laid her altars low,
Nor sent her sons to tramp the hills
Amid the winter snow!

Who spiked the heads of Irish Priests
On Dublin Castle gate?
Who butchered helpless Irish babes,
The lust for blood to sate?
Who outraged Irish maidenhood,
And tortured aged sires,
And spread from Clare to Donegal,
The glare of midnight fires?

Who scourged our land in '98
Spread torture far and wide,
Till Ireland shrieked in woe and pain,
And Hell seemed fair beside?
Who plied the pitch-cap and the sword,
The gibbet and the rack?
O God! that we should ever fail
To pay those devils back.

Who slew the three in Manchester,
One drear November dawn,
While round them howled in fury
The devil's hungry spawn?

Who shattered many a Fenian mind
In dungeons o'er the foam,
And broke the loyal Fenian hearts
That pined for them at home?

Who shot down Clarke and Connolly
And Pearse at dawn of day,
And Plunkett and MacDiarmada
And all who died as they?
Who robbed us of McSwiney brave?
Who murdered Mellows too,
Sent Barry to a felon's grave,
And slaughtered Cathal Brugha?

Not Germany nor Austria,
Not Russia, France nor Spain
That robbed and reaved this land of ours,
That forged her rusty chain;
But England of the wily words—
A crafty, treacherous foe—
'Twas England scourged our Motherland,
'Twas England laid her low!

Rise up, o dead of Ireland!
And rouse her living men;
The chance will come to us at last
To win our own again;
To sweep the English enemy
From hill and glen and bay,
And in your name, o holy dead!
Our sacred debt to pay!

While most of this writing was propagandist rather than
literary, the *Wolfe Tone Weekly* also provided a fifteen-
year-old Dubliner, Brendan Behan, with a vehicle for his
poetic view of the deaths of Rory O'Connor, Liam Mellows, Richard Barrett and Joe McKelvey during the Civil
War. The poem appeared on December 24, 1938, under
the heading 'Four Great Names'.

The tragic events of the war also provided a deluge of pamphlets and broadsheets. One of the most interesting was showered on Dublin on St Patrick's Day, 1942, after George Plant's execution. The leaflet set out the facts from the I.R.A. point of view. But it is not the content so much as the manner of delivery that is memorable. With the aid of friends and relatives, including two Christian brothers, all of whom were subsequently arrested, Seamus G. O'Kelly, a victim of cerebral palsy but the father of four healthy children and a life-long I.R.A. and Republican publicist, arranged for 5,000 copies to be run off and then, while de Valera was attending High Mass in the nearby Pro Cathedral, had them all scattered down on Dublin from the top of Nelson's Pillar.

Brian O'Higgins's *Wolfe Tone Annual* also came out during the war years. This was a compendium of articles on separatist history, something on the lines of the *Wolfe Tone Weekly* though less detailed. In October, 1943 it was banned from appearing as a 1944 issue on the grounds that it contravened the Emergency Powers Order of 1939. It was subsequently published unaltered in 1945 and the banning reverberated through the Dail and the columns of letters to the editors for some years afterwards.

When a regular Republican newspaper, the *United Irishman*, began in July, 1947, the mixture was as before, with articles about I.R.A. leaders who had been executed, accounts of commemoration ceremonies, references to 1916 and a preoccupation with those who died for Ireland rather than with the living conditions of those who wished to live for her in the post-war years. As the younger spirits who masterminded the 1956-62 border campaign came to power, the paper developed a more militant tone and Eamonn Timmoney, O.C. of the I.R.A. group in Derry in that campaign, said, 'This little paper played an important part in developing sympathies with, and support for, the Republican movement.'

It gave articles of interest to Republicans, told the new generation about the indignities suffered by Irish patriots

at the hands of the British and Irish authorities in the past
and blended Fenianism, commentary on the contemporary
political situation in the North and attacks on the Fianna
Fail and Coalition regimes in the South. As the campaign
developed the paper devoted itself to accounts of great
victories won and battles fought. (Many were more apparent
to the editorial staff of the *United Irishman* than to the
public at large.) The contemporary *United Irishman* is well
written and laid out though the Fenian content has been
steadily diminishing and now, while occasional photographs of commemorations (in particular of Bodenstown)
occur, it tends to consist of articles reminiscent of the old
Saor Eire and Republican Congress days. Articles on
Dublin's housing conditions, on emigration and attacks on
Ireland's plan to join the Common Market form the bulk
of its contents. These, like the slogans defacing the walls
around Dublin—'E.E.C. No!'—hardly carry the same
impact as the old 'Up the I.R.A.' which, leaping at you
from dead walls, at least let you know where you stood.

But even in this more sophisticated era of Republicanism, the old dichotomy between armed force and cerebral
political movement is still apparent in the movement's
publications. Glossily produced, *The Separatist* sometimes
appears on newstands showing a map of Ireland on page
one with a Union-jacked hand lifting the six counties out of
it, while in the foreground looms a figure of an I.R.A. man
with a tommy-gun. In its introduction, the publication
states that:

The I.R.A. cannot be dismissed as mere gunmen screaming for blood. There is overwhelming support in the Republican movement today for a more realistic approach to
Ireland's ills. This school of thought is disgusted with the
way Ireland (32 counties) has been ruled for the past forty
years and advocates sweeping social reforms especially in
education. They point out that Britain has changed its
policy towards the 26 Counties and now rules by economic
rather than by political means. They will fight this cheque-

book invasion, changing tactics as it suits them. This does not mean that the I.R.A. will lay down the gun, for they still believe that the final changing of power will come only with the threat of, if not the actual use of, physical force.

As a result of all this pressure towards a sombre, brooding type of patriotism, in which death was used with something of the same spirit of the Japanese suicide flyers in the Second World War, it is not surprising that the I.R.A. should itself inflict death on some of its own members for real or imagined breaches of its code.

A man accused of a capital offence under I.R.A. law is normally given the opportunity to defend himself in a court-martial (though this did not happen in at least one case). I.R.A. court-martial regulations stipulate that the accused be tried before three officers, that he be given the opportunity to nominate a defending counsel and that the prosecution be carried out in the same way as a lawyer for the state presents a case before a judge and jury in ordinary law cases. An accused man may summon witnesses and he is normally served with a copy of the convening order showing the personnel of the court, a copy of the charge sheet and a copy of any exhibits which may be produced, so that he and his 'counsel' may prepare a defence. The regulations provide for a number of oaths, modelled on those taken in legal courts. These are administered to all court members, the legal officer, witnesses and the shorthand clerk.

Much I.R.A. time and energy went, and still goes, into the holding of such courts-martial, courts of enquiry into misdemeanours real or imagined and attendance at commemoration ceremonies. (These are tragically increased by the malfunctioning of some bomb, weapon or ambush.) The more legalistic attach importance to courts-martial, but these can prove to be fairly arbitrary affairs so far as justice is concerned. During the 'Belt and Boot Brigade' era in Belfast one court-martial occurred at which Tarlach

O'hUid was the note-taker when sentence of death was pronounced for a not very heinous misdemeanour. For some reason the principal officer of the court hesitated about sentencing the accused. A discussion began and the officer asked O'hUid, 'Well, should we execute him, or what will we do with him?' O'hUid replied, 'How about reducing him in the ranks?' This compromise was accepted but a compromise was not always forthcoming and a number of 'disappearances' that took place during bombing raids on Belfast were not from falling masonry, but from I.R.A. action. In one of these cases, the widow of the executed man was so well aware of the I.R.A.'s role that she asked a bishop to communicate with the I.R.A. for a certificate stating that her husband had been executed. The insurance company would thus have proof of death and would pay the insurance she badly needed.

The I.R.A. decided that such a document would be too incriminating and refused her request so she never got her money.

No court-martial preceded the Admiral Somerville shooting but there was one for John Egan. I asked a member of the Army Council at the time (all such verdicts have to be sanctioned by the Army Council, in theory at least) how this action could be justified. He replied, 'These things are very necessary in an organisation like the I.R.A. They are very good for morale and they serve to release tension.'

Of all the I.R.A. courts-martial that of Dan Turley on April 5, 1933, in Dublin is probably the most contentious. Turley, who had been a gallant figure during the Anglo-Irish struggle and was for a time O.C. of the Belfast brigade, was at the time of his court-martial, intelligence officer to the brigade. The position of intelligence officer is a delicate one. To get information he has to make contacts with opposing forces, rendering him susceptible to their pressures and suspect to some of his colleagues. Turley fell under suspicion after a number of raids and arrests in

Belfast pointed to an informer in the I.R.A. camp. Because of his position and record he was not informed of the feeling against him and he accompanied two other senior I.R.A. officers (one of whom supplied me with these details) from Belfast to Dublin where he learned that he was not being summoned to a convention but to a court-martial at which Michael Price was the prosecuting officer. He was found guilty of spying and sentenced to death, the sentence being commuted to banishment provided he never returned to the country again—on pain of being shot at sight.

Turley agreed to this and was taken to Glasgow by Sean Russell. However, Glasgow, for an insurance agent with his roots in Belfast and a young family to support, was not an attractive spot in the 1930s, and after about six months he returned. Between then and December 7, 1937, when I.R.A. men shot him dead on the way to Mass, Turley must have lived a haunted life. He remained in a secret room in his house most of the time, only venturing out at night. Several friends visited him and warned him that the I.R.A. was going to kill him but he protested his innocence and refused to leave his native city. After his death his sons continued in the I.R.A., though refusing to believe their father guilty. With extraordinary loyalty to both their father's name and to the organisation that had killed him they continued membership while attempting to build up a dossier proving his innocence.

In addition to Turley I was given the names of three men in the North who, it was claimed, were executed, and four more reputed to have 'disappeared' during bombing raids on Belfast.

North or south of the border, I.R.A. training has always fallen into two categories—military and intelligence work. Recruits were trained in the use of rifles and small arms and in army drill. The guns used in these sessions were always carefully stashed away afterwards and only one or

two weapons were ever available, even for a reasonably
large company. This position did not greatly alter throughout the I.R.A.'s history between 1923 and 1963. Dumps
have always been kept a closely guarded secret, but one
that the police nevertheless penetrate. A Thompson gun at
a drill session was a very rare event and the Derry unit
of the I.R.A. put down a motion at the 1953 convention
that asked that limpet mines and silencers for sten guns be
provided. But they were not available. The chief explosive
was the highly volatile 'paxo', made from potassium chlorate and paraffin wax.

I went, while researching this book, on a drill session
with a group of young I.R.A. men, and watched their
military manoeuvres, mock attacks and advances over rough
country under simulated war conditions, guns at the ready.
This group seemed well armed, as a certain amount of
surplus American war equipment inevitably finds its way
into the hands of those willing to pay for it. The 'soldiers'
wore green battledress with peaked caps and looked a little
like Korean soldiers. Armament was fairly good, with
modern looking sub-machine guns, automatic rifles, walkie-
talkies, bomb-making equipment and useful looking revolvers. Physical fitness was excellent. As this was a military
operation, nobody was anxious to fraternise with me, though
all were courteous enough.

The countryside in many parts of Ireland, even quite
close to Dublin, is mountainous and well covered so there
is little difficulty about concealment. I was told that local
farmers were friendly and interruption by police seemed
unlikely. As a precaution, I was called for at five in the
morning before it was light and I did not reach home
again until after dark, so that I could not divulge the
route, if questioned.

Everyone in that group of twenty-five to thirty people
was a small farmer, a clerk or a labourer. The disquieting
thing was that, apart from the obvious dangers to themselves and others, they had no coherent political or ideo-

logical creed, nor even a sense of humour. Particularly
now with the spread of the ecumenical movement and the
lessening of the horrors attending the word 'Communist',
the I.R.A., I would say, of all revolutionary movements in
Europe, would be the most vulnerable to a Communist
take-over.

The groundwork for the I.R.A.'s intelligence network
was established in a memorandum of February 1, 1924.
The document said that the intelligence information needed
was:

(a) GOVERNMENT OFFICES: A list of Officials, Clerks, etc.,
employed in Government Offices annotated as to whether
they are friendly (R), hostile (F.S.), doubtful (D), or neutral
(N).

(b) NEWSPAPERS: A list of the Staffs on all Dublin daily
and weekly newspapers. (Marked as above.)

(c) RAILWAYS: A list of the permanent employees at all
Dublin Termini. (Marked as in (a).)

(d) OFFICES OF PUBLIC BOARDS: A list of the Staffs and
permanent Officials of Dublin Corporation, Dublin County
Council, Rathmines Council, Employment Offices, Labour
Exchange, etc. (Marked as in (a).)

(e) TRADE UNIONS: A list of Officials, Clerks, etc. of all
Trade Unions. (Marked as in (a).)

(f) CONTRACTS: Names and addresses of all employers,
gaffers, foremen, etc., who have the giving of jobs with
particulars as to their political sympathies, and as to how
best they could be approached to employ released prisoners.

Modifications were introduced to this scheme over the
years. One could today safely add a dossier of television
personnel sympathetic or otherwise. In the 1950s photographs of Special Branch members, their home addresses,
telephone numbers and registration numbers of their cars
were also collected. But the principle remains that each
volunteer is considered to be an intelligence officer who
reports to his company commander anything he considers

may be of assistance to the movement. The amount of reportage depends on the ability of the individual.*

Another continuing source of Republican influence is the annual Bodenstown march, usually held on the Sunday after Wolfe Tone's birth date, June 20. This occupies a position in the Republican calendar, analogous to that of Easter in the Christian religion. Bodenstown is three miles from Sallins in Co. Kildare, about thirty-five miles south-west of Dublin. Visiting Tone's grave on Bodenstown Sunday one can learn a great deal about the I.R.A., and about Ireland itself.

The first procession of the day is by the Irish army. A wreath is laid on the tomb, reveille is sounded and honour paid to the founder of Irish Republicanism. A little later comes the Fianna Fail procession, when the prime minister or some other leading figure lays a wreath to the man from whom the Fianna Fail party derives its inspiration. All is quiet, decorous and generally sunlit.

After lunch comes the I.R.A., the illegal organisation whose existence is not officially recognised, whose name can be mentioned publicly only while keeping a wary eye on the Offences Against the State Act, and the grave of Wolfe Tone is again festooned with wreaths from various Republican organisations. Military commands are given, the flags of I.R.A. detachments are displayed and there is a fiery denunciation of everything symbolised by the previous two processions.

The Bodenstown oration is more than a mere denunciation. It sets the tone for the coming year's Republicanism, explains the policies of the movement, justifies them against criticism and urges those present on to greater efforts. One can judge the direction of I.R.A. policies by a study of the groups and personalities who attend Bodens-

* After the Second World War the paperback revolution inspired many young revolutionaries in the I.R.A. Eamonn Timmoney, O.C. of Derry, and Charlie Murphy, adjutant general of the movement in the early 1950s, both remarked on the influence of books by foreign underground leaders.

town in any given year. In 1931, for instance, though Cumann na Gael cancelled the special trains that normally run for the occasion, and police prevented some of the more openly militaristic from parading, the event was held with members of Fianna Fail marching together in a body. De Valera laid a wreath on Tone's grave after Peadar O'Donnell had called down the customary fire and brimstone on all those who stood in the path of I.R.A. policy. But the following year Fianna Fail were in power and the links between the two movements were becoming more tenuous. In his oration, Sean Russell said of the Dublin parliament, now led by de Valera, what Wolfe Tone had two centuries ago said of Henry Grattan's planters' parliament:

Of all parliaments beyond all comparison the most shameful and abandoned of all sense of virtue, principle or even common decency, was the Dublin government.

However, politics are politics and, this said, Mrs Tom Clarke, widow of the 1916 hero and representing the Fianna Fail, laid a wreath on Tone's grave on behalf of the Fianna Fail national executive. On this particular occasion the official army parade was held a week later, for the times were not propitious for the army and politics to mix safely.

In 1935 Tone's graveyard again rang to the sound of blows between the two sections of the movement, further weakening and embittering both sides. The next year, following the murder of Admiral Somerville the demonstration was banned altogether. It resumed in 1937 but was banned again in 1939. After the war it was the meeting place for those who initiated hostilities on the border in 1955, and was the venue for important public announcements, such as the speech by Christoir O'Neill in 1951 declaring that force would no longer be used against agents of the Southern Irish government but only against those maintaining the *status quo* in 'Occupied Ireland'.

But a casual observer is not normally aware of this

significance. The Bodenstown marchers form up in assembly fields beside the shabby old limestone village of Sallins and then march out to the graveyard itself. All around the area there are encampments of various groups. Stalls do a roaring trade selling teas and ices and people go through the crowds selling booklets with the biographies of various patriots or distributing Republican literature. But the processional route is dotted at intervals by Special Branch cars with walkie-talkies and reputedly more lethal weapons. Special Branch photographers in plain clothes with miniature cameras normally mingle with the crowd taking pictures of those present.

Most of the marchers were, when I was there, young men, generally from country districts, but there were also fathers and mothers wheeling prams, and elderly people. Behind the Republicans marched sympathetic groups. A contingent of Communists marched openly on at least one occasion. Here and there an American is to be seen, taking part in a pilgrimage. I once met one very fat old lady, barely able to walk, who had been coming for nearly fifty years. Although there were political overtones to her gesture she was making it in much the same spirit as any other woman of her generation would pay a visit to a noted shrine.

Men with wives and families chatted quite freely with me and, although the fact of my writing a book about the I.R.A. had aroused controversy within the movement (and throughout the day I was shadowed by two young men detailed to watch me by a senior member of the movement who objected to my writing), no one offered me anything other than friendly conversation and the hope that, whatever my views, I would put their case fairly.

The oration in 1967 was delivered by Cathal Goulding, a good speech which marked a radical turn in Republican policy. He said frankly that the movement's concentration on the removal of partition was a mistake and that social and economic goals must be pursued. Disquietingly and paradoxically, however, he added that to achieve these the option of the use of force must be retained. It was the old bugbear of Republicans manifesting itself again. How to get recruits and retain the support of the militants if force is eschewed? And if it is used how can the support of responsible public opinion be retained?

By a coincidence I listened to his speech in the company of Jack Mulvenna and Roddy Connolly, James Connolly's son. They are old Republican Congress stalwarts who had been involved in fights with the I.R.A. in 1934 and 1935 in that very graveyard for advocating the principles Goulding was putting forward then.

'It's fine but he's thirty years too late,' commented Mulvenna.

As we walked from the graveyard I was chatting with Charlie Murphy, one of the principal organisers of the 1956-62 border campaign. He paused to salute a neighbour, a friendly police superintendent in uniform.

'Force! My God, can you imagine anyone deliberately setting out to kill him?' commented Murphy.

Earlier I had noticed Murphy's wife Carmel standing rigidly to attention as the national anthem was played. She made an attractive picture against the sky, but she had tears in her eyes. As we drove home I asked her why.

'I was just thinking,' she said. 'Poor Wolfe Tone, the man who wanted to unite us all and there today we had three separate commemoration ceremonies and God knows how much bitterness as well.'

Violence and tragedy also fringe the edges of the major Orange parade—that on July 12 to commemorate the Battle of the Boyne. It finishes at Finaghy, about three miles from the centre of Belfast, and thereby takes the Orangemen through Catholic areas, with a consequent rise in tension. The Orange banners are gorgeously sumptuous. Brocaded and tasselled they show in bright colours 'King Billy' on a white horse leading his followers across the Boyne, Queen Victoria bestowing a Bible on a blackamoor or dour-faced men with names and styles such as 'James McFettridge, Founder of the Royal Orange Lodge, Tem-

perance Loyal Lodge, No. 708, Shankill Rd.' Union Jacks
flutter everywhere and, indeed, the Northern Irish march
under symbols of divided allegiance. In the South the
Republicans, divided from the Dublin government, nevertheless carry their country's flag.

The Northern speeches are frequently concerned with
religion and, since Vatican II, increasingly denunciatory
of the ecumenical movement. (Of late, however, some
speakers have found ecumenicism a lesser evil than the
religious indifference which would undermine the grounds
on which the province stands.) Before the resignation in
1969 of Captain Terence O'Neill as Northern prime
minister his liberal policies towards the South came under
constant fire from speakers at this ceremony.

The Orange processions with their bands, banners and
bowlers have a marked Kiplingesque air about them. When
passions and Paisleyism subside in the North it is to be
hoped that the Orange commemoration will be maintained
as a colourful remnant from the past—attended by Irishmen from all parts of Ireland, including those who walk
at Bodenstown. But at the time of writing Wolfe Tone's
hope of abolishing internal dissensions is far from being
fulfilled.

In sport, too, the ugly effects of partition can be felt.
Rugby chooses its international team from both sides of
the border, but soccer is split between the two states. This
prevents Ireland from being a world soccer power as two
weakened teams, each containing some top players in the
English league, are fielded, instead of one good team. The
Gaelic Athletic Association (G.A.A.), the largest sporting
association in Ireland, confines itself to hurling, Gaelic
football and handball, and its social occasions are devoted
to the Irish language and ceile dances. Anyone running
foreign dances, or attempting to play 'foreign games' such
as the former garrison games of rugby, soccer, cricket and
hockey, is liable to be reported by the association's vigilante
committee and expelled. There are very few Protestants

in the G.A.A. and in the North membership of the G.A.A. carries political and religious overtones.

In athletics and cycling too, partition and the shadow of the I.R.A. are noticeable. The Irish Athletic Association, founded in 1885, was the first athletic body to bring working-class people within its scope, thus becoming a national organisation. In 1922, the G.A.A. by then more concerned with hurling and football, handed over control of athletic affairs to a new body, the National Athletics and Cycling Association. Most of the N.A.C.A. trophies were presented by the I.A.A. which joined the new N.A.C.A., offering fine, Republican-sounding awards with names like the Lord Ardilaun Trophy and the Wakefield Cup.

A new athletic association was founded in 1937 to provide an international outlet after the suspension of the N.A.C.A. in 1935 by the International Federation——because the N.A.C.A. maintained an 'anti-treaty' attitude and would not accept the border. The A.A.U. 'accepted' the treaty to gain an outlet for international competitors from the South. Those from the six counties were represented by the Unionist-minded North of Ireland Amateur Athletic Association. In April, 1967, the N.A.C.A. and the A.A.U. combined to form Bord Luithchleas na hEireann (B.L.E.) (something similar, as far as N.A.C.A. was concerned, to Fianna Fail entering the Dail in 1932), which was hailed as a tremendous advance in healing old scars. However, elements in the N.A.C.A. refused to accept this settlement and led by ex-I.R.A. men such as Jim Killeen, Jack Brady and Joe Christle, they could be said to be the contemporary 'Sinn Fein of Irish sport'.

B.L.E. is recognised by the International Federation as controlling cycling and athletics in the Republic of Ireland, but the dissident wing of the N.A.C.A. which, under Christle in the 1950s was perennially engaged in clashes with the R.U.C. over carrying tricolours across the border during cycle races, is unworried by the lack of international outlet and this split will not readily heal.

The thirteen Irish language groups which would, on the face of it, appear to be I.R.A. breeding grounds, tend more to enhance existing tendencies than to sow the seeds of Republicanism. The oldest language group, the Gaelic League, was the avenue through which Tarlach O'hUid, then a young man living in London and rejoicing in the name of Hood, first became interested in an Irish Ireland, and ultimately joined the I.R.A. But he was an exception. Almost all I.R.A. men whom I questioned tended to regard the Gaelic movement as being 'parlour nationalist'. Interest in the language is a facet of their Republicanism rather than its motivating force.

Before 1916 the founder of the Gaelic league, Douglas Hyde, had quit the league because he resented the I.R.B.'s infiltration of it for political purposes. Nevertheless, so many I.R.A. men join language classes, sometimes set up by the I.R.A. as front organisations, that after the 1956-62 campaign a former chief of the Special Branch told me that the branch had to regard the language movement as an I.R.A. stamping ground and to warn superiors of certain schools that individual Irish teachers were inciting classes towards militant Republicanism. Several times the police found that captured I.R.A. lads were from a school class that had been influenced by an Irish language enthusiast.

11 / REPUBLIC AND REPUBLICANS: II

To understand the post-war I.R.A. it is vital to understand also the intellectual and religious atmosphere in Ireland at the time and to look at the educational system under which young I.R.A. men had been raised.

Neutrality had screened Ireland from world affairs, leaving her with the literally insular political problems of partition and the I.R.A. Film and literary censorship had compounded the isolation, cutting off the flow of ideas and helping to stagnate the intellectual climate still further. Television had not come to Ireland except along the south-east coast where B.B.C. programmes could be picked up faintly. And there were the country's religious beliefs affecting the Republican movement through the educational system.

The attitude of Catholics towards Protestants in the South is one of uncertainty rather than of bigotry. An Irish schoolchild speaking of a man who does not go to Mass will not say: 'He is an agnostic.' He will say: 'He's a Protestant', because, to the average child, it is only Protestants who do not go to Mass. Only 5 per cent of the South's population is Protestant, so there is no overt Protestant-Catholic clash. Such visible strains as exist are generally confined to rival pressure organisations with a religious character. For instance, it is a matter of pride to the Roman Catholic Knights of Columbus in Dublin that the order has successfully broken the monopoly of the Protestant Masons on the executive board of the Royal Dublin Society. (The society performs many valuable services for Irish agriculture and bloodstock, and stages the annual horse show.)

Nevertheless the religious divisions run deep and cannot be overlooked. One of de Valera's undoubted achievements was his allaying of the fears of the Protestant minority at his election in 1932. The Protestant *Irish Times* had urged its readers to vote for the Protestant-aiding Cosgrave regime because, 'If Fianna Fail takes office, the wealth and security of every citizen, including the ex-Unionist, will be impaired and perhaps gravely imperilled.' But in office de Valera nominated Douglas Hyde, the Protestant founder of the Gaelic League, as president under his new constitution in 1937. (When Hyde died, the then prime minister, John Costello, and his cabinet did not attend his funeral service because before Vatican II Irish Catholics were forbidden to attend Protestant church services.)

While the fears of Protestants were aroused by the prospect of de Valera in power or by any manifestation of clerical influence, the arms-length attitude which such fears engendered among Protestants was compounded by the fact that, as school children, Catholics learned nothing of phenomena in Church history such as bad popes, the Spanish Inquisition, what the word 'anathema' once signified or that the pope of the day had ordered a *Te Deum* sung in thanksgiving when he heard the outcome of the Battle of the Boyne. But they did learn in their catechisms that, 'There is only one True Church and no one can be saved out of it.' The statement was generally mitigated by a reference to Christ's statement that 'In my Father's house are many mansions' but Protestants were obviously defined as being in a very humble place in the queue for salvation.

Almost no member of my own generation, who left school in the mid-1950s, had the slightest notion of why Protestants should have wanted to remain under British rule in the North, or how religion and politics had become so interwoven that, even in the South, the flags of British regiments can be seen displayed in many Church of Ireland churches and that many Catholic Irishmen will not attend Landsdowne Rugby football ground because there are prominently displayed there the names of former Landsdowne and Wanderers' Rugby Club members who died in the First World War. In some circles, the main entrance to St Stephen's Green Park at the head of Grafton Street, which is similarly inscribed, is known as 'Traitors' Gate'.

The educational system, which furthers such prejudices, shows the marks of British influences and of the struggle between the claims of the Church and Irish nationalism which has been going on since the Act of Union in 1800.

The report of a council on education set up on May 5, 1950, to advise the government on the function of the primary school (for pupils under the age of thirteen) and its curriculum says:

'The school exists to assist and supplement the work of parents. Their first duty is to train the children in the fear and love of God. That duty becomes a first purpose of a Primary School . . . the child must *also* [my italics] take his place in human society as a citizen of the State . . . His training for this is essentially religious and moral.'

Primary schools are under the control of a clerical manager, the local parish priest or vicar, who is responsible for the appointment of teachers and the maintenance of the schools.

So much for the influence of the Church. The Nationalists too have their share. An important guide for parents, *Education in the Irish Republic*, prepared by Professor John O'Meara in 1965, describes the curriculum of a typical primary school of the period as being chiefly concerned with religious doctrine, reading and writing in Irish, and English and arithmetic. In addition there were history, geography, music and (for girls' schools) needlework. One can assess the time spent on these subjects if one remembers the primacy accorded to religious instruction in the council's report and considers the findings of Father John McNamara in his study, *Bilingualism and Primary Education in Ireland*, in which he claims that 42 per cent* of the time spent teaching in national schools was devoted to Irish. Father McNamara is a lecturer in educational psychology in St Patrick's College, Dublin. In his book Father McNamara says that in an English test between two groups of twelve-year-olds, one Irish and the other English, the English children answered three times as many questions correctly as did the Irish. He says that the Irish children had all spent 42 per cent of their time at primary school learning Irish and only 22 per cent of their time learning English.

Arthur Griffith once complained that as a result of British influences, 'Irish education is a means of washing away the original sin of Irish birth'. But in the struggle between the claims of Irish nationalism and those of the Church, neither the Irish primary nor secondary schools' curriculum in the 1940s and 1950s would have given cause to retract his statement. And this was long after the British had left. The Irish language was not restored and if one examines

* In the Dail on July 22, 1969, the minister for education put the figure at 38 per cent in primary school classes and 20 per cent in the senior classes.

the teaching of three subjects—history, English and Irish
—one sees how the effect was to send young people out
into the world generally unenlightened about the division
of their country, with a strong anti-British bias but a
paradoxically strong English bent towards literature, poetry
and mode of expression. The courses for the three subjects
during those years were laid down in the 'Rules and
Programme for Secondary Schools', published annually by
the Stationery Office.

History began with 'Early Christian Ireland, the Mission
of St Patrick and the spread of Christianity' (which to
Irish children, of course, meant the spread of Roman
Catholicism) and ended with 'The Resurgence of 1916'.
In between, the pupil learned of the invasions by Norse-
men and Normans; the Elizabethan wars; the Plantation
of Ulster; Cromwell; the Williamite wars; the penal laws;
the famine, and the movements led by O'Connell, the
Young Irelanders, the Fenians, Parnell and Arthur Griffith;
and finally the 1916 Rising. European and world history
were scarcely taught at all; only a smattering of European
affairs was imparted, ending about the period of the
French Revolution. Almost no Irish schoolchild, to my
knowledge, learned anything about the pre-First World
War era and from the Treaty of Versailles to Yalta was a
time unknown. Moreover the rules stipulated that, 'The
Irish History Course will deal only with the period from
1014 to 1921'. This in practice meant that the teaching of
history ended at 1916 and children never acquired a class-
room knowledge of the Protestant drift away from Catholic
power to the North and the emergence of a situation in
which partition became possible, or the circumstances of
the Anglo-Irish war and the Civil War. These were learned
about later, either from the subjective viewpoint of relatives, or from polemic writings in republican journals.

The English literature course gave the student very
little assistance in broadening his mind, and shut off his
access to the writings of his fellow countrymen. A typical
leaving certificate English course (that for 1951-52) offered

one Shakespearian play, *Hamlet* and one poem each by Shakespeare, Milton, Wordsworth, Shelley, Coleridge, Tennyson, and one by Yeats ('The Lake Isle of Innishfree'). Essays by Lamb, Leigh Hunt, Grey, Thackeray, Belloc, Addison, Ruskin, Newman and R.L. Stevenson were also included. Earlier in the intermediate course pupils would have done slightly better, with one essay by an Irish author, Thomas Davis. Their poetry course would have included one poem each by Aubrey de Vere, Emily Lawless, d'Arcy Magee and James Clarence Mangan.

In the Irish course students read works about the 1916 period such as 'Mo Dha Rosin' (My Two Rosaleens), a tale of young lovers parted by death in the 1916 Rising and 'Mo Sceal Fein', by An tAthair Peadar O'Laoghaire, the story of an Irish parish priest at the turn of the century. This story, describing the priest's battles with the British authorities, gave me, at any rate, the false impression that the clergy were on the side of the language revival. They were, in fact, anti-Irish because a knowledge of English enabled the Irish Church to spread throughout the British Empire.

Irish stories in the secondary school courses reflected the struggle between Church and nationalist ideologies by imparting both a propagandist and religious flavour. Themes such as the great famine were balanced by those about outwitting the power of the devil, as in the book *Seadna*, or supernatural manifestations such as that of the Christ Child in Padraig Pearse's *Isogain*.

Both Church and state were faced with a difficulty in teaching history. The system of education had given the Church a powerful source of strength through its ability to channel so much of the energy and talent of Irish boys and girls into its ranks, and to control the quantity of Irish intellectual life. In Europe, at the time of writing, Ireland, with a population North and South of four million, ranks next to the Netherlands in the actual number of Catholic missionaries sent abroad, and above Germany and France. During 1968, a year of special emphasis by the Church on missionary endeavour, Church apologists pointed with pride to the fact that the proportion of Ireland's resources expended on missionary activity was equal in percentage terms to American military expenditure in the Vietnam war.

This position was achieved by skilful Church diplomacy in playing ball with the British. But the British were, by definition, Ireland's enemies. How could this diplomacy be explained to children? For the state, after the Civil War, the problem was to give children a knowledge of highly contentious issues involving not only living persons in the two major political parties, and hundreds of thousands outside, but also the memories of recent deaths, imprisonments, hunger strikes, burnings and the many brutalities associated with the Civil War, partition and the settling of old scores. The simple answer decided on by both parties was to teach no history after 1916, and to outline very sketchily events of the nineteenth century.

In the North a somewhat similar situation exists. The Catholic children receive much the same historical instruction as do those of the South and some Irish is also taught. But the Protestant children learn almost nothing of Irish history and are instead instructed in the history of Britain. In both cases, North and South, Protestant and Catholic classrooms tend to impart the facts of the past with a gloss which takes note of contemporary politics, though in both quality and volume the educational position has improved considerably since the 1950s. When I left school in Dublin in 1954 some six thousand secondary school pupils sat for their Leaving Certificate Examination. In 1969 this figure had increased to about seventy thousand.

A Telefís Eireann series of illustrated lectures on 'The Course of Irish History' during the 1916 celebrations, edited by Father F. X. Martin of University College, Dublin, and Professor Moody of Trinity College, Dublin, appeared in paperback and had an enormous sale. While writing this book I was shown in confidence a memorandum drawn up by a group of parents, educationalists and historians at the request of the government for use as a guide in creating more realistic history courses. It will certainly go far to improve matters.* In the North a reappraisal of the history situation is also under way and the B.B.C. has done valuable work in televising a series of programmes similar to those by Telefis Eireann and reprinting them in book form. In general, in the wake of enthusiasm for the study of Irish history (generated by the commemoration of the 1916 Rising in 1966) and the goodwill that sprang from meetings between Republican Prime Minister Sean Lemass and the North's Captain Terence O'Neill in January and February, 1965, contemporary interest tends to focus on the civil rights movement rather than on how the border may be blown away.

It was the colourful minister for education, Donough O'Malley, who died in 1968, who led the move to improve the Southern Irish educational system—and it is improving out of all recognition. In the 1950s the kind of educational system I have outlined was the only one available to the vast majority of Irish schoolchildren. The governmental report, 'Investment in Education', prepared under the chairmanship of Professor Patrick Lynch, in 1966, revealed that over 50 per cent of Irish children left school at twelve.

Post-war politics had, of course, a great effect on the policies and organisation of the I.R.A. The general election of February, 1948 reaffirmed the high priority which partition and Republicanism were given in Irish affairs. Ireland had escaped the war but could not escape the post-war unemployment, high taxation, strikes and unrest. Fianna Fail had been in power for sixteen years and the country wanted a change. But while these issues were prominently discussed during the campaign, the political reaction which

* Also appearing in 1966 was my own effort to provide the first attempt at an objective survey of the years 1916-66, *Ireland Since the Rising*. It proved popular and was made recommended reading for university students of history.

they generated was canalised by the Republican movement, or more accurately by a part of it, Clann na Poblachta, which came into prominence concerned not so much with the new problems as with the old problem of partition.

The formation of Clann na Poblachta was the most important break in the ranks of 'physical force' Republicanism since the creation of Fianna Fail in 1926. For Eamon de Valera there was now Sean MacBride, and in place of the land annuities' question the tuberculosis issue presented itself. Some old Republicans, most notably Patrick MacLogan and Maurice Twomey, said 'No' to joining. However, a number of old Republicans, including Con Lehane, Michael Fitzpatrick, Noel Hartnett, Jim Killeen, Donal O'Donoghue, Dr Richard Battenbury and Finian Brenacht came together under MacBride's leadership. At public meetings throughout the country and at private ones in the Teachers' club in Dublin, the new party mushroomed into vigorous life, even enlisting people who had been on opposite sides in the Civil War.

The scheme that most caught the public imagination was a proposal to concentrate on the eradication of tuberculosis, which was then both a social and medical evil. For some reason syphilis today carries less of a social stigma than did tuberculosis in 1948. The tuberculosis issue was the brainchild of Dr Noel Browne, not a Republican but a brilliant young socialist educated at Trinity. The Clann backed him in his programme for new sanatoria and immunisation which proved a success (deaths from tuberculosis had fallen to 431 by 1961 from 3,103 in 1948), but deserted him in 1951 when the Church hierarchy objected to a health act which would have provided sex instruction from state medical staffs and would have thus taken what the hierarchy regarded as *moral* instructions out of the hands of the Church. The hierarchy also objected to free care for anyone, regardless of income. The government fell in the ensuing uproar.

The Clann also introduced the novel idea of seating Northerners in parliament, but as far as ending partition was concerned, this was a flop. In Dublin the seating of the two Northerners in the senate was taken as a sign of cross-border unity but in Belfast the move was regarded with deep suspicion. One of the men was Denis Ireland, who in the Unionist view had shown a renegade's colours by the foundation of the Irish Union movement. The other, Liam Kelly, was known to advocate the use of physical force and did in fact lead armed attacks against the North.

In the South, however, for the moment all was excitement and optimism. Clann na Poblachta which got 173,166 votes won ten seats in the elections of February 4, 1948, and Sean MacBride and Dr Noel Browne, became ministers of external affairs and of health respectively on February 18 when the new Dail met.

The new prime minister was John A. Costello of Fine Gael. He led a heterogeneous coalition which ousted Fianna Fail, 75 votes to 68. The left-wing Clann na Poblachta formed a government with Labour, which was split into two factions: National Labour; and the right-wing Fine Gael. Costello said that 'the principal objective' on which these parties were agreed was the ending of partition.

In September, during a visit to Canada, Costello announced that the government intended to repeal the External Relations Act. The statement aroused considerable surprise in Ireland. MacBride and William Norton of Labour were on record as favouring such a course, but Fine Gael during the election campaign had reaffirmed its traditional support of the Commonwealth and had subsequently said nothing to indicate a change of heart. But despite much controversy and debate the Dail unanimously agreed to pass the Republic of Ireland Act which received the president's signature on December 21. The date when the bill would go into force was held over until the following year.

Then on January 20, 1949, the Northern premier, Sir Basil Brooke, announced that a general election would be held on February 10. On January 25, Costello invited the leaders of all political parties to confer on how their

'assistance can be given to the Anti-Partition candidates
contesting seats at the General Election in the six N.E.
Counties'. Two days later at an all-party meeting in the
Mansion House, Dublin, it was decided that a public subscription should be opened to set up an anti-partition fund.
This Mansion House committee and its offspring the Anti-
Partition League provided a torrent of propaganda about
partition and published a tide of pamphlets describing
discrimination and gerrymandering.

The Mansion House committee collected more than fifty
thousand pounds. Part was devoted to supporting anti-
partition candidates in the North in the general election
and the rest to purposes such as sending anti-partition
speakers like Tom Barry and Denis Ireland on tour of
America and Britain to inveigh against the border. (De
Valera, too, went on a world tour to highlight the partition
issue.) The all-party conference also chose the date of the
Northern Ireland general election, February 10, to announce April 18—Easter Monday—as the date on which
the Republic of Ireland Act would come into force.

All this of course played straight into the Unionists'
hands. For years they had manipulated sectarian fears so
that the average working-class Northern Protestant was
conditioned to believe that if the border went, loyal Protestants would be trampled underfoot by hordes of I.R.A.
gunmen egged on by Catholic clergy. For one instance
there is an alleged version of the Sinn Fein oath which
circulates through the Orange Lodges. It was published in
the April, 1967 issue of the *Protestant Telegraph*, the
organ of the Rev. Ian Paisley. The oath is supposed to read
in part:

These Protestant robbers and brutes, these unbelievers of
our faith, will be driven like the swine they are into the sea
by fire, the knife or by poison cup until we of the Catholic
Faith and avowed supporters of all Sinn Fein action and
principles, clear these heretics from our land . . .
At any cost we must work and seek, using any method of

deception to gain our ends towards the destruction of all
Protestants and the advancement of the priesthood and the
Catholic Faith until the Pope is complete ruler of the
whole world . . .

We must strike at every opportunity, using all methods
of causing ill-feeling within the Protestant ranks and in their
business. The employment of any means will be blessed by
our earthly Fathers, the priests, and thrice blessed by His
Holiness the Pope.

So shall we of the Roman Catholic Church and Faith
destroy with smiles of thanksgiving to our Holy Father the
Pope all who shall not join us and accept our beliefs.

The Northern electorate rallied to the polls for the Unionists in such numbers as to blot out the Northern Ireland
Labour party, even to the exclusion of the outstanding
figure of Jack Beatty who had represented Mount Pottinger
for twenty-four years, and to return the Unionists with the
same majority as they held in 1921: 40 seats to 12.

In the South, however, the coalition government pressed
ahead towards the Republic, which was born to the
accompaniment of a twenty-one gun salute on Easter
Monday. Fianna Fail boycotted the christening because de
Valera said that the party stood for a thirty-two, not a
twenty-six county Republic. The ceremony at the G.P.O.
building was emotional and impressive, recalling memories
of 1916. I was a child of twelve at the time and as I
stood with my mother on the reviewing platform (my
father, the general secretary of Fine Gael, had died shortly
before), the flags, the *feu de joie*, the marching soldiers, all
raised within me emotions which, had I been older, could
well have drawn me towards the I.R.A. and its stand
against the border.

Constitutionally as well as electorally the Unionists
gained from the anti-partition campaign. In response to
their alarm at the declaration of the Republic, British
Prime Minister Clement Attlee introduced the Ireland Act

in the House of Commons on May 3. This contained the following provision:

'It is hereby declared that Northern Ireland remains part of Her Majesty's Dominions of the United Kingdom and it is hereby affirmed that in no event will Northern Ireland or any part thereof cease to be part of Her Majesty's Dominions and the United Kingdom without the consent of the Parliament of Northern Ireland.'

The new Republic was outraged at this reaction to its birth. In the Dail on May 9 all parties agreed to Costello's resolution proclaiming 'indignant protest against the introduction by the British Parliament of legislation purporting to endorse and continue the existing Partition of Ireland', and calling on the British government to 'end the present occupation of our six North Eastern Counties'. Costello in his speech added, 'We can hit the British in their pride, pocket and prestige and every effort we can make we will make if they present us with that horrible alternative.'

The country responded with mass meetings, county council resolutions, thunder from the letters to the editor and editorials in all the leading newspapers. Slogans on walls all over the country announced that the 'Border Must Go'. But the Ireland Act became law the following June and for the I.R.A., trying to pick itself up off the ground after the war years, nothing could have been more welcome than all this concentration on partition.

These were the constitutional events that aided the rebirth of violence and death, a cycle that had for so long characterised Irish Protestant and Catholic failure to stop hating each other.

In the unconstitutional I.R.A., the principal figure in the reorganisation which took place when the detainees were released from the Curragh was the priest-like Anthony Magan, a bachelor and County Meath farmer who had given all his money, time and thought to the I.R.A., a deeply religious man of the old-guard school of Irish Catholicism. In the Curragh he and Michael Conway had been the main leaders of the pro-Irish and pro-Gaelic culture group in the camp. Conway actually went into the Church and several people I interviewed told me that they felt that Magan belonged there too: when he was again interned in the Curragh during the 1956-62 campaign he organised a flourishing branch of the Legion of Mary. He was taken into the I.R.A. by Jim Killeen but after Killeen helped to form Clann na Poblachta Magan ignored him. For a man who contributed most of his waking hours and all of his family inheritance to the Republican movement such deviation was treachery. He was continually in pain from rheumatism during the 1950s but he never allowed this to interfere with his lengthy drives, all-night meetings or day and night organisational activity. A stern, unbending figure whose intransigence drove many people out of the army, he nevertheless had a compassion for his men, especially noticeable after raids when his first question was never, 'How did it go?' but, 'Is everyone all right?'

When Magan, Conway, and to a lesser extent Sean McCool, began to reorganise the I.R.A. the situation was vague and confused, almost like that after the end of the Civil War. Organisation was practically non-existent and both the ex-internees and their sympathisers who had escaped the net were deeply divided. But Magan and Conway persevered. The first general meeting of Republicans came at Bodenstown in June, 1945. There, in the inner assembly field, Magan, Conway and McCool suggested a reorganisation. After Bodenstown the idea spread, very slowly, until an apparent reversal actually enhanced its chances and the post-war strength of the I.R.A. increased.

This was the Ardee Street raid on March 9, 1946, in which a number of prominent Republicans were arrested, including Peadar O'Flaherty, Patrick Fleming, Cathal Goulding and John Joe McGirl. Magan and Conway were also picked up the following morning. What changed this apparent set-back into a springboard for further activity was that a document found at Fleming's home was read out in court and reprinted by the Irish Press. Republicans throughout the country were thus informed that an I.R.A. reorganisation was taking place. The document contained the following:

'That this meeting composed of representatives of the Cork and Dublin, Leitrim and Mayo units and of the surviving members of the 1938 Army Council resolves that the surviving members of the 1938-9 executive be summoned to a meeting for the purpose of bringing the executive up to full strength and electing an executive drawn from active volunteers.'

It was not realised at the time that publication would have an inspirational effect and Magan and Conway were convinced that disaster had befallen. They had arrived for the meeting in the Ardee Bar and found Special Branch men watching the premises as prominent Republicans walked past them, unknowingly, towards certain jail sentences. Their agitation was so great that they never thought of telephoning to warn those inside. Walking around the block, hoping to warn off late arrivals, they exchanged coats, but this ruse was noticed by the watching police who, however, allowed them to go free until the next morning. They were then both picked up at their digs, having spent a sleepless night trying to warn I.R.A. men who might have known of the meeting to prepare for visits from the police. They were given four months each and the eight other young men picked up in the raid received nine to twelve months each.

The I.R.A. also gained useful publicity that year from the death of McCaughey which occurred in the same month that the Stormont released a prominent I.R.A. man, David Fleming, because of ill-health, and from the trial of Harry White. I.R.A. drilling began again and, particularly in the North, 'the Army' began to infiltrate Irish language classes, debating classes, G.A.A. clubs and kindred bodies. The Sinn Fein party was reactivated and a newspaper, the United Irishman, was started in July, 1947. The stage was set for a new outbreak of violence.

Reflecting on the disasters of the war years Magan originated a new policy, stating publicly that it was to be used solely against the Northern administration. This policy was proclaimed at Bodenstown in 1949 by Christoir O'Neill when he said:

'The aim of the Army is simply to drive the invader from the soil of Ireland and to restore the sovereign independent Republic proclaimed in 1916. To that end, the policy is to prosecute a successful military campaign against the British forces of occupation in the Six Counties.'

This aim was unpopular with many of the rank and file, who wanted 'the Army' to turn what they conceived to be its limitless legions against the Special Branch, members of the government, and, above all, against Stephen Hayes. The subject of his elimination was discussed continuously until during a particularly stormy meeting Magan suddenly produced a revolver, handed it to one fire-eater and said, 'Here, you execute him yourself.' The subject was never mentioned again. However, splinter group activities, or some undisciplined I.R.A. man's firing of shots at a neighbour's house or letting off of gelignite bombs became magnified into nation-wide rumours of coups or assassination plots and the I.R.A. had, from time to time, to repeat its avowal concerning the use of force solely against the North lest the Southern government be prompted to take action.

The Army Council statement of Easter 1950 said that 'in order that no excuse may be provided for using coercion and to define quite clearly that the Irish Republican Army had only one enemy, England, no sanction will be given for any type of aggressive military action in the Twenty-Six County area'. The statement for the following Easter said 'all types of aggression in the Twenty-Six County area are ruled out'. But it was not until after the Omagh raid of October, 1954 that the Army Council formally told the various units that this was now official policy and incorporated it into the 'General Army Orders'. From that month, Standing Order Number Eight read as follows:

1. Volunteers are strictly forbidden to take any militant action against 26-Co. Forces *under any circumstances whatsoever*. The importance of this Order in present circumstances especially in the Border areas cannot be overemphasised.

2. Minimum arms drill shall be used in training in the Twenty-Six County area. In the event of a raid every effort shall be made to get the arms away safely. If this fails, the arms shall be rendered useless and abandoned.

3. Maximum security precautions must be taken when training. Scouts must always be posted to warn of emergency. Volunteers arrested during training or in possession of arms will point out that the arms were for use against the British Forces of Occupation only. This statement should be repeated at all subsequent Court proceedings.

4. *At all times* Volunteers must make it clear that the policy of the Army is to drive the British Forces of Occupation out of Ireland.

I.R.A. influence over Sinn Fein grew between 1946 and 1949. Speaking at Bodenstown in 1949 Cristoir O'Neill, at the time vice-president of Sinn Fein, said:

'The Republican movement is divided into two main bodies—the Military and the Civil Arms, The Irish Republican Army and Sinn Fein. Each has an important task to do. In the final analysis the work of either is as important as that of the other.'

The drawbacks of a 'physical force' policy with the I.R.A.'s resources were very much apparent to the survivors of the violent era of the 1940s who now emerged as the principal Republican leaders—the 'three Macs', as they were popularly known, Anthony Magan, Thomas MacCurtain and Padraig MacLogan. For a period of almost ten years after the end of the Second World War they discouraged an armed campaign against the North, and the decade gives evidence of political rather than military activity.

MacLogan, O.C. of South Armagh during the Anglo-Irish war, was the chief political thinker of Sinn Fein. He operated a public house in Portlaoighise and his name became familiar during the agitation to release the prisoners in Portlaoighise jail at the end of the Second World War. Like Magan, he was a man of deep religious conviction. Time-keeping in his pub was meticulous. No drunkenness or profanity was allowed. He met his wife on a pilgrimage to Lourdes and I think it symbolises his combination of religious and conspiratorial outlook that he should have kept his secret I.R.A. papers hidden in an altar that he made himself. He also headed the co-ordinating committee between Sinn Fein and the I.R.A., and one can see how the degree of control which the I.R.A. exercised over the party had extended from the results of the Sinn Fein Ard Fheis of October 7, 1951.

Mrs Margaret Buckley, president of Sinn Fein throughout the war, was demoted to merely a member of the Ard Comhairle (the controlling body) which now included Anthony Magan. MacLogan became president and the vice-presidents were Michael Traynor and Tom Doyle, who had initiated the Magazine Fort raid. Charlie Murphy, who was shortly to become adjutant-general of the I.R.A., became joint secretary with Sean Kearney, who later left to become a priest. Patrick Doyle, who had been sentenced to life imprisonment in Belfast during the war, was also elected to the Ard Comhairle. (There were some differences in policy among them. Traynor, for instance, was not happy that the I.R.A.'s *de jure* position in the eyes of the movement should give the I.R.A. control over democratically elected Sinn Fein representatives and he felt very strongly that the I.R.A. should not control Sinn Fein.)

Traynor and the 'three Macs' shared, however, the view that Ireland's fortunes would improve if the link with England were broken. They all wanted an end to partition.

They also favoured the social teachings of the papal ency-clical *Rerum Novarum*—generally in Ireland in the early 1950s opinion favoured vocationalism—and they opposed the welfare state, which (though they failed to grasp the fact) was steadily driving a wedge between North and South as the standard of living in the North rose because of the British ties they were trying to persuade Northern Catholics to break. The entire Ard Comhairle felt that the welfare state destroyed the concept of the individual, who to them was not a tool to be brought out on election day but a being who should have a continuing influence on his own economic set-up.

Their major political activity then was to draft a Sinn Fein programme to embody these beliefs within a move-ment that had traditionally rallied mass support not for social and economic policies but for the use of force, and which also held to two basic concepts of Republican-ism: Wolfe Tone's 'Breaking the link with England', and Terence MacSwiney's, 'When Ireland was wholly free Ireland was wholly Gaelic. When Ireland was wholly Gaelic, Ireland was wholly free.'

MacLogan, helped by Traynor and another prominent ex-internee, Frank MacGlynn, drew up a new constitution for Sinn Fein along with two other important plans: the 'National Unity and Independence Programme of Sinn Fein', and the 'Social and Economic Programme of Sinn Fein'. All were vetted by sympathetic clergy to ensure that they contained nothing contrary to Catholic teaching. The principles of the new constitution have a familiar look:

'That the allegiance of Irishmen and Irishwomen is due to the sovereign Irish Republic proclaimed in 1916.

'That the sovereignty and unity of the Republic are in-alienable and non-judicable . . .'

Its objectives were:

The complete overthrow of English rule in Ireland.

To bring the Proclamation of the Republic, Easter 1916,

into effective operation and to maintain and consolidate the Government of the Republic, representative of the people of all Ireland, based on that Proclamation.

To establish in the Republic a reign of social justice, based on Christian principles, by a just distribution and effective control of the Nation's wealth and resources, and to institute a system of government suited to the particular needs of the people.

To promote the restoration of the Irish Language and Irish Culture and the widest knowledge of Ireland's history; to make Irish citizens conscious and proud of their traditional and cultural heritage; and to educate the citizens of the Republic in their rights and responsibilities.

Other traditional I.R.A. policies which were retained included the non-recognition of the courts and Dail Eireann. No barrier, however, was placed on membership of local government bodies which levied a large proportion of the taxes without which parliament could not have functioned.

As the Republican movement gathered strength after the war the 'three Macs' planned, not border raids and the blowing up of bridges, but a policy of passive resistance. Michael Traynor told me that a scheme for withholding rates was worked out: the I.R.A. would protect the nationalist sympathisers who supported the idea. But the controversial question of the use of force caused a rupture within the movement as early as 1949 with the founding of the *United Irishman*. (Its first editor was Seamus G. O'Kelly, who worked from an office at 38 King St, Dublin, and produced the first issue in July, 1948.)

The paper was Republican in tone, but not controlled by the I.R.A., owing its origins to sixty pounds collected by members, principally Seamus Doyle and Tom Byrne, of a Republican club named after McCaughey. It was supported strongly by prominent Republicans no longer active in the I.R.A. But during 1948 the I.R.A. became interested in it and MacLogan demanded representation on the editorial board. A row developed over the suggestion that the paper advocate the I.R.A.'s blowing up customs huts along the border, to capitalise on anti-British feelings generated by recent political speeches. The row ended with Doyle, Byrne and O'Kelly severed from their connections with the paper.

Subsequent issues openly urged readers to 'Join the I.R.A.'. The paper was against the 'Free State' (the change to a Republic altered neither the I.R.A.'s attitude nor terminology), anti-Free Mason, anti-Communist, anti-British, and opposed to Irish newspapers carrying advertisements for jobs in England. The difference between the opposing parties was succinctly put in a letter of resignation from the paper which Michael Traynor wrote on January 4, 1949:

'The difference between us is tactical, we are fully agreed on basic principles. Yet, I have stated time after time, on the committee and before the committee was formed, that I would not be a party to organising the youth of Ireland to use force for the mere sake of using force.'

The difference between the activists and those who favoured passive resistance was more than 'tactical'. It was also the difference between one generation and another, between the men who had seen what 'action' could lead to and those who sought excitement without thinking of its consequences. As the movement gathered strength the activists gradually gained in influence and their urgings finally resulted in the campaign which began on December 12, 1956. But prior to this the exponents of force had incited the I.R.A. to carry out six raids, of which four were unsuccessful, and to plan a number of other operations, none of which came off. In this period the movement also suffered three splits: those caused by Brendan O'Boyle, Liam Kelly and Joseph Christle.

Within the I.R.A. proper the leading young activists were Charlie Murphy, Robert Russell, Eamonn Boyce, Tom Mitchell, Rory Brady and Joe Christle.

Charlie Murphy, a young Dubliner, was at the time a

tall, striking-looking figure with prematurely grey hair. A clerk in the Guinness brewery, he had joined the I.R.A. in 1950, at nineteen, after anti-partition slogans such as 'Let's Finish the Job' had put a match to the powder trail laid by a nationalist family and his boyhood reading about the war of independence. He answered an advertisement seeking help for Republican prisoners and met Tom Doyle of Sinn Fein. From the start he showed an unusual aptitude for intelligence work, one of his exploits being to obtain a camera in the shape of a fountain pen with which he photographed the entire Special Branch and compiled a card index system giving their names, addresses and numbers of their automobiles.

Robert Russell joined the movement because of family influences; he was a nephew of Sean Russell. (He later married May Smith who became chairman of Sinn Fein.)

Eamonn Boyce, who led the Omagh raid and was sentenced to ten years, is now happily married and is a bus inspector. In 1953 he had not been aware of the I.R.A.'s existence until one day he passed a large hoarding advertising an English Sunday newspaper series about the I.R.A. and showing a trench-coated figure carrying two guns. By chance, his companion at the time was Matty O'Neill, a former Curragh internee. He remarked on the garishness of the poster thinking that this portrayal had something to do with the war of independence. He was surprised when Matty replied, 'Sure, them that's running it now don't mind.' Amazed that the I.R.A. was still in existence, Boyce made further enquiries which led to his becoming a member when he was twenty-two.

Tom Mitchell, who was also sentenced to ten years for the Omagh raid, became leader of the prisoners at the Crumlin Road jail in Belfast. Elected to Westminster as M.P. for mid-Ulster he was unseated as a convicted felon in 1955 and now works as an official with Dublin Corporation—appropriately enough inspecting dangerous buildings! A formative influence on him was a lay teacher at St Joseph's Christian Brothers school at Marino, North

Co., Dublin. The teacher, later interned, was nationalistic in his interpretation of history and equated Republicanism with religion. Mitchell began to read about the wartime shootings and executions, attended Sinn Fein meetings in Abbey Street, enrolled in Sinn Fein and gravitated to the I.R.A.

Rory Brady is from Roscommon. His mother was a dedicated Republican and he himself took part in some of the most memorable events of the 1950s, including the Arborfield raid and an escape from the Curragh internment camp. He became chief of staff for a brief period in the later stages of the border campaign. (He is now a vocational school teacher.)

These young men went on holidays together, chiefly to the Irish-speaking district in the west, the Gaelteacht, and, apart from their Republicanism, shared a common interest in the Irish language and culture. At the time none of them thought more deeply about the border issue than that the British should be driven out of the North and did not appreciate the part religion played in partition. The social or economic conditions which would follow if they succeeded in their objective did not trouble them greatly. They had only an undefined feeling that the new state ought to be somehow Gaelic.

In the 1940s and early 1950s the number of men coming and going seemed quite large but in fact the movement was neither strong nor widely spread. In Cork there was, of course, Thomas MacCurtain, and older Republicans such as Michael MacCarthy and Gerry MacCarthy (no relation), J. F. Reegan, who had fought with Frank Ryan in Spain, and a number of younger men of Murphy's and Mitchell's generation. In Limerick there was Willie Gleeson. In Portlaoighise, MacLogan's base, there were some reliable men, in particular Terry O'Toole. In Lurgan there was Joe O'Hagan. In Leitrim, a county with a long tradition of rebellion, John Joe McGirl. In Drogheda Larry Grogan, who had signed the proclamation declaring the start of the bombing campaign against England. In Dundalk there was

Liam Fagan. In Derry, Eamonn Timmoney and Seamus Ramsaigh were unusually good men.

In Belfast the movement was numerically strong—Charlie Murphy told me that he remembered inspecting parades, as adjutant-general, at which there must have been hundreds present. But the fire and passion which once animated the Republicans were missing. So was most of their motivation. There had been no sectarian rioting since 1935 and the comradeship of the war years had taken some of the sting out of Protestant-Catholic relationship. Nevertheless, the I.R.A. group in Belfast was, willy-nilly, formed on a sectarian basis. No Protestants now attached themselves to the cause and the movement was almost entirely an armed Catholic one, although not representative of all Catholics. The welfare state having been introduced to the North many former Nationalists were secretly disposed to support the British link. Moreover security was weak. Incidents took place which made the Dublin I.R.A. think that the R.U.C. had sources of information in Belfast which would prejudice any attempted rising there. Bearing these in mind and also the possibility of inciting reprisals against the Catholics, whom they would not be strong enough to protect, the I.R.A. leaders decided to take no action in Belfast when the border campaign began.

The pendulum had swung from the time of the Hayes affair when Northerners went south to direct the I.R.A. —now it was to be Southerners who largely controlled the movement and directed its energies northward.

The major raids initiated before the outbreak of the border campaign were:

June 5, 1951, Ebrington Barracks, Derry.
July 25, 1953, Felstead School Officers' Training Corps, Essex.
June 12, 1954, Gough Barracks, Armagh.
October 17, 1954, Omagh Military Barracks.
April 24, 1955, Eglington Naval Air Base, Derry.
August 13, 1955, Arborfield Depot, Berkshire.

Neither the Ebrington raid nor that on Felstead attracted much attention but they did alert the R.U.C. to the need for strengthening the Northern defence.

Before the Ebrington raid the Derry unit, like every other section of the I.R.A., had been subject to a high turn-over of membership. The unit had been approximately one hundred and fifty strong in the years 1938-39 but wartime imprisonments cut down this strength and the unit was almost non-existent during 1943-45. However, following the release of internees in August, 1945 some reorganisation began, and by 1947 the unit was functioning again, at least to the extent of drilling. But this fact was so well concealed that no one was aware of the unit's existence until the I.R.A. issued a statement from Dublin saying that an arms haul had been made.

Even then a number of people in the North believed that the raid was a figment of some B-Special's imagination. Hugh McAteer's brother Eddie, the Nationalist leader, issued a statement to this effect but the raid was genuine. The I.R.A. seized twenty Lee Enfield rifles, twenty Sten machine-carbines, two Bren light machine-guns, six BESA 7.92 mm. belt-fed machine-guns and a quantity of .303 and .9 mm. ammunition.

After this raid the I.R.A. drills attracted more members and a spate of incidents occurred. R.U.C. intelligence improved and the R.U.C. began to build up defences against any large-scale campaign. R.U.C. commando units were formed, manned by personnel who had seen active service during the Second World War; wireless communications were improved, and security and fortifications at all military installations were considerably tightened.

The raid on the armoury of the Felstead School Officers' Training Corps was more ambitious and was initially successful. The raiders got away with ninety-nine rifles, eight Bren guns, ten Sten guns, a Piat anti-tank gun, a 2-inch mortar and a Browning machine-gun. But the next morning, at Bishop's Stortford, the police, noticing a suspicious van with its rear windows obscured by strips of paper and smeared with whitening material, stopped it and found the weapons inside. Three men were arrested: Cathal Goulding, Sean Stephenson and Manus Canning. The next October they were sentenced to eight years after a jury in Hertfordshire had taken one minute to find a verdict of guilty.

After sentence Goulding, who accepted responsibility as leader of the raid, said, 'We believe that the only way to drive the British Army from our Country is by force of arms, for that purpose we think it no crime to capture arms from our enemies. We make no apology for our action.' However, this declaration by Goulding, a Dublin house-painter whose father had been active in the War of Independence, aroused little echo in Ireland as the raid had been a small one and had occurred in England. It was the Gough raid, in Armagh, which caught the Irish attention. It brought, furthermore, many young men into the movement as well as arousing considerable support in America.

Six months or so before the raid Leo McCormick, training officer for Dublin, noted on a visit to Armagh that the sentry outside the barracks had no magazine in his Sten gun. He felt that some use could be made of this discovery, but his plans were interrupted when he was picked up by the R.U.C. for having incriminating documents on him and sent to jail. Charlie Murphy and Eamonn Boyce then decided that the thing to do was to plant someone in the barracks.

They called on another young Dubliner (nameless as he is still in the I.R.A.) and told him they wanted him to join the British army. He agreed immediately and was posted to Armagh. To keep contact with him, Murphy, Boyce and various girls used to travel to Armagh on Saturday nights to attend the soldiers' dances. They would leave the hall, ostensibly to court the girls but really to contact their plant and reconnoitre the barracks. In this way they learned enough to plan a raid for June 12, 1954.

The operation was launched from a farm outside Dun-

dalk about a mile south of the border. There they struck
a snag when the expected lorry didn't turn up. They therefore sent word to a local haulier telling him that there
was a load of cattle to be shifted, and when he arrived
they hustled him into a tent and took his lorry. They also
had a car, the occupants of which were to take over the
guardroom. There were nineteen raiders, armed with
Thompsons, short-arms, grenades and burglary imple-
ments. Everything worked perfectly. It was nearly three
o'clock on a busy Saturday afternoon when the car drove
through the barracks' gate. The gang held up the guardroom, hurried the sentry away from the gate and in his
place put a man who, because of his training in Ireland's
equivalent of the Territorial Army, was able to march
up and down in front of the gate in convincing fashion.
(The lorry coming behind the car overshot the gate and
had to reverse and a British army lorry, also making for
the gate, courteously pulled up to allow the I.R.A. in first
and drove by without noticing anything amiss.)

Murphy raced up the stairs to the armoury ahead of
the others. He had trouble getting his revolver out of his
pocket and was further embarrassed when the two soldiers
in the armoury refused to put up their hands. However another I.R.A. man arrived carrying a Thompson gun which
overawed the pair. Positioning a Bren gun at the armoury
window to command the barracks' square they started
loading. As each I.R.A. man came into the armoury he
held out his arms and Murphy stacked him up with as many
guns as he could carry. They got away with three hundred
and forty rifles, fifty Sten guns, twelve Bren guns (most
of which were non-operational), and a number of .22 mm.
arms.

During the course of the raid a woman, noticing that
something was wrong, had stopped an officer in the street
and urged him to go into the barracks and do something.
Once inside the gate the officer was taken under control
and, protesting that he was an officer and a gentleman,
refused to be tied until a gun was put to his head. An

N.C.O. then noticed what was happening, got into a lorry and drove for the gate, intending to block the exit. But one of the raiders stood in the gate and brandishing a revolver said, 'Back', and forced the N.C.O. to back the lorry across the barracks' square. Then he too was placed under guard in the guardroom.

The lorry containing the arms was driven away first, Boyce and the group in the car following after locking every gate and door for which they could find keys. (The keys were subsequently auctioned in America to raise funds for the I.R.A.) Luck attended the men in the lorry all the way back across the border. At the Monaghan side of the border an obliging R.U.C. man gave them the right of way and they drove the remaining seven miles without incident. Boyce met them and handed over the small arms that he and the others had carried. Everyone got into the lorry and they drove on to a dump in Co. Meath where they met Magan. His first question was, 'Is everyone all right?'

The men were dismissed, some to find their way back to Dublin by bus, others, including Joe Christle and Eamonn Boyce to return to Dublin in the lorry. Boyce sat in the body of the lorry but Christle got into the driver's cabin and, instead of following the pre-arranged route, he ordered the driver to go by the main road. On the outskirts of Dublin, a squad car, alerted to the fact that the raid had taken place, attempted to block their path. Christle ordered the driver to ram the squad car, which pulled out of the way. Later, when the lorry was being returned to its owner, two men in it were captured and interrogated. They were subsequently released as the Southern government was embarrassed by the whole affair and wished to make as little of it as possible. It was given out that nothing incriminating was found in the truck, although in fact two revolvers were seized.

The raid was a tremendous source of morale for the I.R.A. but fears were aroused by an article in the *Irish Times* speculating that the arms were intended for use in the South. To prevent this idea gaining currency the speaker at Bodenstown the following Sunday, Gearoid O'Broin, repeated once again that I.R.A. policy was directed solely against British forces in the North and said categorically that the guns would not be used against the Southern government or police force.

The raids which the I.R.A. attempted between this time and 1956 were failures, yet the Omagh raid in October, 1954, and its aftermath, brought both recruits and money to the I.R.A.

The raid (which resulted in eight young men going to prison) was made in an attempt to seize ammunition and arms. The I.R.A. had not managed to obtain much information about the layout of the barracks until the same British army agent who had helped in the Armagh raid managed to spend a night in the barracks. With his briefing in hand the raid was fixed for the night of October 16. A week before this date Magan arrived at a house in Dublin with some twenty machine-guns and gave them to Murphy and Eamonn Boyce, who was to lead the raid. Murphy, it had been decided, was too valuable a man in Dublin to risk.

Boyce had thirty-five men in his party, three armed with knives to silence the sentry who patrolled the back wall of the barracks (a duty very few were eager to undertake). Gearoid O'Broin was in charge of transport, which was to consist of two cars and a lorry, and he took equipment with which to start the British army lorries which the raiders hoped to commandeer.

Omagh Barracks, Co. Tyrone, backs on to marshes, its main gate opening on to a narrow street leading to the town. Three sentries patrolled the barracks: two watched the wall facing the town and those at right angles to it, and the third guarded the approximately one hundred yards of the back wall. The raid had been planned for the changing of these sentries but O'Broin had trouble getting a lorry. Eventually he stole one but this had caused a three-hour delay. Boyce and fifteen men then scaled the wall at about

3.30 in the morning, the remaining twenty men staying outside the wall.

The men with the knives headed for an archway in which the sentry was expected to take shelter. When he did not the raiders attacked him, using not their knives but the butts of their revolvers with which they clubbed him. The sentry, however, was an exceptionally strong man and held off the attackers. His shouts both frightened other members of the raiding gang and alerted the British soldiers in the guardroom near the main entrance. In the event of something going wrong the I.R.A. men had planned to use this gate to escape but the soldiers in the guardroom began shooting and made this impossible. The raiders retreated to the back wall and climbed it with no trouble. They escaped into the marshes, leaving their twenty comrades impotently standing outside the main entrance.

The invading party split up and disaster befell Boyce. He was unworried about immediate pursuit and returned towards the I.R.A. lorry, watching for stragglers on his way. When he was fifty yards from the lorry it drove off. He ran for it but could not catch it and, still unworried, tried in vain to unlock an R.U.C. car parked near by. He then began to walk towards the border twenty miles away but, exhausted, hungry and wet he was picked up as he attempted to take off his boiler suit in a ditch.

It is worth briefly examining here how I.R.A. prisoners were treated at this time, not least because stories of their hardships influenced I.R.A. policy and increased its recruitment. These stories also led to an I.R.A. reprisal which cost innocent lives.

Prisoners were certainly roughed up to some degree. Boyce for instance was cuffed about and forced to strip naked and then dress again in his wet clothes six times. But the worst feature of the prisoners' treatment seems to have been the method of their transportation during the time of the taking of depositions. Under English law these had to be taken in the courthouse nearest the scene of the alleged crime. As a result, the I.R.A. prisoners were taken from their cells at 5 a.m. each day, handcuffed to each other and to detectives and taken in a van across the province to Omagh.

Prisoners with weak stomachs got sick shortly after starting, and there was no sanitation available. The trips were never less than seventy miles, sometimes more. The vans often crossed into Donegal to avoid I.R.A. ambushes against the convoy which accompanied the vans. Once in Omagh the police escort was changed but the prisoners, often after a court appearance of only a minute or two, faced another five-hour journey back to jail.

Once, however, the prisoners had been sentenced they were not harshly treated beyond, of course, having to endure normal prison routine. Here the great enemy was 'the bonk', a term coined by Philip Clarke, who, with Tom Mitchell, was elected to Westminster but was later unseated as a convicted felon. 'The bonk' described the terrible depression which would descend on even the best adjusted. One of its effects was that the prisoner became unpredictable, likely to strike out at anyone—a serious matter in such an environment. Prisoners seldom dared become too friendly with each other lest they weaken the will and self-reliance, upon which they depended to get through their sentences.

The Arborfield raid led to the imprisonment of Donal Murphy, Charlie's brother. He had joined the I.R.A. in Dublin by taking much the same route as had Charlie. Interested in history he remembers being influenced in particular by the *Wolfe Tone Annual*, 'Scelig's' pamphlets and Tom Barry's book, *Guerilla Days in Ireland*. Then came the familiar sequence of events: attending Sinn Fein meetings, quite casually at first, merely stopping for a few minutes after the pictures; meeting prominent Republican figures; driving speakers to Sinn Fein meetings at Charlie's request, and finally, in 1953, joining the Dublin unit of the I.R.A., aged twenty-one.

The following year a man who was to play an important role in I.R.A. affairs contacted Donal's brother Charlie through the *United Irishman* offices, and set in train events which led to the I.R.A.'s most ambitious coup of the postwar period—and to Donal's being sentenced to life imprisonment. The man was Frank Skuse, who in autumn 1954 was a serving member of the British forces, stationed in Monmouth. Skuse had a magnificent presence being over six feet tall, red-haired and well proportioned. His father was a lieutenant commander in the British navy, and a brother is in the same organisation today. Born in rebel Cork, Skuse had sufficient Irish blood to make him eager to place such information as he possessed concerning the British military at the disposal of the I.R.A.

The Monmouth Barracks would have been easy for the I.R.A. to attack because the surrounding walls were so low, but Skuse was transferred to Arborfield in Berkshire. There he familiarised himself with its layout and obtained maps for the I.R.A., which eventually decided to attack the Royal Electrical Mechanical Engineering Depot at Arborfield.

Donal Murphy only discovered what was planned by accident but he promptly volunteered for service. After a period of training, which laid special emphasis on things such as walking on tip-toes and small-arms drill, he and a group of eleven others, led by Rory Brady, were briefed in Dublin and shown a film of Arborfield, obtained by Charlie Murphy with Skuse's aid. On August 11, 1955, the party set off for England in the mail boat from Dun Laoghaire, pretending not to recognise each other. There were several other young Irishmen on board, either emigrating to England or returning after the holidays and one of them, in the bunk beneath Murphy, showed no surprise when Murphy's .45 slid out from underneath his pillow and bounced to the floor. Donal accepted the return of his revolver with the same courtesy with which he refused an offer of guidance from a policeman who came up to him at Euston station to ask could he be of assistance. This time Donal was carrying *two* revolvers, a .38 and a .45!

The entire group spent the night in the same London hotel and set off at midnight, August 12, for the raid. They had two hired vans and a car and had spent the day surveying the depot. About a quarter of a mile out Rory Brady lined them up at the roadside, in their dungarees and berets, and warned them not to fire first but if fired on to drop on one knee and aim low. Approaching the barracks they saw a red flare and feared something had gone wrong, but as this was followed by a green one they decided it was merely a routine drill and pressed on. They captured the sentry at the gate, took him into the depot, and left Skuse in his place.

Inside the guardroom the commander of the guard was cooking beans and sausages. He dropped the plate when they appeared and Donal grabbed a sausage—the last one he got for a long time. They tied up the eighteen-man guard without difficulty, but there were five men in the guardhouse serving punishment sentences and they had to use bootlaces and ties to secure them. Then they discovered that the keys to the armoury were not where Skuse had said they would be. He was summoned from the gate, after they had blindfolded the guardroom sergeant to prevent his recognising Skuse, but he couldn't find them either (the armourer had taken them home) and they had to jemmy open the doors. In all they took five *tons* of guns and ammunition.

There were 82,000 rounds of ammunition in the van in which Donal was captured. He should have gone in the car, but Joseph Doyle was unsure of the route back to London and they went together. They were passing Ascot when a patrol car flagged them down on a routine check. They did not use their weapons because they feared that if the police failed to report to their radio control a general alert would ensue and trap their companions who were still in the armoury.

While Doyle and Murphy were being interrogated in

Wokingham police station they heard the other van go by. But the raid had been futile. James Andrew Mary Murphy, in charge of the dump at Pentonville, had hired the vans in his own name and the police traced him easily. He was captured in his digs, lying in bed. The police had little difficulty in recovering the ammunition, although the rest of the raiders got away safely. All of them except Rory Brady were back in Ireland within four hours of the raids. Brady decided to hide out in the Channel Islands for a fortnight before returning to Dublin.

Donal Murphy's imprisonment led to some far-reaching contacts between the I.R.A. and the wider world of revolution. Murphy had settled down to serve his sentence, determined that prison should not break him, when he became friendly with the Russian spy, Gordon Lonsdale, and a number of Greek Cypriots, including the guerrilla Nikos Samson. Lonsdale and he became particular friends and the Cypriots taught him Greek in return for lessons in Irish. Later these lessons developed into contacts between the I.R.A. in Dublin and the Cypriots with a view to having EOKA recruits sent to Ireland to be trained in guerrilla warfare. The I.R.A. also planned to rescue some of the Cypriots but the plans were rendered unnecessary by the signing of the London Agreements.

Murphy regarded Lonsdale as one of the most intelligent men he ever met. He had, Murphy said, an encyclopedic knowledge of world affairs and was able to talk informatively on all aspects of Irish foreign policy at the U.N., Irish domestic policies, the Church and the economy to a degree not then usually equalled by many Irish elected representatives. The warders and the prisoners apparently looked up to him, but apart from Murphy he seems to have made no effort to be friendly with any of them. With Murphy, however, Lonsdale made a point of being friendly, perhaps reasoning that with him he could fulfil the need for companionship which even the most disciplined prisoner must feel without running the risk of being undermined by a British intelligence agent. He would politely decline offers of company from other prisoners on exercise walks, until Donal joined him, and he never attempted to indoctrinate the younger man into Communism. He confided in Donal to a remarkable degree. For instance, the I.R.A. offered to help rescue him but he rejected the offer immediately, not because he thought that the plan could not succeed (at least that is what the I.R.A. says!) but because he was confident that there was no question of his serving his twenty-five-year sentence. 'If anyone thinks there is,' he said, 'they're crazy. My people are just waiting to grab a suitable British spy and they'll exchange him for me.' He was so explicit and forthcoming on the subject that the moment Greville Wynne was arrested neither the Murphys nor anyone in touch with the plan to rescue Lonsdale had the slightest doubt that here was the requisite spy.

Donal was eventually released through the intercession of Carmel Murphy, Charlie's wife, with Cardinal Heenan, a distant relative. The cardinal interested Lord Longford in the case and the earl secured a pardon for him.

In 1956 Magan decided that Cathal Goulding, in prison for the Felstead raid, should be rescued. Plans were laid and during October Sean Cronin's wife Terry chartered an Aer Lingus DC-3 in the name of a fictitious drama group, the 'Scelligs Players' (the title was derived from the name of Cronin's birthplace, Ballinascelig). The plane was filled with Cumann na mBan women and I.R.A. men, the women very curvaceous with sub-machine-gun parts, rope ladders and revolvers stashed in their underwear. Goulding was imprisoned in Wakefield and the plane was scheduled to touch down there. However it was diverted because of bad weather to Huddersfield R.A.F. base, and the party had to charter a bus to Wakefield. The group split up and made separate ways to the prison, intending to fling a rope ladder over the wall to Goulding, who was expecting the attempt. However when the rescuers got to the prison they found that there was a police patrol car circling the walls at regular intervals, and that alarm bells were sounding from within the prison. The raid was called off and the party regrouped at the bus and drove back over the mountains to the air base, unrecognised, and took off safely for Dublin.

The incident was in a way typical of the I.R.A. attitude: concern for a captured comrade, great daring and ingenuity, and a wasteful expenditure of money, energy and potentiality of personnel. The episode took £2,000 of the I.R.A.'s funds and had the police rung down the curtain on the 'Players' practically all of the I.R.A. leadership, with the exception of Magan, of whom Scotland Yard was known to have a description anyway, and MacCurtain, who lived in Cork would have been arrested in England *two months* before the border campaign proper was scheduled to begin.

Another earlier scheme that never came to public knowledge took a tremendous amount of planning and cost life. This was the abortive second Armagh raid, intended as a reprisal for the severity of the sentences imposed on the men captured after the Omagh raid and their treatment. The raiders also wanted ammunition and to boost morale, after the Omagh failure.

Unlike the first Armagh raid this attempt was to have caused destruction and, if necessary, taken life. There were between fifty and seventy picked men involved in the attempt, some of them experienced from the earlier raids. It was made clear to all that this was not merely a raid for arms, but an armed attack on a barracks which was to be burned down if possible. The raid was set for March 6, 1955, but when two trucks containing the raiding party, under Charlie Murphy, approached Keady village en route to Armagh they found it swarming with police.

Murphy decided to try another approach and sent a patrol ahead into Crossmaglen village. The main party retraced its route back over the border so as to reach Crossmaglen from a different direction. They arrived safely outside Crossmaglen, picked up their foot patrol and found that this village too was buzzing with police and B-Specials, and that barricades had been set across the roads. Murphy decided that to attack these forces would tarnish the I.R.A.'s reputation for attacking only British installations and personnel, a reputation which had been gained as a result of the Omagh raid, and he called the attack off. The party got back to Dublin unscathed, where it was learned through Joe O'Hagan of Lurgan, who had a contact on the force, that the R.U.C. had expected a raid that weekend. (For reasons of their own Magan and Murphy decided that the leak in security had come from Belfast and this was a contributory factor in the decision not to begin hostilities in Belfast when the main campaign started the following year.)

The morning after the abortive Armagh raid it was discovered that a boy of eighteen, Arthur Leonard, had been killed when his van was fired on by a B-Special patrol at Keady. Two other young people, a sixteen-year-old girl who was with Leonard and a man whose car was fired on by another jumpy B-Special patrol while driving in Co. Fermanagh, were wounded.

Ironically these happenings played into the hands of the I.R.A. It was widely assumed that the shootings had taken place as a result of Northern trigger happiness engendered by unnecessary mobilisations. Throughout the South, county councils denounced the Stormont regime and demanded that the B-Specials be disbanded. The force was likened to the Mau Mau, protest meetings were addressed by Sinn Fein polemicists and were widely attended by students and young people. In Belfast a visiting Labour deputy from Dublin, Sean Dunne, was expelled from the Distinguished Visitors Gallery for uttering shouts of 'murder' during a Stormont debate on the affair. Even the *Irish Times* became temporarily aggrieved at Stormont, observing huffily on March 8 that it was about time the Northern government developed a sense of proportion in its methods of law enforcement because 'para-military forces are an anachronism in a democratic society'.

Another destructive proposal which occupied a good deal of energy in the early part of 1955 was 'Operation Thermite', intended to inundate Eglington Naval Air Base, Derry, by blasting an embankment retaining the waters of the river Foyle. This scheme was eventually dropped, as was another plan to hi-jack an arms lorry from Omagh barracks. Throughout the period, and indeed as long as the I.R.A. has existed, plans such as these were, and are, continually being made and discarded.

Hoaxes also characterised the period: one at Rhyl, north Wales, involving four junior army officers doing National Service caused a major alert throughout England. Affecting Irish accents the officers tied up a sentry at a royal artillery training camp, and threw him into a truck, making off into the night when another sentry gave the alarm.

This occurred only two days after the Arborfield raid, at a time when English public opinion was outraged by the disclosure that sentries on duty at Arborfield were armed only with pick-axe handles. As a result the minister for war had to return to London from holiday to make a report to the cabinet which also received a special report on I.R.A. activities in Britain from the home secretary, Major Gwylym Lloyd George (later Lord Tenby). No sooner was this meeting over than the two ministers and the chief of the imperial general staff, Field Marshal Sir John Harding, were summoned to a further emergency conference with Prime Minister Sir Anthony Eden. The establishment was bracing itself for a repetition of the 1939 campaign when the four hoaxers confessed to their practical joke five days after the Eden conference, and the war office issued a communiqué apologising to the police for the trouble caused.

On September 13 more hoaxing came to light when it was announced that a sentry who had caused a widespread alarm by falsely reporting that three men had attacked him at St George's Barracks, Gosport, Hants, was to receive psychiatric treatment. On October 26 fifteen R.A.F. stations in the north of England were placed on alert by a false rumour of impending I.R.A. attack. Similar reports of bombs in planes and cinemas required checking and caused a not inconsiderable amount of inconvenience both in England and Ireland.

The public never learned, however, of the most extraordinary 'non-action' of the whole post-war period—the true story behind the attempts on the lives of the inspector general of the R.U.C., Sir Richard Pim, and his deputy, County Inspector A. H. Kennedy.

On September 26, 1957, as Kennedy and a friend, R. D. Ferris, were driving along University Road, Belfast, a bomb fastened underneath the car exploded. It was so slight a blast that the inspector garaged the car and continued his journey, believing merely that some mechanical failure had occurred. Investigation revealed what had happened and police realised that the attempt was similar to one the previous May. Then Sir Richard Pim and his wife were almost blown up by a bomb of the same type attached to their motor launch on Strangford Lough. Further investigation showed that the bombs had not been planted by the I.R.A. but by a disgruntled member of the Northern Security Forces who was, moreover, a relation of one of the leading figures in the Larne gun-running and in the creation of the Northern state. He had been disciplined after his drinking had led to repeated acts of bad conduct which, had they been committed by anyone else, would have resulted in instant dismissal. No influence could have saved him from charges of attempted murder after the bomb incidents, but, being tipped off by a friend, he entered a mental home as a voluntary patient.

In between the raids and abortive raids I.R.A. training and reorganisation went on. A month after the Armagh raid a big camp was established in Ballinascorney above Bohernabreena in the Dublin Mountains. Here over seventy men at a time from different parts of the country were trained for a week, each then returning home and training volunteers in their areas.

Security at this camp was ludicrous. On the normal weekend training sessions volunteers were expected to observe strict precautions to prevent their being followed: not speaking to each other in buses, approaching the camp site in ones and twos and so on. But no sooner would the Rockbrook bus have pulled away from its starting point in Dublin than someone would start singing the old I.R.A. marching song, 'We're off to Dublin in the Green', and before long everyone in the bus would be joining in the chorus. The buses used to pass in front of my aunt's home in Kenilworth Square, in Rathgar, and I often encountered the young singers and thought they were campers. The police knew differently.

As Tom Mitchell put it to me, 'The Special Branch were at one end of a telescope and the I.R.A. were at the other.' He remembers cycling up the Navan Road, a large suburban estate on the northern outskirts of Dublin, with a Bren gun strapped to the crossbar, dismounting under the noses of Special Branch men, who greeted him cheerfully, and then entering a field beside the main road to conduct an arms class in broad daylight.

Relations between the Special Branch and I.R.A. (or at least parts of each group) had become so relaxed since the war that no one considered it unusual for a Special Branch man to greet an I.R.A. man with a friendly 'Hello'. Both Special Branch and I.R.A. members were younger now and had no personal knowledge of the Civil War. In fact some young recruits responded so effusively to the Special Branch that a rule was instituted forbidding volunteers to talk to Special Branch men. Even so, at Ballinascorney no one objected to Special Branch men watching as Charlie Murphy and Tom Mitchell shot a colour film of the training for use in America as propaganda. Bell tents were erected and the training sessions concluded with a shoot-off, using Bren guns, Lee Enfield rifles, a few Thompsons and revolvers.

The pattern of instruction at these training camps* was unrealistic for the conditions obtaining in the North. The theory of warfare used was taken from Tom Barry's book about events thirty years past. This overlooked the fact that in Barry's day reinforcements often took up to two days to arrive at a beleaguered barracks. These young men were going into action when it needed only ten minutes to bring troops, dogs and spotter planes to the scene of an attack. On top of this, of course, was the lack of modern heavy guns and armament.

Recruits were also taught ju jitsu and knife fighting. Some fainted at the thought of knifing (particularly at one especially realistic session in a hired room in Power's Hotel, Dublin, where a medical poster was attacked with carving knives and had a terminal effect on the careers of some would-be freedom fighters) but after the success of the Armagh raid there was great euphoria at classes and in camps. It was assumed that the British would run away when the I.R.A. loomed up out of the night, the faces of the raiders smeared with blacking.

13 / SPLITS IN THE RANKS

While raids and training continued so did another familiar I.R.A. activity—splits in the organisation. In the decade after the war the policies of Brendan O'Boyle, Joseph Christle and Liam Kelly, all of whom diverged from the main stream of 'physical force' Republicanism, occupied almost as much of the I.R.A.'s time as did preparations for the border campaign itself.

---

* At a camp at Kildare before the Omagh raid the I.R.A.'s armaments were almost lost. A short-sighted look-out dashed up to the officer in charge to inform him that there were 'tanks, red lights, white lights everythin' comin' '. As previously arranged, the officer immediately got all the weapons placed in a heap, set explosives around them and prepared to blow up the lot, when someone else reported that the 'tanks' etc. were nothing but the traffic on the main road some distance away!

It is of interest here to turn briefly to America and the Irish-American societies in the post-war period.

The war and close surveillance by the F.B.I. put an end to the Clann na Gael's activities in 1939-46, but in March, 1946, it was reorganised following a convention of the various branches. Despite the war there was almost thirty thousand dollars in the kitty but a split occurred among the clubs and their members over whether this money should be used to build a monument in Dublin to Sean Russell or saved against the day when a new generation of I.R.A. would arise in Ireland and require funds for another uprising. The pro-monument section, led by James Conaty and Joseph Stynes, won the day in 1949 and notified the anti-monument leaders by letter of their expulsion from the movement.

The anti-monument section led by Tadg Brosnan, Paddy Smith, Paddy Thornbury and James Brislanne, was still relatively powerful but it split in 1952, when Brendan O'Boyle went to New York looking for support for a campaign of his own. The pro-monument group healed its row with the Paddy Mahoney section, which had split over the speakeasy issue in 1930, through the good offices of the Dublin I.R.A. which sent over a man called Monaghan to act as peace-maker among all the sundered wings of the Clann. He failed, however, to heal the breach between the pro- and anti-monument sections and in fact the pro-monument section subsequently suffered a split itself in 1956.

Apart from the Clann, which was and is strongest in New York, Chicago and Philadelphia, the many Irish-American groups which exist throughout the States were also likely supporters when bombs began to go off along the border. Some of these societies are little more than a joke. I have on my desk a circular seeking support for a group whose letter-heading proclaims that it has branches in New York, Boston, Philadelphia, Cleveland and San Francisco. Accompanying this was a handbill showing a starving, sad-eyed child behind barbed wire. The caption to the drawing reads:

'This child's father is in a concentration camp in occupied Ireland.'

Now I have very little sympathy with the political troglodytes who so largely comprise the Unionist region of Northern Ireland, but there are no concentration camps in the North of Ireland. I don't think that the originators of that circular were deliberately guilty of dishonesty, but to understand both Irelands, with their constantly shifting groupings and feudings, it is necessary to visit both countries frequently. Irish Americans still suffer from ignorance of the realities of life and politics in Ireland.

A few days before writing these lines I was visited in my office by Roddy Connolly, a life-long Republican socialist. He was accompanied by a young Irish-American priest anxious to make contacts in the North on behalf of a civil rights movement founded in New England to help the Northern Catholics. Because he was in Connolly's company I contented myself with the briefest questioning of his background, and provided him with several introductions. Two days later Eoin MacNamee called in, fresh from Boston, where he told me that he had been told in Clann na Gael circles about a Protestant clergyman, who was seeking support for civil rights—a man of the same name as the young priest. I did not check into the Boston civil rights movement, but if I were in the I.R.A. and a similar confusion arose over a Clann emissary I can understand the tensions and uncertainty which might arise.

Along with the splits and the confusions, the generosity of the average Irish American also exists and is a very real and all-pervasive fact of Irish-American life. Charlie Murphy told me he met with several acts of personal generosity from Americans. Men donated their personal savings to the movement when the border campaign began, or collected money for the movement like the member of the Red Branch Knights' Society of San Francisco who came to Ireland personally to hand over a cheque for $3,000 raised by the Branch. At its peak American aid averaged about £3,000 a month, continuing the tradition of Irish Americans in every decade, whether they were supporting Tom Clarke and his newspaper *Irish Freedom*, or Maurice Twomey and *An Phoblacht*, or Brendan O'Boyle and his ill-fated campaign of 1952-55.

In the hot-house atmosphere of fears and splits after 1945 O'Boyle decided to form his own group. He had joined the I.R.A. while a student at Queen's University, Belfast, in 1940, been captured the following year and was one of the escapees from Derry Jail in the big break-out of March 20, 1943.

His American funds campaign owed its inception to the merest fluke. A Mrs Tom Leonard, formerly of Co. Tyrone where her family and that of her husband were active in the I.R.B. and I.R.A., was holidaying in Dublin with her daughter in 1947 when O'Boyle was pointed out to them in O'Connell Street as 'One of *them*. He's a good lad.' That was the only contact the Leonards had with O'Boyle until two years later when Mrs Leonard, attending a meeting in New York of the United Irish Counties Association, recognised him when he stood up to speak from the floor. He was on a business trip and, seeing the meeting advertised, went to it in the mistaken belief that the association might offer some prospect of revolutionary action. (It is, in fact, a highly constitutional body.) Mrs Leonard spoke to him after the meeting and invited him to her home the following Sunday. Among the guests was Harry Short, a kindly fanatic. Crippled from birth in his native Armagh, he had served with the Fianna in the War of Independence and emigrated to America afterwards. Like Joe McGarrity he devoted his life to the movement.

Short invited O'Boyle to meet some friends, including a member of the pro-monument group of the Clann. Realising that O'Boyle did not have the support of the I.R.A.— otherwise they would have been informed of his visit and he would not have been making himself known in circles

like those of the United Irish Counties Association—
Short and some other members of the group then took him
to the home of Tadg Brosnan from Kerry, a former
I.R.A. leader and, since emigrating to New York, a worker
for Clann na Gael.

After a time of probing and questioning O'Boyle ventured as a general observation the fact that 'there's a good
group at home, if they got support. Do you people think
they could get support?' The others thought this quite
possible despite problems. The Clann was split; O'Boyle
was not 'official'; the Clann men were all in their late
fifties or early sixties; and American law does not look
kindly on the use of its territory and resources for the
fomenting of revolution in other countries (unless of course
such activities are confined to the hands of government
agencies), so there were likely to be difficulties with the
F.B.I. (Indeed it is because of these difficulties that I
must omit dates and names of surviving group members
who still live in the U.S. lest they find themselves behind
bars in the evening of their lives.)

O'Boyle returned to Ireland and tried to get control of
the younger element of the I.R.A. and become chief of
staff. The group in America was to raise funds, purchase
and arrange for the shipping of arms and ammunition to
Ireland.

O'Boyle wrote to Short in August saying that he would
require about ten thousand dollars, five hundred Thompson
sub-machine guns and substantial numbers of rifles, ammunition and hand grenades. He would need these to
achieve any sort of success against the Stormont government, plus the men to use them and a back-up of friendly
houses, doctors, intelligence service and transport, would
be required. However in the conditions obtaining in
Ireland at the time both the request and its execution were
doomed to end in failure and misery. The I.R.A. mistrusted O'Boyle and thought he was getting money for
personal use. Murphy and Magan had him shadowed
constantly and the Special Branch also watched him be-

cause they suspected him of smuggling across the border.

In America also opinion was divided as to the wisdom of helping O'Boyle. One of the most influential figures on the Irish-American scene, the chief representative of the Irish Hospitals Sweepstake's organisation, himself an ex-secretary of the Clann and a man who could smuggle elephants in and out of America if he chose, warned Short on the 'Sweep' grapevine to have nothing to do with the campaign. But Short decided to persevere. He told me that he reasoned, 'O'Boyle is a Northerner. We'll have the fight in Ulster and not in the South. We'll get away from bloody civil war in the South.'

With this in view Short contacted a group of Northern Irish emigrants who, with the addition of one Kerry man, formed the Northern Action Committee. Its members were Felix O'Byrne, Paddy Thornbury, Tom Leonard, Frank Curran, Frank Donnelly, Tommy Guy, like the others a former I.R.A. man but who had taken the Free State side in the Civil War, and Tadg Brosnan, the only non-Ulsterman. They met in August, 1949, in a hotel in Times Square (no minutes were taken for obvious reasons), and Short read O'Boyle's letter to them. The committee was then set up.

Committee organisation was simple. For secrecy the members decided that in correspondence they would always sign their mothers' names. The only hard and fast organ-isational rule was that if Short thought the subject war-ranted it any member of the group must be prepared to meet him without delay at any time. The committee asked for contributions of $100 from friends and associates and had impressive receipt forms printed from a design invented by Joe McGarrity's daughter. In all the group sent about fifteen thousand dollars to Ireland between 1949 and 1960. (About two-thirds of this was sent to Brendan O'Boyle and when he was killed the group transferred its support to Liam Kelly.) They tapped all the county associations for money but the greatest support was from Kerry, Cork, Tipperary, Down, Armagh and Tyrone.

The *modus operandi* for raising funds was to show arms to representatives of different groups and explain the purpose of both weapons and collection, but the committee's motives were sometimes questioned. A problem also arose because part of the Clann was supporting the 'official' I.R.A. and opposed O'Boyle's schemes. Some prominent Irish Americans, such as the 'Sweep' executive, also continually used their influence to scotch support for either organisation on the grounds that both were equally suicidal and futile. Then, too, the minimal secrecy which the committee imposed was sometimes sufficient to cause trouble. One holidaying Tyrone man met Liam Kelly in Ireland and, remembering his subscription in New York, thought that the money was being sent to Kelly. Kelly understandably made it known that he had no money and this caused controversy. Another prominent Irish American, John MacIvor, wrote to Charles MacGleenan (one of the staunchest and best informed Republicans in the country), in Armagh to ask him what he knew about an I.R.A. man called MacAllister who was planning an uprising in the North. Not knowing that O'Boyle was using the name Mac-Allister, MacGleenan replied that he had never heard of him. This kind of incident was always sorted out, but there was enough gossip, among other problems, to make O'Boyle's plans for a campaign very difficult to put into action.

The committee did do away with one convention which had been a continuing source of friction between the I.R.A. and Clann na Gael. Historically the Clann and the I.R.A. were on an equal footing so far as leadership of the joint movement was concerned, but the committee agreed to place itself entirely under the command of O'Boyle, and to ask nothing of him except leadership. Short secretly hoped that O'Boyle would prove himself the strong man of an all-Ireland Republic.

Great ingenuity and daring were shown in securing arms and transporting them to Ireland, not only under the noses of the American and Irish authorities, but also of the hostile wing of the Clann in America and of the equally hostile I.R.A. in Ireland who were ready at any time to commandeer arms intended for O'Boyle. One shipment of ten revolvers and five tear-gas pencil-guns consigned to him at a Dublin hotel was, in fact, hi-jacked by the I.R.A.

The story of the arms procurement activities of the committee reads at times like a film scenario. On the Pulaski Skyway outside New York one evening a car driven by one of O'Boyle's sympathisers developed a flat tyre, which was fixed with the aid of a helpful policeman who duly received a five-dollar bill for his services, unaware that in the boot of the car were two 100-lb. tins of napalm which had just been stolen from the Brooklyn Naval Yard.

One of the most useful suppliers of arms was a gangster whom a member of the group met accidentally. It was he who supplied the tear-gas guns and he was making excellent progress with the supply of revolvers when he decided to expand his activities and began turning up machine-guns. This ceased following a gangland murder involving the use of a machine-gun taken from Brooklyn Pier. The police circulated the serial numbers of stolen weapons and the committee discovered it had been given weapons in the missing serial range.

O'Boyle too proved himself an expert in customs' evasion. He had an almost incredible network of contacts. He once, thanks to a contact, cleared Idlewild Airport with his papers in order but carrying in his luggage several dozen revolvers and many thousand rounds of ammunition. He had the customs at Cobh, where the transatlantic liners from America traditionally call, particularly well organised. A shipment from New York of nine cases of ammunition was once sent to him at Cobh without his being told of the number of cases in the consignment. He only collected eight. One case was left aboard the liner and made a round-the-world cruise before the liner again docked at Cobh and a horrified O'Boyle was telephoned in Dublin by a customs official who told him that there was a case addressed to him awaiting clearance at the docks. His customary helper was off duty when he arrived but he managed to get his case through the customs without opening it to declare the contents.

But all his daring and ingenuity were not proof against the weight of gossip and intrigue that gradually crushed down O'Boyle's spirit. The dour reality of the Northern political scene caused his organisation to dwindle away. By July, 1952, he was dependent on a neighbour and his wife, who were not members of his group to go with him on a mission to blow up Stormont telephone exchange. When the neighbour's baby fell sick O'Boyle's wife Carmel offered to take her place. They got to their destination safely and Carmel and the neighbour stepped out of the car leaving Brendan making adjustments to a mine. Suddenly there was an explosion.

The neighbour led Carmel away from the car, urging her, 'Don't look back.' She was taken to hospital and treated for shock. The neighbour made his escape and despite her terrible condition Carmel resisted all police questioning and refused to reveal the dead man's identity. The Unionists would not allow her to attend her husband's funeral but no charges were brought against her. Ultimately Cardinal d'Alton intervened privately to have her released.

The Liam Kelly split forced its way into the public consciousness on November 26, 1955, when a mine tore the side out of the Roslea R.U.C. barracks, Co. Fermanagh.

Kelly, who had led the raid, was the founder of two Republican organisations, Saor Uladh (Free Ulster), the military wing and Fianna Uladh, its political arm, which ceased to count for very much after the year of its foundation, 1953. Kelly was a figure of some standing in east Tyrone and in Nationalist circles generally, having been imprisoned for nine months in 1953 for sedition shortly after his election to Stormont for mid-Tyrone. On his release his homecoming to the town of Pomeroy was marked by severe clashes between police and Kelly's sympathisers—

afterwards referred to in the North as the Pomeroy riots.

The I.R.A. denounced the Roslea raid on the day after it occurred and issued a statement appealing to young men 'not to join sentimental or microscopic organisations such as those who attacked the R.U.C. Barracks at Roslea.' (The I.R.A. also attacked it with equal lack of success on October 11, 1957.) However Kelly refused to admit to the raid and issued a statement through Fianna Uladh on November 28 which said:

'Fianna Uladh neither admits nor denies responsibility for the raid.

'It is our policy now and always not to felon-set, to inform on political prisoners or to give any information whatsoever to the usurpers of our country that would aid the process of elimination, which in our opinion helps the English army of occupation and its satellites.'

At the time it was not generally realised that there were two militant Republican groups at work. Nor did the public or the I.R.A. know that Connie Green, who had formerly served with the British army and was a member of the Saor Uladh attacking party, had been shot in the raid. His death, or rather the irregularities surrounding the inquest into his death, caused such a storm that Saor Uladh was finally forced to issue a statement, in the Fianna Uladh journal *Gair Uladh* on December 16, accepting responsibility for the raid. The statement also showed the differences between the I.R.A. and Kelly's groups. It said:

'Saor Uladh accepts the Constitution of the Republic enacted on July 1st, 1937, and recognises that Oireachtas Eireann is the sole legitimate authority in Ireland.

'Saor Uladh is organised solely in the Six Counties. Application of the laws enacted under the Constitution is by the Constitution itself restricted to the Twenty-Six County area. It is apparent therefore that these laws are not applicable in the case of Saor Uladh.'

These points are clearly at variance with what was then I.R.A. policy, and there was also the attitude of Magan and the older members of the I.R.A. executive to be considered. Their orthodox Republicanism precluded any official liaison between the I.R.A. and Kelly, although younger members did make unofficial contact with the Kelly organisation. Charlie Murphy told me that Kelly once gave him a large quantity of ammunition for use by the I.R.A. but MacLogan later ordered it to be returned and another young I.R.A. man, Terry O'Toole, told me that when he was on the run he found the Kelly organisation both more helpful and more efficient than that of the I.R.A. network in the North.

This, of course, was because Kelly was a Northerner and despite the fact that many Northerners were acting in the I.R.A. the I.R.A.'s concept of the North was of a place 'up there'. It had to be attacked from the South, according to a plan masterminded from Dublin, which, when the attacks were over, was to be the safe resting place and recruitment area. Militarily however Kelly saw the Northern situation as one to be solved by Northerners. His campaign failed for the usual reasons: lack of popular support and scarcity of weapons of a sufficiently high calibre to breach the defences of R.U.C. barracks (although he tried to purchase arms in America). Like the I.R.A. he also attempted to drive out the British by attacking the Irish constabulary.

While the Fianna Uladh admission of responsibility was important in clarifying the internal situation for Republicans, it was almost completely overshadowed in the public's mind by the events of the raid itself. These show the hesitancy and confusion of governmental policy towards the Republican movement at this time.

The raid began at 5.40 a.m. when a mine went off at the end of the barracks. The debris blocked the doorway from the guardroom which the attackers entered through the breach. As the rubble was being removed Sergeant William Robert Morrow, who was living in the barracks at the time with his wife and two little boys, leaped from bed, grabbed a Sten gun, and beat off the attack, which lasted about fifteen minutes. (He was awarded the George Medal for

this.) In the shooting, a Constable Knowles was hit seven
times, but recovered later and after the raid it was believed
that he was the only casualty.

But rumours, which the *Sunday Independent* published
on November 28, persisted that one of the attackers had
been shot in the raid and buried secretly in Monaghan after
an inquest had been held and a coroner had made the usual
order for burial. After enquiries by journalists the Government Information Bureau in Dublin made the following
announcement:

'In answer to enquiries it was ascertained through the
Government Information Bureau that on Saturday afternoon the Coroner for North Eastern Monaghan was informed that the body of an unknown man who appeared
to have died from gunshot wounds was lying in a farmhouse
in his district. An inquest was held in the evening when it
was found by the jury that the unknown man had died from
shock and haemorrhage and that there was no evidence
to show how the injuries had been received.'

The G.I.B. refused to make any further comment, but a
leading Irish journalist, John Healy, succeeded in getting
the coroner, Dr Thomas Leonard (aged 77), to talk to
him. The old man revealed that prior to the G.I.B. announcement 'no information was to have been given by
anyone who participated in the inquest'.

'That,' he said, 'was the position until today. Then
Dublin let us down with this announcement . . . it was no
longer a secret . . . that is why I am able to talk to you
now.'

Leonard said that the man had died on the morning
following the attack. He had been attended by a local
doctor who had sent for a priest to give the man the last
rites. That afternoon the doctor and two other men called
on Leonard, told him that a man had died (without telling
him when or where) and asked him to hold an inquest.
Leonard explained that he could not do this without inform-
ing the authorities and the men left, apparently to do just
this. Leonard then got in touch with the Gardai and was

visited by a superintendent who at first said he knew nothing about the affair. He later returned and told Leonard that he would be called for at 8 p.m. to carry out an inquest.

That evening Leonard was taken to a farmhouse where he found the body of a 'fine looking man' already in a coffin, and six men ready to act as jurors. Leonard swore them in. The superintendent presided and the inquest was held in his presence and that of a solicitor, a detective, the owner of the farmhouse and the doctor who had examined the man while he was dying. Uniformed guards and members of the detective force were stationed outside the house. Evidence was taken from the owner of the farmhouse and from the doctor, who said that the dead man had had a bullet wound in his left side. A verdict that death was due to shock and haemorrhage was returned.

Leonard went home and made out the death certificate which he described as a 'most unusual one. There is no name. I could not say if the man was married or single, what occupation he had. In the age column I wrote "about 30". That was all.' (The body was buried the following morning at Carrickroe cemetery, about twelve miles north of Monaghan, with the full rites of the church.)

The background to all this was that Liam Kelly sought to have Connie Green buried without an inquest but the doctor insisted that this would not be possible. Kelly telephoned a Clann na Poblachta member who was highly placed in the coalition government, to obtain the permission. However when the Clann na Poblachta contact sought the co-operation of Michael Keyes, the minister for justice, he was informed that an inquest would have to be held but it could be held in secrecy.

The entire episode aroused the strongest feelings both North and South and in England. John J. Horgan of Cork, at the time one of the senior coroners of Ireland, wrote to the papers saying that a secret inquest, at which the coroner made no attempt to identify the deceased or ascertain the cause of death, and following which he denied all knowledge of the event, constituted 'a breach of both law and practice'. The *Irish Times* printed an interview with 'a prominent barrister' who was quoted as saying:

'Let us take an extreme case. Suppose I and some friends of mine decided to commit a murder. Apparently all we have to do is to take out the victim, shoot him, and bring him to the nearest coroner for an inquest and then to a graveyard for burial. We don't even need to say who he was.'

These two quotations reveal the principal worries and the criticisms of the public in the South at the time, though there were subsidiary considerations arising out of there being only six jurymen empanelled. But in the North, where tension had been steadily rising from the time of the Ebrington Barracks raid of 1951, the Roslea affair aroused much sharper reactions and criticism.

During a debate at Stormont a day after Healy's news story, Lord Brookeborough said:

'It is unbelievable that any civilised country which has outlawed the I.R.A. is yet afraid to take action which any civilised country would take to prevent blackguards and scoundrels coming here to commit murder and create antagonism among the people.'

He added that if and when it became necessary to increase the size of the B-Specials, men would join and do their duty 'as their fathers had done in the past . . . We want to assure these blackguards that we won't be shoved around. Nothing is going to put us out of the United Kingdom.'

In the same debate Minister for Home Affairs George B. Hanna announced the banning of Saor Uladh and referring to the inquest said:

'The wisdom of our fathers in refusing to join with the South is evident when one considers the procedure at that inquest, which could not take place in any properly conducted community . . . I charge the Government in the South as being morally responsible for the raid.'

He gave instances of cases wherein the Stormont authorities had given information to the Southern authorities concerning illegal drilling on the Southern side of their border, 'but they took no steps to stop it'. Hanna also pointed out that the Nationalist members who had walked out of the debate claimed to represent the Roman Catholic Church. 'Had the Church no views on what had happened?' he asked. (The Church did in fact have something to say, but it was said too late to have any bearing on the immediate controversy.)

A significant point which emerged from the Stormont debate was the fact that Lord Brookeborough had been in touch with the British prime minister with a view to getting Great Britain to secure an extradition treaty with the Republic. In London, *The Times* seized on this point in a leader headed 'Murder and the I.R.A.':

'Whatever the technicalities in bringing the offenders to book, it should be a point of honour with all three governments . . . to co-operate in overcoming them. If further agreements between the three governments are required they should at once be negotiated . . . these men are, like pirates, the common enemies of all civilised states and it behoves all Governments to combine against them.'

In Belfast the *News Letter* crystallised the feelings of Orangemen at the time, saying:

'Events since the Roslea raid make the Dublin Government look extremely foolish . . . If the Government is not pursuing a policy of hushing up the affair, and thereby shielding the men who were engaged in it, then its authority is being defied in its own territory, it is a weak-kneed and incompetent Administration, and no credit even to the Irish Republic.

'It is the duty of all to give whatever assistance they can and to prove that Ulstermen in 1955 are just as capable of defending themselves, and as ready to do so, as the men who manned the Border and patrolled the gunmen's roads in 1921 and 1922.'

The following day, November 30, the Northern Ireland

Minister of Finance Brian Maginess pressed home the attack on the Dublin government saying:

'Those in the North who look southwards saw a people who were afraid to speak out, and afraid to condemn murderous attacks on police and military establishments. They saw a government that was weak and vacillating. As they saw these things they could thank God that we are part of the United Kingdom.'

On the same day Southern Prime Minister Costello made a major speech in the Dail in the course of which he made three central points:

'We must assert and vindicate the people's right to determine national policy and the right of the Oireachtas and the Government to maintain and to uphold the authority that reposes in them . . .

'We are bound to ensure that unlawful activities of a military character shall cease, and we are resolved to use if necessary all the powers and forces at our disposal to bring such activities effectively to an end . . .

'In order to prevent any future controversy or discussion on this point . . . there can be no question of our handing over, either to the British or to the Six-County authorities, persons whom they may accuse of armed political activities in Britain or in the Six Counties.'

Both Fianna Fail and Clann na Poblachta supported Costello in his stand and on December 4 he attempted to deal with the alleged government complicity in the secrecy surrounding the Monaghan inquest. Speaking at Abbeyfeale, Co. Limerick he said:

'No order or direction to hold the inquest in secrecy or to maintain secrecy was given or suggested by the Government or any member of the Government or by any member of any Government Department, or by the Commissioner or any officer or member of the guards.' He went on to add that as soon as he had heard of the affair he had given a personal direction that 'there should be publication forthwith'.

(I would be inclined to assess Costello's statement as

entirely honest in the light of the information available to him. He was after all the leader of only one party in a coalition supported by Clann na Poblachta which had made Liam Kelly a senator.)

A courageous motion by Dr Owen Sheehy Skeffington in the Senate on December 15 which welcomed the general tenor of Costello's speech, but regretted that he had not actually taken steps to halt 'this crazy militarism, however high its ideals or self-sacrificing its members', failed to attract a seconder.

Nor did church leaders get much further in their efforts to check 'crazy militarism'. At midnight Mass on Christmas Eve Cardinal d'Alton appealed to young men not to use violence in support of their aim in uniting the country, and on January 19 the standing committee of the Irish hierarchy issued a statement condemning the use of force and pointing out the dangers of civil war. The statement was also read out at Masses but it had no effect on the I.R.A.'s recruiting or planning. As Charlie Murphy put it to me, 'When the bishops called down fire and brimstone not a man stirred but when Joe Christle fecked off half the shagging I.R.A. followed him!'

Before describing the 'fecking off' of Joe Christle it is important to pick up the threads of the 'official' I.R.A.'s activities.

Following the Arborfield raid and the severe sentences on his brother and friends, Charlie Murphy began to feel personally responsible for both these and the Omagh imprisonments. A sense of guilt, coupled with the exhaustion engendered by years of sleepless nights and punishing travel, almost drove him out of the I.R.A. This point came one day in November when he found Michael O'Donovan, a life-long Republican, sitting in an office of the United Irishman. He had just been dropped from the staff by Magan. O'Donovan, or 'Pasha' as he was generally known, was such a keen Irish-speaker that he even spoke to his dog in Irish and Murphy like everyone else in the movement had a soft spot for the old man. He tried to get Magan to reinstate him and when he failed he resigned from the headquarters staff of the I.R.A. although he remained an ordinary member of the Dublin unit. A few days later, the Roslea raid took place. Realising that it was not an I.R.A. job but fearing that it might mean a round-up of I.R.A. men Murphy set off for the hills around Dublin in a car and warned the groups drilling there to lie low. Magan then asked him to return, which he did and so began an association that led to large-scale hostilities against the North.

Sean Cronin was thirty-three when he came back from America. He had become known in Clann na Gael circles in New York, and was accepted into the I.R.A. by Magan. He had been an officer in the regular army before emigrating to America where he worked as a journalist and on his return he joined the *Evening Press* as a sub-editor. (Ironically he had known of the editor, Douglas Gageby, in the army where Gageby had earned a reputation for his wartime work in intelligence, as has been mentioned earlier.) From the start Cronin made headway in both the I.R.A. and on the *Evening Press*. On the news-paper he was meticulous about time and used to appear five minutes early in the office every morning. Cronin's American accent earned him the name 'Sheriff' among his colleagues. The staff all liked him and was sorry when he resigned, ostensibly because he had a commission from a newspaper chain in America. A few days later he was picked up on the border and we realised what the com-mission was and how apt had been his nickname.

I had nearly stumbled on the truth some months earlier when I happened to notice him coming out of the *United Irishman* offices. We knew that he used to write for the paper, but pretending not to know this I said to him the next day in the office, 'I hear Sean that you're getting very prominent in Sinn Fein circles.' He nearly rose out of the chair with surprise, grabbed my arm and barked at me, 'What? Where did you hear that? What do you mean?'

He was so intense that I thought he was afraid that I might say something which would harm his prospects on the *Evening Press* and I relented and told him that I had seen him the previous day and was only joking. I was not aware that his relief stemmed from the fact that the I.R.A. had just agreed to a full-scale attack on the North along the lines of a plan drawn up by himself.

From the moment that he arrived back in Dublin in October, 1955 Cronin had been keen on action, but as he had to go through a recruits' course like everyone else it was not until January, 1956 that he began to be listened to in the inner councils of the I.R.A. Then Charlie Murphy invited him to join him as a co-training officer, because of his military background. (At the time, apart from an active service unit of perhaps fifty men who had taken part in raids, the vast majority of the rank and file of the I.R.A. had no experience whatsoever of soldiering.) Cronin gave Murphy a plan, 'Operation Harvest', for an attack on the North aimed at destroying communications, military installations and public property on such a scale as to paralyse the six-county area. Murphy turned the plan over to Magan. It had, of course, very little practical relevance but Magan liked it, and in April, 1956 appointed Murphy and Cronin as joint operating staff. Murphy and Cronin then began repeated visits to the North to meet local I.R.A. units and to reconnoitre targets.

In July, 1956 Murphy and his colleagues arranged for the biggest single operation the I.R.A. carried out, apart from the campaign itself—a battle school in the Wicklow Mountains. The course was devised by a former British officer, a veteran of the Burmese war who had also fought on the Republican side in the Civil War. The site could only be reached by a rope walk over a stream, but he could cross it like a cat, whereas the I.R.A. lads puffed and floundered and very often had to be pushed over.

The day began at 5 a.m. and training involved the use

of live ammunition and simulated attacks over ground along which charges of gelignite had been laid to be detonated by Murphy and Cronin. (A film of this exercise was shot and sent to America.) The school lasted for a fortnight and involved making a considerable amount of noise, but there was no interference from either the Special Branch or the regular army, which during lulls in the firing could be heard at their own practice ranges in the Glen of Imaal just over the mountains. The only complaint received was from traders in a nearby town who objected that the I.R.A. had not bought its supplies locally and to allay such criticism it was decided to invite the locals to a supper which was so lavish* that one shepherd remarked as he laid into a second helping, 'Be Jasus lads if this be war let there never be peace!'

However no date was set for the start of a campaign, nor for security reasons were the rank and file informed of what was afoot. In view of the security position this was necessary but it helped to bring about the Christle split, when most of the active service unit, unaware of what was being planned by the 'Official Army of the Republic', followed Joe Christle in breaking from the I.R.A. because he stood for action against the North and the I.R.A. apparently did not.

Joe Christle has a quality that I can only describe as 'whoosh'—energy, anarchy, male supremacy and learning all canalised into a brand of patriotism that finds its outlet in everything from fomenting strikes and laying up explosives to bicycle racing. Apart from organising the marathon round-Ireland Ras Tailteann he cycles twenty miles before work every day himself. His home in Rath-

---

* This generosity was a cause of the I.R.A.'s running out of meat during the exercise, but despite the presence of large numbers of sheep in the vicinity, no effort was made to eat them, not through honesty but because, despite the fact that the course was held to increase expertise in human slaughter, no one liked the idea of killing a sheep!

gar, Dublin is continually in turmoil. Phones ring. People
rush in and out. Beethoven booms from the record player.
Large young men in track suits carry bicycles through
the hall. (Like most things surrounding Christle there is
more purpose to the activity than meets the eye.) His
three friendly young sons are trained to wash dishes and
do housework. They are intelligent lads who instead of
toy guns are given books at Christmas. One evening
chatting with them while waiting for Joe I was particularly
impressed by their knowledge of Greek mythology.

In 1945, when Christle was still a schoolboy at St
James's Christian Brothers School he founded his first
revolutionary circle. He was sixteen. He made efforts to
contact the I.R.A. but failed and joined the F.C.A. (An
Forsa Cosanta Atiuil) the Irish equivalent of the British
territorial army. As membership involves taking an oath
of allegiance to the state I asked Christle how he squared
this with his conscience.

'Oh,' he said, 'we took the oath like Dev did. To break
the oath.'

In the F.C.A. summer camps he would distribute leaflets asking his fellow F.C.A. members what were they
defending, twenty-six or thirty-two counties? He found a
good deal of support for his views and the authorities
removed him and a number of like-minded enthusiasts
in the summer of 1949. By then he had also joined the
Gaelic League and was a member of its Ard Craobh
(literally 'high branch') of which de Valera was chairman.
That year also he founded the Gate Cycling Club, joined
what was left of the N.C.A. and was taken into the I.R.A.
by 'Pasha' O'Donovan. Everyone in the Gate Club was
a member of the I.R.A. and on the Armagh raid six of
the twenty raiders were club members.

He joined the John Mitchell Club of Sinn Fein in
1952 and became one of its principal speakers along
with Myles Shevlin and Seamus Sorahan. He saw that
'action' brought a mushroom growth in recruiting and he
felt that the movement was too preoccupied with form

and not enough with substance. Because of this view and as that suspicious person, a university student, he gradually found himself isolated from the older leaders of the movement, in particular Anthony Magan, Michael Traynor and Patrick MacLogan. They felt he wanted to take over the movement for himself—and certainly Joe is a leader rather than a follower.

Never a man to allow revolution to interfere with his lawful activities he sat for part of his bachelor of law examination on the morning of the Armagh raid. He had just completed a question asking, 'What are the safeguards in the Irish Constitution against armed insurrection and rebellion?' when he was called for and driven off to take part in a little 'armed insurrection and rebellion' against the Northern Ireland constitution.

He emerged from both tests with second-class honours, hearing from the university some weeks later and being censured by the I.R.A. for taking it on himself to give orders for the disposal of an arms lorry after the raid, an action which resulted in the lorry's being captured. In August he organised the first of his annual eight-day cycling events, the round-Ireland Ras Tailteann. In October he took part in the Omagh raid. In November he organised the National Students Council, embracing every student society in University College, Dublin. He was wounded during the Omagh raid and was on sick leave from his job in the state-run Electricity Supply Board, when he and Martin Campbell, who had been an important I.R.A. fund-raiser around Chicago in 1921-23, set off in December around the country in a car with the slogan 'Let Christmas Day be Prisoners Day', and was so successful that on Christmas Day he and Campbell carried literally buckets of money into the Castle Hotel in Denmark Street for the Prisoners' Dependents Fund.

Christle continued on his ebullient way during 1955 in a manner gravely upsetting to the older men. As part of their contribution towards helping the election of Mitchell and Clarke three of the Christle group decided that if they could get the support of the veteran Nationalist priest, Canon Maguire of Newtownbutler, Co. Fermanagh, they would have gone a long way towards persuading the Nationalists not to stand against either Mitchell or Clarke and so avoid splitting the vote. The three were Seamus Sorahan, a law student and at the time the best public speaker in Sinn Fein, and the brothers Willie and Joe Fogarty. They drafted a letter seeking the canon's co-operation and had it signed by hundreds of students as coming from '. . . University College, Dublin, where Philip Clarke studied and so often spoke of you as the leader of Nationalist thought in Occupied Ireland . . .'

As far as anyone knew at the time Clarke had never mentioned the formidable old canon in his life, but Sorahan and Willie Fogarty affixed Fainnes (gold circles which proclaimed the wearers fluent Irish speakers and Pioneer Pins which proclaimed them teetotallers, which they are not), to their lapels and set off with the letter to the canon. The emissaries and letter so appealed to the old man that he promised to help them.

The I.R.A. leadership, particularly Magan, MacLogan and MacCurtain, eventually decided that Christle would have to go. In June, 1956 Charlie Murphy was ordered to hand him his dismissal notice, ostensibly for addressing a Sinn Fein meeting without permission. This had the easily foreseeable result that those who thought like Christle also left the I.R.A. The bulk of the most active and best trained volunteers, including most of the active service unit and twelve out of fifteen of the officer corps followed him. Like Christle they were unaware that a campaign was being planned by the I.R.A. leadership. But their secession and subsequent activities went so embarrassing to the 'official' leaders that they spent as much time between then and December, 1956 trying to dissuade others from following Christle as on planning the campaign itself.

On his dismissal Christle approached Liam Kelly and

those sections of Clann na Gael which would always support 'action'. Kelly, however, was not too happy and at first suspected Christle of being an I.R.A. plant, but the two groups, about seventy men in all, finally came to agreement in August, 1956 at a meeting in Dublin at which the Northerners arrived carrying arms. The first joint Christle-Kelly operation took place on Armistice Day 1956 when they burned down customs huts along a 150-mile stretch—almost the entire length of the border. The group carried out about twelve attacks, blowing up customs huts, telephone exchanges, bridges, B-Special drill halls, and demolishing the lough gates at Newry.

Kelly and Christle accompanied their groups on all the raids and on a number of ambushes which failed when the R.U.C., the B-Specials or British military did not arrive. Another plot which Christle hatched but which failed through lack of co-operation from his own supporters, including Kelly whom it horrified, was a plan to seize the town of Newry, with the help of the Catholic population, thus forcing the British to engage them and, he reasoned, forcing the Irish army to become involved also. This, Christle hoped, would lead to a situation in which the United Nations would intervene and send a peace-keeping force to replace the British in the North!

There was some evidence of sympathy for Christle's scheme in high places. Michael Fitzpatrick, chief whip of Clann na Poblachta, told me that he favoured sending the Irish army to the border on manoeuvres just to see what the Orangemen would do—engage the Southerners he hoped. I have also been told about Dail deputies parking outside Leinster House with car boots laden with arms and ammunition which they were transporting for the I.R.A. On at least one occasion a ministerial car was used to transport ammunition for Thompson guns from Kerry to Dublin and Christle did have many contacts in the army. (So much so that on one occasion a serving officer, still in the army, took part in a border raid and was very nearly captured, but had the good fortune to find a farmhouse whose occupants put him in contact with a priest who spirited him safely back across the border. Whether or not Christle had intended him to be captured and so provoke a crisis within the army is still a subject of debate.)

Kelly differed from Christle on other matters also. Christle wanted to 'ostracise' British servicemen by using the EOKA tactics of bombing cafés, pubs and dance halls patronised by British soldiers. Kelly disagreed because Catholics might be killed and this he felt would be murder—an attitude towards taking life typical of the thinking concerning the use of force and the I.R.A. It is best illustrated by a story from the 1930s. A man wanted to have a farmer shot because of a dispute over land. The chosen I.R.A. man asked him if he had any sons. He had three, all in their early twenties. Could they not handle the problem for him. The man was horrified.

'My sons shoot him is it? Sure that'd be *murder*.'

Kelly and Christle disagreed again on what the outcome of a successful revolution should be. Kelly did not care who ruled Ireland so long as she were free. Christle saw himself as a socialist revolutionary wanting to create a revolutionary situation by violent methods. To the Northerners, the police were only guarding the peace. Christle argued, 'Let's break the peace so!'

Both men had to acknowledge one fact although in different ways: Kelly by suddenly departing to the States without telling Christle and Christle by laying down his gun, though not his belief in the use of force. That fact was that a campaign such as theirs could not change the position of the Northern Irish government.

In the event the Kelly-Christle partnership cost no lives nor did they lose a man on the border. When in January, 1959 a group of Christle's men were caught by the Gardai and interned he ordered them to sign out. He was arrested himself but was later released.

While the border was the prime source of political discontent in Ireland during 1956, it was also (as it still is) the principal source of revenue for anyone in the area wanting to get rich quickly. Politics, poteen and smuggling are the main preoccupations in a belt of land reaching about forty miles into the hinterland on both sides of the border, which stretches from Derry in the North to Carlingford Lough at its southernmost extremity. Not only does the border divide North from South, it also divides the North. Donegal, which is in the Republic is more northerly than any spot in the six counties and the bewildering loops and curves of the red line marking the division on the map are even more bewildering to an observer standing on a hill a couple of miles north of any of the border counties.

Politically, to the east of the Bann river 80 per cent of the population is Unionist. This is where the good land lies. Driving through the North once with a knowledgeable commentator pointing out the Protestant and Catholic areas to me, I could soon tell for myself which was which —the Orangemen had all the fertile low-lying land, the Catholics generally lived in the hilly marginal areas west of the Bann in east and mid-Tyrone, south Down, west Armagh, south Armagh, south Fermanagh and in the Derry area. At the time of the border campaign these areas were described politically as 'Nationalist' but today they would be better described as at least 50 per cent civil-rights areas, not seeking an all-Ireland Republic led from Dublin but justice under the British crown.

Geographically the 'North' can be either left or right of you, turning in behind you, running along before you, or all unknown to you falling further and further behind as you drive along an 'unapproved road', one on which a customs patrol can stop you when you fondly imagine you are still in the Republic. Of course, if you come to a

sign post you can tell immediately: if you are in the
North the names are printed only in English, in the
Republic they are given in both Irish and English. Also,
rural electrification is further advanced in the Republic
and you can tell by the large number of poles and overhead wires where you are. In 1956 it was usually possible
to tell North from South by the way the fields were kept.
Those in the South looked the way the countryside looks
in childhood or on Christmas cards: overgrown, bounded
by enormous hedges and ditches and as likely to be occupied by rabbits, hares, flocks of crows, flights of pigeons,
or occasional foxes and badgers as by cattle or sheep. The
fields in the North were neat trim agricultural units.

Today, as the South's agriculture improves, it is getting
increasingly hard to tell the two sides apart by looking
at the landscape—and even more difficult to find someone
who knows from living there. Emigration to England, to
America and to the towns on either side of the border, is
draining away the people at a rate that can be measured
better visually than statistically. Stand on a hill at an old
I.R.A. jumping-off point such as Knockatallon, six miles
north of Monaghan town, and you can see the remains of
perhaps thirty homesteads from which people have gone
in the last five or six years.

The man on whose land I stood had memories of a boyhood and adolescence filled with dances and card games,
cups of tea in neighbours' houses, rabbit hunting, hay-
making, bringing in the harvest with the labour shared
between one farmer and another, and the excitement distributed evenly among the hordes of children. Today his
children have no one to play with. It is two miles to the
nearest shop and three to the local school. They have no
car and by the time his wife has looked after the large
family she is lucky if she can manage more than two or
three visits a year to Monaghan. This man is in the I.R.A.
and 'immediate and violent revolution' is his solution to
the problems of life in north Co. Monaghan. It may not
be a good solution but you can at least understand his

feelings if you look over his empty countryside on a wet winter's day. He is a skilful man who could make good money in Dublin, but his father is a widower in his seventies, and will not leave his farm, his only reassurance in his old age, and my friend cannot leave his father alone in the green desert where the pressures of economics have left only the rushes and furze to chase men off the land.

Life was traditionally hard in these counties, which is why the natives made the poteen to keep out the cold and the reality. Then came the border and they started to smuggle after the land annuities dispute and the economic warfare made a field across the road a part of England so far as tariffs were concerned. It is a smuggler's paradise.

The pattern of smuggling changes with the times. During the war any food was welcome in the North. Car batteries, tyres, razor blades and nylons fetched good prices in the Republic. Butter is a perennial favourite, because the cheap food policy of British governments has left a gap ranging from sixpence to two shillings in the pound between the price of butter in the Republic and the North. Whatever the fluctuation, there is always an inducement for someone with a lorry to run four or five tons of butter down south. Dramatic confrontations between customs men and smugglers, midnight car chases and rammings are so frequent that they rarely make any sort of headlines unless the Dublin evening papers are stuck for news.

The border runs through farms, and even through houses, as in the village of Pettigoe, divided between Donegal and Fermanagh, and the entire area is a mass of small, winding roads without signposts. There is a tradition of secrecy in the area as well as the normal suspicion of the law that exists in the Irish countryside. Children mistrust strangers and are trained to regard even the most innocent questions as being aimed at their family's liberty.

While I was driving around the border, inspecting the jumping-off points for raids and the places that were attacked a school teacher told a story which illustrated

the local attitude to the police perfectly. A patrolling squad
car had picked up a child wandering along the side of a
by-road, at a time in the morning which suggested that the
child was either lost or a truant from school. The child, a
boy of about seven, appeared not to know his own name
or where he lived. Neither did anyone at the farms at
which the squad car called. Eventually the police sought
the teacher's help and he immediately recognised the
child as one of his pupils, the son of an established local
family. Everyone the police had called on earlier must have
known this also, but they, and the child, mistrusted the
police's motive in trying to identify the boy. 'Tell them
nothing', is the motto of the border counties.

Such were the traditions of the countryside in which the
I.R.A. launched on December 12, 1956, a campaign
against the North.

The actual beginning of the campaign was as untidy
and as straggling as the countryside itself. One cannot
point to a quickly implemented decision to start the campaign, but shortly after 'Operation Harvest' was proposed
the I.R.A. leadership decided that some such scheme
should be put into effect. The 'three Macs' were not,
however, enthusiastic. MacCurtain argued that they had
no armaments to justify such a campaign, but the urge
for 'action', founded on a lack of appreciation of the real
partition problem and fired by the optimism of youth,
overcame his and other objections (Magan was irresolute
for a time and MacLogan and Traynor were not happy
either). Murphy, Russell, Cronin, Brady and the younger
element in the leadership carried the day, and from
April, 1956 on the I.R.A. made plans for the campaign.

In these early days of the campaign and its planning
Charlie Murphy was comparatively little known. He was,
however, a key man in organising the campaign, was later
involved in a *cause célèbre* and was the central figure in a
dispute which split the I.R.A. internally.

On January 13, 1957, a month after the campaign had

officially started, Murphy, Magan, MacCurtain and Sean
Cronin (not the Cronin of the I.R.A. leadership but a
namesake) were arrested at Murphy's home after they had
attended Mass. The arrests were made by Detective Inspector Philip MacMahon, later head of the Special
Branch and the man who was to prove the nemesis of
Murphy and the movement. Along with the men the
police seized incriminating lists of money sent from
America to the I.R.A.

MacMahon turned the captured evidence over to the
state solicitor's office and ten days later it was produced
in court before Judge Michael Lennon.* Lennon created
something of a sensation by openly siding with the accused men. When the prosecutor produced a copy of the
declaration which brought the Offences Against the State
Act into force, Lennon remarked ironically, 'This proclamation does not end with the words "God save the
King".' The prosecutor asked if he were expected to
reply and the judge said, 'Yes. I remember proclamations
of this kind made in relation to myself and they always
ended with the words, "God save the King".'

Further exchanges followed and at a later hearing
Lennon ordered that the property belonging to the two
I.R.A. men before him—Magan and MacCurtain—be returned to them. The 'property' consisted of ammunition
and, order or no order, MacMahon refused to hand it back.

Lennon's actions cost him his judgeship. After an inquiry
he was retired on a not very impressive pension. But this
stern treatment of an eccentric but humane judge should
be assessed against the background of a time during

* In 1931 Lennon had attacked James Joyce, in the American
Catholic World. He revealed that mixture of shame and chauv-
inism which so many Irish intellectuals show to the 'one who
got away', because they feel that such a person is condemning
them by force of example to the role of timeservers in a land
where, as Joyce put it, 'Christ and Caesar are hand in glove'.
The attack so infuriated Joyce that six years later he wrote to
his friend Constantine Curran refusing to visit Dublin because
the map of Ireland was marked 'Hic Sunt Lennones'.

which many judges were reluctant to include I.R.A. cases on their lists and sentences on I.R.A. defendants tended to be of the order of three to six months. At the same time the I.R.A. was attempting not to recognise the courts.

Murphy had meanwhile served three months and he was to remain at liberty for almost a year. He married on February 16, 1958, the day of the abortive raid on the Blandford military barracks in Dorset, England. (This was another example of daring and planning going to waste. Before the raid Murphy and Frank Skuse paid several visits to the camp and familiarised themselves with the layout. The raiding party of nine men was led by Sean Cronin and included Skuse but the attack was completely bungled. The only result was that a British soldier was shot in the stomach; no arms or ammunition were seized and the raiders were forced to abandon a new car obtained for the occasion.) Shortly afterwards the I.R.A. learned that the Special Branch was about to arrest a captain in the regular army who had been helping the I.R.A. Some-one had to warn him and Murphy volunteered. Mac-Mahon immediately learned of this (the Special Branch by this stage had the I.R.A. riddled with informers) and MacMahon was waiting.

Murphy went back to prison and MacMahon then singled him out as the victim of a ploy designed to split the I.R.A. down the middle—which it did very successfully. Murphy was depressed at his capture, the various disastrous raids and the failure of the campaign in general and was disposed to listen to tales of the hardships which families of imprisoned I.R.A. were suffering. For several days MacMahon tried in vain to talk with Murphy, but eventually MacMahon got him to accept a week's parole during which he was to contact the Army Council and report that if the campaign were called off all the prisoners would be released.

Sean Cronin, the leading man of the hour, was furious at Murphy's action. Cronin believed that if the I.R.A. decided to end the campaign the prisoners would automatically be released, an assumption which was open to question in the light of what had happened during the war. Having encountered great hostility, Murphy returned to jail after two days and refused from then on to have any dealings with MacMahon. But the damage had been done. The I.R.A. was subsequently riven by controversy as to the rights and wrongs of Murphy's action.

The first decision the campaign planners made was to send organisers to a number of centres: north Antrim, south Derry, south-east Derry, south Fermanagh, south Down, south Armagh, Derry city. These were all Nationalist areas and all were easily reached from the border. Belfast did not require a special organiser as Paddy Doyle lived there. Then this was interrupted by the Joe Christle split in June, and the energies of the I.R.A. were devoted to dissuading volunteers from following Christle. (When twelve out of the fifteen officers in the Dublin area did follow him, eighteen-year-olds in some cases succeeded them.) For a time Christle's followers kept their weapons, but tensions subsided when these were handed back. As a result the organisers were not sent in until August, but they managed to remain undetected, despite their Southern accents, until the outbreak of hostilities. There were approximately twenty of these organisers and their job was to train volunteers locally, act as intelligence agents, pick out targets and report back to Dublin in person at regular intervals.

The Army Council had voted to begin the campaign in November, 1956, but the irresolution of some members of the council, and a number of other snags pushed the date into December. During the planning period Paddy Doyle was captured with a Belfast newsletter to local units and the council decided to cut Belfast out of the campaign altogether. It had been feared all along that the I.R.A. might be too weak to defend Belfast Catholics and this setback decided the issue. Then there was a row between the emissary sent from Dublin to Derry con-

cerning the smuggling of arms into the North. Derry
had been chosen as the entry point but as a result of the
row it was decided to send the arms in by south Fermanagh. This caused a twenty-four-hour delay on the very
eve of the campaign, almost getting Charlie Murphy
captured on December 10. He had to drive through the
border areas postponing everything and between the
psychological let-down and the exhaustion caused by travel
and lack of sleep he failed to notice that he was driving
without his lights on. He was stopped by an R.U.C.
man in Pomeroy, Co. Tyrone, but was let off with a
caution. (On Armistice Day he had an even narrower
escape when Joe Christle and Liam Kelly burned down
customs huts. Murphy, Noel Kavanagh and Sean Daly
were in the North casing likely targets. Their method of
operation was to drop a petrol cap off their car as they
passed an R.U.C. barracks and then get out to look for
it, inspecting the area as they did so. They were doing
this outside an R.U.C. barracks when charges went off
under the customs huts, but they escaped.)

Approximately one hundred and fifty men took part in
the opening night of the campaign which between then
and its end in 1962, was to cost, according to figures supplied to me by a Stormont spokesman, £1 million in outright damage (paid for by the British exchequer) and
approximately £10 million in increased police and military
patrols. Six young R.U.C. men and eleven Republicans
were killed. In the South increased patrols and the opening of the Curragh internment camp cost in the region of
£400,000 a year for the campaign's duration. The campaign was certainly a factor in the fall of the government
in Dublin in 1957, and had other effects. An official concerned with attracting new industry to Ireland told me that
some British and Continental investment was scared off
by the disturbances.

But though matters appeared serious to foreigners, and
poisoned the relations of Dublin with both Belfast and
London, the Irish, both North and South, viewed it with

less excitement. In the North the Nationalists refer to the campaign today as 'the incidents', because that is in fact what it was: a series of incidents along the border, impinging very little on Belfast and annoying rather than terrifying the Northern administration. It did, of course, arouse terror in the hearts of Unionist sympathisers living along the border—even on the Southern side. In the early stages of the campaign some Southern Protestants living in border areas made a practice of crossing over to earn pocket money as B-Specials, but after it became known that the I.R.A. was aware of this practice the Gardai warned moonlighting B-men that it would be impossible to guarantee their safety in the South. In the South public interest flared up for the first few days of the campaign or at dramatic moments like the Brooke-borough raid with its subsequent emotive funerals; the opening of the internment camps; the trial which led to Judge Lennon's dismissal; Sean Cronin's trial at which 'Operation Harvest' was read out in court, and the trial of two young Co. Tyrone men for the murder of an R.U.C. sergeant blown to pieces in a booby-trapped cottage. But once it became obvious that the campaign could have no effect on the permanency of the Northern regime public interest diminished.

Interest reached its highest point in the Republic's elections in 1957, when Sinn Fein candidates polled 66,000 votes, but by the 1961 election this total had fallen by half and no Sinn Fein candidates were elected. At no time did this interest ever betoken any hostility to England or indeed towards the North. Most people in the Republic were rather puzzled by the whole thing and were inclined to write the whole thing off as 'the I.R.A. at it again', without any clear appreciation of why it should have been at it again. British tourists were as welcome as ever in the South. In fact, except for the 1916 Rising, or the time of the 'Troubles', it is difficult to find a time in this century when anyone in Ireland would attack an Englishman—despite the efforts of some schoolteachers

T.I.R.A.   N and politicians who, lacking any coherent philosophy of their own, often do make efforts to equate being pro-Irish with being anti-British.

One incident which I can authenticate shows the degree of incomprehension that exists in Irish-English affairs. It occurred at the time of the 1955 Ras Tailteann, the day after the Northern authorities had prohibited the carrying of the tricolour in Northern areas by Ras cyclists. The prohibition, and its breach by some cyclists, had led to violence and a number of cyclists were beaten up by Orangemen. An N.C.A. supporter, employed at Killarney Mental Hospital and normally one of the gentlest of men, was so incensed when he read of this that he swore to take retributory action if he could. He was on his rounds as a van driver on a deserted country road when he saw a British car coming towards him. He stopped his van, halted the car, seized the Union Jack fluttering from the bonnet and tore it into pieces and jumped on them while the middle-aged couple in the car, both visitors from the north of England, looked on in astonishment. The destruction accomplished he drove off leaving Mum saying to Dad (as they later reported), 'Eeh lad. The man in Aer Lingus never said owt about anything like that!' But as the van drove over the hill they noticed in large letters on the rear doors 'Killarney Mental Hospital' and the whole incident thereupon (wrongly) lost all political significance!

The campaign began with a satisfactory bang. Ten different areas were attacked on the night of December 12, 1956, in a ring from Antrim round to Derry. The targets included the B.B.C. relay transmitter at Rosemount, Derry, which was demolished, and Gough Barracks, Armagh, which survived. A Territorial Army headquarters, being built at Enniskillen, was blown down. The Magherafelt Quarter Sessions Courthouse, Co. Derry, was burned down. Near Magherafelt, Toome Bridge was destroyed. At Newtownbutler, Lady Brooke Bridge was damaged and Carry Bridge at Inishmore Island also suffered. In Newry a B-Special hut was partly burned.

Most of the explosions took place early in the morning and in Charlie Murphy's words, 'The place looked like the western front. Bombs going off, flames, Very lights, Sten guns—the lot.' He, together with Magan, Robert Russell and others directed operations from Monaghan, a campaign centre. A guard on his rounds wanted to know what was going on and finally Russell told him that he was a chicken farmer up early to catch the market—a remark rendered nearly inaudible by a loud explosion a few miles to the north. The guard went off complaining that he would have to make a report about this.

The raids were greeted with predictable denunciations in Dublin, London and Belfast, but not in Moscow. On December 29 *Pravda* denied British claims that the raids were only 'isolated actions without popular support' saying: 'The Irish patriots cannot agree with Britain transforming the Six Counties into one of its main military bases in the Atlantic pact.'

In Dublin the government a day later said it would take every action needed to prevent loss of life. In London the government ordered the British ambassador in Dublin, Sir Alexander Clutterbuck, to express Britain's 'very great concern' at the incidents and the hope that Dublin would live up to its promise.

In Belfast of course reaction was more decisive. Lord Brookeborough referred to the I.R.A. as 'hooligans who raid this country' in a speech on December 13 to a meeting of the Shankill Unionist Association which was also addressed by the chairman of the British Conservative party, Oliver Poole. Poole pledged support for the Unionists and promised that as soon as Sir Anthony Eden, then on a visit to Jamaica, returned to London he would inform him of the raids. At this time Eden was under heavy attack from the 'Suez rebels' and the twelve Unionists at Westminster could not be lightly lost by the Conservative government. The price of their support was seen in a strong statement which Eden made in the House of Commons on December 19.

Before this the North had already looked to its own defences. The Special Powers Act's regulations were re-introduced on December 15 (providing for arrest and internment without warrant or trial) and further orders provided for the imposition of curfew, the immobilisation of cars and a strengthened police force. On December 22 the R.U.C. guided British sappers in the drastic step of blowing up unapproved roads in border areas, destroying bridges and spiking roads at intervals. Deep craters greatly restricted transport along the border and the only usable roads were guarded by police and customs posts. Three thousand R.U.C. men and 12,000 B-specials were called into action, and the North became an armed camp.

South of the border the number of guards in border areas was doubled and despite the fact that Belfast con-tinually thundered that Dublin was not doing enough to curb the raiders it was in fact the Southern Gardai who brought off the first large-scale capture of I.R.A. men and who throughout the campaign posed a greater threat to the I.R.A. than did the R.U.C. It was also the Gardai who eventually seized the 'three Macs', Murphy, Cronin, Laurence Grogan and the rest of the principal leaders. If the Southern authorities had not been so vigilant the campaign would have certainly been more destructive.

On December 16 the Gardai and units of the Irish army surrounded a farmhouse at Knockatallon and seized Murphy, Cronin and eleven other I.R.A. but this time released them the same day. Their release caused great annoyance in Stormont where the minister for home affairs, W. B. Topping observed that he hoped that this was not the sort of 'necessary and appropriate' action which the Southern government had referred to in its statement of December 14.

Unionist M.P. Nat Minford, replying to Topping, said that he did not think that the British government was treating the situation seriously enough to 'bring to justice those damned scoundrels nor to bring pressure to bear on the Dublin authorities to stamp out I.R.A. drilling and prevent the raids'.

'We Protestants,' he declaimed, 'are running this country, and are going to run it. We want to live in a country where peace will prevail. If we find that these attacks are going to continue, then we Protestants ourselves will have to determine what the future will be. I'm not content to sit back and see these things continue.'

It was Lord Brookeborough who calmed the atmosphere, saying that Eden had assured him that the North would get the same support in defending itself as any other part of the United Kingdom. He counselled against any efforts to meet force with force, 'no matter how tempted', because such action 'would put the country in a state of chaos, bloodshed and hatred . . . the defence of the country must rest with the Government and no one should take any action on their own.' Eden said the next day that 'The safety of Northern Ireland and of its inhabitants is therefore a direct responsibility on Her Majesty's Government, which they will of course discharge.'

Costello replied to Eden, reiterating his statement of November 30, 1955, saying that the six-county area was a part of the Irish national territory and that any claim that the six counties were 'an integral part of the United Kingdom' could never be accepted by any Irish government. He called on Britain, as being primarily responsible for partition, to take the initiative in doing away with it and wound up by saying again that the government would do everything it could to bring 'unlawful military activities to an end'.

But Costello's government had less influence on the campaign than the campaign had on the government. The campaign helped in bringing down the coalition government, returning Fianna Fail to power and thus ultimately leading to the downfall of the I.R.A. Untroubled by divided councils, as was a coalition having to deal with

I.R.A. sympathisers in Clann na Poblachta, Fianna Fail was able to take vigorous and successful action against the movement.

The end of the coalition came on January 28, 1957, when, on behalf of Clann na Poblachta, Sean MacBride moved a vote of no confidence in the government on economic grounds and because of its 'failure to formulate and to pursue any positive policy calculated to bring about the reunification of Ireland'. Deprived of the Clann's support, Costello had no option but to dissolve the Dail which he did on February 12, 1957. A general election was held on March 5 and in the post-Suez economic crisis the coalition took a bad beating, Fianna Fail winning thirteen more seats than it had held in 1954. Clann na Poblachta lost some thirty thousand of the fifty thousand votes it had got in 1954, but Sinn Fein won almost sixty-six thousand. (Their four seats meant nothing because the candidates refused to sit in the Dail and thus lost, if nothing else, the chance of a national platform to state their case.

One of the most interesting developments of this period was an attempt on the part of the Church to find a solution to the border problem. On March 3, Cardinal d'Alton put forward a plan proposing that each of the six counties be allowed to choose between Dublin and Belfast. If the North agreed to federation with the South, Ireland was then to associate with the Commonwealth as an independent republic on the same basis as India, and offer bases to N.A.T.O. (At the time the cardinal's idea was a non-starter, but so far as Dublin and Westminster were concerned, relations were so harmonious, behind the scenes, on the partition issue that something could well have been worked out. The 'not-an-inch' extremists of the North of course remained a big stumbling block, but even these were considerably weakened by having Harold, rather than Sir Henry Wilson, in London's Corridors of Power. Had Edward Heath found himself dependent on the ten Unionist backbenchers it might have been a different proposition however.)

In the campaign itself the organisation was of course poor as is obvious from the experiences of a typical I.R.A. organiser. Gerry Higginbothom was nineteen when he attended a Sinn Fein meeting in Middle Abbey Street, Dublin, after the Omagh raid in 1954, and he joined first Sinn Fein and then the I.R.A. His feelings about partition were simply a vague notion that Ireland would be better off with thirty-two counties than twenty-six, and he was personally anti-British. He was shaken by the Church's letter of January, 1955, but after a chat with a Jesuit he decided that this need not affect his political activities. An amiable, able lad, the gap left by the Christle defections brought him to the fore rapidly, and in September, 1956 he resigned his job as a clerk and went to Fermanagh under the name of Gerry Cronin. He was joined there by Dave O'Connell from Cork and they began training in Fermanagh and Tyrone.

Young Higginbothom always felt that the predominantly Catholic counties of Derry, Fermanagh and Tyrone, of which he had personal knowledge, were never suitably organised for lengthy guerrilla warfare or even for hit-and-run operations. Training with Thompson and Sten guns and rifles was carried out across the border in Monaghan and was confined to groups of approximately twenty young men at a time. Everyone thought that the movement would snowball when the campaign began, but they were shattered when the Southern police began picking up columns as they recrossed the border and it very soon became clear that no one was going to replace the captured men.

Only luck had kept Higginbothom from being caught before the campaign began. His car had broken down at Derrygonnelly, Co. Fermanagh, and an R.U.C. sergeant asked him his name and what he was doing in the area. Gerry explained that he was interested in exploring caves but he could not answer the policeman's request for the correct name for such activity (he called it archaeology instead of speleology). The sergeant walked off saying resignedly, 'I suppose you'll be coming back some night to put something against the gable end.'

When the campaign began Higginbothom's chosen gable end was Lisanelly Barracks, not far from Omagh. The attack called for the use of gelignite to breach the rear wall, but after obtaining the gelignite from Mountfield quarry, seven miles away, his lorry stuck in a ditch. While the lorry was being extricated sirens went off as other points were attacked and when Higginbothom and his group finally got back to the mustering point the rest of the raiding party had disappeared. Only their possession of two Thompson guns enabled him and his companions to secure a night's lodgings in a mountain farmhouse. (Another young I.R.A. man of the period, Terry O'Toole, told me that in his experience food and lodging had become so hard to find by 1958 as the campaign wore on that he frequently had to brandish a revolver to get in for a night.) There followed eighteen days in a shack with food being supplied at intervals by local sympathisers.

On New Year's Eve 1957 he and his column were ready to attack Carrickmore Barracks about ten miles away from their hideout when they learned of the Brookeborough affair (described below) and Carrickmore had to be abandoned because the area was alive with police and soldiers. They were advised to retreat to Strabane where Saor Uladh members put them up. They crossed the border with the aid of friendly girls who paired off with them as if they were going across to the Republic for a 'court'. In Dublin Higginbothom made contact with the leadership and was asked to return to the North, to Donegal, and to attempt to recross the border and organise a column around Strabane.

By this time, however, the more reliable men in Strabane had been picked up and he could get nothing done. In desperation he took twelve men to Clady one night and let off a mine at an old bridge in the hope that the military would be attracted to the scene and that an ambush could be carried out. However the R.U.C. made it a policy to ignore things that went bang in the night and this ploy failed. He returned to Strabane later dressed as a Franciscan friar and was saluted with due reverence. But he spent the first afternoon in dread because there was a woman dying nearby and for a time it seemed likely that he would be called on to administer the last rites. In the end he gave himself away in a shop by asking for a brand of Southern cigarettes that was not sold in the North. There are no Franciscans in the North anyhow and this slip enabled the R.U.C. to apprehend him. The campaign knew him no more.

A farmhouse at Knockatallon was intended as the operational H.Q. for the border area, the place from which raids could be launched and to which men could return. It was only about a mile and a half to the border from the house but on December 13, a cold, sleety night, to avoid the roads which were alive with police an I.R.A. patrol led by Charlie Murphy followed a route thirty miles over mountain and bog to attack the R.U.C. barracks in the town of Lisnaskea. In the town there were some anxious moments when it was learned that an I.R.A. suspect had been captured and was in a cell at the rear of the barracks. It was feared (wrongly) that he might have given away the raid and while Murphy and the others were going over the final plans in an outhouse not far from the barracks, the woman whose husband owned the farm burst in and exclaimed, 'That - - - - - bollocks has spilt the beans.' Murphy was thunderstruck, not because of the suspected leakage but because he had never heard a woman swear before. However they decided to go ahead.

Lisnaskea Barracks is a three-storeyed building in the main street of Lisnaskea with houses on either side, one of them the local curate's, who was then a Father Fergusson. Across the road lived the parish priest, Canon Donnelly. The I.R.A. party got word to him that they were shortly going to free 'occupied Ireland' and would he care to vacate his part of it in case something nasty came through his window during the war of liberation?

(Solicitude for the welfare of parish priests is not normally a characteristic of the I.R.A., but all had received confession a short time earlier from a Republican-minded young chaplain who had turned his Volkswagen into a roadside confessional.) The old canon sent back word that at his time of life death might as well come to him in his own house and he stayed put.

As the raid began Murphy was just removing a mine from the back of a truck when the driver put his foot on the accelerator instead of the brake, the truck moved forward and the mine dropped at Charlie's feet. The mine, which was made of gelignite, failed to explode. Half of the group then dashed across the road with it, and placed it in position. It went off perfectly at 1.20 a.m. and blew in the side of the barracks, and with it the staircase, which meant that the attackers could not get at the fourteen R.U.C. men. The aim of the raid had been to destroy the barracks and take whatever arms were available, but without heavy weaponry this was impossible. Neither of the two Bren guns used by the attackers functioned properly. The police replied with Sten guns and revolvers and between them the two parties managed to break almost every window in the town. After twenty minutes the I.R.A. broke off the attack and made off in the truck, sheets of tracer bullets pouring down the street after it. 'It made a very pretty sight' one of the residents of the town told me.

Derrylin Barracks was also attacked that night without any damage. Two bridges outside Lisnaskea were blown up to delay pursuit. Everyone concerned got back safely to Knockatallon, arriving in broad daylight, much to Sean Cronin's horror. Here they heard Costello's statement about 'appropriate action' and decided that weapons not immediately needed should be dumped.

The main column then returned across the border hoping to ambush a patrol. Cronin, Murphy and eleven others stayed on, Murphy intending to go next day to south Fermanagh with a sack of ammunition for Noel

Kavanagh. He then fell asleep and was shaken awake a few hours later to find that police and soldiers had surrounded the farm and that the kitchen was full of police. Everyone was very polite. 'Excuse me, sir,' said the soldier who had awakened him. 'Not at all,' he replied and when police and soldiers vanished upon discovering a mine upstairs, Murphy rendered it harmless for them.

There were a number of incriminating documents in the house and when the party was taken to Monaghan police station none of them expected to see home again for some time. But the police officer in charge of the operation telephoned Dublin from the room in which they were detained and to their incredulity they realised from the conversation that they might not be charged.

'No sir, they'd no ammunition,' they heard him say and they were told that they could go—whereupon they immediately refused to move unless they were given transport! The police contended that they had no transport, but Cronin and Murphy persisted and finally two taxis were hired and paid for by the police and the whole party driven to Dublin, Murphy and Cronin in a squad car. The pair walked up Emmet Road, where Murphy lived, in their American army battle dress, but finding that Mrs Murphy had gone to England to visit Donal they called round to a neighbour for breakfast.

A little later Magan came and told them that the campaign had been called off because of their arrest and that Laurence Grogan was in Drogheda contacting those concerned to tell them this. After much argument an Army Council meeting was called and it decided to re-activate the campaign, the men on the border being recalled, however, not only for Christmas but also to regroup and reorganise.

In a sense the Brookeborough ambush explains everything about the I.R.A. and its hold on Irish tradition. It shows all the courage, the self-sacrifice, the blundering and the emotional appeal that have characterised and kept alive the I.R.A. spirit for centuries. The two young men who lost their lives in the Brookeborough affair, Fergal O'Hanlon and Sean South, were given two of the biggest funerals in living memory—but during their lives there was never sufficient public support for their aims for them to receive proper military instruction or even to be correctly briefed on the target that claimed their lives: the R.U.C. barracks in the centre of the little Fermanagh town of Brookeborough.

O'Hanlon was nineteen at the time of his death and South twenty-seven. South was cut from the same cloth as Pearse or Liam Lynch. A clerk in his native Limerick city, he was a prominent member of An Realt, the Irish-speaking branch of the Legion of Mary. The Legion, the physical manifestation of the Mariolatry which characterises so much of Irish Catholicism, is the Irish equivalent of the American Peace Corps or the young Communist Komsommol, except that its members are dedicated to social work and missionary activity in the developing countries, not for nationalism or Communism, but for the Roman Catholic Church. South showed himself in his few writings to be a staunch though not uncritical Catholic and possessed of a social conscience. His attraction to the military calling is shown by the fact that the only photograph of him in circulation shows him in his uniform as an officer in the F.C.A., the regular Irish army reserve.

O'Hanlon was also an outstanding young man in his native Monaghan town. A keen footballer interested in Gaelic culture, he leaves several references in his diaries to the need for training and self-discipline in order to do his duty for Ireland. His I.R.A. comrades remember him as a particularly winning and promising boy.

In the course of writing this book I called on O'Hanlon's parents and visited the farm where he died. Mrs O'Hanlon looked and acted like the mother of a martyred saint. She had the same passionate dedication to the cause which claimed him as had her son and she spoke about his death as something holy as well as patriotic. It hurt her to hear anyone suggest that the cause should be abandoned or that the Republican movement should forswear force as a means of reuniting Ireland. To her, this was a betrayal of all that Fergal and those who went before him died for.

After a meal his father drove me to the place called Baxter's Cross. Hard by the Cross there stands an old-fashioned, two-storeyed farmhouse and beside it a cow-byre. It was in this byre that the bodies of O'Hanlon and South were found. A few miles away to the north is Brookeborough. (Ironically things had become so peaceful that the barracks which was the scene of the raid had become a private house occupied by a family.) Both the farmhouse and the byre at Baxter's Cross are deserted. There are no windows or doors in the byre and one has to look closely to pick out the bullet holes in the wall and the two tiny crosses which Mrs O'Hanlon set into the cement at the spots where her son and his comrade died.

It was frustration after so many failures that led to the Brookeborough raid, plus the fact that the raiders, who had been put out on long, fruitless patrol duty, had been supplied with detailed plans of the barracks by a local. On the night of the raid, January 1, 1957, the raiding party got its first full meal since Christmas at a friendly house and set off in a truck for the attack.

Brookeborough is an Irish town of the sort best described by the quip, 'It has only one main street and the further you go, the mainer it gets.' The barracks was located in the middle of the town in a house which looked no different from those adjoining it. The plan was for the truck to pull up outside the barracks, five men acting as a cover group staying in the truck to open fire and divert attention while an assault group armed with two mines, two Thompson guns and four rifles, augmented by a half-dozen or so home-made grenades, breached the barracks walls and gained entrance. While this was going on, two other men would keep watch on the roads leading into the town.

There was nothing to distinguish the barracks and in the badly lit street the driver, Vincent Conlon, who had given up a job in America to come home when he read of the raids, almost missed it. However, one member of the party, a local man, shouted out, 'Oh Jasus, there's the barracks,' and the truck stopped immediately outside the building. The cover group opened fire with a Bren gun and four rifles while the assault group attempted to let off a landmine. It failed to explode and the party had to dash back and get a second mine from the truck. This also misfired, even when someone tried to trigger it by shooting at it. Then South's Bren gun ran out of ammunition— they had only three magazines for it, a microscopic amount for such a quick-firing gun. As soon as its noise died away the raiders realised that the occupants of the barracks were returning their fire. South was hit first; like the others in the truck he was a sitting target from the upper windows of the barracks. One of the attackers threw a grenade at the barracks, but it bounced off a window-sill and fell under the truck. Just as this happened a burst of Bren-gun fire wounded Phil O'Donaghue, Sean Garland and Fergal O'Hanlon. Then the grenade went off and O'Donaghue was blown off the truck; as he hit the road he was struck by three bullets one of which ran right around his stomach under his belt without scratching him. All it left was a red weal.

Despite the rain of bullets, the party somehow scrambled back into the truck while the R.U.C. concentrated its fire on the driver. The windscreen was cracked and frosted by the bullets. Conlon could not see where he was going, but one of the men who had been guarding the approach to the town came back directly under the windows of the barracks and broke in the windscreen with his rifle butt. Conlon was unhurt but the truck's tipper gears had been shot to pieces and every time the truck went over a bridge or bump its back went up in the air and everyone in it slipped to the rear. Conlon managed to keep going for a few miles despite this damage and the ruined tyres and

then at Baxter's Cross the party halted, realising that the
R.U.C. must be close behind and that Roslea which lay
ahead would be alerted.

There was no one in the farmhouse and the only shelter
for O'Hanlon and South, who were both unconscious,
was the open cow-byre. Four other members of the party
were wounded and one, Sean Garland, wanted them to
leave him behind so that he could make a fight of it and
gain time for the rest to escape. He was dissuaded and
the survivors retreated up the hill a few hundred yards
in the direction of the border. About ten minutes later the
R.U.C. drove up, stopped by the abandoned truck and,
taking no chances, opened fire on it for what seemed like
five minutes. A few minutes later the I.R.A. party heard
one long burst of fire coming from the direction of the
cow-byre and they believed afterwards that this was the
coup de grâce being administered to O'Hanlon and South.
However, Pat Regan (upon whose personal account I
have based this description of the raid) went back to the
spot some years later and found that the line of bullet
holes was approximately waist to chest high on the wall
facing the cow-byre entrance and he concluded that none
of these bullets struck either O'Hanlon or South, unless
perhaps by ricochet. He attributed the firing on the cow-
byre to the normal military tactics, employed when approaching a strongpoint supposedly held by the enemy,
of falling on one knee and firing a burst. However, this
explanation did not percolate through I.R.A. circles for
some years and the deaths of O'Hanlon and South were
a source of intense bitterness.

The survivors reached the Monaghan border safely
where, after resting in a friendly house, they gave themselves up to obtain medical attention for the wounded.
They were treated in the Mater Hospital, Dublin, and
although the police were supposedly keeping a keen eye
on them, and their names were printed in the papers,
they all managed to leave their sick beds at varying inter-

vals and get out of the hospital, which has a long Nationalist tradition, without being detained.

The greatest single disaster of the entire campaign was the Edentubber explosion in Co. Louth which claimed five lives in November, 1957. In some parts of the Irish countryside where tragedy has walked across some green corner it is possible to recreate the event from a relic of some sort—a tumbled-down church, a ruin, a cross perhaps—but at Edentubber today all that remains is a five-barred gate leading into an empty field. Not a stone stands to mark the spot where four young I.R.A. men and the owner of the forester's cottage were blown to pieces when a home-made landmine went off, just before the four set off to cross the Louth border a few yards away. Nearby are homes where you can talk with people who sympathised with the young men and were prepared to help them. Behind the hill there is a lane which leads to a Mass rock inscribed with a cross, a memento of the religious division of the penal days that began the whole affair. Behind rise the Carlingford Mountains, ahead lies Newry, home of one of the dead boys, Oliver Craven, nineteen. In the distance there is Armagh, the birthplace of a second victim, Paul Smith, also nineteen, and away to the south far beyond the reach of eye is Co. Wexford, which gave a title to one of President Kennedy's favourite songs, 'The Boys of Wexford'.

> We are the Boys of Wexford,
> We fought with heart and hand
> To burst in twain our Captive Chains
> And free our native land.

George Keegan, twenty-nine, and Patrick Parle, twenty-seven, had been singing that song since boyhood, and on the night of November 12, 1957, they had left their native Wexford to play a part, as they saw it, in freeing their native land. The fifty-five-year-old bachelor who went to death with them had lived alone since his mother died.

His life and death were symbolic of the Irish: love of his mother denied him a wife; love of his fatherland took his life. Little wonder that the news of this affair shocked Murphy and Cronin. Murphy in particular became prey to a melancholy, suffering for years afterwards, losing weight and frequently waking up sweating in the grip of nightmares.

It is here worth looking briefly at the career of a prominent I.R.A. man of the border campaign period—Terry O'Toole. He saw much active service over a long period, was one of the 'activists' while interned in the Curragh and was very aware of the intrigues and splits that affected the movement.

O'Toole joined the I.R.A. in June, 1954, influenced by the Armagh raid and by the fact that his uncle, Tom Maguire of Mayo, was and is a life-long Republican. He joined the Heath unit (named from the heath near Portlaoighise, another traditionally Republican area where MacLogan had his pub). Nothing happened beyond routine drilling and meetings until August, 1957, despite repeated appeals by Terry and the unit to be sent north. MacLogan was the leading figure in the area and was not in favour of such action.

Then in August word came from Dublin that five men were required immediately for active service. Terry could not supply the request and went to Galmoy in neighbouring Kilkenny to get two volunteers. With these he went to Dublin and was directed to Donegal. The first operation was to be an ambush of British soldiers from Omagh Barracks along the Omagh-Derry road. However the ambush party, about fifteen strong, was forestalled and a police raid seized 150 lbs of gelignite which had been made into mines.

O'Toole and the others withdrew to Mountfield in south Tyrone and began to train about fourteen local youths, there and in Carrickmore. The local people were friendly but the I.R.A. was very poorly organised and Frank

Morris of Convoy, Co. Donegal, who was strictly speaking in Saor Uladh, was their mentor in the area. It was to him that they looked for guidance rather than to Dublin. O'Toole and his group worked with local farmers cutting turf and sharing farmhouse chores. There was no difficulty about freedom of movement by day but night raids by police on suspected houses became so heavy that accommodation was hard to find.

It was decided to build a dug-out in a farmhouse which was used as a piggery by a friendly farmer. Working at night, they removed the floor of one room and dug down eight feet, scattering the yellow clay in a nearby potato field lest it attract attention. The hole was then covered with railway sleepers provided by sympathisers, and the sleepers were covered with concrete. Entry was provided by a shaft which was cut from under a small porch outside the house. Covered by a camouflaged trap-door the shaft and dug-out were completely hidden. After giving the concrete a week to settle straw was sprinkled over it and the pigs were allowed back in. In all it took ten days to build during which the I.R.A. group lived on packets of chicken noodle soup and potatoes from nearby fields. It seemed a small price to pay in return for the safety of the dug-out, but in fact the hiding place nearly killed them all. When they woke up after the first night in the shelter all of them were suffering from excruciating headaches. There was such an acute lack of oxygen that matches would not strike. Worse, they could not force open the trap-door, because the pigs were lying on it. Eventually the tallest man in the group managed to get his shoulder to the door and forced it and a surprised pig into the air. He almost collapsed from the effort. Had his strength not sustained him for the moment all those in the dug-out would have died.

Supplies were now needed for their raids as they had only approximately two hundred rounds of Thompson and three hundred rounds of revolver ammunition. Intelligence was another problem for although the locals were friendly their information was usually so outdated as to be useless. Information about troop movements was finally obtained only after several nights were spent in the open watching B-Specials setting up road blocks a few yards away from them. Then, having discovered when and where to carry out ambushes the supplies problem reasserted itself; four separate lots of equipment sent from Dublin were all seized.

In a hopeless position they decided to move to Monaghan where they thought organisation and opportunities would be better. It took them two days on foot, sleeping out at night, and when they got there they learned that two of their number were named in an R.U.C. leaflet as being wanted in connection with the death of a sergeant the previous August. They could all have faced a capital charge had they been caught, and the fact that they were not informed of the leaflet earlier is indicative of the lack of communication between border units and G.H.Q. in Dublin. Then in December O'Toole, Sean Cronin and J. B. O'Hagan, the leading figure in the North, decided that O'Toole's column should be broken up and that he would try to organise the adjoining areas of Lifford, Co. Donegal, and Strabane, Co. Tyrone.

Between Christmas and Easter his group succeeded in blowing up four transformers on a line between Lifford and Derry, a customs hut and an R.A.F. hut. The plan in each case was to attract the military to the scene and ambush them. The Northerners refused to be drawn and neither shooting nor loss of life took place.

Another operation that failed to materialise was planned for Easter under the direction of a Dubliner, Jimmy McGilligan. Over sixty men were to have taken over the village of Clady and make a stand there, similar to that envisaged by Tom Barry in the 1930s. The approaches to Clady were to have been ambushed for some considerable distance so that Easter Monday 1958 would rival Easter Monday 1916. The scheme fell through when the extra men required from Dublin were not forthcoming. Instead

Sean Cronin ordered a 'demonstration' in the village.

Seven men accordingly entered the village on Easter Monday night. The Army Council's Easter message was read out, a number of I.R.A. leaflets were distributed and the proceedings concluded with the hoisting of the tricolour and the firing of a volley over the post office. The group waited outside the town hoping to stage an ambush but nothing happened until the following day when a tank arrived at the village to supervise the removal of the tricolour. The next day O'Toole and his group had planned to blow up a B-Special hut but their hideout was discovered and they were taken in handcuffs to the Curragh.

While the bombs continued to go off during 1958, particularly during July, the most significant I.R.A. activity was hidden from the public and in fact took place within the Curragh internment camp.

After a number of skirmishes on the border and raids on quarries in the Republic for gelignite de Valera had reintroduced the Offences Against the State Act on July 4. Sixty men were picked up in one swoop on July 8 and by the following March a total of 131 were interned in the reopened Curragh. (The camp, however, did not remain open long. The campaign fell into such disarray that the last of the internees were released on March 11, 1959.)

Compared to the rigours of the war years the Curragh now was almost a rest camp. The food was plentiful if unvaried and could be supplemented from outside or by meals cooked in the huts on electric rings. Tea could be obtained from an immersion boiler. There were four huts at the peak of the internment containing about forty detainees in each. Each hut had its own O.C. and there was a camp council of prisoners with Thomas MacCurtain as O.C. The huts were opened at 7 a.m. and breakfast was served in the dining hall at 8. Anyone who was sick got breakfast in his hut, served by a member of the Legion of

Mary, until he recovered or was transferred to hospital. Everyone did a spell of orderly duty, cleaning out the lavatory (renamed 'Boland's' in honour of the minister for justice), or washing dishes and generally tidying up. Showers were compulsory once a week, and could be had more often. A nearby field was made available for games and the prisoners were also encouraged to read or to make wallets and crosses which were sold outside the camp to raise funds.

The worst feature of internment was the lack of privacy. No one could ever get away from his fellows, or from the sound of chipping and snipping as yet another wallet or cross began its journey to the outside. To a sensitive person the conditions were hell, but several of the internees told me that if you overlooked the defences the place was 'more like a factory than a camp'.

The camp was protected by five sets of fences. Two lay between the camp and a trench six feet deep and eight feet wide, which was booby-trapped with flares and trip-wires, and three more fences had to be surmounted when and if this was negotiated. At the four corners of the camp elevated sentry posts were manned by an armed guard. In addition the perimeter was patrolled by guards armed with revolvers and ammonia grenades.

The prisoners were divided among themselves as to escaping. The camp council frowned on escape attempts believing it best to avoid doing anything that might get someone killed. The activists thought this a cowardly attitude and felt that the proper course for Republicans was to make life difficult for their jailers in the time-honoured manner. Two of the activist group, O'Toole and Conlon, the driver at the Brookeborough raid, brought the debate to a head by trying to escape without the sanction of the camp council.

On first being interned O'Toole was almost glad of the rest and food—apart from the 'patriotic eggs', which were so called because, he claims, when cooked they assumed the national colours of green, white and orange and were apt to turn into concrete if left on a plate. But the novelty wore off soon and he gladly fell in with Conlon's suggestion that they escape. At the time the two men were receiving treatment for slight illnesses in the camp hospital and Conlon thought they could get out through a window in the shower cubicle which was protected only by two iron bars. This window also opened on to clear ground away from the camp defences.

On Whit Sunday they attacked the bars, taking a shower each on each guard's watch and by the following night, although somewhat chilled from their series of unwanted showers, they had sawn through the bars with saws from the handicraft classes. A third occupant of the ward, a young volunteer named Kelly, was to accompany them and he unwittingly caused the escape to fail. Conlon, as arranged, went into the shower first leaving O'Toole playing draughts. A few moments later O'Toole also went to the shower, on the pretext of washing some shirts and underwear. This was the signal for Kelly to follow, first putting some turf on the fire and thus necessitating his washing his hands.

Conlon, a large man, stuck in the window for a moment and had to be pushed through. O'Toole followed more easily. They waited for five minutes for Kelly, unaware that the guard had begun chatting with him just as he made for the shower, and then decided to head for Kilcullen, a village on the main Dublin road. Incredibly they had made no plans for hiding places, although Terry was reared less than twenty miles from the Curragh. After about ten minutes the pursuit began but they got away safely to a place called Yellow Bog, about six miles from the camp. They then decided to knock on the first house they came to, and by good fortune it turned out to be the home of a member of Sinn Fein.

They stayed there for the night, but did not dare to sleep. Next day planes circled the area and soldiers appeared nearby. Kelly, who had finally escaped, had been in the vicinity, attempting unsuccessfully to gain admission to three neighbouring houses, so that their presence in the area was known. They left through the back of the house, deciding not to cross the Liffey which flowed nearby. Later in the day a lorry dropped some troops near their hiding place and they made a run for it. It was now Tuesday and as they had had no sleep since the previous Sunday they slept in a ditch, covering themselves with sacks.

O'Toole awoke to find a young soldier prodding him with a bayonet and that was the end of the escape bid—a fact which was not made any the more pleasant by the officer in charge telling them that had they crossed the Liffey they would have got away as the far side was not being searched.

This short-lived burst for freedom renewed the issue of escape especially when militant members, in particular Charlie Murphy, J. B. O'Hagan and Willie Gleeson, were picked up and interned. These grouped under Murphy's leadership, along with O'Toole and Frank Driver, a phenomenal character who never allows his humorous brand of anti-clericalism (based mainly on the position of the bishops on the Act of Union issue in 1800) to interfere with his Christian charity.

Driver was particularly active in planning escapes. One suggestion of his was that the wife of an internee who had ten children should take them all to the house of the Most Rev. Dr John Charles McQuaid, Archbishop of Dublin, and deposit them on his doorstep for safekeeping until her husband was released! Another was that the wives, female relatives and sympathisers of the internees should make a mass march on the barbed wire from the outside, cutting their way in with wire cutters. 'Jasus,' said Frank, 'think of the publicity if one of them got shot.' The camp council thought of it and turned the proposal down with horror.

When Murphy arrived in camp there were two escape projects in train. One involved cutting a tunnel under the wire, but it came to nothing as a sergeant spotted some of the clay from the tunnel that had been carelessly dumped on a path. The second one worked though not the way the activists had intended.

A blanket was taken from the hut where most of the activists lived (it was called 'Little Rock' after the Arkansas trouble spot) and covered with grass in a corner of the playing field. Two detainees slipped under it while another group stood around to mask them from the sentries. When it was dark the two simply slid under the wire while back in the huts two dummy beds were made up so that the customary inspection found nothing wrong. The trouble was that when the camp council, which had been pressed into sponsoring the escape sent word to Sean Cronin about the scheme, he nominated Dave O'Connell and Rory Brady as his candidates for escape whereas those in the camp wanted Murphy and O'Hagan to go out. Cronin's men went.

Cronin himself was interned not long before the camp elections to choose a new O.C. It had been expected that MacCurtain might stand down and that Murphy would stand in his place, but in the event MacCurtain went forward and Murphy preferred not to stand against him. J. B. O'Hagan stood in Murphy's place and was narrowly defeated. Cronin remained neutral until the night of the election when he advised that policy be left as it was, in the hands of the official leadership, the 'three Macs'.

To the militants the election result meant that if they wanted action they would have to bring it about themselves, and that Murphy was the only leader they could look to to support such a policy. The activist group now gained two supporters, Frank Armstrong, and a young Limerick man, Jimmy Devereux, an expert fitter who could make wire-cutting equipment. The hacksaws used in making souvenirs had all been withdrawn and their only wire-cutting tool was a pair of pliers which a detainee had hidden. But using angle-irons and a six-foot-long poker from the laundry Devereux made three wire-cutters, tempering the steel in the hut fire while members of the group lounged around screening the operation not only from the camp authorities but also from the supporters of the 'no escape' policy, who would certainly have attempted to stymie the attempt if they could. The poker was used to make extended arms for the cutters.

The escape was planned for December, 1958. Twenty-six men were to take part and after getting away they intended to go to Meath to regroup and recommence operations on the border. Everyone went to confession before the escape bid, which in the event failed to come off on the chosen date for it was discovered that soldiers were stationed all around the big trench. The minister for justice was visiting the camp and a general stand-to had been ordered.

The next day, Willie Gleeson, Tom Ferris, Terry O'Toole and Devereux cut their way through the first fence before the guards realised what was happening. Then a guard ran up firing two revolver shots which struck no one. O'Toole noticed as he ran that the sentry in the elevated post nearest to him had his rifle in the air and this seemed to confirm the theory that the escapees would not be fired on. He ran on, passing within eight feet of the guard who was firing the revolver, not knowing that behind him Brian Boylan had already been shot. Charlie Murphy, who had stayed at the gap assisting the others through, went to Boylan's assistance. The rest of the group cleared the second and third fences and reached the dyke without further casualties. Then ammonia grenades were thrown at them. Hampered as they were by trip wires that set off flares they floundered among the coils of barbed wire, everyone injured or cut or temporarily blinded. O'Toole was shot in the right thigh, but kept going. By the time the last fence was reached the cutters had been abandoned and the group, by now reduced to ten, attacked the fence with bare hands and clawed it down while the ground was cut up by flying bullets.*

* The Republicans were particularly bitter about this shooting, but in fairness it should be underlined that the sentries in

It was approximately a mile to the nearest cover, a field with a thick ditch, where they carried out what first aid they could. One of them, Pat McGirl, was completely blind from the ammonia gas and was later captured as was Liam Fagan who had been shot in the knee and had to crawl on his stomach. First aid had to be abandoned as the soldiers drew near again and the group split up. Some of them then went to Moone, near the camp, and called inadvertently at a house where a man was being waked. The widow was not a Republican herself, but her husband had been one and she paused in her grief to arrange that the escapees be taken to friendly houses.

Equipped with maps O'Toole and his companions (Gleeson, Devereux, Gerry Houghey, and Dan Donaghy) circled Kildare and headed for Portarlington town, following a route that took them thirty-five miles instead of the normal eighteen. They reached a friendly house on the outskirts of Portarlington the next morning, wounded and exhausted, and a doctor was sent for (he turned out to be a state medical officer). He tended their wounds and the others moved on but O'Toole's leg prevented him from travelling. He stayed there for two days until the woman of the house dressed him as a woman and drove him to the west of Ireland where a sympathetic surgeon got him into a hospital, and the bullet was removed from his leg, nearly four days after he was shot.

Back in the camp and in the ranks of the I.R.A. throughout the country the escape deepened the split in the movement. To the official leadership, that is to say the remnant that remained of an organisation, the escapees had put themselves outside the movement and almost every Army Council meeting between then and June was

---

the elevated posts could probably have killed many of the escapees had they wished. The number of leg wounds seems to indicate that they deliberately aimed low. The soldier with the revolver who first inflicted casualties was disarmed by an officer as he prepared to fire at some of the escapees from point-blank range.

devoted to discussing what should be done about them. And on top of this issue there was heated argument over the control of Sinn Fein. Should the party be autonomous or should it be controlled by the I.R.A.?

There was one distraction during this arguing. Joseph Christle dumped an unwanted hero into the I.R.A. ranks, James Andrew Mary Murphy whom he had rescued from Wakefield Prison, February 12, 1959. Then the London *Daily Express*, whose Irish correspondent Seamus Brady, was known to be particularly well informed about all levels of Irish politics, constitutional and otherwise, printed a report asking, 'Is Murphy Skuse?' Controversy blew up within and without the I.R.A. as to whether he was Skuse and, if he was, whether he should be extradited to England. Ultimately he was not but for a time this issue drew attention away from what was left of the campaign and from the controversy within the movement, most of it directed against Charlie Murphy for his acceptance of parole at the time of the MacMahon incident and his leadership of the escape.

There were two legal proceedings during the campaign of which mention must be made here. The more important was the case of Gerrard Lawless—the first to be judged by the Court of Human Rights in Strasbourg.

Lawless, who had an I.R.A. record, was arrested by Detective Inspector MacMahon on July 11, 1957, just as he was about to leave Ireland for England. Lawless said that MacMahon offered him a job and money if he would give information about the I.R.A. but that he had refused, claiming that he was not in the I.R.A. (he had sided with Christle in the split). He was then interned in the Curragh where he was, in fact, ostracised by the I.R.A. detainees.

From the Curragh Lawless contacted a Dublin lawyer, Ciaran Mac An Ali, asking him to take his case. Some of the finest lawyers* in Ireland joined Mac An Ali in

* Senior counsels Sean MacBride and Tommy Connolly,

doing so and on November 8, 1957, an application on behalf of Lawless was filed before the European Commission on Human Rights asking immediate release from the Curragh, payment of compensation and damages, and payment of all costs before both the Irish courts and the Court of Human Rights. On the advice of his lawyers Lawless then reluctantly availed himself of the machinery for release from the camp by signing an 'undertaking' and he was freed on December 10.

After a lengthy argument, first through the European Commission and then through the Court of Human Rights to which the Commission's judges had referred the case, judgement was given against Lawless on July 1, 1961, but despite this some important principles were set out. Lawless's lawyers established that the 'undertaking' which Curragh internees signed to release themselves had no legal status as it was not provided for by the Offences Against the State Act to which it referred. More significantly the court set the precedent that it did not have to accept a member country's own opinion as to whether a state of emergency existed within that country sufficient to warrant such measures as internment, but that it could exercise its own judgement as to the extent of the internal crisis, and consequently could rule on the measures adopted to deal with that crisis.

This decision had a direct effect upon Irish politics. When the border campaign flared up again temporarily in 1961-62 the government did not resort to internment camps but instead had recourse to military courts. These imposed sentences of several years—which were quickly commuted to months when the I.R.A. called off the campaign. It is, indeed, doubtful that any Irish government will use internment camps again except in the gravest emergency.

---

junior counsel Seamus Sorahan and one of the country's leading solicitors, P. C. Moore. They continued the tradition of defending the I.R.A. men without payment.

The most dramatic court case of the entire period was the 'Mallon and Talbot affair' which, although it received far more publicity than the Lawless case, had far less long-term significance.

The affair began on August 17, 1957, when R.U.C. Sergeant Arthur Ovens kicked open the door of an unused cottage near Coalisland, Co. Tyrone, and was blown to bits by a mine. The R.U.C., understandably enraged by the death of a colleague who was also the father of three children, nearly took Coalisland apart looking for those responsible. After lengthy interrogations the R.U.C. came up with Kevin Mallon and Patrick Talbot, both twenty-one, as the chief suspects.

In Dublin (where to this day it is not known exactly who set the booby-trap) Charlie Murphy and Sean Cronin decided that regardless of the policy of not recognising the courts Mallon and Talbot would have to be defended or they would be hanged. Again Sean MacBride came to the rescue after Murphy and Cronin had failed to get another Dublin lawyer interested in the case. MacBride advised them that no Unionist lawyer would take the case, that a Nationalist would be too timorous and that the best thing to do was to get an Englishman. He then arranged for Elwys Jones, later a Labour attorney general, to defend the two young men. A vigorous publicity campaign (in which the *New Statesman* was prominent) highlighted the tortures to which Mallon and Talbot were allegedly subjected and a special committee was formed in Dublin to raise funds for the defence. As a result of this, and of Jones's efforts, Mallon and Talbot were sentenced to prison rather than to execution and they were freed when the campaign ended.

The campaign had manifestly failed, although with Irish doggedness the movement was on one hand looking for a scapegoat to blame for the failure and on the other trying to prolong the attacks on the border. It eventually did find a formula whereby the Curragh escapees could be

received back into the fold. They signed readmission
forms, which were a sort of admission that they had been
thrown out but now accepted the authority of the official
section of the movement. In fact O'Toole and the others
planned to eject the 'pacifist' section of the movement
at the convention elections in June, 1959, but for the
moment they co-operated with the existing leadership.

By June the rift in the I.R.A. had become public
knowledge. Reports of a split appeared in the papers and
denials by the I.R.A. publicity bureau certainly failed to
convince the Special Branch at least whose members
frequently accosted I.R.A. men in the streets and asked
them, 'Which I.R.A. do you belong to, Charlie Murphy's
or the official I.R.A.?' without even bothering to arrest
any of them. Worse the authorities publicly showed their
contempt for the movement by gradually releasing the
men in the Curragh. By March, 1959 the movement was
no longer a real threat, despite the British ambassador's
formal protest against the releases and de Valera's angry
exchange with British Prime Minister Harold Mac-
millan. Yet even after de Valera retired on June 17,
1959 (he became president) I.R.A. activity continued to
poison British-Irish relationships. De Valera's successor,
Sean Lemass, worked unavailingly for a revision of the
Anglo-Irish Free Trade Agreement of 1948, which by
the terms of the Agreement should have been revised by
1959. It was not until 1965 under the Labour government
that the Irish secured a new and satisfactory trade agreement.

Within the I.R.A., the campaign against Charlie
Murphy reached a poisonous intensity, and Myles Shevlin
tried to heal the rift at a meeting in Monasterevan, Co.
Kildare, on Spy Wednesday, April, 1959. Everyone reacted amicably and parted friends, but nothing came of
the meeting. In fact for a time relations got worse when,
after the June convention the Murphy wing, having failed
to secure his elevation and the overthrow of the 'pacifists',
resolved to carry out border raids on its own and com-

mandeered weapons from the 'official' I.R.A. These were
given back after Cronin informed O'Toole that his section
had a series of operations planned along the border.
When Murphy heard this he realised that the situation
was drifting not towards war against the North, but towards war within the I.R.A. and he ordered that the captured weapons be handed back.

Charge and countercharge flew with the dum-dum
destructiveness of character that the Irish can so well
employ. When Murphy tried to clear his name by calling
for an inquiry the report praised Murphy with faint damns
in such a way as neither to make the past forgettable nor
the future attractive. Murphy resigned and entered a
black period of self-doubt, financial stringency and read-
justment. Throughout this time the kindness of Sean
MacBride was one of the things that kept him sane.
Murphy's wife Carmel worked as a waitress and he was
taken back by the Guinness brewery. At the time of
writing he and Carmel are the most law abiding and
popular members of their suburban community, devoting
their energies to nothing more revolutionary than residents'
association and bring-and-buy sales. Myles Shevlin and
Thomas MacCurtain also parted with the movement
shortly after the Monasterevan meeting and Sean Cronin
was made the subject of an inquiry after allegations of
Communism were directed against him. The inquiry
found no substance in the allegations but Cronin too
resigned from the army. He is now a successful journalist
in America.

During all this time blood was still being shed. On
July 2, 1958, a police patrol fired on an I.R.A. patrol near
Clontivern, Co. Fermanagh, and killed the column leader,
Aloysius Hand, a twenty-year-old unemployed labourer.
He had a loaded Thompson gun, and according to the
evidence given at the inquest had fired two bursts before
the R.U.C. shot. A verdict of justifiable homicide was
returned.

Later on July 15, 16 and 17 the campaign flared up all

along the border in the major show of activity since its inception in December, 1956. Explosions took place from Down to Derry, resulting in two deaths, a number of injuries and some destruction to customs huts and to bridges.

The first death was deliberate. Constable H. B. Ross, Forkhill, was cycling through Moircastle on the south Armagh border when an electrically triggered mine was detonated from behind a hedge. Although he was badly injured he managed to walk to a nearby house to wait for an ambulance. He died in hospital the next day leaving a wife and child. The second death was caused by the I.R.A.'s faulty bomb-making. Patrick MacManus, twenty-seven, the principal I.R.A. leader at liberty in the North was removing a gelignite mine, made in a biscuit box, from a cache on the roadside at Drumcask, Co. Cavan, when it went off, blowing him to pieces. The physical damage wrought in this short-lived offensive ranged from the destruction of the biggest customs post between North and South, the Killeen post on the main Dundalk-Belfast road, which was wrecked, to craters blown in unapproved roads.

One particularly distasteful killing occurred on August 24, 1958: the shooting of James Crossan by the R.U.C. in ambiguous circumstances at the customs post at Mullan, Co. Fermanagh.

The I.R.A. claimed that Crossan was murdered and this is how his death is described in its roll of honour. The R.U.C. said in a statement that 'the suspicions of a police patrol on duty near the British Customs post at Mullan, Co. Fermanagh, were aroused by persons approaching the post from the direction of Eire. Police called on these persons to halt, whereupon they bolted towards the Border . . . They again called on them to halt. One man stopped but the others continued running. Police opened fire and later . . . the dead body of a young man was found. The other man, who like the dead man is a native of Eire, has been detained.'

However a statement from 'An Enniskillen correspondent', in the *Irish Press* said, 'Crossan and McHugh parted from three Fermanagh friends, two of them Unionists, on the Fermanagh side of the Border at Mullan at about 3.30 a.m. The three Fermanagh friends drove off in a van towards Kinawley and the two Cavan men were walking back again to another van which had brought the five to the Cavan [Southern] side of the Border when Mr Crossan was shot dead by Six County police who had taken up positions near the Customs hut.'

At the inquest a verdict of justifiable homicide was returned and this was met by an indignant press release from the I.R.A. saying that '. . . James Crossan was unarmed. The suggestion that he and Ben McHugh were on a reconnaissance mission at Mullan British Customs post is ridiculous.'

While 1960 was uneventful, 1961 began and ended with deaths, and of all the deaths of the campaign these are the least defensible. Public support for the 'physical force' policy had been falling away and this, combined with new political preoccupations and new political figures and philosophies that greatly improved the standard of living in the South pushed the whole border question well into the background. (In the general election of 1961, Sinn Fein lost all four seats and its poll fell by over 50 per cent.)

Nevertheless the militants struck again. On January 27, 1961, a young R.U.C. man, Corporal Norman Anderson, was taken up a lane shortly after he had said goodnight to his sweetheart, and thirty-four bullets were shot into his back. The I.R.A. believed that he had been spying on its movements. In the wake of condemnation, South and North, the I.R.A. pulled in its horns for the summer, but on November 12, a police patrol was ambushed at Jonesborough, Co. Armagh, and another policeman, Constable William Hunter, was shot dead. There were protests from Belfast, from the British government and from Dublin and the Southern government decided to act.

T.I.R.A. O

On November 22, it was announced that the government was setting up the Special Criminal Court again. The court was composed of army officers and there was no doubt that the government, and in particular the new minister for justice, Charles Haughey, a young man who had come to the fore after the 1961 election, were determined to take the most drastic measures to scotch not alone the campaign but also the I.R.A. at the next possible opportunity. The I.R.A. decided not to give them that opportunity.

On February 26, 1962, the Irish Republican Publicity Bureau announced that:

'The Leadership of the Resistance Movement has ordered the termination of "The Campaign of Resistance to British Occupation" . . . all arms and other materials have been dumped and all full-time active service volunteers have been withdrawn.'

The statement added that one factor responsible for the decision had been the attitude of the public, 'whose minds have been deliberately distracted from the supreme issue facing the Irish people—the unity and freedom of Ireland'.

Press and public welcomed the announcement. Perhaps the best comment was that of the *New York Times* which said:

'The original I.R.A. and Sinn Fein came in like lions . . . and now they go out like lambs . . . they have been condemned by the most deadly of all judgements, public indifference . . . Partition is resented but the present generation know that if Partition is ever to be ended it must be by peaceful arrangements. The few young toughs who make up the tiny remnant that now lays down its arms used a grand and famous name for their organisation, but the Irish Republican Army belongs to history, and it belongs to better men in times that are gone. So does the Sinn Fein. Let us put a wreath of red roses on their grave and move on.'

EPILOGUE

After the campaign ended the dissension within the ranks of the Republicans continued. The dispute centred upon who should control the Republican movement henceforth and again the situation resembled that at the end of the Civil War. The 'physical force' men had been beaten; disillusion and depression had set in; scapegoats had to be found, and there was no clear leadership.

Eamonn Boyce is an example of what I.R.A. men were like at the time and of what they encountered. Boyce emerged from prison to find that his mother had suffered through the loss of his income and through helping his colleagues. She had slept for months with several hundred-weights of gelignite under her bed, worried by his absence and the presence of the explosives and, as Boyce said, 'wondering where she got the headaches'. Eventually he found a job as a bus conductor, but first he had to master his nerves so that he could cross a road unaided, make a simple purchase in a shop, sign on at a Labour Exchange, or do any of the normal things which prison keeps a man from doing. Many of Boyce's comrades decided they could take no more and dropped out of the movement completely. Patrick MacLogan was found dead in his back garden with a revolver beside him, causing allegations and counter-allegations in the I.R.A. as to how he died.

Gradually, after 1964, the movement began to build it-self up again. The most significant single individual was perhaps Roy Johnston, a young Marxist computer scientist who became so trusted by the I.R.A. leaders that he was appointed to the Army Council as a kind of education officer cum political commissar. Under his influence I.R.A. policy moved steadily left. The absence of a strong ideological grounding (apart from the crusading to end partition by force), made this a relatively easy process, at least at leadership level; among the grass-roots members and those of a right-wing cast of mind the new developments were worrying.

In 1965 the political arm of the movement, Sinn Fein, announced that it would continue to sit on local government bodies but would also continue to boycott Stormont, the Dail and Westminster. However the party decided, somewhat paradoxically, that in the event of Sinn Fein winning an over-all majority, which would enable it to take over the Dail, the party would do so: constitutionalism, too, was growing during this period. In the North Sean McCaughey, who had been a vice-president of Sinn Fein, resigned and concentrated on building up an Irish union movement along much the same lines as Denis Ireland's efforts of the 1940s. Helped by the emotionalism of the 1916 anniversary celebrations in 1966 Sinn Fein increased its strength, openly in the South and in the North under the guise of Republican clubs. At the 1966 Ard Fheis Sinn Fein was pledged by its president, Tomas McGoilla, to an effort to win a majority in the Dail within five years. At Bodenstown in 1967 Cathal Goulding made his speech in favour of socialist policies and decried the movement's concentration on the 'physical force' policy found in the writings of Dan Breen.

But the activist tradition inevitably re-emerged and throughout 1966 several incidents and bombings took place, the most celebrated being the destruction of Nelson's Pillar. One young Republican, Richard Behal, in jail in Limerick on charges arising out of a visit to Ireland by Princess Margaret, made a dramatic escape at midnight on New Year's Eve 1966, and for the greater part of the year, on the run from both the left-wing I.R.A. and the Special Branch, was openly associated with some of these incidents. Another group of Republicans which favoured the use of force began to coalesce into what became known as the Saor Eire Action Group and this took a hand at bank raids. Between 1967 and mid-April 1970 either it or the I.R.A. carried out seventeen bank raids. In the last, disavowed by the official I.R.A., a garda was killed.

Throughout this period the *United Irishman* struck up a medley of Fenian and Marxist airs despite the fact that there were rumblings from Clann na Gael in America that the leftward swing was not to its liking. In England the movement made some ground by dropping the title Sinn Fein and trying to amalgamate all the various emigré Irish parties and associations under the banner of a new grouping: Clann na hEireann, 'the family of Gaels'. In Dublin the Republicans' greatest success in terms of publicity was the sponsorship of the Dublin Housing Action Committee, a body which existed independently of the I.R.A. to do something for Dublin's homeless. The I.R.A. put muscle into its demonstrations and sit-ins, and in the country also, wherever disputes arose over small farmers seeking to have large estates broken up, the I.R.A. became active in land leagues. Foreigners who owned land in Ireland or who held Irish ground-rents were singled out for verbal and sometimes physical attack. In May, 1968 the I.R.A. burned out £60,000 worth of buses used to take workers to a factory owned by an American company, the E.I. Company of Shannon, during a dispute over union recognition. In the west, in Rossaveal on the Connemara coast, a £6,000 fishing boat owned by an American-financed company was wrecked in August by an I.R.A. bomb, and in June, 1969 a number of buildings on farms owned by Germans were set alight.

But the I.R.A.'s most significant initiative was its behind-the-scenes involvement in the Northern civil rights movement. The broad-based civil rights movement, which captured the world's headlines, began with a private meeting of interested parties in Derry in August, 1967, and a public meeting the following October in Maghera. Cathal Goulding attended the Derry meeting and while he said frankly that he did not think it would work, he pledged the I.R.A. to give it a trial. The association worked brilliantly: Unionist spokesmen continually thundered that C.R.A. (Civil Rights Association) was only another way of saying I.R.A., but never a shot was fired, never an I.R.A. man showed himself as such and the I.R.A. deserves some of the credit for the great success of the civil rights movement, although politically it got swallowed by it much as it did in Fianna Fail's success in 1932.

As the civil rights movement spread figures such as John Hume, Ivan Cooper, Gerry Fitt and Bernadette Devlin came to national and then international prominence and the radical movement, People's Democracy, received much publicity. Behind the scenes, however, many older Republicans of the generation of 1940 disagreed violently with the passive resistance policy. The idea of going up to a policeman at a barricade and allowing him to baton one into the ground without any attempt at retaliation was common ground with the Southern opponents of the socialist policy generally but all criticism was stifled by the enormous publicity the civil rights movement received after October 5, 1968. Then a peaceful march in Derry was batonned by the R.U.C. and there began the decline into anarchy, the erosion of respect for the R.U.C. as an impartial force and the build-up of Protestant feeling which on August 12, 1969, made of the Apprentice Boys' march in Derry a torch that very nearly lit a powder keg in all Ireland.

As Protestant passions mounted, inside Stormont hardline Unionists such as William Craig, began to rail against Prime Minister Terence O'Neill and his policy of liberal Unionism and a gradualistic approach to friendship with Dublin. Unconstitutional leaders and movements began to make themselves felt on the Protestant side. The Ulster Volunteer Force was heard of again and in May, 1969 a group of I.R.A. leaders in Belfast became worried enough at the build-up of Protestant strength and emotion that it went to Dublin to ask the Army Council for large supplies of arms without delay.

The request was not granted. In the first place the

I.R.A. had become almost de-militarised and was virtually without funds. (The *United Irishman* was only saved by an emergency appeal for money.) To have given the few arms at its disposal to Belfast would have left the I.R.A. in the South unarmed. Then too, in the event of weapons being discovered in the North, the work for the civil rights movement would have been discredited and a stick given to Stormont to beat the I.R.A. out into the open from behind its façade of Republican clubs. Moreover, Belfast had not distinguished itself during the border campaign and the conversion to militancy did not wholly convince the Dublin leaders. The Northerners went away unhappy and from then on there were suggestions that a separate Northern Command be formed.

Outside the ranks of the I.R.A. events built up to a climax. O'Neill resigned as prime minister after an election in which the Rev. Ian Paisley recorded a high poll in O'Neill's own constituency. On the other hand the People's Democracy movement, had it had a little more political savvy, might have returned more than the lone figure of Miss Bernadette Devlin to Westminster. The U.V.F. stepped up its preparations. In its quest for arms, the U.V.F. has apparently made contacts with Iron Curtain countries and there are reports that large consignments of weapons have arrived in the Northern state. But while the movement claims widespread Protestant support its potential political leadership is extremely low. The only likely leaders it might hope to find at Stormont—the right-wingers Craig, Laird, Boal and West—were routed in a vote of confidence debate which they had forced at Stormont on March 19, 1969. (Paisley's election to Stormont and Westminster in 1970 could change this assessment drastically. He is the most able Irish politician in decades.)

On August 12 the Apprentice Boys were allowed to hold their traditional march in Derry despite warnings that this could lead to a bloodbath. In the event, the procession passed off peaceably enough but eventually, maddened by the provocations of some Catholic hooligans who had been pelting them with stones, the R.U.C. instead of being withdrawn from the Bogside area baton-charged its assailants and hurled stones back at them. Batons and bricks failed to dislodge the Bogsiders from behind their barricades and, for several days, there was enacted another siege of Derry. This time history was reversed and the Catholic defenders withstood the Protestant onslaught.

In Dublin the prime minister was Jack Lynch, a quiet, pipe-smoking Corkman who had never shown himself a militant in any sense. He had continued the hands-across-the-border policy initiated by his predecessor, Sean Lemass, visiting Stormont and being entertained by O'Neill, and having O'Neill on a return visit to Dublin. But Lynch now escalated the partition issue to a plane it had not reached since the days of the treaty debates. Speaking mildly, with sincerity in his voice and a haggard look about the eyes, he went on television to announce that he had moved units of the Irish army up to the border and was opening field hospitals so that people injured in the Bogside battles could be treated without fear of being reported to the R.U.C. Refugee centres were set up in military installations in the South.

London was immediately forced to take notice of a situation which raised the spectre of Irish troops being engaged against British forces. In Belfast, the news was received with fear and horror by Protestant extremists and rioting broke out in which millions of pounds worth of property and some lives were lost. Whether the rioting would have come anyway as a result of the summer's build-up of tension and the fighting in Derry or whether the Irish government's action precipitated it will always be arguable but, once and for all, it forced the British government to take the most decisive action it had taken on the North of Ireland since the creation of the state itself. British troops poured into the North and British politicians poured in after them; a spate of commissions and tribunals ensued, and the British government guaranteed, publicly, that all the reforms sought by the civil rights movement would be conceded and, privately, that if the government of Major Chichester Clarke, who had succeeded O'Neill, fell, there would be no further Northern government. Westminster would take over.

In one year the civil rights movement had done more to end injustice than fifty years of anti-partition policies had begun to do. Where was the I.R.A. during all this? Apparently not there at all as an organised body. As far as can be reasonably ascertained, approximately six Republicans took to the streets of Belfast during the rioting which broke out after August 12 to defend the Catholic areas. One of these, at least, was a middle-aged man who had not been active since the 1940s. He somewhere got a tommy-gun and for his exploits that night has forever earned himself an honoured place in the hearts of Belfast Catholics. There seems little doubt that had the handful of I.R.A. men not been present, Orange mobs led by B-Specials would have burned the Falls Road to the ground and, with it, every Catholic family which did not flee. But this circumstance, much as it may have redounded to the credit of the individuals concerned, redounded very badly indeed on the I.R.A.'s public image.

The principal public activity of the I.R.A. during this period was to issue a ridiculous statement claiming that units of the I.R.A. were active in the North and ready to take any and every action, short of throwing the British Crown into the Thames, in the defence of Catholics and liberation of the North. It did nothing except bolster the charges by hard-line Unionists that the C.R.A. and the I.R.A. were identical. Relations between Belfast and Dublin reached their nadir. Republicans congregated in farmhouses along the border waiting for arms from Dublin that never came and once again the Northern I.R.A. decided to act on its own and the plan for a Northern Command began to take shape. Distraught Republicans began scurrying around the country to lay hands on weapons to give to the desperate Catholics—

with sometimes bizarre results. A Dublin Capuchin monk, for instance, gave five rounds of revolver bullets and a Dominican dressed five I.R.A. men as priests to enable them to get into Belfast undetected.

Concomitant with the I.R.A. troop movements, the Irish government mounted an ill-advised publicity campaign to draw world attention to the partition issue, a campaign which recalled the anti-partition efforts of 1948. The government also appealed to the United Nations, where Irish Foreign Minister Dr Patrick Hillery did surprisingly well in his efforts to get support for the Irish position. Privately, however, some of his colleagues reportedly began taking more unconventional initiatives. Allegedly some of the arms which began to find their way to the North did so as a result of a prominent Dublin politician's action and at one stage there were rumours of £50,000 being paid to the I.R.A. But this referred to the total cost of an arms shipment to the international market and, I am told, only approximately £2,300 was paid to the I.R.A. for arms purchases to assist the Northern Catholics. Catholics could also receive training in the Donegal area and at some of the military centres set up in the South for refugees. Reports that six Irish army officers were sent across the border to co-ordinate Citizens' Defence Committees, again with Republican co-operation, circulated in Dublin and a columnist writing in *Hibernia* said bluntly that the ultimate boss of the Northern Command was a member of the Fianna Fail cabinet.

Certainly the Fianna Fail government appeared to speak at times with two voices on the North. Two ministers in particular, Neil T. Blaney and Kevin Boland, took harder attitudes than did Lynch. Boland laid the continuing blame on Britain and Blaney repeatedly said that the use of force was not ruled out on the part of the Irish government as a means of ending partition. Rumours that some of Lynch's colleagues had not wished him to stop short of the border but to push on to Derry gained currency but on December 28 Lynch gave a very frank radio interview in which he said that he had had a 'firm chat' with Blaney. 'He understands,' Lynch said, 'that the members of the government must adhere to government policy. In fact, he does.'

Whether this broadcast had anything to do with governmental policy towards the I.R.A. is a matter of conjecture, but it is a fact that six Derry youths who had been training openly under arms near Buncrana, Co. Donegal, were suddenly arrested in early January, 1970, charged under the Firearms Act and lodged in prison in Dublin before being released under the Probation Act. Despite this leniency the arrests were clearly designed to indicate that the blind-eye policy regarding drilling was at an end and Lynch won a thunderous ovation at the Fianna Fail Ard Fheis on January 18 when he again ruled out force, challenged anybody (his audience included Blaney and Boland) to oppose him, refused to allow organising for Fianna Fail in the North and said frankly that the South would have to recognise the fact that the majority of the North's inhabitants wanted to remain linked with Britain.

Exactly one week before Lynch's speech the Republican movement had split down the middle in a crisis that was as public and almost as damaging as that which led to the formation of Fianna Fail itself. The stated issue was the recognition of the 'partition parliaments' of Dublin, Stormont and Westminster. The I.R.A. had held a secret convention in mid-December which had voted 39 to 12 in favour of recognition and the Sinn Fein Ard Fheis meeting (in the incongruous surroundings of the American-financed Intercontinental Hotel), was supposed to do likewise and give Sinn Fein a mandate to oppose foreign investment and set about the 'reconquest of Ireland, shop by shop and factory by factory'. There seemed little doubt that the Ard Fheis would give the required two-thirds majority.

A commission set up by the 1968 Ard Fheis to examine the movement and make recommendations as to its future had circulated a report, 'Ireland Today', in March, 1969, saying that there was no need for the leadership of Sinn Fein and the I.R.A. to be amalgamated as 'the present degree of mutual understanding of overall policy and strategy renders any such amalgamation unnecessary'. The usual overlapping of membership had occurred and many of those who had voted to recognise the parliaments at the I.R.A. convention were highly placed on the Sinn Fein executive.

News of the I.R.A. vote was leaked to the press and the *Sunday Press* carried the story two weeks after the convention, on December 28. The report helped to crystallise opposition to the new policies. The March document had recommended that 'all embargoes on political participation in parliament be removed from the Constitution and Rules of both bodies [Sinn Fein and I.R.A.]', but this was accompanied by a directive 'that the undermining of confidence in existing parliaments and eventual abstention from them in order to establish an alternative form of government must be a major objective of the movement'. Now, however, it was out in the public press that Sinn Fein was going to recognise the 'partition parliaments' without any provisos. A new 'provisional' Army Council was set up and various I.R.A. units and Sinn Fein bodies around the country gave the 'provisional' council their allegiance. These groups included important figures such as Tom Maguire, John Joe Sheehy and eighty-nine-year-old Joe Clarke, who fought in 1916. By the time the crucial vote was taken at the Ard Fheis on January 11, the traditionalists had so rallied their forces that the proposal to abandon the abstentionist policy was only carried by 153 votes to 104, less than the required two-thirds majority.

Far from agreeing on the 'creation of the National Liberation Front' called for by the March policy document, Sinn Fein was as split as ever it was. The 'Provisional Army Council' has brought out its own newspaper,

An Phoblacht, and as I write these lines it is hard to prophesy what the future holds.

There may have been other, deeper motives behind the proposals to enter parliament. The 'Ireland Today' document posed the possibility of a link-up with the Southern Irish Communist Party and, interestingly enough, in mid-March the Southern and Northern Communist Parties completed a merger at a meeting attended by several Russian journalists. The idea of a 'National Liberation Front' had come very close to giving Moscow a voice in an Irish national movement for the first time in history.

In America, the older members of Clann na Gael will probably support the 'provisional' side but the more vigorous and influential Association for Justice in Northern Ireland led by Brian Heron, a grandson of James Connolly and equally revolutionary, would probably prefer the leftists whom it has already supplied with considerable funds since the August rioting—some of this money, the civil rights movement claims, having been destined for it and wrongly seized by the I.R.A. In England Clann na hEireann suffered serious internal dissensions on the matter of recognising the 'partition parliaments'.

Constitutionally, the border issue seems as intractable as ever. Possibly some external change, such as entrance to the Common Market, might hasten progress towards a federal solution. Another possible solution, although one which has not yet been seriously discussed, is a voluntary British withdrawal from the six counties. The Britain which withdrew from Malta can hardly enjoy subsidising Belfast to the tune of £170 million a year. It is reasonable to suppose that at present only fears of greatly increased national sentiment in Scotland and Wales keep this alternative from the forefront of British planning. The future could well be different.

Certainly nothing is better calculated to prolong the division than bigoted and ignorant statements from the

South concerning force. Eire has four obsolete Vampire
jets and three ancient corvettes (one of which actually sails)
to back up this shamrock-rattling. The army is outnum-
bered by the combined B-Special and R.U.C. forces, to
say nothing of the contingent of British troops at present
in the North. (But Britain should remember that even
the most placid Southern Irishman is liable to take up
arms in defence of the Catholics of the North, civil war
or no civil war, should Britain fail to keep the peace and
allow a general conflagration to break out. The feeling
in the South of solidarity with the Catholics in Derry
and Belfast in the days following Lynch's speech was
unprecedented in my experience. The most pacific of
men were prepared to mobilise. With such latent emotion
on both sides of the border a policy of restraint is obviously essential.)

Such a policy, of course, will not please the emigrant in
New York who likes to saunter into an Irish bar, where
the record player is blaring out 'Lovely Leitrim', hoping
that his trench-coat will make him look like an I.R.A.
man and therefore worthy of respect, and it certainly
will not appeal to the I.R.A. men back in Ireland. Theirs
is a tradition that will be neither jailed nor wound up
in this century or probably the next. The cyclical nature
of the movement will continue to bruise its members
against jagged political reality. The present split may be
seen as a reoccurrence of the Republican Congress and
Saor Eire upheavals, brought about this time by Roy
Johnston's appearance on the Republican scene at a time
when the movement was trying to re-establish itself. But
if the movement were not in schism itself it would be in
dispute with the Dublin or Stormont governments.

The I.R.A. tradition is one of physical action and
separatism. It is not an intellectual one, which is why I
have carefully refrained in this book from discussing
events or personalities which some historians might feel
were influential in the Republican story: the constitution

of 1937 or the declaration of a Republic in Ireland in 1948, for examples on the political side, or the writings of Sean O'Faolain or of Brendan Behan on the literary one. These are not important to Republicans of the 'physical force' school. Deaths, commemorations, holding firm with the past—these are and will be the preoccupations that nourish the I.R.A.

For those who think this is a cheerless prospect, let me quote a letter (published in the *Irish Press*, November 6, 1969) to his mother from Canor Lynch, son of a prominent I.R.A. man of the 1930s, who had just received a seven-year sentence in England.

'Cheer up, Mother,' he wrote. 'It could have been worse, I could have got seven years and a month.'

I can do nothing but admire that young man's spirit and hope that in some small way this book may help to remove the suspicions and hatreds that caused him to sacrifice his youth. For if we Irish, North and South, can learn to stop hating each other in the name of God and develop the moral courage to prevent others, even those in high places, from inciting us to such bigotry, other young men will have no cause to follow the example of Lynch or of Fergal O'Hanlon. If we fail to learn wisdom from their histories we are doing nothing save turning the keys in the cells and throwing sods on the graves of the future. The British created the partition problem—only the Irish can solve it.

But as I close the British Army GOC in Northern Ireland, General Freeland, has warned that his men will shoot to kill at any petrol bombers; the 'provisional I.R.A.' has said it will shoot a British soldier for every Catholic shot; and the U.V.F. (its ranks presumably swollen by ex-members of the just disbanded B-Special Corps) has threatened to shoot a Catholic in retaliation for every soldier killed. This is where we came in. God knows where we will go out. My personal belief is that the forces of moderation are most likely to triumph, but in the present circumstances this has to be said more in hope than in confidence—and even this confidence must be considerably weakened by the shooting of Protestants in Belfast during the June, 1970 rioting and by the arrest and trial of former Southern cabinet ministers Haughey and Blaney on gun-running charges which have provoked Boland into resignation and open hostility to Lynch.

SELECTED REFERENCES

The principal source material for this book was, of course, the more than five hundred interviews I conducted with persons either in or connected with the I.R.A. I also made use of a wealth of Republican publications: I.R.A. directives, regulations, proclamations, pamphlets, newspapers, records of courts-martial and of county brigade activities, letters and personal statements of various kinds. These, and other material not normally available to the public, such as the ritual (adopted 1931) and constitution (adopted 1946) of the Clann na Gael were given to me through the kindness of individuals.

The principal Republican newspapers, such as *An Phoblacht*, the *Republican Congress*, *Republican File* and the contemporary *United Irishman* provided useful information, as did the national press, in particular the *Irish Press, Irish Times, Irish Independent, Irish News* and *Belfast Telegraph*. A series of articles in *The People* by Joseph Gallagher (commencing December 10, 1961) shed a good deal of light on Nazi-I.R.A. activities.

These activities and other indications of German policy towards Ireland may be studied more formally in the captured documents on German foreign policy published by the Allies after the Second World War. (Some are in German.) Telegram 101410, dated November 24, 1941, is a lengthy assessment of the Irish position, the worth of Goertz's mission, the I.R.A.'s strength and an interpretation of the Hayes affair. It is particularly interesting and well worth translation. But the most comprehensive and easily available study of this aspect of Irish history is Enno Stephan's very fine work, *Spies in Ireland*.

Readers wishing material on other relevant aspects of Irish history may, with confidence, be recommended to the first twelve of the following titles and with diffidence to the thirteenth:

Michael Davitt's *Fall of Feudalism in Ireland* charts the

growth of agrarian reforms by the principal reformer. A contemporary reformer, Dr Conor Cruise O'Brien, charts the rise and fall of Parnell in *Parnell and His Party* with elegance and authority.

P. S. O'Hegarty's *Ireland under the Union*, by an ardent and erudite member of the I.R.B. will take a reader to the Civil War and if, en route, one acquires a somewhat jaundiced view of the Irish parliamentary party, Professor T. S. Lyons's *Irish Parliamentary Party* will help to redress the balance.

Balance of another kind is provided by P. S. Beaslai's fiercely partisan *Michael Collins and the Making of a New Ireland*, which treats of the 1916-21 period in an encyclopedic fashion, matched only by Dorothy MacArdle's *Irish Republic*—which brings the reader past the Civil War as convinced that Eamon de Valera was right as Beaslai would have him wrong.

Donal O'Sullivan's fine *Irish Free State and Its Senate* takes readers to the outbreak of the Second World War and is unashamedly anti-de Valera. Unfortunately no pro-de Valera work of similar stature exists for the same period, with the possible exception of Desmond Ryan's *Unique Dictator*. One of the best books on the whole period is Professor P. T. A. Stewart's *The Ulster Crisis*, which gives unequalled insight into the establishment of the Northern state and is as relevant to today's situation as Miss Bernadette Devlin's *Price of My Soul*.

The Thomas Davis lectures, available in book form as *The Shaping of Modern Ireland* and *The Years of the Great Test*, are a series of essays on various aspects of contemporary Irish history.

My own *Ireland Since the Rising* surveys Irish history from 1916 to 1966 and attempts to give the reader some indication of the part played by the Church, language revival movements and other interest groups in Irish life.

INDEX OF NAMES

GENERAL INDEX

Abbey Theatre, 33, 139

Act of Union (1800), 18-19, 39, 256, 314

Albania, 59

America: Catholic Church in, 130; de Valera in, 131; relations with Ireland, 124, 126-37; in Second World War, 262-7 (*see also* Irish Americans)

American Association for Recognition of Irish Republic ('Growl'), 134

American Civil War, 256

Anglo-Irish Treaty (The Treaty, 1921), 46-52, 55, 59-62, 77-8, 260; reactions to, 136-7, 292-3; signing of, 135 (*see also* Treaty ports)

Anglo-Irish war, 42-7, 53, 150-1, 225, 316; casualties in, 44; guns from U.S.A., 127-8; truce declared, 44

An Phoblacht, 70, 73, 91, 98, 105, 120, 211, 212, 270, 285, 293-4, 355

Anti-Imperialist League, 124

Anti-Partition League, 322

An tOglach, 42

Apprentice Boys' March (Derry 1969), 422-4

Arborfield raid, 334, 336, 342-5, 349, 368

Arbour Hill jail, 90, 120, 124, 152, 179, 184, 187, 257, 287

Ardee Street raid (Dublin, 1946), 326

Argument on behalf of the Catholics of Ireland, 17

Armagh: Gough raid (1954), 335, 337-9, 347, 352, 373; abortive raid (1955), 347-8; Gough attack (1956), 386

Army Comrades' Association, 91, 92, 97, 98

Army Convention (1933), 93-7

Army Council: establishment of (1922), 51; as 'legitimate rulers of Ireland', 159

Association for Justice in Northern Ireland, 429-30

Athletic Associations, 310-11

Athlone manifesto, 107-8

Australia, Fenians in, 30

Austria-Hungary, 39

Baldonnell Aerodrome, 187

Ballinascorney I.R.A. camp, 350-2

Ballykinlar camp raids, 177n, 181

Bank raids, 206, 420

'Barry Plan', 150

Battle school (Wicklow Mts.), 370-1

Belfast, 16, 21, 26; 179, Catholic and Protestant areas of, 208-9, 220; Churchill in, 224; Crumlin Road jail break-out, 237-41; Falls Road, 220, 240, 425; I.R.A. in, 176, 179, 181, 195-6, 208-11, 226, 229, 301-3, 332-5; no action in border campaign, 246, 335, 348; prisoners on strike, 241-2, 245-6; riots and acts of violence, 45, 209n, 210-11, 231-7, 240-1, 281, 425; *Social Geography of*, 20; social welfare introduced, 246; subsidy from Britain, 430

Belfast News Letter, 366

'Belt and Boot' brigade, 229-30

Berlin Congress (1930), 125

Bilingualism and Primary Education, 315

Bishops, criticism of, 291

Bishops' pastorals, 54

Blandford camp raid, 385

Blenheim Palace, 23

Blueshirts, 97-104, 107, 123, 151

Bodenstown: general meeting of Republicans at, 325; new I.R.A. policy proclaimed, 327-8; oration, 306-9; pilgrimage, 90-1, 110, 123-4, 142, 152, 168, 173, 224, 300

Boer War, 140

Bolivia, McGarrity in, 150

Bombing campaign in England, 31, 55, 154-73, 175, 202, 268; deportees from, 207; effect of, 173; preliminary ultimatum, 164-5, 334

'Bonfire on the Border' (ballad), 175

Border campaign (1956-62), 174-8, 380-418; court cases during, 411-13; early raids by young activists, 332-3, 335-41; effects of, 384-5; financial cost, 384; opening night, 384, 386-7; poor organization in, 390-3; prelude to, 327-32, 373-5; resumed (final flare-up and end of), 412-18

Border countryside, description of, 377-80

Boundary Commission (1925), 76, 214

Fontana History

Fontana History includes the well-known History of Europe, edited by J. H. Plumb, and the Fontana Economic History of Europe, edited by Carlo Cipolla. New series are in preparation. Books now available include:

The Practice of History G. R. Elton

Debates with Historians Pieter Geyl

The English Reformation A. G. Dickens

The Nation State and National Self-Determination
Alfred Cobban

Europe and the French Revolution Albert Sorel

Russia 1917: The February Revolution George Katkov

The Trial of Charles I C. V. Wedgwood

The King's Peace 1637-1641 C. V. Wedgwood

The King's War 1641-1647 C. V. Wedgwood

Britain and the Second World War Henry Pelling